Prussian Army Soldiers and the Seven Years' War

Prussian Army Soldiers and the Seven Years' War

The Psychology of Honour

Katrin Möbius and Sascha Möbius

BLOOMSBURY ACADEMIC
LONDON • NEW YORK • OXFORD • NEW DELHI • SYDNEY

BLOOMSBURY ACADEMIC
Bloomsbury Publishing Plc
50 Bedford Square, London, WC1B 3DP, UK
1385 Broadway, New York, NY 10018, USA
29 Earlsfort Terrace, Dublin 2, Ireland

BLOOMSBURY, BLOOMSBURY ACADEMIC and the Diana logo are trademarks of
Bloomsbury Publishing Plc

First published in Great Britain 2020
This paperback edition published in 2021

Copyright © Katrin Möbius and Sascha Möbius 2020

Katrin Möbius and Sascha Möbius have asserted their right under the Copyright, Designs
and Patents Act, 1988, to be identified as Authors of this work.

Cover image: Knötel III, 56 (© Historic Images/Alamy Stock Photo)

All rights reserved. No part of this publication may be reproduced or transmitted
in any form or by any means, electronic or mechanical, including photocopying,
recording, or any information storage or retrieval system, without prior
permission in writing from the publishers.

Bloomsbury Publishing Plc does not have any control over, or responsibility for, any
third-party websites referred to or in this book. All internet addresses given in this
book were correct at the time of going to press. The author and publisher regret
any inconvenience caused if addresses have changed or sites have ceased to exist,
but can accept no responsibility for any such changes.

A catalogue record for this book is available from the British Library.

A catalog record for this book is available from the Library of Congress.

ISBN: HB: 978-1-3500-8157-4
PB: 978-1-3502-4507-5
ePDF: 978-1-3500-8158-1
eBook: 978-1-3500-8159-8

Typeset by RefineCatch Limited, Bungay, Suffolk

To find out more about our authors and books, visit www.bloomsbury.com
and sign up for our newsletters.

Contents

List of Illustrations and Table	vii
Acknowledgements	viii
Introduction	1
Current state of research	2
Sources and methods	9
1 Drilling on the Job: About a Soldier's Brain	19
'The men': Origin, recruitment, beliefs and expectations for the future	19
Linear tactics: Forming the men's instincts	39
Shocking with cold steel: Psychological warfare	43
2 Between 'Emasculating Fear' and 'Heat': Emotions and Psychology in Combat	57
The men's reflections: The soldiers who wrote about their emotions	57
Sheltered by the Almighty: How should one read the sources?	75
The soldiers' letters and their emotions in battle	79
Statements about soldiers' emotions in combat	99
Prague and the 'Little War': Successfully formed instincts?	115
3 The Components of Prussian Honour: What Made the Men Fight?	129
The honour of professionalism and the soldiers' estate	129
Religion	135
National and cultural concepts	137
Gender and honour	143
The soldiers' interactions with their officers	146
Music: The fine-tuning of military honour	151
Material incentives	159
Discipline by force	163
4 Summary	169

Appendix I Sources: Regulations, military history and theory, journals	173
Reglements and orders	173
Military history and theory	174
Appendix II Twelve Prussian Soldiers' Letters from the Seven Years' War	177
The letters	178
Glossary	205
Bibliography	207
Index	223

Illustrations and Table

Illustrations

1.1 A Prussian battalion and platoon ready for battle. 46

2.1 Charge of the third battalion of the Alt-Anhalt Regiment at the Battle of Prague. 119

3.1 Oboists of the Von Bevern Regiment (No. 7) during the Battle of Zorndorf. 157

6.1 Letter from Johan Matthias Zander, Dorschulze of Nitzahn, to Major-General Philipp Bogeslav von Schwerin, Nitzahn, 18 June 1749, in Christian F. Zander, *Fundstücke – Dokumente und Briefe einer preußischen Bauernfamilie (1747–1953)* (Hamburg: Verlag Dr. Kovač, 2015), 25. 199

Table

1.1 Organizational and tactical units of the Prussian army. 21

Acknowledgements

We would like to thank several colleagues and friends who gave their generous support to this project and to us during the time of writing this book.

Dennis Showalter and his works on eighteenth-century warfare were a source of inspiration and stood at the cradle of our research. He also assisted us in various ways and encouraged us to write this book. Hermann Wellenreuther also championed our endeavour from its early beginnings and supported us wherever help was needed. Ilya Berkovich read the manuscript carefully and made many friendly and extremely useful suggestions. He provided important sources which were out of our reach and we owe a lot to him. We are also indebted to Jörg Muth and his research on the Potsdam garrison for many insightful discussions and hints. Our Spanish friends Agustín Guimerá and Manuel Reyes Garcia Hurtado always gave their support and friendly advice and helped by providing valuable sources. Manuel Moreno Alonso and Eduardo de Mesa Gallego gave invaluable assistance in two forerunner projects on Prussian and Austrian influences on the eighteenth-century Spanish military. Horst Pietschmann, Ivan Valdez-Bubnov, José Covarrubias and Martín F. Rios Saloma kindly provided the opportunity to exchange ideas with many Mexican and Spanish colleagues at the UNAM in Mexico City. Peter Way generously supported our work by sharing his research. We owe a lot to the cheerful and helpful support of Daniel Krebs, Kathryn Barbier and Eva Labouvie who helped us in more than one way as we wrote this book. We are also indebted to Jürgen Kloosterhuis for many constructive remarks.

Jorge Corada painted the illustrations. Developing them with him was a pleasure. We also want to thank Rhodri Mogford and the team at Bloomsbury Academic for all their support and collaboration. The Bavarian State Library in Munich, Library of the Ibero-American Institute Berlin, the State Archive of Saxony-Anhalt, Franke Foundations, especially Thomas Grunewald, the Library of the Center for Military History and Social Sciences of the Bundeswehr and the Biblioteca Central Militar in Madrid were always helpful and supportive. We also thank the publishing house Dr. Kovač and Christian Friedrich Zander for giving us permission to translate the letters of the Prussian soldiers Christian Friedrich and Johann Dietrich Zander and providing the facsimiles.

Introduction

11 May 1745 near Fontenoy in Belgium: the *Gardes Françaises* and the British Guards brigade met during the battle between the royal French army and a combined British and German force. Legend has it that the British officers stepped forward and asked their French opponents to fire the first volley. Initially, the French declined this polite offer but accepted it after a short debate. Their fire had little effect, but the British answer was devastating, leaving more than 400 Frenchmen dead, maimed or wounded and putting the rest to flight.[1] True or not, the scene has been presented as the archetype of rococo warfare ever since. Well-drilled armies of press-ganged mercenaries in colourful uniforms, their hair powdered and twisted into long plaits, drawn up in endless lines and commanded by noble officers fighting a gentlemen's war. The noble generals were not aiming to secure victory in battle but rather to preserve their expensive soldiers and follow a code of conduct which suited a royal court more than a bloody battlefield. And everybody was keen to spare the civilian population another blow like that dealt by the Thirty Years' War. To achieve this, all armies maintained hundreds of magazines along their routes to minimize the need to plunder and loot.

The modern spectator of model-soldier dioramas or paintings of eighteenth-century battles is also captivated by the geometrical order of the combat formations. Immediately, the question arises about how it had been possible to position and move these massive formations of men, horses and weapons. From a bird's eye view, we witness a highly artificial machine, in which the individual soldier was only a tiny cog, subjected to chivalrous – if unpractical – rules of war.

The heroic anecdotes and paintings that imply a graceful and aesthetic 'Art of War' in the Age of reason stand in sharp contrast to the vast numbers of dead and wounded left behind by these wars. Many participants of the hostilities wrote horrified accounts of the images of fellow combatants who were torn apart by enemy bullets or burnt to death, beyond all recognition, as a result of exploding ammunition carts. The men speak in their letters and diaries about mortal agony and thoughts of fleeing the field, of their deep apprehension ahead of battle, and their reactions to the suffocating threat of violence during the individual attacks.

Overcoming the conflict between the necessary order and military effectiveness on the one hand and the sheer fear of death on the other hand, was a central goal of soldiers' training. As one might guess, only tough methods of drill kept the soldiers in

[1] Reed Browning, *The War of the Austrian Succession* (New York: St. Martin's Press, 1993), 206–13.

line, made them fearless and beat into them an unquestioning and blind obedience to their superiors. Even today, one of the most infamous punishments in the Prussian army, 'running the gauntlet' (*Spießrutenlaufen*), is still a proverb in German and English for being forced to deal with a host of public and painful criticisms. Likewise, the Soldier King's *Lange Kerls* (literally: long men; Potsdam Giants), who would later become the famous Grenadier Guards (Regiment No. 6) of Frederick II, are still seen as the archetype of Prussian order and subordination.

Most scholars dealing with the mentalities of *ancien régime* armies still regard the soldiers' fear of the officers, and the latters' outright use of force, as the main factors which 'motivated' soldiers in combat; they had already been reduced to numb automatons on the drill square. And to be sure force, fear and drill did play a role, but what these scholars did not take into account was the fact that an army full of psychologically crippled and traumatized soldiers could never have been able to stand side by side in the line or to trust their leaders or comrades during an attack. Fighting automatons could not react properly and with creative solutions to a threat, like the Prussian Army did many times during the Seven Years' War. Furthermore, it would have been almost suicidal for any officer to go into battle with soldiers who hated him and were eager to get their revenge for the inhuman drill inflicted on them on the parade ground. Thus, the question remains, which mental and psychological factors made the Prussian army so effective, that its enemies never dared to attack it without a vast superiority in numbers?

This book will question thoroughly the deeply entrenched idea that the old Prussian army was filled by ranks of psychologically damaged 'robo-soldiers'. It offers a view into the psychology of the Prussian man on the battlefield and his family at home. For the soldiers, another factor helped them cope with all hardships and fight so effectively: their honour.

The psychology of the soldiers of *ancien régime* armies in combat has to date been treated only in Sascha Möbius' previous study, published in German alone, 'Mehr Angst vor dem Offizier als vor dem Feind?' ('Fear the Officer more than the Enemy?'). Together with some other studies by German, British and US historians, it marked the beginning of a turn towards a more balanced approach in dealing with the mentality of the old Prussian army.

This book is the first in-depth investigation of the long-dismissed idea of a characteristic sense of honour held and shared by common (that is, non-commissioned) Prussian soldiers and their families, based on their own accounts. *The Psychology of Honour* shows how deeply the fighters were embedded in a system of religious beliefs, estate, reputation and honour. It presents an intimate view into soldier's families and their compassionate and professional support for their husbands and sons. This book draws on a multifaceted concept of honour, at the core of which is Ernest Gellner's notion that honour is the 'defence of one's status'.

Current state of research

Ancien régime armies, and their Prussian apogee, have been thoroughly reappraised during the last twenty years, resulting in a scissor movement between military historians in the stricter sense and general historiography. This shift was first linked to the development of modern 'new military history', a move from the operational and political towards social and mental questions being asked by military historians. It was also linked, secondly, to German military historians catching up with their Anglo-Saxon colleagues and turning to the aforementioned 'new military history'.[2]

Until the second half of the 1990s, there was a broad consensus between military and general historians that the common soldiers of the armies of absolutist Europe were 'scum' drawn from the lowest strata of society, recruited by strong-arm methods and driven by fear of their officers and the brutal punishments imposed for fleeing the battlefield.[3] This view is still held by many general historians and on screen[4] and canvas[5] today, but more recent studies of specialised historians have taken another direction. This 'new school' suggests a differentiated picture of the social status of the soldiers, their living conditions and the impact of the establishment of standing armies on society as a whole. Yet the question of the common soldiers' emotions and influences on their behaviour during combat in eighteenth-century warfare has been the subject of just a handful of studies.

The analyses offered by German military historians during the first quarter of the twentieth century focused heavily on organizational questions and, above all, operational matters. They were written mainly by professional soldiers like Curt Jany[6] or those officers of the Great General Staff[7] with a historical education. These historians were influenced significantly by the prevailing glorification of Frederick II and a tendency to present the Prussian king as a Napoleon before Napoleon, leading conscript armies[8] with the aim of annihilating his enemies in a single Armageddon-like battle.[9]

Until the early 2000s, a broad majority of historians saw the military in the Age of Enlightenment as a highly repressive institution that existed only to carry out the will of kings and princes, and to fight in wars characterized by changing coalitions. The result was, according to Otto Büsch's influential German study,[10] a social militarization

---

[2] Ralf Pröve, 'Vom Schmuddelkind zur anerkannten Subdisziplin? Die "neue Militärgeschichte" der Frühen Neuzeit: Perspektiven, Entwicklungen, Probleme', *Geschichte in Wissenschaft und Unterricht* 51 (2000): 598–99.
[3] Ilya Berkovich, 'Fear, Honour and Emotional Control on the Eighteenth-Century Battlefield', in *Battlefield Emotions 1500–1800: Practices, Experience, Imagination*, ed. Erika Kuijpers and Cornelis van der Haven (Basingstoke: Palgrave Macmillan, 2016), 95–6.
[4] E.g. Prof. Dr. Johannes Kunisch's and Prof. Dr. Wolfgang Neugebauer's appearance in *Die Deutschen: Preußens Friedrich und die Kaiserin Duell zwischen Preußen und Österreich* (2008), [TV Programme] ZdF (Germany), 11 November.
[5] E.g. the machine-like appearance of the British line-infantry in *The Patriot* (2000), [Film] Dir. Roland Emmerich, USA: Centropolis Entertainment, Mutual Film Company.
[6] Curt Jany, *Geschichte der Preußischen Armee*, vol. 2 (Osnabrück: Biblio, [1928] 1967).
[7] *Der Siebenjährige Krieg 1756–1763*, ed. Großer Generalstab, 13 vols. (Berlin: Mittler, 1901–14). The enterprise was stopped in 1914 and covers the war from the beginning to the time shortly before the Battle of Torgau (3 November 1760).
[8] Martin Winter: *Untertanengeist durch Militärpflicht? Das preußische Kantonsystem in brandenburgischen Städten im 18. Jahrhundert* (Bielefeld: Verlag für Regionalgeschichte, 2005), 16–17.
[9] See Gerhard P. Gross, *The Myth and Reality of German Warfare. Operational Thinking from Moltke the Elder to Heusinger* (Lexington, KY: The University Press of Kentucky, 2016), 57–98.
[10] Otto Büsch, *Militärsystem und Sozialleben im alten Preußen 1713–1807. Die Anfänge der sozialen Militarisierung der preußisch-deutschen Gesellschaft* (1962; Frankfurt/Main et al: Ullstein, 1981), 43.

during the eighteenth century, which resulted in the infamous Prussian / German *Untertanengeist* (subservience), which in its turn formed one of the pillars of the Nazi dictatorship in the twentieth century.[11] Similar theories exist in countries such as Spain.[12] Consequently, the old school insisted, the machine-like armies of feudal Europe were easy prey for the revolutionary citizens' armies of the new-born USA[13] and the French Republic and Empire.[14]

Christopher Duffy, one of the most influential English-language historiographers of Frederick II's army, had produced a differentiated picture of soldiers during the Age of Enlightenment from the 1980s on.[15] Thus, the 'old school's' position was shaken but not completely changed, as far as specialists in eighteenth-century armies are concerned, while general historiography is still strongly influenced by the more traditional view.[16] Together with Duffy's book on Frederick the Great, it was Timothy C.W. Blanning who shed serious doubt on the assumed moral superiority of the armies of the French Revolution over their old regime adversaries[17] and Dennis Showalter's studies were the starting point of the 'new school'. Showalter presented the thesis that European eighteenth-century armies, and especially the Prussian one, were characterized not by brutal methods of recruitment and drill, but rather by their professionalism.[18] The notion of servile Prussian soldiers serving all-powerful *Junker* officers and a specific Prussian social militarization was also challenged by Peter H. Wilson and William W. Hagen's detailed study of the Brandenburg manor (*Rittergut*) of Stavenow.[19] More recent studies by Jennine Hurl-Eamon,[20] Peter

---

[11] See: Olaf Jessen: Review of Martin Winter, Untertanengeist durch Militärpflicht, *Militär und Gesellschaft in der frühen Neuzeit* 9, no. 2 (2008), 206—09.

[12] Heidi Ly Beirich, *The birth of Spanish militarism: the Bourbon military reforms, 1766–1808* (San Diego: MA Thesis San Diego State University, 1994); Geoffrey Jensen, *Irrational Triumph. Cultural Despair, Military Nationalism, and the Ideological Origins of Franco's Spain* (Reno and Las Vegas: University of Nevada Press, 2002), 26–7.

[13] Peter Way, 'Class and the Common Soldier in the Seven Years' War', *Labor History*, 44, no. 4 (2003): 456–57.

[14] Gerd Fesser, *Die Schlacht bei Jena und Auerstedt 1806* (Berlin: Deutscher Verlag der Wissenschaften, 1986).

[15] Duffy, *Frederick the Great*, 336–7.

[16] Armstrong Starkey, *War in the Age of Enlightenment, 1700–1789* (Westport, CT: Greenwood Publishing Group, 2003), 60–62.

[17] Timothy C. W. Blanning, *The French Revolutionary Wars, 1787–1802* (London: Arnold, 1996), 119, quoted after Ilya Berkovich, *Motivation in War: The Experience of Common Soldiers in Old-Regime Europe* (Cambridge: Cambridge University Press, 2017), 2.

[18] Dennis E. Showalter, *The Wars of Frederick the Great* (Boston, MA: Addison-Wesley Longman, 1995), 7; Dennis E. Showalter, 'Tactics and Recruitment in Eighteenth Century Prussia', *Studies in History and Politics/Etudes d'Histoire et de Politique* III, no. 3 (1993/1994): 15–41; Dennis E. Showalter, 'Hubertusberg to Auerstädt: The Prussian Army in Decline?', *German History* 12, no. 3 (1994): 308–33; Dennis E. Showalter, *Frederick the Great: A Military History* (1996; Kindle ed. Barnsley: Frontline Books, 2012).

[19] William W. Hagen, *Ordinary Prussians: Brandenburg Junkers and Villagers, 1500–1840* (Cambridge: Cambridge University Press, 2003), 122, 468.

[20] 'Deadbeat Dads? A Closer look at the Married Men Who Joined the Army in Eighteenth-Century Britain', Dr. Jennine Hurl-Eamon, History. https://www.youtube.com/watch?v=RM6f4UgHSvI (accessed 22 August 2018). Jennine Hurl-Eamon, *Marriage and the British Army in the Long Eighteenth Century: 'The Girl I Left Behind Me'* (Oxford: Oxford University Press, 2014).

Way,[21] Nicholas Mansfield[22], Matthew McCormack, Kevin Linch[23] and Joe Cozens[24] on the British army of the time have drawn a differentiated picture of the soldiers serving His Britannic Majesty, some leaning more toward the old school and some to the new, but all presenting fresh perspectives. The new trend is perhaps summed up best by Yuval Noah Harari, who stresses the centrality of 'drill' and 'harsh external supervision' for ensuring discipline but concedes: 'Old regime soldiers – after being properly trained – were often highly motivated, not only by fear and greed, but also by professional pride, *esprit de corps*, small unit cohesion, personal honour, masculinist ideals, and occasionally by patriotism and even religious fervour.'[25] Timothy C.W. Blanning has given the following summary in his biography of Fredrick the Great: 'Recent research has shown that the harshness of Prussian discipline has been exaggerated and that the soldiers were motivated by honour, esprit de corps, professionalism, Protestantism and patriotism as well as fear.'[26] Christopher Clark stressed the bonds between men coming from the same region and village serving in the regiments.[27]

German scholars were way behind their American and British colleagues. Only a tiny minority of them dealt with military questions and Otto Büsch's analysis dominated the field for several decades, finding its way into other influential works by Johannes Kunisch[28] and Ulrich Bröckling.[29] Their 'old school' position on Frederician soldiers in combat was summed up in Klaus Latzel's article *Schlachtbank oder Feld der Ehre?* ('Slaughterhouse or Field of Honour?')[30], presenting them as numbed by iron discipline and apathetically enduring the horrors of combat. Just a handful of historians presented

---

[21] Peter Way, 'Rebellion of the Regulars: Working Soldiers and the Mutiny of 1763–1764', *William and Mary Quarterly*, 57, no. 4 (2000): 761–92; Way, *Class*: 455–81; 'Venus and Mars: Women and the British Army in America during the Seven Years' War', in *Britain and America Go to War: The Impact of War and Warfare in Anglo-America, 1754–1815*, ed. Julie Flavell and Stephen Conway (Gainesville, FL: Florida University Press, 2004), 41–68; 'Militarizing the Atlantic World: Army Discipline, Coerced Labor, and Britain's Commercial Empire', *Atlantic Studies: Global Currents*, 13, no. 3 (2016): 345–69.
[22] Nicholas Mansfield, *Soldiers as Workers: Class, Employment, Conflict and the Nineteenth-century Military* (Liverpool: Liverpool University Press, 2016).
[23] Kevin Linch and Matthew McCormack, 'Introduction', in *Britain's Soldiers. Rethinking War and Society, 1715–1815*, ed. Kevin Linch and Matthew McCormack (Liverpool: Liverpool University Press), 2–3; Matthew McCormack, *Embodying the Militia in Georgian England* (Oxford: Oxford University Press, 2015); Kevin Linch, *Britain and Wellington's Army. Recruitment, Society and Tradition, 1807–15* (Houndsmills and New York: Palgrave Macmillan, 2011).
[24] Joe Cozens, '"The Blackest Perjury": Desertion, Military Justice, and Popular Politics in England, 1803–1805', *Labour History Review* 79, no. 3 (2014): 255–80.
[25] Yuval Noah Harari, *The Ultimate Experience. Battlefield Revelations and the Making of Modern War Culture, 1450–2000* (Basingstoke: Palgrave, 2008), 164.
[26] Timothy C. W. Blanning, *Frederick the Great. King of Prussia* (London: Penguin, 2015), 271.
[27] Christopher Clark, *Iron Kingdom: The Rise and Downfall of Prussia, 1600–1947* (New York: Penguin, 2007), 99–100.
[28] Johannes Kunisch, *Der Kleine Krieg. Studien zum Heerwesen des Absolutismus* (Wiesbaden: F. Steiner, 1973); Johannes Kunisch, *Das Mirakel des Hauses Brandenburg. Studien zum Verhältnis von Kabinettspolitik und Kriegführung im Zeitalter des Siebenjährigen Krieges* (München and Vienna: Oldenbourg, 1978).
[29] Ulrich Bröckling, *Disziplin: Soziologie und Geschichte militärischer Gehorsamsproduktion* (Munich: Verlag Wilhelm Fink, 1997).
[30] Klaus Latzel, '„Schlachtbank" oder „Feld der Ehre"? Der Beginn des Einstellungswandels gegenüber Krieg und Tod 1756–1815', in *Der Krieg des kleinen Mannes. Eine Militärgeschichte von unten*, ed. Wolfram Wette, 2nd ed. (1992; Munich and Zürich: Piper, 1995), 76–92.

a more favourable view of the rank and file of the Prussian army.[31] A link between the 'old' and the 'new' school was Michael Sikora's study *Disziplin und Desertion* ('Discipline and Desertion').[32] Focusing on combat behaviour, Sikora stresses the central importance of religion. Triggered by Sikora's book and Ralf Pröve's groundbreaking earlier study on the Göttingen garrison of the Elector of Hannover's army,[33] a series of important case studies on the Prussian army began to appear, like the fine studies done by Jörg Muth[34] on desertion in the Potsdam garrison and Martin Winter[35] on recruitment and mentalities in Brandenburg, or indeed various writings by Jürgen Kloosterhuis dealing with the army of Friedrich Wilhelm, the Soldier King, and his son[36] as well as an important revaluation of Ulrich Bräker's autobiography.[37] Beate Engelen's book on soldiers' women in Prussia[38] and Frank Zielsdorf's study of military cultures of remembrance in Prussia[39] were also valuable contributions to a more balanced picture. Stefan Kroll[40] and Jutta Nowosadtko[41] produced important studies of two other German territories, the electorate of Saxony and the principality of Munster respectively.

Concerning our question of combat emotions and motivations, both English- and German language research are closely linked and represent a productive synthesis of both Anglo-Saxon and German new military history. It was German and English-language historians who produced the fundamental studies on *ancien régime* battle tactics. These books by Ross, Nosworthy and Ortenburg do not deal with the soldiers' motivation in detail but are still invaluable sources for anybody interested in eighteenth-century battles, and show that linear tactics were not a static concept but underwent

---

[31] Ernst Willi Hansen, 'Zur Problematik einer Sozialgeschichte des deutschen Militärs im 17. und 18. Jahrhundert', *Zeitschrift für Historische Forschung* 6 (1979): 425–60; Hans Bleckwenn, 'Bauernfreiheit durch Wehrpflicht: ein neues Bild der altpreußischen Armee', in *Friedrich der Große und das Militärwesen seiner Zeit*, ed. Johann Christoph Allmayer-Beck (Herford: Mittler, 1987): 55–72.
[32] Michael Sikora, *Disziplin und Desertion: Strukturprobleme militärischer Organisation im 18. Jahrhundert* (Berlin: Duncker & Humblot, 1996).
[33] Ralf Pröve, *Stehendes Heer und städtische Gesellschaft im 18. Jahrhundert. Göttingen und seine Militärbevölkerung 1713–1756* (Munich: Oldenbourg, 1995).
[34] Jörg Muth, *Flucht aus dem militärischen Alltag. Ursachen und individuelle Ausprägung der Desertion in der Armee Friedrichs des Großen. Mit besonderer Berücksichtigung der Infanterieregimenter der Potsdamer Garnison* (Freiburg in Breisgau: Rombach, 2003).
[35] Martin Winter, *Untertanengeist durch Militärpflicht? Das preußische Kantonsystem in brandenburgischen Städten im 18. Jahrhundert* (Bielefeld: Verlag für Regionalgeschichte, 2005).
[36] Jürgen Kloosterhuis, *Bauern, Bürger und Soldaten. Quellen zur Sozialisation des Militärsystems im preußischen Westfalen 1713–1803* (Münster: Selbstverlag des Nordrhein-Westfälischen Staatsarchivs, 1992); Jürgen Kloosterhuis, *Legendäre 'lange Kerls'. Quellen zur Regimentskultur der Königsgrenadiere Friedrich Wilhelms I., 1713–1740* (Berlin: Geheimes Staatsarchiv Preussischer Kulturbesitz, 2003);
[37] Jürgen Kloosterhuis, 'Donner, Blitz und Bräker: Der Soldatendienst des "armen Mannes im Tockenburg" aus der Sicht des preußischen Militärsystems', in *Schreibsucht: autobiographische Schriften des Pietisten Ulrich Bräker (1735–1798)*, ed. Alfred Messerli and Adolf Muschg (Göttingen: Vandenhoeck & Ruprecht, 2004), 129–87.
[38] Beate Engelen, *Soldatenfrauen in Preußen. Eine Strukturanalyse der Garnisonsgesellschaft im späten 17. und 18. Jahrhundert* (Münster: Lit Verlag, 2005).
[39] Frank Zielsdorf, *Militärische Erinnerunskulturen in Preußen im 18. Jahrhundert. Akteure – Medien – Dynamiken* (Göttingen: V&R unipress, 2016).
[40] Stefan Kroll, *Soldaten im 18. Jahrhundert zwischen Friedensalltag und Kriegserfahrung. Lebenswelten und Kultur in der kursächsischen Armee 1728–1796* (Paderborn: Ferdinand Schöningh, 2006).
[41] Jutta Nowosadtko, *Stehendes Heer im Ständestaat. Das Zusammenleben von Militär- und Zivilbevölkerung im Fürstbistum Münster 1650–1803* (Paderborn: Ferdinand Schöningh, 2011).

important changes from the late seventeenth to nineteenth centuries.[42] Sascha Möbius produced the first case studies on emotions and motivations of *ancien régime* soldiers in combat in 2002[43] and 2007[44], pointing out that they played a much more decisive part in the battles of the Seven Years' War than hitherto acknowledged and that their feelings ranged from horror over fear and 'heat' to bloodlust; it also became clear that their motivations were centred around their religious faith and the fulfilment of their duties as members of the soldiers' estate. Stefan Kroll underlined not only the importance of religion but also that of an early patriotism for the Saxon army during the Seven Years' War.[45] The anthology on *Battlefield Emotions* by Erika Kuijpers and Cornelis van der Haven appeared in 2016, with contributions by Ilya Berkovich[46] and Marian Füssel[47] covering the Seven Years' War. Berkovich highlights a triangular relationship between fear, honour and shame.[48]

The most recent English study on the motivations and mentalities of soldiers in the age of Frederick II is Ilya Berkovich's fine and thorough analysis *Motivation in War*, which focuses on the experience of (mainly English-speaking) common soldiers in old-regime Europe. Berkovich argues that these men were motivated by a complex network of incentives ranging from the prospect of plunder to a strong sense of military honour, and stresses the significance of the soldiers' peer group and unit cohesion.

The notion of *military* honour in the eighteenth century has not yet been a major field of debate in Germany, especially with regard to common soldiers.[49] That said, the concept of honour in general has been a perennial area of interest for English- and German-speaking early-modern historians and has produced valuable methodological results.[50] While the older school viewed honour mainly as a concept that distinguished

---

[42] Steven T. Ross, *From Flintlock to rifle: Infantry tactics, 1740–1866* (London: Routledge, 1979); Brent Nosworthy, *Anatomy of Victory: Battle Tactics 1689–1763* (New York: Hippocrene Books, 1990); Georg Ortenburg, *Waffe und Waffengebrauch im Zeitalter der Kabinettskriege* (Koblenz: Bernard & Graefe, 1986).

[43] Sascha Möbius, 'Von Jast und Hitze wie vertaumelt'. Überlegungen zur Wahrnehmung von Gewalt durch preußische Soldaten im Siebenjährigen Krieg, *Forschungen zur Brandenburgischen und Preußischen Geschichte, Neue Folge* 12 (2002), 1–34.

[44] Sascha Möbius, *Mehr Angst vor dem Offizier als vor dem Feind? Eine mentalitätsgeschichtliche Studie zur preußischen Taktik im Siebenjährigen Krieg* (Saarbrücken: VDM / Akademikerverlag, 2007).

[45] Kroll, *Soldaten*, 361.

[46] Berkovich, *Fear*, 93–110.

[47] Marian Füssel, 'Emotions in the Making: The Transformation of Battlefield Experiences during the Seven Years' War (1756–1763), in *Battlefield Emotions 1500–1800. Practices, Experience, Imagination*, ed. Erika Kuijpers and Cornelis van der Haven (Basingstoke: Palgrave Macmillan, 2016), 149–72.

[48] Berkovich, *Fear*, 99.

[49] Ulrike Ludwig and John Zimmermann, 'Ehre und Pflichterfüllung als Codes militärischer Tugenden – einführende Bemerkungen', in *Ehre und Pflichterfüllung als Codes militärischer Tugenden*, ed. Ulrike Ludwig, Markus Pöhlmann and John Zimmermann (Paderborn: Ferdinand Schöningh, 2014), 14–15.

[50] *Ehre, Fallstudien zu einem anthropologischen Phänomen in der Vormoderne*, ed. Dorothea Klein (Würzburg: Königshausen und Neumann, 2019); Eberhard Isenmann, *Ehre. Die Ehre und die Stadt im Spätmittelalter und zu Beginn der frühen Neuzeit* (Würzburg: Königshausen und Neumann, 2019); Arnaud Guinier, *L'honneur du soldat: éthique martiale et discipline guerrière dans la France des Lumières* (Ceyzérieu: Champ Vallon, 2014); *Honour, Violence and Emotions in History*, ed. Carolyn Strange (London: Bloomsbury, 2014); Anja Lobenstein-Reichmann, *Sprachliche Ausgrenzung im*

the nobility from the other estates, modern research has shown that *all* estates developed their own concepts of honour:[51] 'Honour is understood as a medium by which social estimation can be awarded or distracted.'[52] English-language literature is more abundant and in-depth debate of military honour as a motivating factor is to be found in Berkovich's study.[53] He uses a definition of honour which stresses the common soldiers' 'inner feelings of self-worth'.[54]

This overview of modern research on eighteenth-century soldiers and their behaviour in combat shows why a new study on the *Prussian* army is a useful undertaking. First, many military historians, even of the 'new school', still see it as the archetype of ensuring effectiveness by iron discipline and brutal methods.[55] Second, the question of actual combat behaviour and feelings has largely been ignored, and thus still offers plenty of space for new studies. The time has surely come for in-depth studies of culture of the different armies, and even regiments. While all soldiers in all armies could (and did) feel fear, their mechanisms of dealing with it surely were different.

Our study wants to add to the different debates. The great English (military revolution) and German (social militarization and state-building) debates can be enhanced by our look at the attendant mental factors. Thus, we can contribute to a more nuanced overall picture of *ancien régime* warfare. We are part of the debate among military historians on how to weight the different emotions and motivations of soldiers in the age of enlightenment.

---

späten Mittelalter und in der frühen Neuzeit (Berlin and Boston: De Gruyter, 2013); *Ehre und Recht. Ehrkonzepte, Ehrverletzungen und Ehrverteidigungen vom späten Mittelalter bis zur Moderne*, ed. Sylvia Kesper-Biermann (Magdeburg: Meine, 2011); Matthew H. Spring, *With Zeal and With Bayonets Only: The British Army on Campaign in North America, 1775–1783* (Norman, OK: University of Oklahoma Press, 2010); Kathy Stuart, *Unehrliche Berufe. Status und Stigma in der Frühen Neuzeit am Beispiel Augsburgs* (Augsburg: Wißner, 2008); Dagmar Burkhart, *Eine Geschichte der Ehre* (Darmstadt: Wiss. Buchgesellschaft, 2006); Tina Braun and Elke Liermann, *Feinde, Freunde, Zechkumpane. Freiburger Studentenkultur in der frühen Neuzeit* (Münster: Waxmann, 2007), 35–6; James Bowman, *Honor: A History* (New York: Encounter Books, 2006); Caroline Cox, *A Proper Sense of Honor: Service and Sacrifice in George Washington's Army* (Chapel Hill, NC: University of North Carolina Press, 2004); Elizabeth A. Foyster, *Manhood in Early Modern England: Honour, Sex and Marriage* (Harlow: Longman, 1999.); Richard van Dülmen, *Der ehrlose Mensch. Unehrlichkeit und soziale Ausgrenzung in der frühen Neuzeit* (Cologne: Böhlau, 1999); *Ehrkonzepte in der frühen Neuzeit. Identitäten und Abgrenzungen*, ed. Sibylle Backmann and Ute Ecker-Offenhäußer (Berlin: Akademie-Verlag, 1998).

[51] Klaus Schreiner and Gerd Schwerhoff, 'Verletzte Ehre – Überlegungen zu einem Forschungskonzept', in *Verletzte Ehre. Ehrkonflikte in Gesellschaften des Mittelalters und der Frühen Neuzeit*, ed. Klaus Schreiner and Gerd Schwerhoff (Cologne, Weimar, Vienna: Böhlau), 1–28; Martin Dinges, 'Die Ehre als Thema der historischen Anthropologie. Bemerkungen zur Wissenschaftsgeschichte und zur Konzeptualisierung', in *Verletzte Ehre. Ehrkonflikte in Gesellschaften des Mittelalters und der Frühen Neuzeit*, ed. Klaus Schreiner and Gerd Schwerhoff (Cologne, Weimar, Vienna: Böhlau), 29–62.

[52] Sibylle Backmann and Hans-Jörg Künast, Einführung, in *Ehrkonzepte in der Frühen Neuzeit*, ed. Sibylle Backmann, Hans-Jörg Künast, Sabine Ullmann and B. Ann Tlusty, 2nd ed. (1998; Berlin: Akademie, 2018), 15.

[53] Ibid., 12.

[54] Berkovich, *Motivation*, 10.

[55] Starkey, *War*, 60.

Introduction 9

Sources and methods

Sources

The sources used for this book can be divided into two main categories. The first one consists of writings on military theory, which can be subdivided into three subcategories:

1. regulations and instructions for officers;
2. military history / theory;
3. diaries of certain units – the *Journals*.[56]

Regulations and instructions are necessary to analyze the basis of military tactics and the desired reactions of the soldiers in combat. The most important source is the Prussian Infantry *Reglement* of 1743 / 1750.[57] Eighteenth-century military history and military theory must also be taken into account. Their authors were officers presenting their own tactical analyses of combat in the Seven Years' War to the public of their time. They wrote military history to advance their own military theories and their theoretical texts were always based on practical examples and the author's personal experience with their men. At the same time, officers and generals used texts from categories 1 and 2 above to educate themselves, and for the training and drill of the troops entrusted to them. The *Journals* contain information on the regiments' movements, which facilitate the contextualization of the 'ego-documents' (see below). And they relate those actions that were regarded as especially honourable for the unit.[58] This makes them a unique source for the Prussian army's notion of honour. Thus, these texts form the theoretical background and context for the interpretation of the second category, the ego-documents.

The ego-documents[59] are texts written by common soldiers, NCOs and line-officers. These texts are characterized by their highly personal and emotional style. Most of them were written for private use and the addressees were typically close relatives. The types of text concerned are mainly informal: letters, diaries, memoires and personal records. The carefully published writings of the military chaplain Daniel Küster are an exception, but his unique and very personal analyses of the soldiers' psychological conditions demand his incorporation into this group.

---

[56] A detailed list of these sources can be found in Appendix I on pages 173–6.
[57] Frederick II issued new regulations in 1743. The *Reglement* of 1750 is identical to that of 1743. *Reglement vor die Königl. Preußische Infanterie, Worinn enthalten: Die Evolutions, das Manual und die Chargirung, und Wie der Dienst im Felde und in der Garnison geschehen soll, Auch Wornach die sämtliche Officiers sich sonst zu verhalten haben. Desgleichen wie viel an Tractament bezahlet und darvon abgezogen wird, auch wie die Mundirung gemachet werden soll. Ordnung halber In XII. Theile / ein jeder Theil in gewisse Titules, ein jeder Titul in gewisse Articles abgefasset* (Berlin, 1743). https://play.google.com/books/reader?id=WysPAAAAQAAJ&hl=de&pg=GBS.PA3 (accessed 10 September 2018). For the sake of readability, it will be cited as *Prussian Infantry Reglement of 1743* in the text.
[58] Möbius, *Mehr Angst*, 33–4; Zielsdorf, *Militärische Erinnerungskulturen*, 73–9.
[59] In Germany, there was a debate regarding whether sources such as letters or diaries should be called *Selbstzeugnisse* ('self-testimonials') or *Ego-Dokumente*. As there is no adequate English translation for *Selbstzeugnisse* ('self-testimonials' is a more or less clumsy translation), we chose to name them ego-documents, which is easier to translate.

Of the ego-documents, the three collections of soldiers' letters are at the core of this study:

1. the *Letters of Prussian Soldiers from the Campaigns of 1756 and 1757*, published by the Prussian General Staff;[60]
2. the *Prussian Soldiers' Letters from the region of the Province of Saxony*[61] from the 18th Century, published by Georg Liebe;[62]
3. the *Prussian Soldiers' Letters 1747–1758* of Christian Friedrich and Johann Dietrich Zander from Brandenburg, an uncle and nephew serving in the infantry von Itzenplitz Regiment (no. 13), published by Christian Friedrich Zander;[63]
4. a letter by the Grenadier Johann Hermann Dresel from Prussian Westphalia, serving in infantry regiment no. 9.[64]

The following diaries and memoires[65] have been used for comparison and contextualization of the letters:

1. the diary of the Musketeer Dominicus, serving in infantry regiment no. 9;[66]
2. the memoires of the NCO J. F Dreyer of the Prussian light infantry (*Freiregiment*);[67]
3. the memoires of the Hessian Chasseur-NCO Georg Beß;[68]
4. letters of the Brunswick Musketeer-NCO Johann Heinrich Ludwig Grotehenn;[69]
5. the surviving fragments of the diary of Lieutenant Lemcke from the Alt-Anhalt Regiment (no. 3);[70]

---

[60] *Briefe preußischer Soldaten aus den Feldzügen 1756 und 1757*, ed. Großer Generalstab (Berlin: Mittler, 1901).
[61] Today a part of the *Bundesland* (state) of Saxony-Anhalt, one of the former core provinces of the Prussian monarchy.
[62] *Preußische Soldatenbriefe aus dem Gebiet der Provinz Sachsen im 18. Jahrhundert*, ed. Georg Liebe (Halle/ Saale: Gebauer-Schwetschke, 1912).
[63] Christian F. Zander, *Fundstücke – Dokumente und Briefe einer preußischen Bauernfamilie (1747-1953)* (Hamburg: Verlag Dr. Kovač, 2015), 15-113.
[64] Rolf Dieter Kahl, 'Ein Brief des Wiblingwerder Bauernsohnes Johann Hermann Dresel aus dem Siebenjährigen Krieg', *Der Märker* 28, vol. 3 (1979): 82–4.
[65] There is an ongoing discussion around whether printed memoires can be used for investigating soldiers' mentalities. We decided to use those passages, which are reliable in our specific context, especially, when their content matches with other ego-documents and theoretical writings.
[66] *Aus dem Siebenjährigen Krieg. Tagebuch des preußischen Musketiers Dominicus*, ed. Dietrich Kerler (München: Beck'sche Verlagsbuchhandlung, 1891). Below cited as *Tagebuch des Musketiers Dominicus*.
[67] Joseph Ferdinand Dreyer, *Leben und Taten eines preußischen Regiments-Tambours* (1810; repr., Osnabrück: Biblio, 1975).
[68] George Beß, *Aus dem Tagebuch eines Veteranen des Siebenjährigen Krieges* (s.l. & t.).
[69] Johann Heinrich Ludwig Grotehenn, *Briefe und kleine Nachrichten, die ich während dem Kriege, welcher sich Anno 1757 im Monat April eräugnete, an meinen Vater geschrieben*, ed. Hans Hölscher (Kirchbrak, 1991); *Johann Heinrich Ludwig Grotehenn. Briefe aus dem Siebenjährigen Krieg, Lebensbeschreibung und Tagebuch*, ed. Marian Füssel and Sven Petersen (Potsdam: Militärgeschichtliches Forschungsamt, 2012).
[70] Jakob Friedrich von Lemcke, 'Kriegs- und Friedensbilder aus den Jahren 1754–1759. Nach dem Tagebuch des Leutnants Jakob Friedrich Lemcke', ed. R. Walz *Preußische Jahrbücher* 138 (1909): 19–43.

6. the reminiscences of Lieutenant von Hülsen from the East Prussian infantry von Below Regiment (no. 11), written for his children;[71]
7. the diary of Lieutenant, and later Captain, von Barsewisch from the von Meyerinck Regiment (no. 26), taken from an edition published in the 1930s;[72]
8. the complete memoirs of the Silesian Lieutenant von Prittwitz, who served in the Alt-Bevern regiment (no. 7) during the war and wrote them for his children.[73]

The publications of the regimental chaplain and *Oberkonsistorialrat*[74] Carl Daniel Küster are of particular importance. He went to war with the Markgraf Karl Regiment (no. 19). As a trusted pastor, he gained an intense and immediate insight into the soldiers' minds in the aftermath of battle. He used his pastoral experiences when writing and publishing his relation of the Battle of Hochkirch and his journal *Officier-Lesebuch* ('The Officer's Reading Book').

Methods

The praxeological method of historical anthropology is the core approach adopted in this study. It starts from the assumption that human behaviour is conditioned by 'elementary situations' –, as in our case, the threat to one's life – and feelings and their cultural framework, which set the limits for human reactions to and perceptions of these elementary situations and feelings. We have chosen the praxeological method to analyse the soldiers' behaviour in combat because it is most useful for exploring the cultural meaning of honour and honourable behaviour. Praxeology takes as its point of departure the concept that human beings shape and develop their culture by their day-to-day actions ('doing culture' in the terms of the theory of action).[75] Those social actions are of special importance, which are carried out unconsciously. They can also be described as day-to-day, unconscious actions. Yet, these cultural actions must not be confused with instincts or reflexes. They have to be acquired in the framework of a given society and are guided by certain intentions. Once implemented, they are carried out automatically and are usually neither called into question nor changed independently.

Any study of the early modern Prussian concept of soldiers' honour must be aware that we are dealing with a separate social group, which played a central role in shaping the culture of the macro-sociological framework of the Prussian state. To a high degree,

---

[71] *Unter Friedrich dem Großen. Aus den Memoiren des Aeltervaters. 1752–1773*, ed. Helene von Hülsen (Berlin, 1890).
[72] Ernst Friedrich Rudolf von Barsewisch. *Von Rossbach bis Freiberg 1757–1763. Tagebuchblätter eines friderizianischen Fahnenjunkers und Offiziers*, ed. Jürgen Olmes (1863; Krefeld: Verlag Hermann Rühl, 1959). Cited below as Barsewisch, *Von Rossbach*.
[73] Christian Wilhelm von Prittwitz, *"Ich bin ein Preuße ..."*. *Jugend und Kriegsleben eines preußischen Offiziers im Siebenjährigen Krieg* (Paderborn: Verlag für historische Publikationen und Reprints, 1989).
[74] Leading member of the highest administrative body of the Lutheran church in a given German region.
[75] Karl H. Hörning and Julia Reuter, 'Doing Culture: Kultur als Praxis', in *Doing Culture. Neue Positionen zum Verhältnis von Kultur und sozialer Praxis*, ed. Karl H. Hörning and Julia Reuter (Bielefeld: Transcript, 2004), 9–18.

this is also true for the common soldier, as will be shown in the course of our investigation.

With regard to soldiers, our analysis has to focus on the experience of war culminating in the exposure to excessive violence and death on the battlefield.[76] But what does 'experience of war' mean? Although the phrase might appear self-explanatory, the way in which experiences are formed and processed is often unclear.[77] As German native-speakers, we must clarify an important linguistic issue at this juncture. The English word 'experience' covers the German terms *Erleben* (witnessing) and *Erfahrung* (experience). We use 'experience' in the sense of the German word *Erfahrung*. For example, a soldier *erlebt* (witnesses) the death of a comrade when he is directly present when the awful event takes place. He creates the *Erfahrung* (experience) of the comrade's death when he (for example) writing about it after having – however briefly – reflected and created sense of it / or acknowledged his failure to create sense of it. The sociological notion of 'experience' is part of the discourse on the living environments of social groups or individuals. The concept of a social 'space of experience' (*Erfahrungsraum*)[78] is based on a spatial movement. Here, we have to keep in mind that the German word *Erfahrung* contains part of the verb *fahren* (to go or travel). From a morphological perspective, *erfahren* means 'to go *through* something' or to be on your way, en route. Thus, *Erfahrungen* (experiences) are realizations generated on your way, on your journey. The space traversed during this journey is the space of experience. This journey – like all others – also requires time. Experiences are those observations (or parts of them) that people remember after the journey and which affect their future actions and thoughts. The ongoing repetition of an experience creates an entrenched mode of behaviour.[79]

What does this mean for our analysis of the early modern Prussian soldier?

1. His experience is formed during his 'journey'. That means in combat, on the drill square, at the dressing station *but not* at the journey's end after the war was over. Again, we have to stress the unique character of the soldiers' letters as a historical source as they provide the most immediate and unmitigated insight into the men's experience.
2. Experiences of war and their repetition lead to stabilized experiences and entrenched modes of behaviour. These also form the day-to-day life of the soldier

---

[76] Gerd Dressel, *Historische Anthropologie. Eine Einführung* (Vienna: Böhlau, 1996), 77.
[77] As German native-speakers, we have to clarify an important linguistic issue here. The English term 'experience' covers the German terms *Erleben* (witnessing) and *Erfahrung* (experience). We use 'experience' in the sense of the German word *Erfahrung*. A soldier e.g. *erlebt* (witnesses) the death of a comrade, when he is directly present and senses the horrible event. He makes the *Erfahrung* (experience) of the comrade's death, when he e.g. writes about it after having – however briefly – reflected and created sense of it / or acknowledged his failure to create sense of it.
[78] Michael Kauppert, 'Wie erschließt sich der Erfahrungsraum? Zur Transformation des Lebenswelttheorems, in *Phänomenologie und Soziologie. Theoretische Positionen, aktuelle Problemfelder und empirische Umsetzungen*, ed. Jürgen Raab et al. (Wiesbaden: Verlag für Sozialwissenschaften, 2008), 247.
[79] Kauppert, *Erfahrungsraum*, 248; Reinhart Koselleck, *Vergangene Zukunft. Zur Semantik geschichtlicher Zeiten* (Frankfurt / M: Suhrkamp, 1979), 356.

and enter his living environment. Thus, cultural practices emerge which form and define the notion of honour, as it can be found, for example, in the regulations and *Journals*. The cultural notion of honour is thus formed by experiences of war.

We have to stress that the specific space of experience of the soldiers' estate is the battlefield. This space of experience distinguishes them from all other estates, regardless of their place of origin. That is why simply equating a soldier's honour with that of a noble or an artisan is not possible.

Our book will present an analysis of the psychology and ideology of the Prussian army in combat during the Seven Years' War. To clarify this, we want to draw on findings of the American literary historian Paul Fussell. He pointed to two facts that are important for our enterprise. On the one hand, even the most erudite civilian historian is separated quite dramatically from the experience of war possessed by the objects of his investigation. This deep gulf between the images of war held by non-combatants and the soldiers' experience is highlighted by the deep ambivalence many veterans of the Second World War felt towards their own public heroization by war correspondents and the media.[80] On the other hand, as Fussell pointed out, any debate on motivation and ideologies in war must make a careful distinction between the prevailing ideology of the given society involved in the war and the soldiers' thoughts during combat.[81] Concerning our soldiers' letters, this means that:

1. there can be considerable differences between memoires, *Journals* and regulations on the one hand, and the letters on the other hand. This is not only due to the temporal distance but also to the different audiences.
2. these differences may be linked to the process of reflection and sometimes transfiguration typical for memoires, *Journals* and regulations.
3. there can be considerable differences between the image of the soldier as a cog in the machine – carefully constructed by the king – and the soldiers' self-perception.

We do not want to try to analyse the psyche of those soldiers who took part in the Seven Years' War based on a certain psychological theory, as there are simply not enough sources on consequential traumatization or the psychological effects of their exposure to violence. Yet we can state that the soldiers witnessed all of the causes of severe psychological traumatization listed in the Diagnostic and Statistical Manual of Mental Disorders (DSM-5)[82]: exposure 'to death, threatened death, actual or threatened serious injury, or actual or threatened sexual violence' by 'direct exposure, witnessing the trauma, learning that a relative or close friend was exposed to

---

[80] Paul Fussell, *Wartime. Understanding and Behavior in the Second World War* (New York and Oxford: Oxford University Press, 1989), 270.
[81] Fussell, *Wartime*, 296.
[82] See the criteria for PTSD on the homepage of the US Department of Veterans Affairs: https://www.ptsd.va.gov/professional/PTSD-overview/dsm5_criteria_ptsd.asp (accessed 28 May 2018). We will not go into the debate on problems of the DSM: https://www.theodysseyonline.com/criticisms-dsm-5 (accessed 28 May 2018); https://www.psychologytoday.com/us/blog/dsm5-in-distress/201212/dsm-5-is-guide-not-bible-ignore-its-ten-worst-changes (accessed 28 May 2018).

a trauma, indirect exposure to aversive details of the trauma, usually in the course of professional duties.'[83] These factors caused fear, and sometimes panic, in nearly every soldier.[84]

As far as our sources are concerned, the word 'psychology' first appeared in the writings of the former army chaplain and *Oberkonsistorialrat*[85] in Magdeburg, Carl Daniel Küster.[86] The conscientious chaplain had reflected on the soul of the soldiers and used his findings to influence the hearts and minds of the men by conversations,[87] sermons[88] and his personal intervention during the Battle of Hochkirch.[89] Although Küster was a very meticulous observer, *his* notion of psychology must not be mixed up with twentieth-century scientific psychology. Modern military psychology developed only before the First World War.[90] 'The Russian Army in the Russo-Japanese War (1904–1905) was apparently the first army in modern times to establish a system of forward psychiatric clearing hospitals equipped with its own specialists.'[91] Military psychologists served in the American and British armies during the First World War in order to return traumatized soldiers to the trenches. The corresponding mental illness was called 'shell shock' at that time, and the psychologists presented differing interpretations for its causes, ranging from tiny steel-particles having penetrated the victim's spinal cord to more serious psychological reasons.[92] Military psychology, and psychology in general, became established sciences during the Second World War. This is highlighted by the fact that more psychologists and psychiatrists were trained by the US armed forces during that conflict than there had been members of the *American Psychiatric Association* before 1941.[93]

---

[83] https://www.ptsd.va.gov/professional/PTSD-overview/dsm5_criteria_ptsd.asp (accessed 28 May 2018).

[84] For example, thousands of Austrian soldiers fled during the Battle of Leuthen, but there is no evidence that all of those who were terrified by the advancing Prussians developed PTSD. Jörg Muth, 'Leuthen: contra una abrumadora superioridad', *Desperta Ferro: Historia Moderna* 24 (2016): 48–55. The same is true for the Prussian Lieutenant von Prittwitz, who fled in 'panic' together with his regiment at the Battle of Zorndorf but did not develop PTSD. Prittwitz, *'Ich bin ein Preuße...'*, 95. Today, about one-quarter of all soldiers exposed to violence in war develops PTSD. Arieh Shalev, Israel Liberzon and Charles Marmar, 'Post-Traumatic Stress Disorder', *The New England Journal of Medicine* 376 (2017): 2459–69.

[85] There is no equivalent term in English. An *Oberkonsistorialrat* is a member of the *Konsistorium*, the highest administrative body of the Lutheran church, in this case in the church province of Saxony. It consisted of theologians and jurists.

[86] [Carl Daniel Küster], 'Einige psychologische Erfahrungen über Vergnügen und Misvergnügen der Krieger im Getümmel der Schlacht', in *Officier-Lesebuch*, vol. 2, 88–91. [Carl Daniel Küster], Des Preußischen Staatsfeldpredigers Küster, Bruchstück seines Campagnelebens im siebenjährigen Kriege (Berlin: Karl Mathdorffs Buchhandlung, 1791), XV, 191, 112–14.

[87] Küster, *Bruchstück*, 61, fn. *

[88] Küster, *Bruchstück*, 158.

[89] Küster, *Bruchstück*, 41–3, 49, 63.

[90] Martin Lengwiler, 'Jenseits der "Schule der Männlichkeit". Hysterie in der deutschen Armee vor dem Ersten Weltkrieg', in *Landsknechte, Soldatenfrauen und Nationalkrieger. Militär, Krieg und Geschlechterordnung im historischen Wandel*, ed. Karen Hagemann and Ralf Pröve (Frankfurt/Main and New York: Campus, 1998), 145–170.

[91] Eric T. Dean Jr., *Shook over Hell: Post-Traumatic Stress, Vietnam, and the Civil War* (Cambridge, MA, and London: Harvard University Press, 1997), 31.

[92] Ibid., 33.

[93] Ibid., 38.

But it took another twenty years – and the experience of the Vietnam War – to establish a synthesis between military psychology and general psychology. The analysis of the 'Vietnam Syndrome' developed into research on the Post-Traumatic Stress Disorder, PTSD.

Basing our argument on the comparison between the reactions to violence by soldiers of the American Civil War and the Vietnam War, we can take as a point of departure that there is a set of emotions which *can* appear when human beings are exposed to life-threatening violence.[94] The resulting actions are conditioned by the soldiers' individual psychological condition, their previous conditioning by allegiance to different estates (artisans, peasants, noblemen), religion, family ties, as well as military formation and the interaction with comrades and officers during combat. It is exactly this variety of reactions that prompted us to include the translated soldiers' letters in the appendix in order to show the broad variety of potential soldier-types and emotions.

While our analysis of the sources carefully draws on key concepts in modern psychology as methodological aids, we remain fully aware of the limitations of such a modern psychological analysis of ancien régime soldiers. The same is even truer for the vast amount of literature on primary unit cohesion. Ilya Berkovich has written an excellent overview and discussion of this concept in his study on motivation in war, which we recommend here without re-stating it.[95] We must highlight that the specific nature of our sources and of the Prussian army make it difficult to use this twentieth-century sociological concept for our undertaking. 30 to 50 per cent of the rank and file of the Prussian army were mercenaries and we have just two memoires from this group. Their relationship to the drafted *Kantonisten*,[96] who made up the rest of the regiment, cannot be derived from the sources. But this would be essential, as the Prussian battle formation tore apart the small groups of men who lived together and put men side by side who scarcely knew each other. And the letters and diaries of the *Kantonisten* do not contain enough information to gather sufficient data. At the same time, we encounter the same problem in applying this concept as did Omer Bartov in his study of Wehrmacht divisions fighting on the Eastern front.[97] Prussian regiments, especially those of the authors of our letters, often lost two-thirds of their men on one day and three times their full strength between 1756 and 1763. Even the argument that the *Kantonisten* of each regiment came from the same region does not permit the conclusion that these men provided the units with ever-renewed cohesive small groups enhancing their fighting capacity. This was true for nearly all infantry regiments and their battle records differ substantially. Again, an in-depth study of at least a small number of regiments is almost impossible on the basis of the surviving known sources. Thus, the concept of small-group cohesion is difficult to apply to our special case as a central methodological tool and other factors have to be studied.

---

[94] Ibid., 70–90.
[95] Berkovich, *Motivation*, 23–30.
[96] See pp. 24–5.
[97] Omer Bartov, *The Eastern Front, 1941–45: German Troops and the Barbarisation of Warfare* (Basingstoke: Palgrave Macmillan, 2001).

The soldiers' honour

When we talk about soldiers' honour in the old Prussian army, we have to stress that the mid-eighteenth-century notion of honour amongst Prussian soldiers differed substantially from nineteenth- or even twentieth-century notions of honour. The link between honour and the nation, nationalism or even chauvinism did not exist in the minds of most Prussian soldiers. Due to the fact that we are talking about the early modern era, the letters show us unequivocally that the soldiers' mentality is more connected to the ideas of the Renaissance than to those of the modern nation state. And we must not forget the specific German context. At that time, there was no unified German nation state; instead, bitter conflicts raged between the different entities making up the Holy Roman Empire of the German Nation.[98] Thus Germany differs substantially from Great Britain, France or Spain, and this had substantial repercussions for the armed forces.

The idea that men had to fight without fear, or that war in itself was both honourable and desirable, or battle the ultimate proof of male courage and honour, would have sounded strange, ridiculous and even sinful to them. And they would have considered it idiotic to seek personal honour that was not linked to any material or social recompense. Analysing their concept of honour, we base ourselves on the following definition:

> Honour is a medium, by which social estimation can be awarded or distracted and which fixes the social reputation of a person in their community. (...) Thus, the position of the individual on the social market of esteem was decisive for his room of manoeuvre in his society. It secured the approachability of material and social support through informal networks or institutions of social and economic collaboration.[99]

We want to stress that notions of honour can change and are basically open systems for defining social groups.[100] Time and place also play a crucial role in why modern concepts of honour are not useful for our investigation. Thus, we have to define the elements of honour in the thinking of the individual Prussian soldiers and analyse how these can be traced in the letters and diaries of the soldiers or the writings about soldiers by officers and chaplains.

Without anticipating our results, we can outline some cornerstones of the Prussian soldiers' notion of honour:

- fighting *because* of honour and glory and not *for* honour and glory: soldiers saw themselves as honourable beings and tried to fight effectively in order not to lose their and their families' honour.

---

[98] The word 'Nation' in this term implies a common language and culture but not a political national consciousness.
[99] Sibylle Backmann and Hans-Jörg Künast, 'Einführung', in *Ehrkonzepte in der Frühen Neuzeit*, ed. Sibylle Backmann, Hans-Jörg Künast, Sabine Ullmann and B. Ann Tlusty, 2nd ed. (1998; Berlin: Akademie, 2018), 15.
[100] Ludwig and Zimmermann, *Ehre und Pflichterfüllung*, 12.

- combat effectiveness to a reasonable degree earned a regiment and its members honour.[101] Foolish bravado, 'Ramboism' or fighting to the last man without tactical need decreased or even wiped out their honour.
- desertion in battle or premature flight were branded as cowardice and led to the total loss of honour, but crying, shaking or other signs of fear were viewed more leniently.
- the adherence to certain rules of honourable behaviour during combat, like not using certain types of ammunition and sparing wounded and helpless enemies, was of crucial importance, because actions to the contrary made the soldiers lose the right to being taken prisoner after throwing down their arms if surrender was the only option.
- enduring the hardships of marching and campaigning was in itself honourable.[102]
- the honour of God, king and regiment were to be defended.
- the physical defence of their homes and above all their friends' and the families' lives was an important part of the soldiers' honour.
- decent behaviour towards unarmed civilians and helpless enemy soldiers was deemed honourable but less important than effectiveness in battle.
- honour was always linked to social and material gains.
- the notions of honour in the *Reglements* and theoretical writings and in the soldiers' private letters do not show significant differences. There is no difference between the authorities' notion of honour and the soldier's notion of honour.

---

[101] The case of the first battalion of Guards (No. 15) is especially instructive. The battalion had managed to fire two complete rounds of platoon fire during the Battle of Mollwitz. It had lost many men but contributed to the Prussian victory by following this order. Platoon fire was very effective, and the soldiers practised it daily, but it was extremely difficult to get it right in battle situations. The king led the battalion to the drill square and made it fire two rounds of platoon fire every year on the anniversary of the Battle of Mollwitz. Zielsdorf, *Militärische Erinnerungskulturen*, 230.

[102] Zielsdorf, *Militärische Erinnerungskulturen*, 69.

1

Drilling on the Job

About a Soldier's Brain

This chapter contains three parts. The first one will deal with the basic features of the eighteenth-century Prussian army, and we will discuss its structures, social composition and general mentalities. The second will deal with linear tactics and early modern European combat in general, while the third analyses the Prussian army's elementary tactics and training. A special focus will be on the psychological aspects of the new tactics developed in the years before the Seven Years' War.

'The men': Origin, recruitment, beliefs and expectations for the future

The Prussian *Reglement* uses the German term *Kerls* for the ordinary soldiers. Unlike today, *Kerl* normally had no pejorative meaning in the first half of the eighteenth century. It could be used in a derogatory sense, but this had to be clarified by corresponding adjectives. *Kerl* encompassed meanings ranging from 'man of peasant origin' to 'tough and manly guy' and even 'hero'.[1] Thus, a noble officer could not be called a *Kerl*, but for a private it was no insult but could actually stress his military ability, and his peasant or artisan origins. The term captures a good proportion of what the king wanted his soldiers to be and how they saw themselves: as humble, yet brave and honourable men. There is no real equivalent to the Early Modern German *Kerl* in modern English. 'Man' is the nearest.[2]

---

[1] *Zedler's Universal-Lexicon* 15 (1737), 484.
[2] 'Lad' or 'fellow' could also be used. But 'lad' normally refers only to a very young man and many soldiers were in their late twenties to early forties. 'Fellow' stresses a comradely relationship, which would have been unthinkable for the king to express in the official regulations and does not fit with the meaning of *Kerl*.

The organizational framework

Numbers and organization of troops

The Prussian army numbered 153,700 men at the beginning of the Seven Years' War. It lost 180,000 altogether in the course of the conflict.[3] Indeed, in some regiments, only around fifty soldiers survived the war.[4] Taking into account that a standard-sized infantry regiment had a complement of just under 1,850 men, it was nearly impossible to make it through alive.

The basic types of soldiers in all European *ancien régime* armies were the infantry (foot soldiers), cavalry (mounted troops) and artillery (gunners). Infantry and cavalry were divided into organizational as well as tactical units. The basic organizational unit was a regiment comprising 1,832 infantrymen of all ranks or 984 cavalry in 1756.[5] The men wore the same uniform and the owner[6] of the regiment and its commanding officer[7] were decisive for the handling and the working atmosphere of the regiment. The latter could vary to a high degree. While some units were ruled by fear and bullying, others were characterized by a humane treatment of the men. An infantry regiment consisted of ten companies of musketeers or fusiliers and two of grenadiers.[8] The companies were the basic organizational units, commanded by captains, who were responsible for all organizational matters ranging from recruitment to uniforms and equipment. In combat situations, the structure changed. Every five musketeer / fusilier companies formed one battalion, which was the basic tactical unit of European infantry in the eighteenth century. The two grenadier companies of the regiment formed a battalion together with the grenadier companies of another regiment. Every battalion was broken down into eight, later[9] ten platoons, which were the essential subdivisions of the battalion for moving and firing. The soldiers were organized in small units, known as 'tent comradeships'. Men from these units used to eat, march and sleep together.[10] The soldiers were assigned to the tent comradeships according to their place in the line of battle and were thus also fighting together.[11] Yet the letters indicate, that the soldiers' social frame of reference was not the tent comradeship but either the other *Kantonisten* from his home village or other

---

[3] Winter, *Untertanengeist*, 124.
[4] Zielsdorf, *Militärische Erinnerungskulturen*, 111.
[5] Johann Heilmann, *Die Kriegskunst der Preußen unter König Friedrich dem Großen*, vol. 1 (Leipzig and Meißen: F.W. Goedsche'sche Buchhandlung, 1852), 97.
[6] The owner (*Inhaber* or *Chef*) of the regiment was normally a general. Although basic funding was provided by the Crown, the owner often used substantial sums of his own money to hire good soldiers and buy high-quality uniforms.
[7] The commanding officer (*Kommandeur*) was a colonel. Responsible for the day-to-day running of the regiment, he also commanded it in battle.
[8] On the differences between musketeers, fusiliers and grenadiers, see pp. 21–2.
[9] From 1757 onwards.
[10] Engelen, *Soldatenfrauen*, 365.
[11] Gabriel Christian Benjamin Busch, *Handbuch der Erfindungen*, vol. 8 (Eisenach: Wittekindsche Hofbuchhandlung, 1816), 16.

mercenaries from the same country or region as they themselves.[12] A standardized drill and training assured every soldier that any comrade next to him was a professional who had the same understanding of honour, and who would help survive. All of this was also true for the cavalry, the only difference being that its regiments consisted of ten companies, two of which formed a tactical unit, a squadron.[13]

Table 1.1 Organizational and tactical units of the Prussian army. Note that brigades, divisions and corps are not permanent institutions but grouped together for one campaign or even immediately prior to battle

Organizational unit	Tactical unit
Infantry	**Infantry**
Army	Army
	Corps (several divisions)
	Division (normally two brigades)
	Brigade (normally four battalions)
Regiment (12 companies = 10 musketeer and 2 grenadier companies)	
	Battalion (8-10 platoons)[14]
Company	
	Platoon
Tent comradeship	
Cavalry	**Cavalry**
Army	Army
	Division (normally two brigades)
	Brigade (normally 10 squadrons)
Regiment (10 companies)	
	Squadron[15]
Company	
Tent comradeship	

Different types of troops

Most Prussian soldiers were infantrymen. On the eve of the Seven Years' War, the Prussian infantry amounted to 84,284 men in ninety-nine battalions.[16] They had to march thousands of miles when on campaign, carry their own baggage and weapons and it was they who also bore the brunt of fighting and who suffered the most casualties. Unlike other European armies, the Prussian army granted the infantry the place of honour on parade and by giving trumpets to its regimental bands. This queen

---

[12] Writing soldiers do not mention their tent comrades unless they are from the same village. When they write about the losses suffered by their unit, the tent comradeship is not mentioned specifically. Dominicus' letter is especially interesting, as he describes the gruesome death of some of the men standing next to him. His resulting depression and inability to thank God for his survival is caused by his expectation of immediate death but he writes nothing about feeling pity for his fallen tent-comrades.
[13] *Prussian Cavalry Reglement of 1743*, 3.
[14] Five musketeer or four grenadier companies form a battalion.
[15] Two companies form a squadron.
[16] http://www.kronoskaf.com/syw/index.php?title=Prussian_Army#Line_Infantry (accessed 22 June 2018). The site gives manifold and well researched background information on the Seven Years' War.

of baroque instruments was normally a privilege of the heavy cavalry alone.[17] The ordinary line infantry was made up of musketeers (*Musketiere*) and fusiliers (*Füsiliere*). The musketeers were regiments raised before the accession of Frederick II in 1740. These 'tall regiments' had to consist of recruits between five feet seven inches[18] (*c.* 176 cm) and five feet ten inches tall (*c.* 184 cm). The fusilier regiments were mainly[19] raised between 1740 and 1744[20] and consisted of smaller men between five feet six inches (*c.* 173 cm) and five feet seven inches (*c.* 176 cm). Nevertheless, some regiments had not a single man under 176 cm.[21] Another difference to the musketeers was that the musketeer wore tricorn hats, while the fusiliers wore a cap with a shield,[22] evoking the image of a smaller version of the grenadiers' mitre caps.[23] The grenadiers[24] – elite infantry deployed for shock action and the 'Little War' of skirmishes, foraging and reconnaissance – were taken from the ranks of their musketeer and fusilier regiments.[25] They were shorter[26] and had to be agile and 'men, who are able to march well, are not over 35 years of age, look good, which means that their noses shall not be to short and they shall not have meagre or thin faces'. This was prescribed in the 1726 regulations.[27] From 1743, there were no special regulations for selection of grenadiers. As they were often used in the Little War, they must have been trustworthy and able to fight in open order. Yet it seems that sometimes the captains of the musketeer companies used the opportunity to transfer men to the grenadiers to get rid of unwanted subordinates.[28]

There were also small specialist contingents of *Jägers* (huntsmen / chasseurs) for reconnaissance, the Little War and raids, similar to today's special forces. They were mostly volunteers recruited amongst the professional huntsmen of the kingdom. As

---

[17] Sascha Möbius, '"Ein feste Burg ist unser Gott" und "Das furchtbare Lärmen ihrer Trommeln". Preußische Militärmusik in der Kultur des Kampfes in den Schlesischen Kriegen', in *Mars und die Musen. Das Wechselspiel zwischen Militär und Gesellschaft in der frühen Neuzeit*, eds. Jutta Nowosadtko and Matthias Rogg (Münster: Lit Verlag, 2008), 270.
[18] The German measurement units are *Fuß* (foot) and *Zoll* (inch). There are few differences between the old German and the modern English units.
[19] Four were raised during the reign of Frederick William I (No. 28–31), but later made musketeers. Winter, *Untertanengeist*, 157.
[20] An exception was No. 48, which was created in 1755. http://www.kronoskaf.com/syw/index.php?title=Erbprinz_von_Hessen-Cassel_Fusiliers (accessed 3 September 2018).
[21] Winter, *Untertanengeist*, 157. Amongst these was No. 3, Alt-Anhalt. This is true for peacetime (1733), but these regiments tried to keep themselves large.
[22] See the picture of the cap of No. 35. http://www.kronoskaf.com/syw/index.php?title=Prinz_Heinrich_von_Preu%C3%9Fen_Fusiliers (accessed 3 September 2018).
[23] See the replica of a mitre cap of the grenadiers of No. 2. http://www.kronoskaf.com/syw/index.php?title=File:Prussian_Kanitz_Infantry_Mitre_Cap.jpg (accessed 3 September 2018).
[24] The name stems from the original use of these men in the Royal French Army of the late seventeenth century. There, they were specialists for storming enemy fortifications and defences armed with hand-grenades. As grenades were not used on the battlefield in the Seven Years' War, they were called grenadiers only as a mark of their elite status.
[25] Winter, *Untertanengeist*, 107.
[26] Möbius, *Mehr Angst*, 20. The grenadiers of the converged grenadier battalions, stemming from the musketeer and fusilier regiments must not be confused with the 'giants' of No. 6 (Grenadier Guards) or No. 15 (First Battalion of Guards).
[27] Reglement vor die Königl. Preußische Infanterie von 1726 (1726; repr., Osnabrück: Biblio, 1968), 8. It will be cited as *Prussian Infantry Reglement of 1726*.
[28] C.F. Zander, 17 February 1757, in *Fundstücke*, 48. Zander tells his nephew that another relative or friend had been handed over to the grenadiers for being lazy.

sharpshooters, they were armed with rifles, which were much more precise than the standard muskets of the infantry. In the hands of an experienced hunter or marksman, these were highly lethal weapons. They also played the role of an early military police force, especially to hunt down deserters. Even today the German military police are referred to as *Feldjäger* (literally: field-hunter).

There were also a number of so called *Freibataillone* (free battalions), which were raised to combat the numerous Austrian light troops in the Little War.[29] They were composed of volunteers, but also of deserters from other armies. Although most of them were not very effective, a minority proved valuable in the Little War. Those specialists were mainly recruited amongst butchers' apprentices, to make sure that they were used to killing with their own hands.[30]

Garrisons were manned by special garrison regiments. These were organized like musketeer regiments, but consisted of smaller or less physically able men and were charged with protecting their garrison towns. They were normally not used in the field. Out of these regiments, the best men were given to the 'standing grenadier battalions'.[31] While the other grenadier battalions were formed only in wartime, the standing grenadier battalions were permanent units who worked and trained together in peacetime too. These battalions were extremely effective in battle and counted amongst the elite units of the army.

The *Land Regimenter* (provincial regiments) and the militias raised in 1757 were normally not used in combat but as a recruiting pool for the field regiments.[32] There is not enough research on these units to draw a clear picture.

The mounted arm, the cavalry, was smaller in number but had many advantages for the men. The troopers could travel on horseback, and in battle the casualties of cavalry regiments were always lighter than those of the infantry. Furthermore, mounted men could loot more easily and had a realistic chance of turning a profit in war. As in other European armies, the Prussian cavalry consisted of heavy cavalry, the cuirassiers, medium cavalry, the dragoons and light units, the hussars.[33] Although the cuirassiers had breastplates made of steel and heavier horses for shock action in battle, and the hussars had become experts of reconnaissance and the Little War during the War of the Austrian Succession (1740-48), all cavalry regiments had to be able to fulfil the tasks of the other branches.[34] Thus cuirassiers were often used in the Little War and hussars and dragoons could successfully charge enemy infantry and heavy cavalry on the battlefield. Like the infantry, the cavalry regiments had their *Kantone*, from which they drew half of their men; the other half were volunteers. The cavalry's *Kantone* were located in rural areas to make sure that their men were able to ride and work with horses. The physical demands on the troopers differed from those on the infantrymen, as being tall was no

---

[29] Muth, *Flucht*, 83.
[30] Dreyer, *Leben*, 28.
[31] They were called 'standing' because they were also an organizational unit in peacetime, while the 'composite grenadier battalions' consisting of the two grenadier companies of two infantry regiments were put together only in times of war.
[32] Winter, *Untertanengeist*, 126-30.
[33] Muth, *Flucht*, 80-2.
[34] Peter Wilson, 'Warfare in the Old Regime 1648-1789', in *European Warfare 1453-1815*, ed. Jeremy Black (London: Routledge, 1999), 92.

prerequisite for the cavalry. Thus, cavalry and infantry regiments often shared a *Kanton* without problems.[35]

The artillery was the smallest branch of the army, but it grew substantially during the Seven Years' War, and the gun became the decisive weapon in the later phase of the war.[36] Artillerymen were the intellectuals of the army, because they had to be able to read and calculate to a high level. Amongst their tasks was the calculation of trajectories, the right amount of powder and the handling of time-fuses.[37] Thus, it is no surprise that they were heavily overrepresented amongst military writers and theoreticians. Artillerymen could serve with the heavy artillery, which formed batteries in battle and during sieges, and which mainly consisted of 'twelve-pounders' (guns firing projectiles, which weighed twelve pounds). Smaller pieces accompanied the infantry, normally two six- or three-pounders for each battalion.[38]

Recruitment and daily life

There were three ways via which a man could become a soldier in mid-eighteenth century Prussia. About half of the men in Frederick II's service were so called *Kantonisten* (cantonists). Frederick's grandfather, Frederick I, and his father, the *Soldatenkönig* (soldier king) had introduced a system that distributed the countryside and small towns amongst the regiments of infantry and cavalry. It was codified in 1733, but its forerunners can be traced back to the War of the Spanish Succession (1701–14).[39] Many *Kantonisten* were first drawn into the militia and then into the field regiments.[40] At the end of the Seven Years' War, roughly two-thirds of the army were *Kantonisten*. The regiment as the basic organizational unit had its own area of recruitment. There, all male peasants, artisans and small traders who reached a certain height and were not only sons[41] were enrolled at the age of thirteen and drilled for two months during the summer each year once they reached the age of twenty. Soldiers were obliged to serve in the army between the age of twenty and forty and older.[42] Some were even younger.[43] Who was actually called up was decided by the regiment together with the local authorities. More than half of those who had been enrolled were able to evade service.[44] The community had to provide a new recruit if one of its members deserted. Not unreasonably, all *Kantonisten* wanted to avoid service in wartime, yet service in peacetime could mean a substantial increase in legal power for the whole family, when the regiment's soldiers had the right to address the king

---

[35] Showalter, *Frederick*, pos. 443.
[36] Möbius, *Mehr Angst*, 96.
[37] *Zur Ausbildung und Taktik der Artillerie*, ed. Hans Bleckwenn (Münster: Biblio, 1982), 26–7.
[38] Muth, *Flucht*, 81–2.
[39] Winter, *Untertanengeist*, 95–6.
[40] Ibid., 150.
[41] The eldest son could also be recruited if a family had more than one son. *Fundstücke*, 84.
[42] Winter, *Untertanengeist*, 201.
[43] Kaspar Kalberlah, who was killed in the Battle of Kay, had served the king since he was seventeen years old. Letter from Kaspar Kalberlah, 26 September 1758, in *Soldatenbriefe*, 29.
[44] Showalter, *Frederick*, pos. 462.

directly.⁴⁵ The letters show that sons of the peasant elite, the *Dorfschulzen* (village administrators), were also drawn into the army. Given their literacy and position in peasant society, they seem to have been crucial for maintaining the information network between the village and the front and could serve as mediators between other soldiers and the officers.⁴⁶

Only the nobility, the burghers of certain larger cities (Berlin, Potsdam, Brandenburg), rich merchants and certain religious groups like Mennonites, Quakers and Jews, were exempt. Thus, the army had a large reservoir of trained men who were not lost for the rural and urban economy. The system should not be confused with modern conscription, but it supplied enough men to keep the army's numbers steady and to avoid a total dependence on strong-arm methods.

The introduction of the *Kantonsystem* did not meet with much resistance. This was partly due to the integration of the local magistrates and elites into the recruitment process, which made it preferable to arbitrary recruitment by the regiments' press gangs. It might also have profited from an old medieval idea of all able-bodied men being responsible for the defence of the realm.⁴⁷ Most of our sources, letters and a diary, were written by these men.

The other half of the army consisted of *Ausländer*.⁴⁸ This German term is highly misleading, as its most common English translation is 'foreigner'. Yet in the Prussian muster lists, it simply means that the person came from outside the *Kanton*, or was a mercenary, who came from the *Kanton* but was not required to serve.⁴⁹ A euphemistic translation would be 'volunteer', but only some of the *Ausländer* were genuine volunteers. This latter group, who entered the Prussian service of their own free will, normally signed contracts for six years of service,⁵⁰ and were mainly artisans or peasants from the surrounding principalities and imperial cities, principally Mecklenburg, or were Prussian subjects who were exempt from military service as *Kantonisten*. A smaller proportion came from outside the German-speaking realm.⁵¹ Many of these men saw military service as an alternative to unemployment, while others looked for plunder and booty, evading family obligations, fleeing prosecution for crimes or bankruptcy, and some simply wanted to be soldiers. The Prussian king paid regularly, and the Prussian army had won all its battles during the War of the Austrian Succession (1740–48). For these men, its service was hard but attractive.

Other *Ausländer* were not volunteers at all. They were recruited by violence, deceit and the infamous press gangs. During wartime in particular, recruitment in occupied countries like Saxony took the form of illegal man-hunts, resulting in human tragedies, as able-bodied men were simply torn from their families and forced to serve a cause

---

[45] See the letters of the Zanders, pp. 197–204.
[46] See the introduction to the Zanders, pp. 83–5.
[47] Dennis Showalter stresses the old feudal bonds between the men and the officers. Showalter, *Frederick*, pos. 768–47.
[48] Winter, *Untertanengeist*, 167–70.
[49] Matthias Ludwig von Lossow, *Denkwürdigkeiten zur Charakteristik der preußischen Armee unter dem Grossen König Friedrich II. Aus dem Nachlasse eines alten preußischen Offiziers* (Glogau: Carl Heymann, 1826), 2–7.
[50] Kloosterhuis, *Donner*, 156.
[51] Ibid., 159.

that was not theirs.⁵² Johann Dietrich Zander tells his family about this kind of forced recruitment in March 1757 in Dresden: 'Yea, there was upheaval and lamentation in the city, they took servants, Heiducks⁵³, runners, merchant's apprentices, young craftsmen, day-labourers, Bohemian peasants, and their women ran besides them and were nagging and lamenting. To sum it up, they were from many nations and it did not matter, how many women or children they had.'⁵⁴ The press-ganging was conducted not just by the army but also by local authorities trying to furnish their share of the recruitment process.⁵⁵

Contrary to many accepted tales, the soldiers were not recruited from the lowest or most immoral groups of society.⁵⁶ Indeed Many *Kantonisten* were from well-off peasant and artisan families, and the *Ausländer* were also often from a background that was more middle class than lower class.⁵⁷

In peacetime, the soldiers were firmly rooted in civil society. The *Kantonisten* lived with their families, while unmarried *Ausländer* were billeted in the homes of burghers and peasants. Professional soldiers with families were accommodated in barracks, where only army families lived. For the genuine 'foreigners', this would often become a means of integration: marrying one of the daughters of their landlord might even lead to naturalization, and their becoming a subject of the Prussian king.

Soldiers' 'women' and families

There were also four main groups of soldiers' women and women in Prussia's 'garrison society'.⁵⁸

1. *Wives*: The wives of the soldiers, who were legally married to them. Some of them travelled back and forth between the army and the *Kanton* and served as messengers between the two.
2. *Sweethearts*: A Prussian idiosyncrasy was the legalization of the *Liebsten* (sweethearts). Soldiers, who were not allowed to marry due to a lack of money or permission by their master, could get a *Liebstenschein* (sweetheart diploma).

---

⁵² This was the case in the many neighbouring countries from which the Prussian army forceably recruited young men. Winter, *Untertanengeist*, 146.
⁵³ Heiduck: The able-bodied and tall servant of a Polish noble. *Zedler's* 12 (1735), 1142.
⁵⁴ J. D. Zander, 11 April 1757, in *Fundstücke*, 50–1. It is interesting to see that the Prussian king had first tried to reach an agreement with the local government of Dresden. After its refusal to provide recruits, the king used force. We have to note that the Prussian press-gangs took people who were not protected by the Saxon authorities, namely foreigners and apprentices and unskilled workers. According to Zander, Prussian subjects who had been accidentally caught during the manhunt were released.
⁵⁵ Winter, *Untertanengeist*, 130.
⁵⁶ See: Showalter, *Tactics*, 27–8. Duffy takes the middle ground: Christopher Duffy, *The Military Experience in the Age of Reason* (1987; Ware (GB): Routledge, 1998), 96–104; Lossow, *Denkwürdigkeiten*, 1–18.
⁵⁷ Way, *Class*, 461–2.
⁵⁸ Beate Engelen, *Soldatenfrauen in Preußen. Eine Strukturanalyse der Garnisonsgesellschaft im späten 17. und 18. Jahrhundert* (Münster et al: Lit Verlag, 2005), 203–06. The book is the most detailed study of Prussian soldiers' women.

With this, the army recognized the girlfriend of a soldier as a legitimate companion, cared for the women in times of war and made the relationship honourable.[59]
3. These first two groups were called *Soldatenfrauen* (soldiers' women) in contemporary German.[60]
4. *Family members*: Other women in the soldier's family, like sisters, cousins, mothers etc.[61]
5. *Sutlers and workers*: Many women followed the army and worked as traders, laundresses or cooks.[62]

The women in most soldiers' families, especially when they were *Ausländer*[63] living in the garrison towns, had to take on paid work in addition to their duties in the home.[64] Soldiers' wives could also take over the military duties of their absent men, such as guard duties or supervising the cleaning of stables.[65] This underlines that they were familiar with the soldier's trade. Most soldiers also had to pursue a second occupation. In peacetime, soldiers' families needed two to three additional jobs to survive, like harvest-worker, porter, seamstress or cook. When the men had to march into the field, the economic situation of many soldiers' families deteriorated and became worse still when a man was killed in battle. The government took some hesitant steps to address this problem after the War of the Austrian Succession, so that poor women, whose men were on campaign, could apply for aid.[66] It has to be stressed that this was possible only for the women in the garrison towns, however; wives of the rural *Kantonisten* were not eligible and instead were regarded as part of the rural mutual support network. In other words, they were supported by their families and the village or church community. Thus, the government did not deem it necessary to support them and they were not considered a juridical part of the soldiers' estate by the government.[67] Most widows were not supported by the royal government either, and had to ask the local authorities for assistance. Only the widows of the elite regiments of the Potsdam garrison got some support.[68] As in other cases, official support from the government or the regiment depended on the soldier's service and his honour. The families of those men who had deserted or been dismissed for 'bad conduct' did not get any money.[69] Yet the government knew how important the connection between the soldiers and their families at home was and Frederick II established a postal service that was free for the soldiers and their families.[70]

---

[59] Engelen, *Soldatenfrauen*, 109–11.
[60] Ibid., 26–7.
[61] See the letters on pp. 178, 183, 191, 194, 195.
[62] See: Engelen, *Soldatenfrauen*, 350.
[63] Half of the bridegrooms of the regiment no. 13 were *Ausländer*. Kloosterhuis, *Donner*, 159.
[64] Engelen, *Soldatenfrauen*, 149.
[65] Ibid., 162–64, 377.
[66] Ibid., 144.
[67] Ibid., 387–91.
[68] Ibid., 421.
[69] Ibid., 474–5.
[70] Duffy, *Military Experience*, 128.

Many women followed their men into the field or went there of their own volition, sometimes even accompanied by their children. They worked as sutlers, took on the selling of looted goods, washed and repaired clothes, cooked or served as messengers between the soldiers and their rural or urban communities. There must have been a considerable number of women in the field, as every company was allowed to take up to six women into the field after 1745.[71] Thus, every regiment could take seventy-two women on campaign. And we know that many more women went into the field without official permission. Some of the women even read military literature.[72] The women to whom the soldiers were writing knew their men's trade well and shared their values. Above all, the women's honour was inextricably linked to that of their men. A regiment's flight out of fear would not only dishonour the unit but could mean defeat for the whole army. This meant poverty, humiliation, rape or death for the female camp-followers and their offspring.

Training

Military training was more intense in the Prussian forces than in any other contemporary army. An insightful Spanish military observer, the Duque de Almodóvar, saw the physical hardships and the intensity of the training[73] as a reason for many suicides amongst Prussian soldiers.[74] The basic training took between two months and a year. During this time the soldier spent a good proportion of his working hours training. These exercises were held five days a week in the morning, but also included many hours in the afternoon for cleaning uniforms etc.[75] The *Kantonisten* had to serve for two months a year[76] after their basic training had been finished. The *Ausländer* were drilled more intensely as they were permanently in the garrison, but their service became less demanding after the basic training. Plenty of time was left for doing other jobs to earn money to boost the meagre payment they received for soldiering.

During exercise and manoeuvre periods, drill could start at 2 a.m. and end at 12 p.m. or 1 p.m. and could be extremely demanding, or, as the *Kantonist* Christian Friedrich Zander put it: 'we were thoroughly sheared'.[77] And being physical unable to keep up with the training could lead to punishments, which aggravated the soldiers' grievances.[78] This was also true for the cavalry. Frederick is said to have exclaimed that he would prefer to lose thirty horses more per regiment during training than to suffer his cavalry being unable to attack the enemy or to defend itself in any

---

[71] Jany, *Geschichte*, vol. II, 252.
[72] Möbius, *Mehr Angst*, 82.
[73] NOT punishments or abuse of soldiers.
[74] Anonima Carta del castellano de Avilés á un amigo en Madrid, sobre la presente guerra de Alemania, la córte y estados del Rey de Prusia, su vida, tropa, gobierno, etc., in Epistolario español: colección de cartas de españoles ilustres antiguos y modernos, vol. II (Madrid: Imprenta y Estereotipia de M. Rivadeneyra, 1870), p. 190 r.
[75] Winter, *Untertanengeist*, 196.
[76] Ibid., 200. The *Kantonisten* had to serve for three months per year prior to 1743, and two months a year thereafter.
[77] C.F. Zander, 21 August 1753, in *Fundstücke*, 27.
[78] Winter, *Untertanengeist*, 416–17.

given situation.[79] The drill procedures were tiring and demanding but not senseless. The aim was not to produce blind obedience to meaningless or even stupid commands, but rather to result in expert knowledge on the battlefield. The soldier was trained 'to do precisely what he will execute on the day of battle, and nothing superfluous'.[80] The training was demanding but kept the soldiers healthy, too. Handling a musket weighing more than 4.5 kg improved their strength. Although alcoholism was widespread in society at that time, the drill sessions prevented the soldiers from drinking too much. It was simply not possible to participate in the training with a hangover and soldiers would have feared punishment for this transgression.[81]

Punishments and abuse

The extent to which soldiers were beaten or abused by their superiors is still an open question.[82] First of all, we have to distinguish between *corporal punishments during the drill sessions*, e.g. for being slow, not loading the musket fast enough, or turning in the wrong direction, and *corporal punishments for offences against military law*, and *physical and mental abuse* of soldiers by their superiors. These have been mixed together in many later debates. Time and time again, contemporary engravings of running the gauntlet are reprinted and explained by the 'brutal drill' of the Prussian army. Yet the Prussian regulations did not allow superiors to make their men run the gauntlet for being too slow at a drill session, and physical abuses were forbidden. This does not mean that abuses did not occur, but the regulations show that a clear distinction between rigorous training, military law and abuses has to be made.

The older image of an army kept together and 'motivated' by the sergeant's stick is too simplistic.[83] It discounts the fact that a certain amount of corporal punishment was normal in eighteenth-century education and beating an apprentice or student did not affect his honour.[84] Actually, it was expected in the context of any kind of education, and thus military training did not differ from other kinds of education. There was, in fact, one major difference: soldiers were able to complain, while apprentices or students did not have this opportunity.[85] The soldier who was slowest in loading his musket was beaten

---

[79] Biblioteca Central Militar. Sig. 1758-M4, 133–4. The observers are two Spanish captains in the Royal Guards, Juan José Vertiz y Salced and Martin Alvarez de Sotomayor.
[80] Duffy, *Frederick*, 337.
[81] This is reflected by the advice given to Ulrich Bräker by one of his comrades to buy light beer for the night. http://gutenberg.spiegel.de/buch/lebensgeschichte-und-naturliche-ebentheuer-des-armen-mannes-im-tockenburg-1825/13 (accessed 28 August 2018).
[82] Way gives evidence for a lavish use of punishments, including death sentences, by the British forces in America during the Seven Years' War. Way, *Militarizing*, 356. An alternative view is to be found in Berkovich, *Motivation*, 96. The Prussian army does in fact seem less brutal in punishing its members. This could have been due to the large number of *Kantonisten*, who were subject to military jurisdiction after actually joining the regiment, but who also had a landlord, whose rights had to be considered. See Winter, *Untertanengeist*, 202–07.
[83] Jürgen Kloosterhuis, probably the most learned expert on the subject of the Prussian army's culture, gives a differentiated account of Regiment No. 13 and refutes the old school's stress on military punishments. Kloosterhuis, *Donner*, 166–70.
[84] Muth, *Flucht*, 72.
[85] Ibid, 73.

three times. These procedures were obviously accepted as normal. Arbitrary beatings were forbidden by the *Reglement* and the king made it clear that this ran contrary to the conduct expected from a noble officer.[86] But abuse did occur and ran the gamut from overdoing normal punishments to outright mistreatment of soldiers and subordinates. This could include letting troopers run the gauntlet for falling off their horses[87] to beatings and verbal abuse for no reason. This does not seem to have been the rule,[88] and excessive beatings could lead to uprisings 'like in Potsdam and Berlin'[89] or revenge being taken in battle, when mistreated soldiers got the opportunity to shoot sadistic officers. But sadistic officers could use the general acceptance of corporal punishments to satisfy their proclivities, which is why some influential generals forbade physical punishment during the exercises altogether. The famous cavalry general Friedrich Wilhelm von Seydlitz did just that, arguing that the soldiers' estate was an estate of honour and being beaten for minor lapses or without any reason at all ran contrary to this.[90] General von Natzmer favoured a humane treatment of his soldiers for religious reasons.[91] Again, the differences between the individual regiments were enormous.[92]

The punishments meted out to disobedient soldiers could be draconic indeed. A Prussian soldier could be disciplined by running the gauntlet (twenty times through 200 men) for arguing with his superiors and outright disobedience was to be punished by death[93] or 'most rigorous punishment'.[94] Desertion was to be punished by death. Yet, most deserters were in fact not executed but often enough pardoned and re-admitted to the service if they requested a pardon.[95] Desertion on the battlefield seems to have merited execution immediately after the conclusion of hostilities, but simply running away on the battlefield was dealt with by dishonouring the man or the unit involved. Sometimes, though, it was not punished at all, particularly when the leadership concluded that fleeing had been a reasonable alternative to being slaughtered.[96] 'Summary executions' for 'cowardice' are not a feature of the Prussian army[97] of the

---

[86] *Prussian Infantry* Reglement *of 1743*, 422.
[87] Colonel von Eberstein, commander of the von Plettenberg Dragoons (No. 7) made a trooper run the gauntlet four times for falling off his horse during exercises. Muth, *Flucht*, 69.
[88] Duffy, *Frederick*, 336.
[89] Wolfgang Heil, *Die Gemeinen Soldaten – Das Sozialleben der militärischen Unterschicht im altpreußischen Heer und seine Rolle in der altständischen Gesellschaft 1754–1807* (Hagen: PhD thesis, 2001), 367, cited after: *Fundstücke*, 124.
[90] Muth, *Flucht*, 69.
[91] Sikora, *Disziplin*, 288.
[92] Winter, *Untertanengeist*, 196–7, fn. 208.
[93] *Prussian Infantry Reglement of 1743*, 437.
[94] Ibid., 429.
[95] Sikora, *Disziplin*, 140.
[96] The rout and panic of the Prussian left wing in the opening of the Battle of Prague resulted in a rebuke from the king but nobody was shot or publicly dishonoured, like the Alt-Anhalt Regiment had been during the siege of Dresden in 1760.
[97] There are some sources that relate the hanging for desertion in battle, but this is different from cowardice or running away for good reason, such as those originating from the camp near Lobositz, dated 3 October 1756, and written by an NCO [J.S. Liebler] from the Alt-Anhalt Regiment to Halle, in *Briefe*, 19. Liebler relates the hanging of three soldiers for desertion. When Brian Ditcham writes about 'summary executions' to keep the troops in line, he provides no evidence for this. Brian G.H. Ditcham, Review of Sascha Möbius 'Mehr Angst vor dem Offizier als vor dem Feind', H-German, April 2008. https://networks.h-net.org/node/35008/reviews/45433/ditcham-m%C3%B6bius-mehr-angst-vor-dem-offizier-als-vor-dem-feind-eine (accessed 29 May 2018).

eighteenth century. Mass trials and hundreds of death sentences for failing to attack were a phenomenon of the twentieth century, to be sure, but not the eighteenth. It seems that like in many other cases of early modern military justice[98], it was mainly *the threat of* brutal corporal punishments and the death penalty that kept the men in line than an actual lavish use of them by the authorities. Unfortunately, the loss of the Prussian army files and a lack of modern research[99] do not allow us to draw any definite conclusions. Surely, the common soldiers at least of the elite regiments would have had the right to appeal to the king. It can also be taken for granted that there were huge differences between the individual regiments and that corporal punishments were one, but not the only,[100] means of enforcing discipline and obedience. We should also take into account that punishments were not only a way to intimidate soldiers but could also be seen as a means of protecting them. A negligent musketeer could ruin a whole battalion, while a sadist or rapist could taint the honour of a whole regiment.[101] And another fact has long been overlooked: a regiment's colonel had to pay for all expenses in connection with corporal punishments. The *Reglement* says: 'When *Executions*[102] are carried out by the regiment and the regiment has any expenses for them, only the Colonel has to pay them.'[103] Even a sadistic colonel like von Manstein (Regiment No. 3, Alt-Anhalt, killed in the Battle of Prague)[104], would have thought twice before over-using the gauntlet when he had to pay for all expenses related to any associated injury.

Again, we must stress that when we talk about an absolute monarchy in early modern Europe, there was no such thing like democratic debates about war, debates about military service or conscientious objectors (with the exception of special religious minorities like Mennonites or Quakers). There was a broad consensus in Prussian society that serving the king even in war was a duty before God

---

[98] Maren Lorenz, *Das Rad der Gewalt. Militär und Zivilbevölkerung in Norddeutschland nach dem Dreißigjährigen Krieg (1650–1700)* (Cologne: Böhlau, 2007), 209–18. Lorenz analyzes the Swedish jurisdiction in Pomerania. Although rape should have been punished by death, there were nearly no executions for this offence.

[99] Jutta Nowosadtko, 'Militärjustiz in der Frühen Neuzeit. Anmerkungen zu einem vernachlässigten Feld der historischen Kriminalitätsforschung', in *Unrecht und Recht. Kriminalität und Gesellschaft im Wandel von 1500–2000. Gemeinsame Landesausstellung der rheinland-pfälzischen und saarländischen Archive*, ed. Heinz-Günther Borck (Koblenz: Verlag der Landesarchivverwaltung Rheinland-Pfalz, 2002), 638. Markus Meumann, '"j'ay dit plusieurs fois aux officiers principaux d'en faire des exemples". Institutionen, Intentionen und Praxis der französischen Militärgerichtsbarkeit im 16. und 17. Jahrhundert', in *Militär und Recht vom 16. bis 19. Jahrhundert*, ed. Jutta Nowosadtko, Diethelm Klippel and Kai Lohsträter (Göttingen: V&R unipress, 2016), 87. An analysis for trials against deserters exists only for the time *after* the Seven Years' War: Martin Winter, 'Desertionsprozesse in der preußischen Armee nach dem Siebenjährigen Krieg', in *Militär und Recht vom 16. bis 19. Jahrhundert*, ed. Jutta Nowosadtko, Diethelm Klippel and Kai Lohsträter (Göttingen: V&R unipress, 2016), 187–208.

[100] Berkovich, *Motivation*, 228.

[101] Showalter, *Frederick*, Pos. 522, 2563.

[102] The early modern German meaning of *Execution* is 'regulated and lawful corporal punishment'. It does not necessarily mean, that the delinquent is killed.

[103] *Prussian Infantry Reglement of 1743*, 478.

[104] *Aus dem Nachlasse von Georg Heinrich von Berenhorst*, ed. Eduard von Bülow, vol. 1 (Dessau: Verlag von Aue, 1845), XVI; Lemcke, *Kriegs- und Friedensbilder*, 28.

and was, as part of their destiny, not to be questioned.[105] Modern ideas of having an individual choice about one's way of life simply do not work in mid-eighteenth-century Europe.[106]

Care for disabled soldiers and the families of the dead

There was no adequate system of social care for disabled veterans and the families of soldiers killed in action. Some long-serving veterans were eligible for a small pension, and certain families were also given monthly payments when their menfolk died in the field. But this was the exception to the rule. Normally, widows and orphans had to rely on their rural and urban communities and networks in order to avoid impoverishment. As losses mounted during wartime, the strain on these networks also became unbearable and poverty and starvation was the lot of many families deprived of their husbands, fathers, sons and brothers. One of the darkest chapters of the Prussian army's history was the handling of the military orphanage in Potsdam. While Frederick William I had carefully built up the orphanage and provided the inmates with spiritual guidance and a good education by Pietist chaplains and musical instructors, Frederick II sent the children to the arms factories, where many of them perished due to a harsh labour regime and long working hours.[107]

Desertion

So why didn't those who had been forced to join the colours simply run away? This question has been at the core of German research for many decades. The myriad provisions against desertion and the severe punishments levied against deserters on paper have been seen as proof of the thesis that most men were forcibly recruited and would desert as soon as they could. More recent research has shown that it was rather easy to escape military service in spite of all these provisions, and that only a small percentage of those deserters who were caught were actually sent to the gallows.[108] Scholars have also questioned whether desertion was caused by the brutality or the hardships of the service and have pointed to a set of individual reasons.[109]

It has become clear that the men were not kept together by physical violence – or the threat of it[110] – although this would have played a role to a certain degree.[111] In fact, desertion rates in the Prussian army were fairly low.[112] Precautions against desertion were in place, but when large numbers of soldiers concluded than fleeing was a

---

[105] Möbius, *Mehr Angst*, 101–02.
[106] Sikora, *Disziplin*, 283.
[107] René Schreiter, 'Das Große Militärwaisenhaus zu Potsdam 1724–1952. Ein Kapitel preußisch-deutscher Erziehungsgeschichte', *Militär und Gesellschaft in der frühen Neuzeit* 7, no. 1 (2003): 77.
[108] Berkovich, *Motivation*, 228.
[109] Muth, *Flucht*, 85–104.
[110] Berkovich, *Motivation*, 110–14.
[111] Way sees physical punishment as the 'ultimate weapon of motivation and discipline' besides other ideological and social means 'to secure their hearts and minds to the conflict'. Way, *Militarization*: 347.
[112] See Winter, *Untertanengeist*, 364–6.

preferable alternative to service, leave they did. This was certainly the case in the winter of 1744, when the Prussian king was unable to feed his men and many of them left rather than starve.[113] It was also the case with many regiments of Saxon soldiers pressed into the Prussian service after the capitulation of the Saxon army at Pirna in 1756. Most Saxons had been left in their old formations but allocated Prussian officers. As the Saxons remained loyal to their Elector, they chased away the Prussian officers and went away to join the allied French army or left for Poland.[114] But in most other cases, the Prussian soldiers did not even try to desert. This was due to a wide range reasons:

- the *Kantonisten* would have to give up their social existence and leave their families behind, and their goods would be confiscated.[115]
- the Protestant and Pietist upbringing of many soldiers saw service for the king as fulfilling God's will.[116]
- every soldier would break his oath by deserting, which was not only a capital offence before any worldly court but also before God.[117]
- every deserter needed a place to go to and an alternative way of making a living. With the exception of joining another army[118], both were often hard to come by, especially in time of war.[119]
- the army was a space of survival, as long as it provided basic foodstuffs and had a chance to win.[120]
- a deserter could not only be caught by his own fellow soldiers, but also by enemy soldiers, who could rob or even kill him.[121]
- civilians chased deserters to get a bounty and deliver them to the authorities.

Beliefs and expectations

Below, we present an overview of the beliefs of the Prussian soldiers during the Seven Years' War. These points will also be discussed in more detail in Chapters 2 and 3.

Honour and the estate: As members of the soldiers' estate, they were the king's servants and had to defend the king's honour as well as their own.[122]

A belief in their professional abilities: Prussian soldiers knew that they were better drilled and prepared than their enemies. Their honour was also linked to their professional behaviour. It was not courage alone which secured the men's honour but also their execution of effective tactics.[123] A trooper who moved out of the line of his

---

[113] Showalter, *Frederick*, pos. 1415–21.
[114] Kroll, *Soldaten*, 352–63.
[115] Engelen, *Soldatenfrauen*, 130; Sikora, *Disziplin*, 160.
[116] Möbius, *Mehr Angst*, 134.
[117] Sikora, *Disziplin*, 218. Kloosterhuis, *Donner*, 157.
[118] Sikora, *Disziplin*, 151.
[119] A striking example is the Prussian regrouping after the Battle of Kunersdorf. In spite of the total defeat of the Prussian army, more than 20,000 men returned to the army after having been dispersed by the Russians and Austrians. See Muth, *Flucht*, 160.
[120] Muth, *Flucht*, 42.
[121] See: Showalter, *Frederick*, Pos. 5682.
[122] See p. 130 Loss of honour as an incentive: Berkovich, *Motivation*, 173.
[123] Zielsdorf, *Militärische Erinnerungskulturen*, 248–249.

advancing squadron lost his honour. Even the unwilling *Ausländer* Bräker was at least proud of his ability to shoot fast[124] and the more than willing Dreyer joined the Prussian army to be among the elite of European soldiers.[125]

A belief in their contractual rights: Soldiers saw their service as being based on a contract between themselves and the army / the king.[126] It was not a contract on equal terms, but soldiers had rights and defended them. This was also true for the enlisted *Kantonisten*, proven by Christian Friedrich Zander's attempt to be discharged from the army. Both Christian Friedrich and his civilian elder brother even challenged royal decrees prohibiting the intervention of civilians in military affairs, because they interpreted their rights differently. In the end, Christian Friedrich had to remain a soldier, but seems to have gained a long period of leave before being called to arms at the outbreak of the war. Linked to the soldiers' contract also was a concept of *Subordination*[127] and discipline, which stressed respect for the needs of *all* soldiers in a regiment.[128] The unity of rights and subordination was called *Harmonie* in the *Reglement of the Prussian Army*.[129]

Their comrades and friends:[130] All *Kantonisten* were part of a close-knit network of men from their village and the surrounding ones. They were not only bound to the men marching and fighting with them, but also to their families and the rural community. This is proven by all letters from Kantonisten.

For the *Ausländer,* the situation was quite similar; even the *Ausländer* Bräker has a group of four friends with whom he is quartered. One of them, Bräker's mentor Christian Zittemann, calls the group 'brothers'[131] and teaches Bräker the basic drill procedures.[132] Bräker is also in close contact with the other Swiss mercenaries in the regiment; one of them even plans to desert with him.[133] These mercenaries supported each other economically and emotionally, thus taking the place of the *Kantonisten* families. Bräker – as well as the Zanders and other soldiers – write a lot about their

---

[124] Bräker boasts that he fired all his sixty cartridges, one after the other. Although this is an obvious lie, he shows his pride in his training. Soldiers could fire all their cartridges in one battle, but not one after the other, as this would have made the barrel of the gun too hot. Ulrich Bräker, *Der arme Mann im Tockenburg*, ed. Eduard Bülow (Leipzig: Georg Wigand's Verlag, 1852), 150. http://gutenberg.spiegel.de/buch/lebensgeschichte-und-naturliche-ebentheuer-des-armen-mannes-im-tockenburg-1825/16 (accessed 14 October 2018).

[125] Dreyer, *Leben*, 13.

[126] A common feature of *ancien régime* armies, although historians disagree on the balance between entering a contract with obligations for both parties and sheer force on the side of the government. Way, *Class*: 468; Way, *Militarizing*: 347 vs. Berkovich, *Motivation*, 56–8; Showalter, *Frederick*, pos. 186, 188, 1743.

[127] Subordination is a central term in the Prussian Reglement. *Prussian Infantry Reglement* of 1743, 423–30.

[128] Duffy, *Frederick*, 337. Sascha Möbius, 'Die Kommunikation zwischen preußischen Soldaten und Offizieren im Siebenjärigen Krieg zwischen Gewalt und Konsens', *Militärgeschichtliche Zeitschrift* 63, vol. 2 (2004): 325–53.

[129] *Prussian Infantry Reglement* of 1743, 423–4.

[130] Duffy, *Frederick*, 337; Berkovich, *Motivation*, 35–6.

[131] This is no invention of Bräker, but an expression also used by Tempelhof, who knew the army much better. Georg Friedrich von Tempelhof, *Geschichte des Siebenjährigen Krieges*, vol. 1 (Berlin: Unger, 1783), 69.

[132] Bräker, *Arme Mann*, 116, 120–1. http://gutenberg.spiegel.de/buch/lebensgeschichte-und-naturliche-ebentheuer-des-armen-mannes-im-tockenburg-1825/13 (accessed 28 August 2018).

[133] Bräker, *Arme Mann*, 127. http://gutenberg.spiegel.de/buch/lebensgeschichte-und-naturliche-ebentheuer-des-armen-mannes-im-tockenburg-1825/14 (accessed 28 August 2018).

comrades and friends, but as soon as the first musket is fired, most of them seem to think only of themselves and their families.[134]

Religious faith: The Protestant religion of the Pietist branch was an important factor. The soldiers believed that their service for the *Obrigkeit*[135] was a divine service and would lead their souls to heaven. Anti-Catholic feelings also played a role. Protestant soldiers feared a forced Counter-Reformation. This is reflected in the Zanders' letters, when they relate the rumour that Catholic monks had been caught with six wagons of thumbscrews for torturing Protestants not willing to convert to Catholicism.[136] Another soldier, Sergeant Liebler, calls the Austrians the 'enemies of the gospel'.[137]

Defence of the fatherland and hatred of the enemy: Fatherland in the mid-eighteenth century meaning of the German word *Vaterland* meant, in a very limited geographical sense, the region a soldier came from and only in a few cases the realm of the entire Prussian monarchy. The term is derived from the idea that one's fatherland is the land inherited from one's father. And the soldiers saw the defence of this fatherland as one of the duties they owed to their families and ancestors. Their patriotism differs substantially from the nationalist fervour of the French revolution.[138] The idea of defending the fatherland appears in their writings when their region of origin is in danger of enemy occupation; very seldom is the defence of the fatherland, in the broader sense of the whole country, mentioned as a general duty of the soldier. It is in sharp contrast to later nationalist or even chauvinist notions of the fatherland and is not to be confused with modern ideas.

Negative notions of the enemy are linked to cultural and religious stereotypes as well as the soldiers' experience of these enemies. Hatred of the enemy is often linked to accusations of breaking the rules of war. Thus, the Austrians are the main target of negative religious connotations, while the Russians are seen as barbarians who eat children.[139] Interestingly, the soldiers view all their enemies as effective and courageous soldiers.

[134] Bräker writes that other soldiers hurried to help their brothers-in-arms fight the Austrian light troops on the Lobosch mountain, but his thoughts are focused only on deserting and he does not mention his comrades from his housing in the garrison or the other Swiss soldiers during combat. Bräker, *Arme Mann*, 150–1. http://gutenberg.spiegel.de/buch/lebensgeschichte-und-naturliche-ebentheuer-des-armen-mannes-im-tockenburg-1825/16 (accessed 14 October 2018).

[135] There is no satisfactory translation for the German term *Obrigkeit* in English. 'Authorities' is not too far off the mark, but for Early Modern Germans *Obrigkeit* had a much wider sense. According to the teachings of Martin Luther, the *Obrigkeit* (ranging from the Emperor to the city councils) was installed by God and had to be obeyed like the heavenly ruler. It has to be stressed that in the Holy Roman Empire of the German Nation, the Protestant princes were also the rulers of the church in their realms, thus uniting spiritual and secular authorities. However, this sacred position of the German authorities did not mean that the subjects were forced to – or actually did – follow their orders blindly.

[136] Johan Dietrich Zander, 14 December 1756, in *Fundstücke*, 42.

[137] Letter of Sergeant G.S. Liebler, 7 May 1757, in *Briefe*, 45.

[138] Sascha Möbius, '"Haß gegen alles, was nur den Namen eines Franzosen führet"? Die Schlacht bei Rossbach und nationale Stereotype in der deutschsprachigen Militärliteratur der zweiten Hälfte des 18. Jahrhunderts', in *Gallophobie im 18. Jahrhundert*, ed. Jens Häsler and Albert Meier (Berlin: Deutscher Wissenschaftsverlag, 2005), 123–58.

[139] Russian brutality is a common stereotype in German eighteenth-century military literature. Fleming, *Vollkommene Teutsche Soldat*, 41. Yet Fleming states that they have been 'civilised' and become able warriors.

Gender roles and behaviour towards women and defenceless persons: The soldiers see themselves as the defenders of their families and their families' honour. At the same time, their honour also rests in their behaviour towards women and other defenceless persons. This is mainly shown by the image of the enemy in the soldiers' letters, who 'threw the womenfolk into the straw and burned them, yeah, they ate young children, stabbed and burned everything in the towns and villages'.[140] The enemy wreaks havoc, 'as we [the Prussians] never do'.[141] Interestingly, nineteenth- or twentieth-century notions of combat as the ultimate test of the 'real man' were alien to the Prussian soldiers.[142] Being courageous is never called 'manly' in the soldiers' letters, and being brave is not seen as a special quality of the male gender. What we do see, however, is that it is manly to be a good and faithful husband.[143] If they are too young to be married, it is also manly to fulfil their obligations to the heads of their family.

Trust in the officers and the king: All soldiers show a high degree of trust in their superiors, which was mainly due to the latter's military competence and their willingness to share the hardships of campaigning and combat with them.[144] Contrary to later nineteenth-century legends, the soldiers did not 'adore' the king but felt buoyed up by the fact that he 'was at the front all the time', could grasp a flag and lead his 'children' into the fray.[145] The king could also be criticized and his decisions were open to debate.[146] Their trust in the king's decisions had been based on an uninterrupted series of victories during the War of the Austrian Succession. Prussian soldiers trusted in theirs and their commanders' expertise and experience to win battles and assumed that risks to be calculated.

During the Seven Years' War – and as a result of the defeats at Kolin, Hochkirch and Kunersdorf – this changed, and soldiers began to criticize tactical decisions,[147] particularly launching attacks against enemy troops positioned on heights.[148] These

---

[140] Letter from Kaspar Kalberlah, written between Dresden and Pirna, 26 September 1758, in *Soldatenbriefe*, 29.

[141] Letter of Sergeant G.S. Liebler from the camp near Prague, 7 May 1757, in *Briefe*, 45.

[142] Sascha Möbius, '"Bravthun","entmannende Furcht" and "schöne Überläuferinnen" – Zum Männlichkeitsbild preußischer Soldaten im Siebenjährigen Krieg in Magdeburg, Halle und der Altmark', in *Leben in der Stadt. Eine Kultur- und Geschlechtergeschichte Magdeburgs* (Cologne, Weimar, Vienna: Boehlau, 2004), 95–6.

[143] Letter from Corporal Binn, 18 April 1759, in *Soldatenbriefe*, 20–1.

[144] Duffy, *Frederick*, 337–8. Concerning the king, this behaviour was well calculated. Ute Frevert, *Gefühlspolitik. Friedrich II. als Herr über die Herzen* (Göttingen: Wallstein, 2012, Kindle edition), pos. 781–816.

[145] Letter from Musketeer Dominicus, 25 August 1759, in *Tagebuch des Musketiers Dominicus*, 65. See p. 180.

[146] Beschreibung der Lobositzer Bataille, datirt 1. Oktober 1756, in *Soldatenbriefe*, 4. Letter of Lt. Seiler, 8 November 1757, in *Soldatenbriefe*, 36. C. F. Zander, 16 September 1757, in *Fundstücke*, 62. All of these letters relate debates between the king and his generals in which the king wants to attack a well-defended enemy position, and his generals persuade him to abstain from it. Seiler openly states, that General von Seydlitz was responsible for the victory at Roßbach, because he dissuaded the king from attacking the Austrians in a position 'like that at Kolin'.

[147] Beschreibung der Lobositzer Bataille, datiert 1. Oktober 1756, in *Soldatenbriefe*, 4. Lager vor Prag, den 8. Mai. Schreiben eines Musketiers des Regiments Anhalt zu Fuß 1757, in *Briefe*, 51. Letter of Lt. Seiler, 8 November 1757, in *Soldatenbriefe*, 36. C. F. Zander, 16 September 1757, in *Fundstücke*, 62.

[148] Charles Emmanuel de Warnery, *Feldzüge Friedrichs des Zweyten*, vol. 1 (Hannover: Helwing, 1789), 224.

had been at the root of the heavy Prussian casualties at Lobositz, Prague, Kolin, Kunersdorf and Torgau.

Overall the soldiers were convinced that they could beat any enemy when their generals led them to fight on even terrain, where the soldiers could make use of their superior training and firing speed cadence.[149]

Being used to it: The Kantonisten were enlisted by the age of thirteen. In the period of time between seventeen and twenty, they were able to learn their trade as soldiers and join the regiment. In many cases, their fathers[150], elder brothers or cousins were (or had also been) in the king's service. Thus, they and their peers were used to becoming soldiers. The result of this was a 'soldiers' spirit', which consisted of toughness, obedience and professional knowledge. Obedience did not mean blind obedience, but carrying out orders in a professional way, as outlined in their contractual obligations. The notorious Prussian *Kadavergehorsam*[151] was a feature of nineteenth- and twentieth-century armies. And their toughness was not the militancy of a nationalist zealot, but rather the ability to bear hardships and danger in the framework of a calculated risk.[152]

A lack of social alternatives: In order to avoid military service or to leave the Prussian army, anecdotal evidence suggests that soldiers could try to mutilate themselves by damaging or cutting off the parts of their bodies that were essential for handling their arms, like the thumb of the right hand or their front teeth. We do not, however, have any valid sources that this actually happened.[153] And we should add that self-mutilation was extremely dangerous: an effective mutilation could cause gangrene and prove deadly.[154] The other possibility was desertion. The soldiers write about desertions, mostly those of *Ausländer*,[155] but also a few from the ranks of the *Kantonisten*.[156] A *Kantonist*, who deserted had to be ready to give up his former life.[157] For most soldiers this would have been impossible, as they would also have lost their property and been unable to find a new job as farmer or artisan. Even the *Ausländer* who had been in the Prussian service for a while would have had encountered difficulties in finding alternative employment and accommodation. During conflicts, the army was often the sole means of sustaining oneself and the only alternative to the Prussian army would have been another European army, as armies were the largest employer in Europe during wartime. Defecting to another army would not have improved deserters' situations, because payment and provisions were not as good as those offered by the Prussians.

---

[149] C.F. Zander, 21 July 1757, in *Fundstücke*, 54. Möbius, *Mehr Angst*, 62.
[150] E.g. father and son Liebler, see p. 66.
[151] Literally translated the term means 'obedience of a corpse'. It stands for blind obedience, however stupid or even amoral an order might be.
[152] Liebler's description of his conduct in the Battle of Prague shows this very clearly. Möbius, *Mehr Angst*, 130.
[153] Winter, *Untertanengeist*, 351–3.
[154] Harold Ellis, *A History of Surgery* (London: Greenwich Medical Media Limited, [2001] 2002), 55–61.
[155] C.F. Zander writes that the '*Ausländer* are deserting' after the defeat at Kolin. C.F. Zander, 21 July 1757, in *Fundstücke*, 55.
[156] Corporal Binn, 30 December 1757, in *Soldatenbriefe*, 11.
[157] A Kantonist, who had fled in 1783 had handed over his complete uniform, an old coat and his marriage certificate (!) to his brother-in-law while running away. Winter, *Untertanengeist*, 415.

Expectations for the future: As the vast majority of the letters were written during wartime, we have a rather good image of soldiers' expectations while they were in the field: getting home without serious injuries[158] and keeping their honour intact were key. This desire contributed substantially to the Prussian army's effectiveness. Rising through the ranks and earning a commission as an officer was most probably no incentive for common soldiers during peacetime, as this was reserved for the nobility. This seems to have changed to a certain degree in wartime, when the king needed officers and proofs of 'nobility' were not checked too closely.

In fact, some soldiers simply faked such certificates when they got a chance at promotion. Christian Friedrich Zander speaks about five non-noble NCOs from his region who were promoted or could have been promoted. It is most obvious that the officers in charge had not cared one iota whether their nobility was real or not. There was only one rejection, and that was because the soldier was married.[159] Promotion was also linked to a substantial raise in wages. While a soldier got two *Reichsthaler* per month, an NCO received between three and four *Reichsthaler*. Becoming an ensign or second lieutenant brought eleven *Reichsthaler* and meant that the soldier no longer had to rely on other part-time jobs. Thus, the Zanders' letters show that officers of humble origins *could* rise through the ranks without being bullied by their noble colleagues and that promotion was possible in wartime.[160]

Soldiers also hoped for material gains. This could start with the bounty gained following victory, which was in some cases quite considerable and end with expectations of plunder and looting. They might also receive a financial bonus for military successes. Yet the number of those who acquired a fortune during the war was minimal, so such hopes were often in vain.

The most important expectation for the future seems to have been survival without serious injuries. It was based on the intensive training of the men, their experience and a record of victories of their army and regiment.

All of this chapter's points form the mental framework of the soldiers, which kept most of them in the ranks of their regiments even after a total catastrophe like the Prussian defeat at Kunersdorf. Even then, most of the Prussian soldiers who had fled from the field after the dissolution of the army came back several days later.[161] In the evening of 12 August 1759, after an extremely violent battle, Frederick II was left with only 3,000 men out of the 50,000 who had been at his disposal in the morning. 19,000 had died or been wounded and the rest had dispersed during the panic following the breakdown of the Prussian army. But just a week later, 28,000 had rejoined the colours.[162]

---

[158] Johann Christian Riemann, s.d. [Summer 1762], in *Soldatenbriefe*, 34.
[159] C.F. Zander, 16 May 1758, in *Fundstücke*, 76.
[160] Duffy, *Frederick*, 336.
[161] Showalter, *Frederick*, pos. 4433. See also Dominicus' description of his flight after the Battle of Kay, pp. 178–9.
[162] Blanning, *Frederick*, 239–41.

Linear tactics: Forming the men's instincts

Weapons

The line infantry was armed with a muzzle-loading musket, the model 1740.[163] It was a smooth-bore gun and could be fired by a mechanism called flintlock.[164] It was possible to fix a socket-bayonet on the muzzle, thus transforming the musket into a short pike.[165] Well-trained troops were able to fire two to three shots per minute under combat conditions.[166] Elite regiments were probably able to fire four or five shots in battle, when the circumstances were favourable for orderly fire.[167] The acceleration of the firing rate was an important part of the men's training, as their firearms were inaccurate.[168] The recoil of the weapon was so severe, that it could irritate a well trained and experienced soldier who used a precision gun with a rifled[169] barrel.[170] Christopher Duffy gives an overview of the effect of a flintlock musket: 'Many veterans could tell of battalions or entire lines of battle which had fired without causing any perceptible casualties. In combat conditions the hits at 450 paces (300 yards [c. 270 m]) were negligible; there were a few losses at 300 paces (200 yards [c. 180 m]), some more at 150 paces (100 yards [c. 90 m]), and real execution at 75 paces (50 yards [c. 45 m]) and below.'[171]

Thus, the standard weapon of the infantry was almost useless when a single musket was fired from a long distance. But when as many weapons as possible were concentrated in a small space and fired from a short (or point-blank) range, they could cause a massacre.[172] Line cavalry cuirassiers and dragoons were armed with a straight sword,

---

[163] http://www.kronoskaf.com/syw/index.php?title=Prussian_Line_Infantry_Weapons (accessed 6 September 2018).
[164] The mechanism consisted of a cock supporting a flintstone. When the trigger was pulled, the cock with the flintstone hit the pan cover. The latter was opened by the collision with the cock and let the resulting sparks ignite the powder in the pan. The resulting ignition produced a darting flame, which went through the ignition channel and ignited the propelling charge. Ortenburg, *Waffe*, 59–60; Nosworthy, *Anatomy*, 39.
[165] The predecessor of the socket bayonet, the plug-bayonet, was inserted into the muzzle, thus also making a short pike but leaving the soldier unable to shoot. The socket bayonet allowed for this. Ortenburg, *Waffe*, 48. The pike itself disappeared from most armies – except as a weapon for NCOs – during the War of the Spanish Succession. Hans Delbrück, *Geschichte der Kriegskunst im Rahmen der politischen Geschichte*, vol. 4 (Berlin: De Gruyter, [1920] 1962), 305–06 and fn. 2 on p. 306.
[166] Hans Delbrück, 'Exkurs über die Feuergeschwindigkeit im 18. Jahrhundert', in: Delbrück, *Geschichte*, vol. 4, 329–32.
[167] Nosworthy, *Anatomy*, 145.
[168] The smooth bore barrel became blocked by powder remnants after just a few shots. Thus there had to be a small free space between the barrel and the bullet so that the latter could be pushed down the barrel under combat conditions. Once fired, the projectile 'toddled' through the barrel thanks to the free space. Ortenburg, *Waffe*, 55.
[169] Rifles are small parallel grooves inside the barrel that are structured like a helix. They make the projectile spin and thus fly straight out of the barrel. In order to cause the desired spin, the bullet had to fit inside the barrel snugly and be pressed down with the ramrod. Due to the amount of physical strength required to achieve this, the loading process took much longer than that for a smooth bore musket. Ortenburg, *Waffe*, 63–4.
[170] We thank Prof. Dr. Thomas Barker for this information.
[171] Duffy, *Military Experience*, 208.
[172] See the incident at the Battle of Fontenoy mentioned at the beginning of this book. More than 2,500 muskets were fired at a distance of less than thirty metres. More than 400 Frenchmen were killed or wounded. Showalter, *Tactics*, 19–20; Browning, *War of the Austrian Succession*, 206–13.

while light cavalry such as hussars or chevau-légers carried a curved sabre. They also carried two pistols and a short musket called a carabine.[173] But the most dangerous weapon at a trooper's disposal would have been his horse. Just like the infantry's muskets, it was the ordered *mass* of riders that made them 'dreadful'.[174]

The Prussians used two main classes of artillery on the battlefield: infantry battalions were supported by two light guns positioned at the flanks of each battalion that fired projectiles weighing three to six pounds,[175] while heavy guns fired cannonballs of twelve[176] or twenty-four pounds. Howitzers and mortars comprised a third category of gun. Howitzers were able to fire all kinds of shot but were designed specifically to fire different kinds of cannister.[177] Light howitzers were also attached to the infantry battalions to augment their firepower. Mortars fired hollow projectiles filled with powder in a high-arching trajectory. The artillery train of the field army was increased substantially over the course of the Seven Years' War. While the army had 120 heavy pieces (heavy cannon as well as howitzers and mortars) in the summer of 1756, there were 298 of these guns in 1759.[178] Four kinds of shot used by European gunners in the eighteenth century:

1. solid shot or round shot was fired from longer distances (1.5 to 0.5 km). These could be fired directly at the target in a horizontal trajectory, yet it was more usual to 'ricochet' them on the battlefield. Here, the cannonball hits a point well in front of the target at a flat angle so that it rebounds / ricochets off the ground and continues to rebound in the same way until it hits the enemy formation. It is more accurate than direct fire and has a profound psychological impact on the enemy, who can see the ball ricocheting off the ground and heading towards them.[179]
2. when the enemy had advanced close enough (300–400 m), the gunners switched to canisters. These were dozens, or even hundreds, of small iron or lead balls wrapped in tar, boxes or bags, which made the cannon function like a giant shotgun.[180] Grapeshot was similar, but in that case larger and fewer balls were used. 'Canister was the tactical equivalent of machine gun fire, and in the Seven Years' War it probably inflicted more casualties on the Prussian infantry than any other weapon.'[181]
3. howitzers or mortars were able to fire 'bombs', or hollow shells filled with powder. The gunners used a fuse to time the explosion of the bomb. Well-trained and experienced gunners could make them explode some metres above the ground,

---

[173] Ortenburg, *Waffe*, 106–15.
[174] Warnery, *Feldzüge*, vol. 1, 119.
[175] There were mainly three-pounders.
[176] There were light as well as heavy twelve-pounders. The latter were called *Brummer* (hummer / growler).
[177] http://www.kronoskaf.com/syw/index.php?title=Prussian_Howitzers (accessed 7 September 2018).
[178] http://www.kronoskaf.com/syw/index.php?title=Prussian_Artillery_Equipment#Howitzers (accessed 7 September 2018).
[179] Ortenburg, *Waffe*, 82.
[180] Ibid., 74; Bleckwenn, *Ausbildung*, 26–7.
[181] Duffy, *Military Experience*, 217. See also the soldiers' descriptions of their attacks against enemy artillery firing canister and grapeshot, p. 178.

thus injuring many soldiers with the resulting splinters. They were also extremely effective against cavalry as they hit and frightened the horses.[182]
4. guns could also be used to fire types of shot that were against the rules of war, such as chain-shot[183] or scrap metal.[184] They were extremely effective but the gunners using them were normally put to the sword when taken prisoner.

The development of linear tactics

The crucial question for all tactical innovations, was how to make the most effective use of the infantry's muskets, as they were by far the most numerous branch of all European armies in the eighteenth century.[185] Yet all reformers had to keep in mind that while the infantry was dominant on the battlefield, it was not alone there. A sudden attack by enemy cavalry could annihilate several battalions, as occurred at Hohenfriedberg in 1745[186] or Kolin in 1757,[187] and the artillery could ruin the fastest firing unit of grenadiers. These basic questions were addressed by the development of linear tactics.[188] We have to refute the thesis that these were devised to keep control of unwilling foreign mercenaries,[189] as in the next century the battlefields of the American Civil War were still dominated by them. Both the Union and the Confederate Armies consisted of volunteers and no mercenaries were recruited by strong-arm methods.[190]

Linear tactics as they were used in the Seven Years' War had been developed during the Nine Years War (1689–97) but particularly during the course of the War of the Spanish Succession (1701–13/14). The most basic measure involved deploying two to six lines (ranks) behind each other.[191] Thus, the smallest tactical units were formed, namely infantry battalions (300–1,000 men) and cavalry squadrons (100–150 troopers). A number of these battalions or squadrons were placed next to each other, leaving larger or smaller distances between the individual units, depending on the tactical situation. It is from these long lines that the concept of linear tactics derives its name.

The first line of battalions, in German *erstes Treffen*,[192] was supported by a second line, in German *zweites Treffen*, which was set up in parallel, 300 paces[193] behind.[194] The

---

[182] Ortenburg, *Waffe*, 75.
[183] Two cannonballs linked by a chain, Normally, there were used on warships to tear down the rigging and sails of the enemy.
[184] See Musketeer Dominicus' description of the Russian use of this kind of projectile, p. 178.
[185] Delbrück, *Geschichte*, vol. 4, 328.
[186] Here, the famous charge of the Prussian Bayreuth Dragoons (No. 5) decided the battle and cost the Austrians more than 2,500 prisoners and above all sixty-seven colours and five guns. Showalter, *Frederick*, pos. 1504.
[187] Here, the Austrians and especially Saxons settled the score for Hohenfriedberg by riding down the Prussian infantry. Duffy, *Frederick*, 129.
[188] Nosworthy, *Anatomy*, 15.
[189] Reinhard Höhn, *Revolution, Heer, Kriegsbild* (Darmstadt: Wittich, 1944), 31–2; Bröckling, *Disziplin*, 68.
[190] James M. McPherson, *Für die Freiheit sterben. Die Geschichte des amerikanischen Bürgerkrieges* (München: List and Leipzig, 1988), 464–9.
[191] Nosworthy, *Anatomy*, 5.
[192] Best translated as 'first line of battle', as *Treffen* means a line of battalions as well as 'battle'.
[193] A pace is a *Schritt* in German. An old Prussian *Schritt* was 75.325 cm long. Thus, the distance was roughly 225 metres.
[194] Nosworthy, *Anatomy*, 70 and 82; *Prussian Infantry Reglement of 1743*, 271.

normal rule was to position the infantry in the centre and the cavalry on the wings of the formation.

This was the framework for different uses of the different weapons and branches of the service. From the Nine Years War on, the Dutch and British infantry were trained to fire most effectively. The battalion was broken up into eighteen platoons. These were in their turn ordered into three 'firings'. Every firing was made up of six platoons, distributed over the length of the battalion. Thus, seen from the right, the first firing contained platoons 1, 4, 7, 10, 13, 16, the second one platoons 2, 5, 8, 11, 14, 17 and the third one platoons 3, 6, 9, 12, 15, 18. When the battalion was advancing, it halted after the first volley fired by the enemy. Then, '*Halt!*' was ordered and the British started to fire. The first firing shot first, then the second and then the third. After having discharged their weapons, each firing started to reload immediately. The cadence of fire was calculated to enable one firing at a time to have its weapons loaded.[195] In case the enemy stood its ground, the battalion moved forward a few paces and repeated this firing procedure. This was a means to permanently hit the entire front of the enemy while always having one firing with arms shouldered and loaded to fend off any attacking enemy cavalry.

The cavalry of most European armies also used its firearms. To do this, troopers advanced at a trot, halted near the enemy and fired their pistols or carabines. After one discharge, they drew their sabers and galloped towards the enemy. Another tactic was to fire at an attacking enemy standing firm and trying to put the charging foe to flight.[196] Counterposed to this 'fire-school' was the 'cold-steel school', championed by the Swedish army.[197] The Swedes constantly had to cope with the problem of insufficient manpower and were thus keen to win quick victories that minimized their losses. The aim of the Swedes from Gustavus Adolphus (1594–1634) to Charles XII (1682–1718) was not so much to physically destroy the enemy by firing at it, but to use the psychological effect of a quick assault and the fear instilled by cold steel. The infantry battalions of Charles XII were ordered to advance up to fifty paces away from the enemy. The last two of the four ranks of the battalion were to fire, while the first two ranks knelt down. The battalion advanced a few paces further until they 'could see the whites of their enemies' eyes' and the first two ranks fired. After that, the entire formation would fall upon their enemy at full speed, bayonets levelled and shouting 'With God's help!'.[198] The Swedish forces were accompanied by a large number of chaplains. In order to prepare the soldiers psychologically for these cold-steel tactics, they preached that God's providence alone decided whether a man was hit or not by enemy fire.[199] Swedish cavalry squadrons had strict orders to charge at a gallop and not to fire at all.[200] Many French generals also preferred their infantry to charge with

---

[195] Nosworthy, *Anatomy*, 56–8.
[196] Ibid., 7.
[197] See: Geoffrey Parker, *The Military Revolution: Military Innovation and the Rise of the West, 1500–1800* (Cambridge: Cambridge University Press, [1996] 1998), 23.
[198] Nosworthy, *Anatomy*, 107–08.
[199] Ragnhild Mary Hatton, *Charles XII of Sweden* (London: Weidenfeld and Nicolson, 1968), 115–16.
[200] Ibid., 116.

bayonets fixed and to abstain from long fire-fights with the better-trained British or German troops.[201]

Shocking with cold steel: Psychological warfare

Elementary tactics of the Prussian army

The basic training of the Prussian infantry before the Seven Years' War was based mainly on the regulations established by Frederick William I (1688–1740), the 'Soldier King'. He issued a corresponding *Reglement* in 1726[202], which formed the basis for the *Reglement* of 1743 by Frederick II, his son. The Prussian army's equipment did not differ substantially from that used by other European armies of the period. Yet there were some peculiarities. It had been the only major army to use the iron ramrod well into the 1740s; the smaller force of the Electorate of Hannover had also used it from 1724 onwards.[203] Leopold of Anhalt-Dessau had introduced it to his regiment in 1698 and it was deployed across the entire army in 1718.[204] It was more robust than its wooden counterpart and allowed the weapons to be loaded faster.

The Prussian *Reglement* of 1726 was unique due to its sheer existence. Austria, Great Britain and France simply did not have any authoritative regulations for their respective whole armies well unto the 1740s. Maria Theresa of Austria issued her regulations in 1749, for example, [205] although Spain was an exception, as Philip V had issued binding regulations in 1728.[206] The first Prussian manuals were issued by Frederick I as early as 1702 and 1705, however. In the main they covered the coordinated loading and firing of muskets. The first *Reglement* of the Soldier King was published in 1714, another one in 1718.[207] The most important and enduring set of guidelines was issued in 1726. It was based on two sources. The first was a training manual for the Swedish army, which had been published in Reval in 1701.[208] The Prussians implemented the Swedish way of manoeuvring the battalions, but as noted above, they did not embrace the Scandinavians' method of firing plus infantry charge. The second source was the platoon-fire approach

---

[201] Nosworthy, *Anatomy*, 100; J. Michael Hill, 'Killiecrankie and the Evolution of Highland Warfare', *War in History* 1, no. 2 (1994): 125–39.
[202] Reglement vor die Königl. Preußische Infanterie von 1726 (Osnabrück: Biblio, [1726] 1968). It will be cited as *Prussian Infantry Reglement of 1726*.
[203] 'Brief des Grafen von Mirabeau an den Herrn Grafen von **** Betreffend die Lobrede des Herrn von Guibert auf Friedrichen und den allgemeinen Versuch über die Taktik desselben Verfassers', *Neues Militärisches Journal*, 3 (1790):19, fn. *).
[204] Austria introduced it between 1742 and 1744, France from 1745 onwards. Ortenburg, *Waffe*, 64–5.
[205] Alexander Balisch, 'Die Entstehung des Exerzierreglements von 1749. Ein Kapitel der Militärreform von 1748/49', *Mitteilungen des Österreichischen Staatsarchivs* 27 (1974): 170–9.
[206] Ordenanzas de su Magestad, para el Regimen, Disciplina, subordinacion, y servicio de la Infanteria, Cavalleria, y Dragones de sus Exercitos en Guarnicion, y en Campaña. Dividas en dos Tomos (Madrid: Imprenta de Juan de Ariztia, 1728).
[207] Balisch, *Entstehung*, 173–5.
[208] Carl Binder von Kriegelstein, *Geist und Stoff im Kriege*, vol. 1 (Vienna and Leipzig: Wilhelm Braumüller, 1896), 104, fn. 1.

used by the British and Dutch infantry, which had been adopted by the Prussians in 1705 (and subsequently modified).[209]

By 1743, a Prussian infantry regiment was made up of ten companies of musketeers and two of grenadiers. In times of war, the ten musketeer companies formed two battalions, while the two grenadier companies were removed from the regiment. Together with the two grenadier companies of another regiment, they would form one composite grenadier battalion.

In peacetime the grenadiers were trained alongside the musketeers. Thus, a battalion on the drill square consisted of five musketeer companies and one grenadier company, and the battalion was made up of the following types of soldiers:

- 25 commissioned Officers, amongst whom one subaltern officer[210] as aide-de-camp.[211]
- 59 NCOs.
- 3 fifers.[212]
- 19 drummers.
- 126 grenadiers.
- 570 musketeers.[213]

These numbers were steadily increased before and during the Seven Years' War.[214] The 1726 *Reglement* remarks on the grenadiers' selection: 'The grenadiers shall be taken from the third rank, and must be men, who can march well, are not older than 35 years, look good, must not have short noses or meagre and thin faces, for which reason all grenadiers must be grown men. Those grenadiers, who happen to have moustaches, shall keep them and wear them in the Polish manner.'[215] There were no other criteria.[216] The 1743 *Reglement* does not regulate the selection of grenadiers.[217] The order that the grenadiers had to be taken from the 'third rank' means that they had to be the smallest men.[218] A battalion was *rangiret* (ranked/ordered according to the height of the soldiers) in four ranks. The tallest men were to stand in the first rank, the second tallest in the fourth rank, the next tallest in the second rank and the smallest men in the third rank.[219] When the battalion was ordered to fire, it re-formed into three ranks.[220] When the first rank knelt down for firing, the second rank stood upright aiming their muskets

---

[209] Balisch, *Entstehung*, 174.
[210] Not to be confused with an NCO. The subaltern officers are those below the rank of captain, e.g. lieutenants or ensigns.
[211] Adjutant to the Colonel.
[212] Flutists and trumpeters. Here, 'piper' also seems to include the 'Hautbois', the oboe and bassoon players.
[213] *Prussian Infantry Reglement of 1743*, 4.
[214] http://www.kronoskaf.com/syw/index.php?title=Prussian_Line_Infantry_Organisation (accessed 13 October 2018).
[215] *Prussian Infantry Reglement of 1726*, 8.
[216] Ibid., 548.
[217] See p. 22
[218] This was also true for the drummers of the grenadiers: 'N[ota] B[ene]. The drummers of the grenadiers shall be the smallest and have good faces.' *Prussian Infantry Reglement of 1726*, 18.
[219] Ibid., 7.
[220] 'Three men high': ordered in three ranks. Ibid., 96.

over the heads of the kneeling first rank. The third rank, now standing upright and thus being physically higher than the two front ranks, could aim their muskets at the level of the ears of the men in front of them, thus forming a deadly cascade of muskets, firing bullets from three angles with machine-like efficiency.

The new recruits were taught a new posture at the very beginning of their basic training:

> The first exercise must be to train a man and teach him the air of a soldier, that the peasant gets out of him. This means teaching the man:
> How he is to support his head, particularly [that he should] not to bow it, not look down to the ground, but hold his head upright when carrying his gun and to look over his right shoulder to his right hand and to look into the eyes [of the officer] when marching past him ... That a man holds his body straight, does not sag backwards and push his belly out, but pushes his breast out well and straightens his back.[221]

The *Reglement* stresses the need to make the soldiers internalize their posture: 'All officers and NCOs must make the soldiers to develop the ambition to stand straight. Because if a man does not like his own body, he is still a peasant and not a soldier.'[222]

The upright posture was useful in the tightly packed formation of the battalion, because it helped to avoid disorder and gave the impression of a well-trained and well-ordered group. Eliminating the 'peasant's posture' of servility also made the soldier look more imposing and the martial 'air' that imitated noble behaviour could also make the soldier more self-confident. The soldier was taught the basic movements by an NCO or an experienced private who was ordered not to yell at the soldier or to beat him, but to explain everything patiently so that he would 'love the service'.[223] The loading procedure and the different movements were not especially difficult, but the soldier needed a good teacher to internalize the unfamiliar ways of moving.[224] Before taking part in the drill sessions, the recruits were ordered to 'repeatedly fire on their own ... so that he does not fear the powder and learns how to handle his gun correctly and how to load with cartridges correctly'.[225] 'Cartridges' were made of paper and contained the bullet as well as the powder needed for one shot.[226] The soldier had to bite it open, pour a small portion of powder on the pan, pour the rest into the barrel and ram the bullet with his ramrod into the barrel. As the musket's shot was extremely loud and the recoil caused bruises, the soldiers had to get used to firing their guns.

After the recruit had learned the basic movements, he was allowed to take part in exercises on the drill square together with the other men. When the battalion was

---

[221] *Prussian Infantry Reglement of 1743*, 33–4.
[222] Ibid., 508.
[223] Ibid., 147; *Prussian Infantry Reglement of 1726*, 222.
[224] Bräker, *Arme Mann*, 121–2. Although Bräker thought that his friend and comrade had taught him the basic movements for avoiding the drill sergeant's stick, his comrade was just executing the *Reglement* by teaching the new man the basics.
[225] *Prussian Infantry Reglement of 1743*, 148–9; *Prussian Infantry Reglement of 1726*, 224.
[226] Ortenburg, *Waffe*, 65–6.

Figure 1.1 A Prussian battalion and platoon ready for battle. © Jorge M. Corada.

exercising, it was divided into eight – subsequently[227] ten – platoons of musketeers.[228] The five colours of the battalion[229] were located in the middle of the battalion. Together with the musicians and their escorts, they formed the 'colours platoon'. The commander had the most exposed position, as he was riding in front of the colours platoon so that he could be seen by all of his subordinates.[230]

Prussian combat training was based on platoon fire. When the battalion was preparing for combat, the first rank fell on the right knee, so that 'the second rank had the right foot of the first rank between their feet'. 'But the third rank must move into the gaps of the second rank,[231] which must be observed with the utmost care as any failure to do so would lead to the men getting burned.'[232] This order was necessary to avoid the muzzle flash burning the faces of the second rank. Nevertheless, the noise of a volley on the height of their ears would have been enough to make their eardrums burst. The eight[233] platoons were numbered sequentially from right to left. No. 1 was to fire first, followed by no. 8, then no. 2, no. 7, etc.:

---

[227] Autumn 1757.
[228] Also grenadiers and fusiliers.
[229] Every company had one colour.
[230] *Prussian Infantry Reglement of 1743*, 27–8.
[231] The small gaps between the individual soldiers, who stood elbow to elbow. The soldiers in the third rank put their guns through these small gaps as far as possible to avoid the risk of burning their 'brothers' in the second rank by the fire coming out of the muzzle.
[232] *Prussian Infantry Reglement of 1726*, 79. The section on getting burned is left out in the Reglement of 1743. *Prussian Infantry Reglement of 1743*, 57.
[233] All this also applies to the formation with ten platoons.

Numbers of the platoons:	8	7	6	5	4	3	2	1
Sequence when firing:	2	4	6	8	7	5	3	1[234]

This firing sequence allowed the Prussians to keep up an uninterrupted hail of bullets, because when platoon 5 fired, the first four platoons had already reloaded and were ready for the next session of platoon fire. Taking into account the three ranks of every platoon firing on three levels using platoon fire, you can compare the output of deadly bullets to the efficiency of modern automatic weapons. And that was exactly what the enemy feared, especially when the enemy was forced to face this 'weapon' standing in the same tightly packed formation, but without the training to fire back in that way. In combat conditions, two rounds of platoon fire were possible, after which every man started to fire at will, but the initial two rounds were often enough to put the enemy to flight.

Using platoon fire when advancing was another specifically Prussian tactic, which had been introduced as early as 1705.[235] When the battalion fired while advancing, it had to move by taking small steps. The platoon would run forward with three big steps, the first rank would fall on its right knee and the rest fired. After the volley, the first rank jumped up and the platoon loaded while again advancing with small steps. The musket butt was never allowed to hit the ground when exercising in order to get the soldiers used to reloading their weapons while advancing. The soldier had to ram down the ramrod with his right hand while holding the musket with his left and ram down the bullet with all strength and both arms, while still moving forward. This could be done only by tall and strong men, which is one of the reasons why the Prussians had stringent requirements concerning the physical condition of their soldiers.

Platoon fire could also be used while retreating. The whole battalion had to move backwards taking large steps, while still facing the enemy. The platoon that was due to fire would then stand still, fire and follow the others in moving back with similarly large steps while the next platoon to fire stood still to discharge their weapons and thus cover the others. This was repeated until the battalion was ordered to halt. Georg Heinrich von Berenhorst, son of Leopold of Anhalt-Dessau, and officer in the Prussian army and military theoretician, summed up the concept behind this kind of training: 'that it was the fire, but physical fire mixed with moral fire, which brought victory and that good aiming, quick loading, intrepidity and courageous attack will lead to victory.'[236]

The training of the Prussian cavalry under the Soldier King did not reflect these aggressive principles. The Soldier King and his Field-Marshal had given total priority to the infantry, in sharp contrast to other European armies.[237] Even the cavalry troopers were well-drilled foot soldiers, but their horsemanship was unsatisfactory. The 1727

---

[234] *Prussian Infantry Reglement of 1743*, 93–6.
[235] Balisch, *Entstehung*, 174; *Prussian Infantry Reglement of 1743*, 98–103.
[236] Georg Heinrich von Berenhorst, *Betrachtungen über die Kriegskunst*, 3rd ed. (1797; Leipzig: Fleischer, 1827), 54–5.
[237] See Kurt and Kati Spillmann, 'Friedrich Wilhelm I und die preußische Armee. Versuch einer psychohistorischen Deutung', *Historische Zeitschrift* 246 (1988): 549–89.

Prussian cavalry *Reglement* did not order the charge at a gallop. Instead, the troopers had to fire their pistols and carabines and move towards the enemy at a trot.[238]

Concepts developed by Frederick II

The basic training of the infantry did not change after the death of the Soldier King and the accession of Frederick II in 1740.

> The main innovations concerning the training affected the grenadier companies, which had not been established in 1726. They were positioned at the right wing of their respective battalion in peacetime, while detached completely from their regiments in the field ... The bayonet [of every infantryman, K & S.M.] was to be fixed permanently during the exercises ... Every battalion was assigned two cannons with the corresponding gunners.[239]

The orders for giving battle were also changed. The *Reglement* of 1726 only mentions the disciplined way of firing: 'As fire cannot be delivered with the same accuracy during combat as it can during exercises, you have to see to it that at least every platoon fires when it is its turn, in order to keep up a continuous fire of the battalions and to avoid getting out of ammunition. All officers have to pay attention to this. Also, no officer must give the order to open fire before the colonel or commander of the battalion has done so.'[240] The 1743 *Reglement* did, however, change this due to a more realistic perception of the soldiers' ability to keep up any kind of orderly platoon fire in combat:[241]

> Keeping up an orderly fire with platoons according to the regulations is best. But as this is difficult to manage, the commanders and Majors have to see to it, that four platoons have their arms shouldered at any given time, that no fire by divisions[242] and no volleys by the entire battalion are delivered. This is only allowed when retreating.[243]

The most important alteration was the introduction of a paragraph on the aggressive use of the bayonet, which was followed by several tactical essays pointing in the same direction. Contemporary military critics[244], the German General Staff,[245] as well as a

---

[238] Jany, *Geschichte*, vol. 2, 93.
[239] Ibid., 91.
[240] *Prussian Infantry Reglement of 1726*, 360.
[241] As Frederick praised the Guards' (1st Battalion, No. 15) ability to fire two rounds of platoon fire during the Battle of Mollwitz, he must have believed that even one round was hard to manage. See p. 17, fn. 101.
[242] Two platoons form one division.
[243] *Prussian Infantry Reglement of 1743*, 272.
[244] Warnery, *Feldzüge*, vol. 1, 100.
[245] *Die Taktische Schulung der Preußischen Armee durch König Friedrich den Großen während der Friedenszeit 1745 bis 1756*, ed. Großer Generalstab (Berlin: Mittler, 1900).

good number of English-speaking historians[246] have interpreted Frederick's focus on the bayonet as a ruinous doctrine of prioritizing cold steel over gunfire and one of his major tactical blunders. More recent German authors have more or less neglected this aspect of Prussian tactics.[247]

The paragraph on the use of the bayonet reads as follows: 'Every officer, NCO and private must know for sure that the ultimate goal of combat is to make the enemy quit the place he had hitherto occupied. Thus, victory in battle totally depends on not halting without order, but that you advance and fire in good order against the enemy. As the strength of the men and its good order make the Prussian infantry invincible, the men must know for sure that – if the enemy, against all odds, stands firm – their surest and most certain advantage would consist in pushing into the enemy's lines with levelled bayonets. If this is done, the king pledges that none of them will stab back.'[248] This passage alone shows that Frederick II did not preach a doctrine of the bayonet.[249] Otherwise, he would not have ordered the troops to fire at the enemy before charging with cold steel. Another paragraph underlines this: 'In particular, His Majesty most graciously orders that fire is delivered accurately and according to the *Reglement*, as you have seen how well rapid loading and orderly fire fit the infantry.'[250] The passages are even more significant when we analyse their mental and psychological implications. In general, the *Reglement* deals only with technical and organizational issues. When the king, as author of the *Reglement*, deals with a problem, he either threatens his readers or explains a solution to them. But this paragraph is the only one where the king gives his word and thus puts his honour at stake to encourage his men. By this, the highly valued honour of their king[251] is used to have a psychological effect on his men, who in their turn are ordered to use 'psychological warfare' against their enemies. We have to remind ourselves that eighteenth-century military theoreticians agreed that a bayonet charge was first and foremost a psychological measure to frighten off the enemy.[252] Berenhorst explained this in detail: 'Those who take the decision to settle the matter with the bayonet ... are convinced that the other side will not await them. In this, they seldom fail, as the enemy shows by standing still, that he is not keen on fighting it out.'[253] While the *Reglement* of 1743 sees the bayonet charge as a last psychological resort when the physical superiority of Prussian firepower is not sufficient to drive the enemy off the field, the king's analysis of the Prussian victories in the War of the Austrian Succession seems to have led him to the conclusion that the enemy could be defeated by psychological means alone. 'When battle really commences, those generals

---

[246] Christopher Duffy, *Friedrich der Große und seine Armee* (Stuttgart: Motorbuch, 1978), 131; Nosworthy, *Anatomy*, 145.
[247] Johannes Kunisch, *Das Mirakel des Hauses Brandenburg* (München: Oldenbourg, 1978), 62.
[248] *Prussian Infantry Reglement of 1743*, 275–6.
[249] Duffy, *Friedrich der Große und seine Armee*, 132.
[250] *Prussian Infantry Reglement of 1743*, 511.
[251] Musketier Johann Christian Riemann, 16 Juni 1762, in *Soldatenbriefe*, 32; Dreyer, *Memoiren*, 22.
[252] Duffy, *Military Experience*, 204–06.
[253] Berenhorst, *Aus dem Nachlasse*, 135. See also: Georg Friedrich von Tempelhof, *Geschichte des Siebenjährigen Krieges*, vol. 1 (Berlin: Unger, 1783), 66–7; J.G. Thielke, 'Von dem Angriff und Vertheidigung der unverschanzten Berge und Anhöhen', in *Beyträge zur Kriegs-Kunst*, ed. J. G. Thielke, vol. 1 (Freiberg: Bartels, 1775), 60–70.

will recommend themselves most, who charge the enemy with shouldered arms and who manage to silence their men, when they start shooting on their own and who attack the enemy with the bayonet and only order their men to shoot, when the enemy turns his back unto them.'[254] The background of this quotation is that the king and his generals knew that the soldiers had been trained in shooting fast and fighting from a distance, but were not used to killing their foe with a bayonet face to face. This is the reason why the Prussian soldiers started shooting without being ordered to do so when they were ordered to charge with the bayonet. They feared being killed by enemy fire while being deprived of their main advantage, rapid fire.

The Political Testament of 1752 contains two passages dealing with the bayonet charge. Under the headline 'Recruitment', the king explains to his successor his search for tall soldiers: 'the height is necessary, because tall people are stronger than the others. No army in the world will be able to withstand their charge with fixed bayonets.'[255] He writes in more detail some paragraphs later:

> I have trained the officers to judge the terrain and occupy it advantageously, especially to secure their flanks. I have educated them to fall upon the enemy in a quick step, without firing, only with the bayonet. Because you will surely put the enemy to flight when you charge boldly and lose much less compared to a slow advance. To win a battle means to force the enemy to leave his positions to you. If you march against him at a slow pace, his fire will cause heavy casualties amongst your men. If you march against him at a quick step, you preserve your soldiers. Your firm stance defeats him and forces him to retreat in disorder.[256]

A similar note is struck in the 'Thoughts and general rules of war' from 1755:

> Always, when you want to attack the enemy, your way of fighting will be determined by the terrain and the advantages, the enemy can gain ... The infantry is to shoot as little as possible, but has to charge with the bayonet ... Never use my attack column when the enemy has his well-ordered cavalry ready behind his infantry. It is only useful when the infantry line starts to fire. Then, if no cavalry is behind the enemy infantry, you form a column out of one battalion from the second line, support it by four squadrons and cut through the enemy line.[257]

Frederick wanted to weaken the enemies by the battalions' cannon and then drive them off by a charge with cold steel. Compared to his father's views, he clearly accentuates psychological factors. The fear of the Prussian bayonets will frighten off

---

[254] Friederich II, 'Instruction für die General-Majors von der Infanterie', in Gesammelte Werke Friederichs des Grossen in Prosa, ed. Isaak Marcus Jost (Berlin: Lewent, 1837), 532. http://friedrich.uni-trier.de/de/jost/532/ (accessed 11 September 2018).

[255] Friederich II, 'Das Politische Testament von 1752', Friedrich der Große, ed. Otto Bardong (Darmstadt: Wissenschaftliche Buchgesellschaft, 1982), 239.

[256] Frederick II, Das Politische Testament, 243.

[257] Frederick II, 'Gedanken und allgemeine Regeln für den Krieg', in Die Werke Friedrichs des Großen, ed. Gustav Berthold Volz, vol. 6 (Berlin: Reimar Hobbing, 1913), 91–2.

the enemy. The soldiers' needs and wishes are also addressed, when the king tells them that their chance to survive will be enhanced when they charge with bayonets fixed. He knows that the soldiers want to use their muskets and fear advancing with them shouldered, because they feel defenceless. He calls upon the officers to address this problem and promises honour and promotion to them if they make their men stop firing.

Training and manoeuvres

The daily training of the Prussian infantry between the end of the Second Silesian War (1744–45) and the Seven Years' War continued to be characterized by drilling manoeuvres, evolutions and above all rapid fire:

> The new method of attack was only slowly introduced into the daily training during peacetime. To be sure, it was sometimes part of the training, e.g. during manoeuvres held at Potsdam on 19 August 1748, where the corps of the Prince of Prussia advanced 50 paces up to the enemy. There are also various 'dispositions'[258] of Moritz of Anhalt-Dessau, which resemble the afore-mentioned procedure, written in the following years. In August 1750, an exercise was held in Tempelhof,[259] where the infantry fired only after the enemy had turned around. Most of the exercises were held in the traditional way of the *Reglement* with the battalions advancing and firing. Of course, the battalion pieces supported the new method of attack like before by firing canister.[260]

The equipment of the infantry was also adjusted to the new tactical concepts:

> The king had new bayonets produced for the first rank [of each battalion], which were two *Zoll*[261] longer than the old ones. They were issued [to the soldiers] from the end of August 1753 on.[262]

In February 1755, the NCOs were issued new pikes,

> which were very long and very sharp … and as these were still too short, they were made 9 to 10 feet long and the old ones were sent to the arsenal in Berlin. The NCOs were ordered to level their pikes, too, when the lads[263] were being commanded to level their bayonets. They should stick their pikes through the files,

---

[258] Dispositions are the commanders plans for military actions like manoeuvres, marches, sieges and battles.
[259] Today a district of Berlin.
[260] *Die Taktische Schulung*, 445.
[261] 5.6 cm.
[262] Jany, *Geschichte*, vol. 2, 283.
[263] Scheelen uses the German term *Burschen*, which is not like *Kerl*, but definitely means a young man. In this case, Scheelen does not stress the age, but the difference in rank between the 'lads' (= privates) and the senior ones (= NCOs).

but they were too short and at the same time too heavy. Thus, the NCO does not possess enough strength to make good use of it.²⁶⁴

Intensive exercises for the bayonet charge seem to have taken place as late as 1755.²⁶⁵ The king instructed his officers on this point in the camp at Spandau on 25 August 1755. Frederick underlined the 'material' advantages of attacking with the bayonet, as 'you would lose far fewer men if you did not bother with shooting but marched against the enemy head on.'²⁶⁶ The monarch conducted an experiment with three platoons of the Guards to underline his point. One of them posed as the enemy, one advanced firing and the other one with levelled bayonets. Frederick summed up the result with the following words:

> Even if the enemy shoots only half as fast [as our Guards did in the experiment], you will draw three times more fire if you bother to shoot compared to the fire you draw when you march against the enemy head-on. And with the latter method you also advance three times faster than with the former, when you shoot.

The literary estate of Moritz of Anhalt-Dessau contains a similar calculation. In both cases a crucial factor is missing: the effect of the Prussian fire on the enemy and its capacity to inflict casualties. It might be that Frederick did not intend to conduct a 'scientific' experiment, but rather that the exercise was meant to condition his officers and through them his men. A hint in this direction is Frederick's renewed stress on the psychological effect of this bayonet charge in his explanation:

> Our quick advance will arouse the lad's heat, so that he does not start to make considerations but only tries to reach the enemy, because he knows that this will bring him out of danger ... anyway, a brisk charge will enormously boost the [lads'] courage. But the enemy will lose his courage and composure when he sees that you advance that daring in spite of his heavy fire.²⁶⁷

This opinion was shared by several contemporaries.²⁶⁸

On 26 November 1755, 'the new way of levelling the bayonets was first shown by the king at the Guard Parade', Captain von Scheelen from the First Battalion of Guards noted in his diary.²⁶⁹ Thereby, the first rank 'lowered the bayonet points to the ground, the second levelled it horizontally, so that the bayonets of both ranks formed a "fork or

---

[264] Ernst Gottlob von Scheelen, 'Aus Scheelens Tagebüchern', in *Potsdamer Tagebücher 1740-1756*, ed. Großer Generalstab (Berlin: Mittler, 1906), 37.
[265] Großer Generalstab, *Die Taktische Schulung*, 445–6.
[266] Ibid., 446.
[267] Ibid., 447.
[268] Kriegelstein, *Geist und Stoff*, vol. 1, 103, fn. 1; See also: 'Schreiben eines Königl. Hungarischen Offiziers aus Neiß vom 14. Apr. 1741 über die Schlacht bei Mollwitz', in *Sammlung*, vol. 1 (Dresden: Waltherische Hofbuchhandlung, 1782), 35.
[269] The First Battalion of the three-battalion strong regiment no. 15. Scheelen, *Aus Scheelens Tagebüchern*, 70.

cheval de frise".²⁷⁰ The actual effect on the enemy in the case of an actual clash was obviously almost negligible. The second rank could not stab the enemy, while the first could only reach shoes or calves. Again, the king counted on the psychological effect on the enemy. A battalion using this method would have been a terrifying prospect, as two rows of bayonets protruded from the ranks. Together with the pikes of the NCOs, it would have given the impression of a deadly hedgehog that was permanently advancing and bringing death closer with every step.

This survey shows that the king stressed psychological factors in his tactical deliberations. Yet, the daily training of the infantry still consisted of loading and firing as fast as possible. This seems to be contradictory but can be solved by taking into account that rapid fire could be learned on the drill square, while the problems of the bayonet charge stemmed exclusively from real battlefield conditions. The psychological stress of marching towards a firing enemy while not being able to fight back could not be imitated on the drill square.

The cavalry

The Prussian cavalry *Reglement* of 1743 contained the following orders for the mounted arm:

> As soon as they advance, they have to attack the enemy, march against the enemy with sabres drawn and flying standards, and all trumpets shall sound the charge. Thus, no squadron leader shall make his men shoot, if he does not want to forfeit his honour and reputation. The squadrons shall but attack the enemy sword in hand, for which the generals of the brigades will be responsible … When the enemy charges, the officers must see to it that they are not attacked themselves but that they attack the enemy. They also have to make it crystal clear to their men that they must keep their composure and teach them that the enemy is totally inferior to us. Furthermore, the officers must order the men most strongly not to spare the enemy, but to kill and cut down as many as possible. When the enemy is put to flight, he shall not be pursued in heat, but the troopers shall quickly join their squadrons when the rallying signal is sounded, because a single trooper can obtain nothing, and an ordered squadron very much … When the enemy is attacked, it shall be done according to the evolutions, starting with a fast trot and in the end in a full gallop, yet with tightly closed ranks. When you attack the enemy in this way, His Majesty is assured that the enemy will always be beaten.²⁷¹

Again, the psychological focus is obvious. Close order and speed shall frighten the enemy. In striking similarity to the infantry *Reglement*, the king himself promises that

---

[270] Ibid., 70, fn. 3. The *cheval de frise* is a movable obstacle used against cavalry. It consists of a several metres long beam, into which four rows of shorter pikes or sharpened wooden sticks are fixed. Viewed from the side, they form a cross. See: https://markerhunter.wordpress.com/2016/06/03/fort-fri-obstacles-pt7/ (accessed 13 September 2018).
[271] *Prussian Cavalry Reglement of 1743*, 176–8.

the enemy will be put to flight. In fact, cavalry combat was a game of nerves. It was an accepted rule that charging cavalry would always defeat enemy cavalry that were standing fast.[272] The 'waiting' enemy could either flee before actually engaging the enemy or after a short but bloody melee.[273] The explicit order 'to kill and cut down as many as possible' showed that many soldiers were reluctant to kill – otherwise the king would not have had to command his officers to issue this order 'most strongly'. This reluctance was, on the one hand, a natural reflex by men who were not brutes. On the other hand, many soldiers seem to have feared that by staining their hands with human blood, they would come to the fringe of infamy. An explicit order by the king could make killing honourable, however. Teaching the men 'that the enemy is totally inferior to us' seems to be a psychological means to combat the feelings of inferiority amongst Prussian cavalrymen after their ignominious defeat at the Battle of Mollwitz (10 April 1741).[274]

Troopers' training began with the 'air' that the soldier had to adopt, similar to the 'air' of the infantry. After that, the officers had to teach the men to ride. This might sound strange, but good horsemanship was not that common among European troopers, especially not those serving in heavy regiments.[275] Training good riders was expensive, and many generals saw the main task of heavy cavalry in putting an already shaken enemy to flight by one hammer-blow-like charge. For this, they thought it sufficient to teach them to stay in the saddle while maintaining a fast trot. That said, the Prussian cavalry was trained very carefully between the end of the Second Silesian War (1744–45) and the outbreak of the Seven Years' War.[276] Charles-Emmanuel de Warnery, major-general of the Prussian hussars and one of the most prolific military theoreticians of his time, saw their expertise in riding as the only, but decisive, advantage of the Prussians over their enemies.[277] Beating the troopers during the exercises was nearly abolished in the Prussian cavalry regiments.[278] A Prussian peculiarity was the harmonization of the different types of cavalry regiments. Officers of heavy cuirassier regiments were transferred to the hussars for a certain amount of time and vice versa. The generals also saw to it that heavy and light cavalry were trained together.[279] This was a means of enhancing the manoeuvrability of the heavy cavalry and at the same time getting the hussars ready for shock tactics.

---

[272] Charles-Emmanuel de Warnery, 'Bemerkungen über die Kavallerie', in Charles-Emmanuel de Warnery, *Des Herrn Generalmajor von Warnery sämtliche Schriften*, vol. 1 (Hannover: Helwingsche Hofbuchhandlung, 1785), 23.

[273] Warnery, *Bemerkungen*, 77–8.

[274] The Prussian cavalry was chased off the battlefield by the attacking Austrians. Only the steadfastness and skill of the Prussian infantry saved the day. Similar approaches seem to have been used by the Saxons. See 'Disposition des Herzogs von Sachsen-Weissenfels, zu der Bataille bey Hohenfriedberg. Landshut, den 1. Jun. 1745', in *Sammlung* 1 (1782), 326.

[275] Nosworthy, *Anatomy*, 4.

[276] 'Zur Geschichte des Königlich Preußischen Fünften Husarenregiments, genannt Blücher'sches, ehemals Belling'sches', in *Militärischer Nachlaß des Königlich Preußischen Generallieutenants, Gouverneurs von Königsberg und General-Inspekteurs der Ostpreußischen Infanterie, Viktor Amadäus, Grafen Henckel von Donnersmarck*, ed Karl Zabeler, vol. 1 (Zerbst: Kummersche Buchhandlung, 1846), 30–42.

[277] Warnery, *Bemerkungen*, VI; Biblioteca Central Militar. Sig. 1758-M4, 133–4.

[278] Warnery, *Bemerkungen*, VII.

[279] Ibid., 15.

Frederick II extended the distance from the enemy from which a cavalry charge had to start: 'While he had been content with attacks bridging 700 paces in 1748, he demanded a distance of 1,800 paces in 1755, the last part of which had to be covered at the fastest gallop [Karriere].'[280] The troopers were ordered to yell loudly during the charge. Warnery explains that this was above all for psychological reasons:

> On this day, I became convinced that it was best for the cavalry to yell loudly as the Turks do when they attack the infantry, because you do not hear the whizz of the bullets, which instils more fear in the men than anything else.[281]

The principle aim of Prussian training before the Seven Years' War was to: reach maximum combat efficiency by conveying the necessary knowledge to the soldiers; enable them to use this knowledge in battle by internalizing the manoeuvres and movements; and to prepare them psychologically. The last aim in particular was to be achieved by convincing the soldiers of the effectiveness of their training and the usefulness of their battle tactics. Resigned 'numbness', or sheer fear of the officers and NCOs walking behind the lines, was not a stated aim of the army's leadership. And we must stress that the two-month manoeuvre periods for the *Kantonisten,* and not even the more regular training of the *Ausländer,* were simply not enough to create emotionless automatons.[282]

Summary

The majority of the common soldiers of the Prussian army came from the lands of the Hohenzollern monarchy. Roughly 50 to 70 per cent depending on the phase of the war, were *Kantonisten,* draftees from the recruiting districts (*Kantone*) of the regiments. They were the second, third or fourth sons of peasants and craftsmen, solid members of Prussian society. Most of them were Lutheran Protestants of the Pietist branch, who believed that the faithful and professional fulfilment of their duties would secure them a place in heaven. The other 30 to 50 per cent were *Ausländer* (foreigners), of whom a majority originated in Prussian lands or neighbouring principalities like Mecklenburg. Only a few would have been 'foreigner's in the modern sense of the word. Many of them joined the colours for financial reasons, while others had an individual inclination to the soldiers' trade, but let us not forget that a large number was press-ganged during the war. Training periods were intense for eighteenth-century standards and ensured the professional functioning of the Prussian battalions. Yet the soldiers had plenty of spare time in which to follow other occupations to boost their pay. Most of the men were quartered in the homes of civilians and were not under the permanent control of their officers. Thus, the means of creating totally controlled battle-automatons in peacetime simply did not exist.

---

[280] Delbrück, *Geschichte,* vol. 4, 325.
[281] Warnery, *Feldzüge,* vol. 1, 42.
[282] Winter, *Untertanengeist,* 194–202; Möbius, *Mehr Angst,* 31.

Women were a central component of the soldiers' estate. Without the mothers, wives, sweethearts, sisters and daughters of the serving men, an army family could not survive economically, as the soldier's pay would not have been enough to feed a family. The men depended to a large extent on their families' support when they were in the field. Many women followed their men into the field or maintained the flow of communication between the community at home and the front by visiting them.

The basic tactics of the Prussian army were the linear tactics adopted by all European armies of the time. Battalions of 300–1,000 stood two to four ranks deep in close order and applied different methods of fire to bring as many muskets to bear on a certain point as possible. Permanent drill in formation made the men close their ranks instinctively and fire without harming themselves or their comrades. It also made them believe in the efficiency of their fire and strengthened a state of mind, which saw collective action as the central means of individual survival.

The elementary tactics introduced by Frederick II of Prussia before the Seven Years' War were also characterized by a high degree of psychological considerations. He trained the infantry and cavalry to charge with cold steel without firing in order to cause panic amongst the enemy. Concerning his own soldiers, the king wanted to use their interest in their own survival to prepare them for the bayonet-charge by pledging that the enemy would not dare to stand fast and assuring them that a prolonged stand fire-fight would cost more lives than a lively attack with cold steel.

2

Between 'Emasculating Fear' and 'Heat'

Emotions and Psychology in Combat

In this chapter, we will firstly give an overview of the ego-documents written by common soldiers and NCOs and present the most significant writers, whose letters will also be reproduced in translation at the end of the book. The next part of this chapter will deal with our method of analysing the letters and their central common features. The third part will present the soldiers' perception of combat and their emotions as described by the chaplain, Küster, and in pieces of writing from other Prussian officers. The fourth and final part will deal with soldiers' behaviour in the Battle of Prague and the Little War.

The men's reflections: The soldiers who wrote about their emotions

Three printed collections of soldiers' letters, two memoires, and one diary including a letter to the author's brother, form the core of the sources of this book:

- the collection of the letters sent home by the soldiers Christian Friedrich and Joachim Dietrich Zander;
- the collection of soldiers' letters by the Prussian General Staff;
- the collection of soldiers' letters edited by Georg Liebe;
- the memoires of Ulrich Bräker;
- the memoires of Joseph Ferdinand Dreyer;
- the diary and a letter to his brother from Musketeer Dominicus.[1]
- a single letter from Grenadier Johann Hermann Dresel.

There is a collection of eighteen surviving letters from Christian Friedrich (thirteen letters) and Joachim Dietrich Zander (five letters), uncle and nephew in a village administrators' family from Brandenburg, both serving in the famous von Itzenplitz Regiment.[2] The letters were published by a descendant of the family, C.F. Zander, and the printing house Dr. Kovač in 2015. Another five letters sent by the two had been

---

[1] See p. 178.
[2] http://www.kronoskaf.com/syw/index.php?title=Itzenplitz_Infantry (accessed 13 October 2018); *Fundstücke*, 88.

excerpted by a relative of the family, Prof. Friedrich Schultze, when he visited the Zanders' farmhouse in 1919 but were lost subsequently. Schultze was also able to provide some information provided by his relatives about other letters, which had already been lost by 1919. This is especially important for our study, as these lost letters probably contain the description of the regiment's participation in the Battles of Lobositz, Roßbach and Leuthen respectively.[3] Schultze's information on these letters is very meagre. This collection forms the most extensive coverage of the war by common soldiers.

The Generalstab's and Liebe's editions present letters from different soldiers. The publication of both collections was politically motivated and was supposed to answer the memoires of Ulrich Bräker. Georg Liebe states:

Too long the Swiss deserter Ulrich Bräker (The Poor Man from Toggenburg), who was introduced by Gustav Freytag in his 'images',[4] has been seen as the archetypal Frederician soldier. Even the latest edition of his autobiography does this without any reason. But no, most of the men who fought Frederick's battles were cut from a different cloth.[5]

The Great General Staff also makes a sharp distinction between *Landeskinder* (natives), and 'foreign mercenaries'. The editors want to show that the native Prussian soldiers who wrote the letters were 'adoring and blindly following their king' and even 'sensing, what future times were to call the German vocation of Prussia'.[6]

The letters edited by the Great General Staff originated from the Household Archive of the Princes of Stolberg-Wernigerode (*Fürstlich Stolberg'sches Hausarchiv*). They were copied directly after having been sent to the Prince of Stolberg-Wernigerode during the Seven Years' War and kept together with other documents from that conflict.[7] The repository could still be found in the inventory of the Landeshauptarchiv Sachsen-Anhalt, Außenstelle Wernigerode[8] in 2000, but the documents were missing. Unfortunately, the Household Archive could not be accessed at the time of writing as the heirs of the Prince of Stolberg-Wernigerode and the state of Sachsen-Anhalt are involved in a legal dispute about the further use of the Archive. The repository was most probably brought to the Soviet Union by the Soviet occupational authorities after 1945, a fate shared by many repositories on subjects of war and conflict. The General Staff's introduction does not mention any kind of selection of the printed letters from a larger number of pieces in the archive. The editors state only that there were no more recently written letters in the repository.[9] The letters cover the Battles of Lobositz and

---

[3] *Fundstücke*, 15–16.
[4] *Bilder aus der deutschen Vergangenheit*, ed. Gustav Freytag (Dachau: OK Publishing / musaicum, Kindle edition, [1859–1867] 2017). Freytag (1816–95) was one of the most influential German national-liberal writers of the second half of the nineteenth century.
[5] *Soldatenbriefe*, 2.
[6] *Briefe*, VI.
[7] Ibid., V.
[8] Landeshauptarchiv Magdeburg, Außenstelle Wernigerode, Rep. H Stolberg-Wernigerode.
[9] *Briefe*, VI.

Prague and five are 'extracts' from more extensive letters, which present these battles alone and the actions surrounding them, obviously leaving out passages not related to the battles. All these facts make it most likely that the Prince of Stolberg-Wernigerode obtained these documents from the families of the writing soldiers via an unknown source, probably Pietist chaplains,[10] and that he had collected them with the aim of gleaning information about these battles. Both of the regiments represented in the letters were involved in the fighting[11] and a part of Hülsen's *Kanton* regiment were also a part of Stolberg-Wernigerode's realm, as the regiment had Wernigerode as a *Kanton*. The *Kantons* of the Anhalt Regiment bordered on Stolberg-Wernigerode's county.[12] Why – and by which means – Stolberg acquired the letters is not known. Yet there is no indication that the General Staff or Liebe excluded existing letters from their editions. Had that been the case, Liebe would have left out the letter written by Corporal Binn dated 30 December 1757, where he writes that 'Grete's husband [obviously a *Kantonist* well known to the Binn family, K.&S.M.] has deserted'[13], as Liebe's stated aim was to show that the writing *Kantonisten* were not cut from the same cloth as the 'deserted Swiss' Ulrich Bräker. We can assumed that the letters survived by chance and were not extracted from a greater surviving pool of letters that presented differing opinions and mindsets. This is also true for the letters written by Dominicus[14] and Dresel from Westphalia. Dominicus was a musketeer and *Kantonist* in the infantry regiment no. 9, stationed in Hamm and Soest in the Prussian County of Mark in today's North Rhine-Westphalia.[15] He was a prosperous merchant. Dresel came from the same region and regiment but was a grenadier and son of a wealthy peasant family.[16] Berkovich's research in European archives, and the recent discovery and editing of the Zanders' letters, indicates that future research could also produce more letters.[17]

If we add the letters from the collections of the Zanders, the General Staff and Liebe, as well as the letters by Dominicus and Dresel, we have fifty-five letters by twenty-five different authors: seventeen soldiers contributed one letter each; three soldiers wrote two letters each (of which one letter was written together with the author's brother); one NCO wrote four letters; one private five; one cavalry NCO ten; and one musketeer thirteen. Judging from the writers' names, frequent mentions of relatives and friends from the villages and cities of the authors, most of them were *Kantonisten*. They came from the region of today's state of Saxony-Anhalt. Concerning the General Staff's collection, six authors were from the von Hülsen Regiment (No. 21), stationed in

---

[10] Stolberg-Wernigerode was a prominent adherent of Pietism. See: *'Mit göttlicher Güte geadelt'. Adel und Hallescher Pietismus im Spiegel der fürstlichen Sammlungen Stolberg-Wernigerode: Katalog zur Ausstellung der Franckeschen Stiftungen*, ed. Claus Veltmann and Thomas Ruhland (Wiesbaden: Harrassowitz, 2014).
[11] Hülsen at Lobositz, while being spectators at Prague, Alt-Anhalt at Prague, while being spectators at Lobositz.
[12] http://www.preussenweb.de/regiment1.htm (accessed 24 October 2018). http://www.kronoskaf.com/syw/index.php?title=H%C3%BClsen_Infantry (accessed 24 October 2018).
[13] Corporal Binn, 30 December 1757, in *Soldatenbriefe*, 11.
[14] Kerler, *Tagebuch*, 61–6.
[15] Ibid., I.
[16] Kohl, *Ein Brief*, 82.
[17] Berkovich, *Motivation*, 40–5.

Halberstadt and Quedlinburg. One author was a grenadier from the same regiment, serving in the converged grenadier battalion commanded by Johann Christian Karl von Lengefeld.[18] Another six writers of single letters were from the Alt-Anhalt / Anhalt-Bernburg Regiment (No. 3) from Halle/ Saale.[19] The NCO who wrote the series of four letters, Sergeant Liebler, was also a member of this regiment. Concerning Georg Liebe's edition, the writers came from the infantry regiments No. 3, No. 20 (from Magdeburg, the capital of today's Saxony-Anhalt)[20] and No. 27 (from Stendal and Gardelegen, minor cities in the same federal state).[21] Dominicus and Dresel were from the Westphalian No. 9 regiment. All these regiments were amongst the most effective in the whole army, yet many of their soldiers were killed or maimed during the war.[22] One letter probably stems from a dragoon and the long series of ten letters was written by a corporal from the cuirassier von Driesen Regiment (No. 7), stationed around Salzwedel and Tangermünde in the north-west of today's Saxony-Anhalt.[23]

The letters edited by the General Staff exclusively cover the years 1756 and 1757 and the Battles of Lobositz and Prague. Liebe's collection contains letters written mainly between 1756 and 1759 but also two texts from 1762, near the end of the war. Thus, all authors of the surviving letters were from the core regions of the Prussian monarchy and from regiments, which were particularly effective[24] and whose soldiers were considered to be especially loyal, competent and zealous.[25] The authors were aged from their mid-twenties to fifty years old, had served for a long period and half of them were married. This was typical for Prussian soldiers, particularly those serving during the first two years of the war.[26] There are seventeen privates and seven NCOs amongst the writers of our letters. One author was probably a lieutenant.[27] 28 per cent of the authors were NCOs, while the percentage of NCOs in a regiment was only 6.4 in 1756 (118 NCOs out of a total 1,832 men of all ranks).[28] Thus, NCOs are heavily overrepresented amongst the writers of the letters.

---

[18] The other two grenadier companies of the battalion came from Infantry Regiment No. 27. http://www.kronoskaf.com/syw/index.php?title=21/27_Lengefeld_Grenadiers (accessed 13 October 2018).

[19] Halle / Saale is a major town in today's Saxony-Anhalt and was the centre of German Pietism, also called Halle Pietism. It was also a cultural centre of the Brandenburg monarchy. The most famous British composer of the eighteenth century, George Frideric Handel, was born in Halle.

[20] Günther Gieraths, *Die Kampfhandlungen der Brandenburgisch-Preussischen Armee 1626–1807. Ein Quellenhandbuch* (Berlin: Walter de Gruyter & Co., 1964), 71.

[21] Gieraths, *Kampfhandlungen*, 92.

[22] Ibid., 73 and 94.

[23] Ibid., 216.

[24] The von Itzenplitz Regiment was the third-best in the army according to the king. Tempelhof, *Geschichte*, vol. 1, 328. The Alt-Anhalt Regiment (No. 3) was considered to be as good as the Guards for many years. After having been dishonoured by the king after its failure during the siege of Dresden in 1760, it rehabilitated itself during the Battle of Liegnitz, when it attacked and routed Austrian cavalry by a furious bayonet charge. Friedrich August von Retzow, *Charakteristik der wichtigsten Ereignisse des siebenjährigen Krieges, in Rücksicht auf Ursachen und Wirkungen*, vol. 2 (Berlin: Himburg, 1802), 244.

[25] Tempelhof, *Geschichte*, vol. 1, 67 and Tempelhof, *Geschichte*, vol. 2, 9, fn. *9.

[26] Willerd R. Fann, 'On the Infantryman's Age in Eighteenth Century Prussia', *Military Affairs* 41, no. 4 (1977): 165–70.

[27] He signs his letter 'Lt. Seiler' (Liebe, *Soldatenbriefe*, 37.). It was not uncommon to sign private letters with the rank and surname, as can be shown by a letter of Corporal Binn. Liebe, *Soldatenbriefe*, 11.)

[28] See Chapter 1.

The authors' general ability to read and write was not exceptional in the Prussian army; indeed being able to write was a prerequisite for becoming an NCO.[29] Younger officers and also many NCOs and soldiers wrote 'marching' diaries that documented the whereabouts and actions of the soldier and his unit.[30] Exchanging letters was common in the Prussian army, as indicated by C.F. Zander's claim that 'all our comrades are eagerly waiting for mail from home'.[31] The overall educational level of the authors is good, which reflects the high standard of education in the heartlands of the Prussian monarchy facilitated by the large sums of money and time parents invested in their children's education.[32] We must stress that the German orthography of the men cannot be taken as a measure of their literacy, as German spelling was not standardized at this time.[33] Unlike, (for example) Spanish, there was no single authority that determined how a word should be written; only the spelling of foreign words from French or Latin can serve as an indication of soldiers' reading and writing capacities as these *were* standardized. Some soldiers tend to write as they spoke. This is most obvious when C.F. Zander relates his conversation with his major and the regiment's auditor. The Zanders and other authors vocalize foreign words.[34] Thus, we have to look at the men's ability to communicate differentiated knowledge to varying audiences. We will show that the writers had a good knowledge of military affairs[35], social structures, cultural and religious standards and their economic affairs.

Three of the writers are obviously used to abstract literary products, as indicated by the way they use typical literary expressions of their time. One NCO from the Alt-Anhalt Regiment (no. 3) is able to read Latin and knows the works of Pufendorf.[36] The General Staff viewed him as an 'unsuccessful student of Halle University',[37] but this is doubtful given that the general level of literacy in Halle was high and guildmasters and village administrators were sometimes as learned as the anonymous NCO. Another example of a highly literate NCO is Sergeant Liebler, of whom four letters have survived. He is very well acquainted with the Bible and able to write long

---

[29] *Prussian Infantry Reglement of 1743*, 444–5.
[30] Kloosterhuis, *Donner*, 142.
[31] C.F. Zander, 04 December 1756, in *Fundstücke*, 38.
[32] Unlike many later legends, there was no public school system at this time in Prussia. We are dealing with a cultural phenomenon, which is reflected in Corporal Binn's letters, who pays for a private tutor to teach his son how to read and write. See p. 191. C.F. Zander also stresses the need for one of his younger relatives to learn to write well. C.F. Zander, 29 January 1758, in *Fundstücke*, 67 and C.F. Zander, 16 May 1758, in *Fundstücke*, 77.
[33] Liebe, *Soldatenbriefe*, 3.
[34] Corporal Binn, 19 June 1745, in *Soldatenbriefe*, 4. Binn uses *Patali* for the French loanword *Bataille* (battle). J.D. Zander, 14 December 1756, in *Fundstücke*, 38. Zander uses *Contong* for *Kanton* and *Fractemente* for the French loanword *Tractement*.
[35] This analysis is supported by contemporary military writers. Musketier Hoppe, 'Wahrhafte Beschreibung der blutigen Schlacht bei Zorndorf, von einem alten preußischen Soldaten, welcher 34 Jahr gedient und jetzt (1793) noch lebt. Von ihm selbst beschrieben', in *Officier-Lesebuch*, vol. 1, 195–6, fn. *). Tempelhof, *Geschichte*, vol. 1, 147. We can also point at the descriptions of the Battle of Lobositz by soldiers from the Alt-Anhalt Regiment, which mirror the official reports. See Frederick II, *Geschichte des Siebenjährigen Krieges* (Die Werke Friedrichs des Großen, vol. 3) (Berlin: Hobbing, 1913), vol. 1, 47–9, and Beschreibung der Lobositzer Bataille, datirt 1. Oktober 1756, in *Briefe*, 1–7.
[36] 'Beschreibung der Lobositzer Bataille, datirt 1. Oktober 1756, in *Briefe*, 1–7.
[37] *Briefe*, 7, fn. **.

letters very quickly given his enormous workload at the front.[38] The General Staff assumed that he had 'fallen prey to a convention of awakened Christians'.[39] Being a wealthy merchant, Dominicus was also able to read and write.[40] He managed a substantial inheritance while he was at the front and also had a deep knowledge of the bible.

We will now take a closer look at some of the soldier authors.

The Zanders

Johann Matthias Zander was *Dorfschulze*[41] of Nitzahn, a Brandenburg village near Plaue an der Havel. As head of his family, he was exempt from military service but his position did not prevent his relatives from being drafted into the army. His younger brother, Christian Friedrich Zander (21 August 1725–14 October 1758), and his eldest son, Johann Dietrich (15 December 1729–14 October 1758),[42] both served in the von Itzenplitz Regiment (no. 13). Christian Friedrich was a 'brewer'[43] and burgher of Plaue and had unsuccessfully tried to leave the army in 1749,[44] but seems to have gained a substantial spell of leave.[45] Johann Matthias Zander died in 1752 and his second son, Johann Wilhelm Zander, inherited the position as *Dorfschulze*. Johann Wilhelm was Christian Friedrich's nephew and Christian Friedrich addresses him as 'Vetter' (nephew) in his letters.[46] That they were from a prosperous and educated peasant family of village administrators does not seem to be exceptional. Two of the other authors were privates[47] and also sons of the local *Dorfschulzen* (village administrators), and C.F. Zander mentions the death of the son of the *Dorfschulze* of Möthlitz, a village bordering on the Zanders' village of Nitzahn.[48]

The king valued their von Itzenplitz Regiment as an elite unit.[49] For the soldiers, this meant that they had *Immediatverkehr* with the king, and were thus allowed to address him directly in all matters concerning their service. The two Zanders did not take part in the Battle of Prague due to illness but seven months later, both were present at the regiment's famous charge as part of the vanguard of the army at the Battle of Leuthen. They also took part in some minor actions and were killed during the Battle of Hochkirch along with the other *Kantonisten* from their village.

---

[38] Schreiben des Feldwebels Liebler, 7. Mai 1757, in *Briefe*, 48.
[39] *Briefe*, VI.
[40] Kerler, *Tagebuch*, VI and VIII.
[41] Village administrator. The *Schulze* was normally from a well-off peasant family with a relatively high level of education.
[42] *Fundstücke*, 83–4.
[43] This did not necessarily mean that he worked as a brewer, as every house-owner had the right to brew beer. *Fundstücke*, 86.
[44] See pp. 197–8.
[45] There are only two letters between 1749 and the outbreak of the war. They stem from the manoeuvre period of 1753.
[46] This can be misleading for modern readers as the modern German word *Vetter* is translated as 'cousin', while in early modern German it means 'uncle' or 'nephew'. *Zedler's*, 48 (1746), 373.
[47] Arnholz, Kamiet See his letter on p. 194.
[48] C.F. Zander, 17 February 1757, in *Fundstücke*, 49.
[49] Kloosterhuis, *Donner*, 135.

The Zanders played a central role in the community of *Kantonisten* from their village as they were the hub for exchanging information by letters between the village and the army due to their reading and writing skills and their affiliation to the family of the *Dorfschulzen*.⁵⁰ Christian Friedrich and Johann Dietrich were central to a network that secured the 'presence' of the village at the front and the presence of the front at the village. At the same time, their position as intermediaries between the noble authorities and the peasantry in civil life is reflected by their way of dealing with their officers. Christian Friedrich does not hesitate to approach the owner of his regiment and even the king to request that he be dismissed, while Johann Dietrich approaches his captain on behalf of an acquaintance from the village whom they try to prevent from becoming a grenadier. They fail in both cases, but their challenge to the officers' decisions is perceived as a perfectly normal action by them and their commanding officers alike. The strong position of the Zanders stems from their rank in civil society: the officers needed the support of local administrators for recruiting the *Kantonisten*.⁵¹

While not all their friends and relatives were in the same company – two of them served in one of the grenadier companies, for example – it seems that they meant more to them than did the men with whom they fought side by side. Their letters are mainly written to their nephew and show how they care for their relatives, who were also to receive the information contained in their letters. Most striking is their fear, that younger relatives will also be drafted. They are honourable men in their village and also honourable soldiers at the front. Their direct influence on the draft is small but that it exists at all, increases their standing.

The Zanders took part in the Battles of Lobositz, Roßbach and Leuthen, but the corresponding letters did not survive.⁵² Yet when they write about their role in combat, they seem to be very reluctant to provide details, although they were part of one of the elite regiments of the Prussian army and their relatives were often asking for details from the front. The Zanders are not as religious as other soldiers but their religious allusions multiply when they write about the hardships of their service or the danger of combat.⁵³ Their writing strategy will be discussed in detail below because it is different from the other authors' and shows their goal of improving their social standing in the village.

Johann Jacob Dominicus

Johann Jacob Dominicus is the soldier about whom we have the most extensive information about his life on campaign and as a POW. He wrote a diary and a long letter to his brother covering the Battle of Paltzig (also called Kay or Züllichau) in 1759. Dominicus was born in Harhausen near Gummersbach⁵⁴ on 13 November 1731. His

---

⁵⁰ This corresponded to the role of the *Dorfschulzen* as 'brokers of information' (*Informationsmakler*) in civil life. Löffler, *Dörfliche Amtsträger*, 185.
⁵¹ Which was also a source of corruption. Winter, *Untertanengeist*, 311.
⁵² *Fundstücke*, 91, fn. 196.
⁵³ Ibid., 99.
⁵⁴ In today's North Rhine-Westphalia, 50 km east of Cologne.

father died when he was still a child and his stepfather took on responsibility for his education, which enabled Dominicus to become a merchant's apprentice in Iserlohn.[55] He was drafted into the army aged 19, and joined Regiment No. 9 due to his extraordinary height (although this is not known, sadly). Normally a well-off merchant's son would have been able to avoid the draft, because he was a valuable tax-payer and important for the economic wellbeing of his town. As he possessed a considerable fortune, he was granted leave from the regiment for a long period, but had to join the colours again at the outbreak of the Seven Years' War.[56] Together with his regiment, Dominicus fought in some of the major battles of the war, such as Lobositz (1 October 1756), where his colonel was mortally wounded, and Prague (6 May 1757), where the regiment was extremely successful but lost roughly half of its men. At Roßbach (5 November 1757) No. 9 and No. 5 (Alt-Braunschweig from Magdeburg) were among the few infantry units which exchanged fire with the Allied French and Imperial troops before routing them. Dominicus and his comrades then fought the Russian army on 23 July 1759 at Kay. Although the Prussians lost the battle, Dominicus' regiment – and some others – managed to break through the first Russian line by intense musket fire and bayonet charges. It is important to bear this in mind when comparing Dominicus' letter and the description of the battle in his diary. While the diary stresses the courageous behaviour of his regiment, the letter does not mention any close combat but instead focuses on Dominicus' suffering, the danger he had been in and his plea for his brother to pray for him. It also shows that Dominicus was overwhelmed by the sight of his comrades being killed in a most gruesome way.[57] He admits that the normal religious strategies used to cope with exposure to violence do not work and calls upon his brother to help him to regain his ability to pray and thank God. Dominicus survived the disaster at Kunersdorf and was captured together with his regiment at Maxen. After the war he stayed with the regiment as *capitain des armes* and was charged with overseeing the stores of the regiment at Hamm. He died in 1775.[58]

Musketeer Frantz Reiß from the von Hülsen Regiment (No. 21)

Franz Reiß was a private, most probably a *Kantonist*, serving in the von Hülsen Regiment (No. 21). The regiment was stationed in Halberstadt and Quedlinburg and got its *Kantonisten* from there and the surrounding areas. It lost twelve officers and 265 men during the Battle of Lobositz, which is described in Frantz Reiß' only surviving letter. Reiß' regiment was with General Keith's corps during the Battle of Prague and thus did not take part in the bloody fighting of that day. Yet it was amongst those troops that met the Austrian relief force at Kolin (18 June 1757) and perished during the disaster, losing just under 1,000 men in the battle. Later on, its first battalion would participate in the victory at Roßbach against the French and Imperial forces. The

---

[55] A few kilometres south-east of Dortmund.
[56] Kerler, *Tagebuch*, VI–VII.
[57] Dominicus does mourn his tent-comrades explicitly, writing only that he had been overwhelmed by seeing them die and his own fear.
[58] Kerler, *Tagebuch*, VI–VII.

regiment lost 700 men in the Battle of Kunersdorf (12 August 1759) and was captured at Maxen in November of that year. In 1760, the regiment participated in the Battle of Torgau.[59] As our only source of information on Franz Reiß' life is this letter, we do not know where or when he died.

We do know, however, that Frantz Reiß was married and had a child.[60] Reiß gives one of the most detailed descriptions of a soldier's involvement in combat. He stresses the horror of combat, when he tells his wife how a comrade near him had his head shot off. And he is one of the few soldiers who relates his thoughts during combat. Due to the very emotional content of his letter, where he stresses having thought of 'God, you [my wife] and the child',[61] it is one of the most moving pieces of writing we have from the Seven Years' War. Reiß was still shocked when he wrote his letter and it becomes clear that he cannot get to grips with the appalling death suffered by so many comrades. Although he stresses the importance of the help he felt God had given him, and is proud of the king's visit to his regiment, Reiß expresses his anger about the carnage and of not having had the opportunity to prepare for the forthcoming battle. Reiß also shows that he is able to critically reflect a sermon given by the regiment's chaplain. The bible reading for the thanksgiving service for the victory at Lobositz given to the soldiers by the chaplain, was reinterpreted by Reiß to express his anger. The regimental chaplain had preached about Romans 8:36–37:

> As it is written: 'For your sake we face death all day long; we are considered as sheep to be slaughtered.' No, in all these things we are more than conquerors through him who loved us.

Reiß takes the Gospel's image of the slaughtering block and inserts it into his expression of anger:

> Now, dearest child, think about this, how we must have felt, led to the scaffold with empty stomachs[62] in the morning, not knowing what was to happen. We and another three regiments suffered the heaviest losses.[63]

When Reiß writes that he and his comrades were left unaware of 'what was to happen', he means that they were not able to prepare themselves with prayers or farewell letters and had been purposefully sacrificed like sheep. He clearly uses religious terms to show his rage.

---

[59] http://www.kronoskaf.com/syw/index.php?title=H%C3%BClsen_Infantry (accessed 22 October 2018).
[60] Extrakt Schreibens eines Soldaten Hülsischen Regiments Namens Frantz Reiß, Lobositz, 6. Oktober 1756, in *Briefe*, 32. (Excerpt of a letter by a soldier from the Huelsen Regiment, named Frantz Reiss, written near Lobositz, 6 October 1756.)
[61] Ibid.
[62] The German original has *nüchtern*. *Nüchtern* can either mean 'not drunk' or 'empty', 'with an empty stomach'. *Zedler's* 24 (1740), 1589–60. As Reiß writes that they had been led to the scaffold *in the morning*, we can assume that he is angry about not having been able to eat and not that he had not been able to drink alcohol.
[63] Frantz Reiß, Lobositz, 6. Oktober 1756, in *Briefe*, 31.

Reiß does something that could be interpreted as a symptom of PTSD. In his letter he starts to attack his wife rudely, even though she is no way responsible for his plight.[64] First, he is annoyed, because he thinks that she had written too extensively about a quarrel with a neighbour. Then he tells her not to think that the battle had been 'child's play' and is still angry with her. But immediately thereafter, he displays emotional switching and the tone of his letter becomes friendly and loving. What we see is a deeply distressed man, disoriented in his emotions and beliefs, who has been hurt severely on many levels by the brutal slaughter he had been forced to witness.

Sergeant G.S. Liebler from the Alt-Anhalt Regiment

Sergeant Liebler of the Alt-Anhalt Regiment (No. 3) was married with several children; one son also served as an NCO in the same regiment. Liebler must have been relatively old, as his son was also married and had a child. His regiment was stationed in Halle / Saale, where one-third of the population were soldiers or their relatives.[65] It had ranked second only to the guards during the reign of the Soldier King and counted amongst the most effective during the first two Silesian Wars. It had been the model-regiment of Leopold von Anhalt-Dessau, the famous Field-Marshal, and closest adviser, of the Soldier King. During the Seven Years' War, it was present at the Battle of Lobositz but took no active part. It suffered heavy casualties at Prague, and lost an entire battalion at Kolin. The regiment did take part in the Battle of Kay, where it was able to overrun the gun positions on the Russian left wing, but was driven back due to a lack of support.[66] It fought valiantly against vastly superior Austrian forces at Meißen on 4 December 1759 but seven companies had to surrender (although they did not lose colours, which had been taken to safety earlier).[67]

The regiment's fortunes reached their nadir in late July 1760, when two of its companies were shattered by a night-time sortie by Austrian troops during the Prussians' abortive siege of Dresden. Most observers agreed that the flight of the Prussian musketeers had not been their fault, but the king wanted to make an example of them: not even this renowned and hard-fighting regiment would evade his wrath if he considered its soldiers to be cowards. The regiment lost its 'braid and ornament from their uniforms. The rank and file also lost their swords'.[68] Thus, the regiment was deprived of its honour[69] and the deeply humiliated officers tried to leave the service but were not allowed to do so.[70] On 15 August 1760, the regiment got the chance to

---

[64] http://www.veterans.gc.ca/eng/services/health/mental-health/publications/ptsd-families#b5 (accessed 22 October 2018.)

[65] Ute Fahrig, *Militär und Gesellschaft. Die Integration Halles in den brandenburgisch-preußischen Staat (1680–1740/50)* (MA diss. Institut für Geschichte, Universität Potsdam, Potsdam, 2000).

[66] Showalter, *Frederick*, pos. 4262. A very good map of the battle is to be found here: http://www.kronoskaf.com/syw/images/4/49/1759-07-23_-_Battle_of_Paltzig.jpg (accessed 23 October 2018).

[67] http://www.preussenweb.de/regiment1.htm (accessed 23 October 2018). See also: Tempelhof, *Geschichte*, vol. 3 (Berlin: Johann Friedrich Unger, 1795), 321.

[68] Showalter, *Frederick*, pos. 4787.

[69] The soldiers' swords were not to be used in battle, but rather served as a symbol of their honour. Showalter; *Frederick*, pos. 2874.

[70] Johann Wilhelm von Archenholz, *Geschichte des Siebenjährigen Krieges in Deutschland von 1756 bis 1763* (Mannheim: Schwan und Götz, 1788), 176.

vindicate its injured honour. At the Battle of Liegnitz, it surged forward, defeated enemy cavalry with a furious bayonet-charge and was rehabilitated by the king. Remarkably, four privates approached the king after the battle and asked him to get their laces and swords back, while the officers hung back and waited for the king to show his approval.[71]

The regiment's history during the war was tragic. It was a well-trained unit with a proud history[72] and obviously consisted of literate and educated NCOs and privates. At the Battle of Prague, though, the regiment was sent into a series of suicidal attacks, a pattern repeated at Kolin and Kay and even the restoration of its honour at Liegnitz left many of its men dead or maimed.

Halle / Saale, where Liebler's regiment was garrisoned, was the hometown of the *Hallesche Pietismus*, a branch of Lutheran Orthodoxy. Even today the *Franckesche Stiftungen*,[73] a vast complex of buildings, which were used as a well-run orphanage in the eighteenth century, show the former influence of the Pietists on the city. Pietism stressed the individual faith of the Christian believer and the fulfilment of one's duties towards the authorities as divine service. The Soldier King had already seen the potential of this creed and had formed an alliance[74] with the Pietists to influence the officers and soldiers through Pietist army chaplains,[75] thereby creating 'a state organ completely divorced from the civilian church'.[76] It is no surprise, then, that the Pietist influence is also reflected in the soldiers' letters from the regiment stationed in Halle / Saale.[77]

Both trends, the professional military[78] and the religious,[79] are most sharply reflected in Liebler's letters, which depict a deeply pious man who knows many sections of the Bible by heart and acts like the chaplain of his family. He is able to grasp tactical situations, gets the high command's dispositions for marching[80] to organize everything for his company[81] and cares for the safety of the companies' colours during the Battle of Prague.[82] Liebler's faith seems to enable him to cope well with the horror of the

---

[71] Archenholz, *Geschichte*, 186. Retzow, *Charakteristik*, vol. 2, 244.
[72] See: Johann Friedrich Seyfarth, *Geschichte des Infanterie-Regiments von Anhalt-Bernburg* (Halle / Saale: J.G. Trampe, 1767).
[73] https://www.francke-halle.de/ (accessed 23 October 2018).
[74] Benjamin Marschke, *Absolutely Pietist. Patronage, Factionalism, and State-Building in the Early Eighteenth-Century Prussian Army Chaplaincy* (Tübingen: Niemeyer, 2005), 184.
[75] Johannes Wallmann, *Pietismus-Studien. Gesammelte Aufsätze II* (Tübingen: Mohr-Siebeck, 2008), 384.
[76] Marschke, *Absolutely Pietist*, 38.
[77] Lager vor Prag, den 8. Mai. Schreiben eines Musketiers des Regiments Anhalt zu Fuß 1757, in *Briefe*, 52. (Camp outside Prague, 8 May. Letter by a musketeer of the Anhalt foot regiment.)
[78] Von einem Unteroffizier, 6. Oktober 1756, in *Briefe*, 24–29. Klauel gives a detailed account of the Battle of Lobositz, which displays a high degree of military expertise. His religious allusions are few, but still more numerous than those in (for example) the Zanders' letters. Schreiben eines Musketiers des Regiments Anhalt zu Fuß 1757, in *Briefe*, 49–51. He gives a professional description of the Battle of Prague.
[79] Von einem [anonymen] Unteroffizier, 6. Oktober 1756, in *Briefe*, 23–4. Barthel Linck, im Lager bei Lobositz, 3. Oktober 1756, in *Briefe*, 11–15. Schreiben eines Musketiers des Regiments Anhalt zu Fuß 1757, in *Briefe,* 52. The musketeer is deeply convinced that intercession influences God's decisions.
[80] G.S. Liebler, den 10. April 1757, in *Briefe*, 41.
[81] G.S. Liebler, in *Briefe*, 48.
[82] Ibid., 47.

slaughter he witnesses during combat. Although he is afraid, he views himself as one of the chosen of the Lord fighting the 'enemies of the Gospel' and is full of praise for God's mercy upon his survival.[83] His thoughts during the murderous attack on the Austrian positions are religious only and centred on his own salvation.[84] Pity for fallen comrades or horror at their deaths are completely missing.[85] Given the regiment's losses during the war, it is very unlikely that either Liebler or his son survived the war, but we do not know for sure whether they survived or when they died.

An Anonymous Musketeer of the Alt-Anhalt Regiment

The Musketeer was from the same regiment as Sergeant Liebler. The surviving passages we have of his have been taken from a longer letter or correspondence. We do not know to whom the letter is addressed, but it must have been a close relative, and is probably the musketeer's wife. He also expected other relatives to read his letter.[86] The man served together with his brother, who also stood next to him in the ranks, as he writes that 'it was only a matter of a finger's breadth for me and my brother to be sent to the other world by a cannonball'.[87] He gives a detailed description of the operations of the Prussian army and even evaluates them, when he writes critically about the order to attack without firing:

> ... many of our men perished. This was also due to the order that our men were not to fire before being ordered to do so, as they were to charge into the enemy [lines] with fixed bayonets.[88] Because of this, many of our men were pitifully maimed, but the enemy had to flee from the bayonets – even if the mountains had been two times higher and even if there had been another 120 cannon.[89]

Although his religious allusions are not nearly as numerous as that of Sergeant Liebler, he also gives thanks to the Lord and calls upon his relatives to pray and thank God. He speaks frankly about his fear and prayer during the night before the battle[90] and stresses how important the intercession of those Prussian troops who had not

---

[83] Ibid., 45.
[84] Ibid., 47.
[85] This might be due to the writing strategy of making his relatives praise the Lord together with him, but also the individualistic trend in Pietism and perhaps also an egocentric character. Similar trends can be traced in the Pietist discourse on the Seven Years' War: Anti-Catholicism, praise for God for the salvation of Halle and no compassion for the killed or maimed soldiers, especially when they are enemies.
[86] Schreiben eines Musketiers des Regiments Anhalt zu Fuß 1757, in *Briefe*, 52. The author writes of 'my brother', who is also a soldier and asks an undefined group of people to praise God for his mercy towards them. Mark Häberlein and Michaela Schmölz-Häberlein, *Der Siebenjährige Krieg und das Kommunikationsnetz des Halleschen Pietismus*, to be published in *The Seven Years' War 1756–1763: Micro- and Macroperspectives* (Schriftenreihe des Historischen Kollegs München), ed. Marian Füssel (Berlin and Boston, MA: De Gruyter/Oldenbourg, 2021).
[87] Schreiben eines Musketiers des Regiments Anhalt zu Fuß 1757, in *Briefe*, 52.
[88] See p. 189.
[89] Schreiben eines Musketiers des Regiments Anhalt zu Fuß 1757, in *Briefe*, 51.
[90] Ibid., 50.

been able to take part in the fighting.⁹¹ Like many other men, he stresses the suffering of the soldiers. During combat, he was aware only of the danger to himself and his brother.⁹² We do not know whether he survived the war or when he died.

Corporal Nikolaus Binn from von Driesen Cuirassier Regiment (No. 7)

The letters of Corporal Nikolaus Binn of the von Driesen Cuirassier Regiment (No. 7) form the longest surviving series of letters next to the Zanders'. Ten of his letters, and one written by his son, were kept by one of his descendants. The first letter dates from 1745, shortly after the Prussian victory at Hohenfriedberg. Nikolaus Binn's last letter is from 1759, some three weeks before the Battle of Kunersdorf. Binn survived the disaster, as the letter from his son dates from 1776 and is addressed to him and his wife.

We do not know whether Binn had been a *Kantonist* or a volunteer. It is certain that he came from Erxleben, that his family was deeply rooted in the community and that he was a professional NCO at the time he wrote his letters.⁹³ He was married and had two sons; his letters are addressed to his wife but would also have been read by his parents and other relatives. His mother seems to have died between 1745 and 1757.⁹⁴ Binn and his brother served in the same company.⁹⁵ His brother died in February or March 1758 of the wounds received during an encounter at the beginning of that year.⁹⁶ He also played the role of a hub between his fellow soldiers and their hometown, as his letters pass on information and greetings from several of his comrades.⁹⁷ The relationship to some of his comrades from his hometown seems to have been quite uneasy, as they had accused him of adultery. The accusation made him write an extensive letter to his wife explaining the good relationship between him and the preacher's family, especially his two daughters, in a village where he had been quartered. In spite of his regiment's heavy losses, he survived the war.

The von Driesen Cuirassier Regiment was a very effective unit. It fought with distinction at Lobositz, Kolin, Roßbach, Kay and Kunersdorf. At Kunersdorf alone, thirteen officers and 136 men were killed or wounded.⁹⁸ Compared to the infantry, these numbers were low, but for a cavalry regiment they were high. The whole regiment was captured at Maxen (20 November 1759), which probably saved Binn's life and that of many of his comrades.⁹⁹ These factors may explain why there are no surviving letters from Binn after July 1759, shortly before the Battle of Kunersdorf (12 August 1759).

---

⁹¹ Ibid., 52.
⁹² Ibid., 52.
⁹³ This is proven by Binn's remark that he wants his son to learn to read and write in order to get a better job than Binn himself had been forced to accept.
⁹⁴ Compare, Letter no. 1 by Corporal Binn, 19. Juni 1745, in *Soldatenbriefe*, 4 and letter no. 3 by Corporal Binn, 30. Dezember 1757, in *Soldatenbriefe*, 8.
⁹⁵ Letter no. 7 by Corporal Binn, 1758, in *Soldatenbriefe*, 16.
⁹⁶ Ibid.
⁹⁷ Letter no. 3 by Corporal Binn, 30 December 1757, in *Soldatenbriefe*, 10. Letter no. 7 by Corporal Binn, 30 December 1757, in *Soldatenbriefe*, 17–18. Letter no. 9 by Corporal Binn, 18 April 1759, in *Soldatenbriefe*, 21.
⁹⁸ http://www.preussenweb.de/regiment4.htm (accessed 24 October 2018).
⁹⁹ http://www.kronoskaf.com/syw/index.php?title=Driesen_Cuirassiers (accessed 24 October 2018).

Like most of the other writers, Binn does not like his job but for him, there is no contradiction between this dislike and a certain pride in the achievements of the Prussian army. Binn's letters contain features that are of special importance for our study. He sees himself as a good and faithful husband in the face of the accusations from men from his hometown that he had cheated on his wife. We will never know which version is true, but Binn's panicky reaction[100] shows that womanizing was despised in his social group. And while he appears to be a rather calm man during combat, he becomes furious at his son's poor spelling.[101] Like the Zanders, he tries to maintain his place in the family and permanently intervenes in family affairs, when (for example) he tells his wife that he has sent money to her and how she should use it.[102] Binn's first letters do not contain many religious allusions, but his last surviving letter, written shortly before Kunersdorf, is full of them. Binn's fear of the Russians, whom he calls 'tyrannical enemies', is obvious and he encourages himself by writing that he will 'not give anything away for free and do what a righteous soldier is supposed to do in battles'.[103] Binn had already fought the Russians at Kay and knew that they were hard to beat; he was definitely thinking about his death and shows much more fear at this point than after Hohenfriedberg or Prague. Binn thought that this letter could be his last,[104] but he lived on to see his son grow up to become a soldier – albeit one with bad orthography.[105]

Musekteer Christian Arnholtz from the von Kleist Regiment (No. 27)

Christian Arnholtz came from Zethlingen near Salzwedel in today's Saxony-Anhalt. He served in the von Kleist regiment (from January 1757 on, renamed as von der Asseburg, No. 27) and was most probably a *Kantonist*. Georg Liebe tells us that he was, like J. D. Zander, the son of the *Dorfschulze* of Zethlingen and that Christian was born in 1730, so was thus in his mid-twenties when he had to go to war.

His regiment was amongst the most efficient in the Prussian army, although many of its men were killed or wounded during the war. It had proved its abilities during the War of the Austrian Succession. During the Battle of Lobositz, the regiment was on the left wing and had to break the fierce resistance of the Austrian infantry on the Loboschberg.[106] In the final phase of the battle, the regiment ran out of ammunition and charged with levelled bayonets, driving the enemy off the field.[107] It fought well too at the Battle of Breslau (22 November 1757) and was deployed in the vanguard at Leuthen together with the Zanders' regiment (No. 13). The regiment lost twelve officers and 623 men at Zorndorf, where it helped avert defeat on the right wing of the Prussian position[108] amidst scenes of horrible slaughter in hand-to-hand

---

[100] Letter no. 9 by Corporal Binn, 18. April 1759, in *Soldatenbriefe*, 20.
[101] Letter no. 8 by Corporal Binn, 8. April 1759, in *Soldatenbriefe*, 18.
[102] Ibid., 19.
[103] Letter no. 10 by Corporal Binn, 20. Juli 1759, in *Soldatenbriefe*, 22.
[104] Ibid., 23.
[105] Joachim Nikolaus Binn, 18. April 1776, in *Soldatenbriefe*, 24.
[106] Duffy, *Frederick*, 345.
[107] http://www.preussenweb.de/regiment2.htm (accessed, 25 October 2018).
[108] http://www.preussenweb.de/regiment2.htm (accessed, 25 October 2018).

fighting.¹⁰⁹ It did not take part in the defeats at Hochkirch and Kunersdorf, however, or the dearly won victory at Torgau.¹¹⁰

Christian's letter to his brother is proof of the important position occupied by relations of village administrators. These people were part of the prosperous peasantry and the letters indicate that their writing capacities also contributed to their important position as points of contact between the front and the village of the *Kantonisten*.¹¹¹ Arnholtz cites nine men from his and neighbouring villages who sent greetings and health updates back home. He explicitly asks his brother that he and the mentioned families gather and write one single letter back to him. He also asks them to send the letter to 'cutler Rinke' in Gardelegen, so that it will reach the regiment safely.¹¹² The address also hints at the fact that there might have been some kind of army postal service, but many men had other, and obviously more trusted, ways of sending and receiving their mail. Again, Arnholtz's public letter stresses the soldiers' exhaustion and suffering and asks for God's help.¹¹³ We do not know anything further about the fate of Arnholtz and his comrades.

Musketeer Kaspar Kalberlah from the Alt-Anhalt Regiment (No. 3)¹¹⁴

Kasper Kalberlah came from Behnsdorf near Weferlingen in the north-west of today's Saxony-Anhalt. He was born on 4 May 1732 and killed on 23 July 1759, two months after his twenty-seventh birthday, during the Battle of Kay. He had been a soldier for ten years.¹¹⁵ He served together with his brother, who survived at least until the end of September 1758.¹¹⁶

His regiment's service was outline in Sergeant Liebler's biography above, but it is surely noteworthy that his second letter from 1758 is the last surviving letter of a soldier in this regiment. Unlike the NCOs Liebler and Klauel,¹¹⁷ but like his fellow private Barthel Linck,¹¹⁸ Kalberlah took no delight in watching the Battle of Lobositz. His letter is full of thanks to God that he was not involved and he and his brother tell

---

¹⁰⁹ Duffy, *Frederick*, 169.
¹¹⁰ http://www.kronoskaf.com/syw/index.php?title=Kleist_Infantry (accessed 25 October 2018). Duffy, *Frederick*, 365, 370, 374.
¹¹¹ This is underlined by Dresel's role as communication hub for his conrades and their families. Kohl, *Ein Brief*, 84.
¹¹² Christian Arnholtz, 21. September 1756, in *Soldatenbriefe*, 25.
¹¹³ Ibid., 26.
¹¹⁴ Liebe, the editor of the letters, does not give any information on Kalberlah's regiment. Given his home region and the facts that his company lost one man during the Battle of Lobositz and that he himself was killed at Kay, it must have been regiment No. 3. The only regiment present at Kay with *Kantons* in his region was Alt-Anhalt (http://www.kronoskaf.com/syw/index.php?title=1759-07-23_-_Battle_of_Paltzig#Prussian_Order_of_Battle (accessed 25 October 2018)). Alt-Anhalt had also inucrred very few casualties at Lobositz. Von einem [anonymen] Unteroffizier des Anhaltischen Regiments, 6. Oktober 1756, in *Briefe*, 24.
¹¹⁵ Georg Liebe cites an entry in the farm's housebook by Kalberlah's stepbrother. *Soldatenbriefe*, 28.
¹¹⁶ Kaspar Kalberlah, 11. November 1756, in *Soldatenbriefe*, 29. Kaspar Kalberlah, 26 September 1758, in *Soldatenbriefe*, 29.
¹¹⁷ Von einem Unteroffizier des Alt-Anhaltischen Regiments, in *Briefe*, 15. Von einem Unteroffizier [C.G. Klauel] Anhaltischen Regiments, in *Briefe*, 28.
¹¹⁸ Barthel Linck, im Lager bei Lobositz, 3. Oktober 1756, in *Briefe*, 11–15.

their relatives that because of the battle, they were 'so fed up with life, that they could eat it with spoons'.[119] The expression means that both brothers were deeply depressed and their mental state can be interpreted as a result of PTSD, especially as Kalberlah names the battle as the cause of their psychological problems.

We do not know anything about Kalberlah's role in the following encounters, only that he and his brother survived them.[120] The most important feature of his letter from 26 September 1758 is his description of the Russians, which reflects rumours in the Prussian army. These were on the one hand based on crimes committed by the light Russian troops[121] and on the other hand on exaggerated stories spread out by the Prussian high command to motivate the Prussian soldiers to take on a 'barbarian' enemy.[122] Yet Kalberlah and many of his comrades simply began to fear the Russians:[123]

> Dear brother,[124] you informed me that the king had beaten the Russian,[125] we heard of this just two days after the victory [and] how they [the Russians] behaved, how they tortured the people, cut off their hands, threw the womenfolk into the straw and burned them, yeah, they ate young children, stabbed and burned everything in the towns and villages. Pray every day, that God does not allow this enemy to get too mighty and conquer us, otherwise we and you will fare badly.[126]

Kalberlah thus reflects not only rumours and propaganda, but also the information provided by the men from the king's army, which had returned to Saxony from the eastern theatre after the bloody Battle of Zorndorf.[127] King Frederick had tried to present it as a glorious victory over a clumsy and brutal enemy, even reducing the number of Prussian casualties in his official report from roughly 13,000[128] to around 1,200.[129] Kalberlah and his fellow soldiers seem to have heard very different stories from the Prussian survivors of the carnage at Zorndorf, which made them fear the Russian enemy,[130] a fear that would cause many problems in later battles. One of them was the Battle of Kay, where Kaspar Kalberlah was killed.

---

[119] Kaspar Kalberlah, 11. November 1756, in *Soldatenbriefe*, 28.
[120] Kaspar Kalberlah, 26. September 1758, in *Soldatenbriefe*, 29.
[121] Tempelhof, *Geschichte*, vol. 2, 230.
[122] Retzow, *Charakteristik*, vol. 1, 320. Retzow relates the atrocities committed by Cossacks. True or not, his text reflects the Prussian image of the Russian light troops and claims that the rumors of Russian atrocities had infuriated the Prussian troops marching towards the field of Zorndorf.
[123] Tempelhof, *Geschichte*, vol. 3, 216.
[124] We may assume that the brother is a more fluent reader and all participants know that he will pass on the letter's contents to the other relatives.
[125] Kalberlah is referring to the bloody Battle of Zorndorf (25 August 1758). In fact it was a gory draw, with the Prussians losing more than 13,000 men and the Russians approximately 18,000.
[126] Kaspar Kalberlah, 26. September 1758, in *Soldatenbriefe*, 29–30.
[127] On Prussian images of the Russians and the Battle of Zorndorf, see Sascha Möbius, 'Kriegsgreuel in den Schlachten des Siebenjährigen Krieges in Europa', in *Kriegsgreuel: Die Entgrenzung der Gewalt in kriegerischen Konflikten vom Mittelalter bis ins 20. Jahrhundert*, ed. Sönke Neitzel and Daniel Hohrath (Paderborn: Ferdinand Schöningh, 2008), 202–03.
[128] Showalter, *Frederick*, pos. 3853.
[129] Friedrich der Große, *Geschichte des Siebenjährigen Krieges*, 139.
[130] Tempelhof, *Geschichte*, vol. 3, 216.

Musketeer Johann Christian Riemann from the von Jung-Stutterheim Regiment (No. 20)

Johann Christian Riemann was a *Kantonist* from No. 20 regiment, stationed in Magdeburg. He had a brother, Benjamin, who died on 7 June 1762, probably in a military hospital between Wittenberg and Torgau after having been wounded around Pentecost 1762 near Geringswalde. His brother did not serve in the same company and probably in another regiment.[131] Benjamin Riemann had been married, and his death left one or more children orphaned.[132] Johann Christian had a sister, was unmarried and his parents had already died.[133]

As we do not know when Riemann was enlisted or when he died, it is impossible to say anything about his whereabouts during the war. His regiment had a good reputation,[134] however, and was very effective.[135]

Riemann's two letters from June 1762 are remarkable as they show the pain and anguish of a man who had lost a close relative. We do not even need to look at modern psychological research on PTSD after the death of a loved one[136] to imagine how depressed Johann Christian was. He tells his relatives that his heart 'into pieces does break'[137] and in the following letter, that he still weeps for hours because of his brother's death.[138] There are also remarks which show that Johann Christian Riemann also wants to die:

---

[131] Johann Christian Riemann, 16. Juni 1762, in *Soldatenbriefe*, 31. Gieraths, who has compiled the most complete list of encounters of the Prussian army, cites a skirmish near Geringswalde, but here only two cavalry regiments were present, Cuirassier Regiment No. 4 and Hussar Regiment No. 4, which were beaten on that day. Gieraths, *Kampfhandlungen*, 209, 277. The von Jung-Stutterheim Regiment was deployed in the area but on 1 June 1762, the grenadiers alone were involved in a rearguard action near Reichstädt (Gieraths, *Kampfhandlungen*, 72). One explanation might be that Riemann's brother had been on a commando mission (a detachment of the regiment assigned to some special duty like foraging or defending a field bakery or transport, etc.), as indicated in Riemann's second letter (pp. 33–4). As Riemann writes about a visit by his brother to Gera, both cannot have been in the same company, battalion or regiment. Thus, Riemann was either with the grenadiers of Regiment No. 20 or in another regiment.

[132] Johann Christian Riemann, 16. Juni 1762, in *Soldatenbriefe*, 32.

[133] His letters are addressed to his uncles / nephews, cousins, brother-in-law, friends and above all his 'heartily beloved sister'. His parents are not mentioned, nor is a wife. Johann Christian Riemann, 16 June 1762, in *Soldatenbriefe*, 30; Johann Christian Riemann, 1762, in *Soldatenbriefe*, 33.

[134] Tempelhof remarks that the recruits from Magdeburg were amongst those who were able to 'fight it out with the bayonet', which was considered to be especially honourable. Tempelhof, *Geschichte*, vol. 1, 67.

[135] Indeed it won forty-seven skirmishes and lost only two. The skirmishes are more indicative than battles won or lost, because here the regiment was directly involved and one of a few Prussian units engaged.

[136] Katherine M. Keynes et al., 'The burden of loss: Unexpected death of a loved one and psychiatric disorders across the life course in a national study', *American Journal of Psychiatry* 171, vol. 8 (2014): 864–71. The article shows that the unexpected death of a relative or loved one 'provokes especially strong responses'. We have to stress that 'unexpected' in a modern (contemporary US) context means an accident or murder. Although Riemann and other soldiers knew that death could happen, he had not anticipated losing his brother. In Riemann's case, Benjamin's death was also unexpected as he had already recovered from his wound. https://www.ncbi.nlm.nih.gov/pmc/articles/PMC4119479/ (accessed 3 November 2018)

[137] Johann Christian Riemann, 16 June 1762, in *Soldatenbriefe*, 33.

[138] Johann Christian Riemann, 1762, in *Soldatenbriefe*, 34.

...hunger hurts and we have to live miserably, so that no man has ever heard of nor experienced the like. Thus, we ask God every day that he has mercy upon us and delivers putting an end to this misery-life.[139]

Riemann tries to comfort himself in every possible way. He stresses that his brother has been decently buried in a well-made coffin.[140] It is also important for him to know where his brother is interred and that his sister knows as well, in case he is killed.[141] Johann Christian also points out that his brother would have been a 'miserable cripple' had he survived.[142] His words of comfort give a moving and economically expressed insight into Prussian soldiers' concept of honour:

> Let us comfort ourselves with our brother's honour, he has let his glory in this world, that as a faithful soldier he shed his blood courageously and bravely and lost his life for his right, for his king's honour, for his fatherland and its allies and for the good of us all. May our gracious God give him eternal bliss for this, he has escaped all hardships and has gone to a place, where all war and war cries have an end. No cannon blast can frighten him any more.[143]

This paragraph will be discussed in detail in Chapter 2.[144] The letter's intention is to make the relatives pray for his brother and remember him and help Johann Christian to cope with his brother's death.

Our overview, as well as this short list of biographies, shows that the writing soldiers hailed from the core regions of the Prussian monarchy and from some of the most distinguished regiments of the army. Although their writing abilities were not unusual, they were also not shared by all soldiers, as many men relied on the writers to send information and greetings to their relatives at home. The soldiers' 'information network'

---

[139] Ibid. The *German* original has *Jammer Leben*. Thus it is not totally clear whether Riemann means that God shall end their *lives* or only the misery. Given the fact that Riemann praises the other world as a realm where no harm can be done to him and his relatives, he seems to mean that he and his comrades want to end their lives. Asking God for one's own death is a common idea in mid-eighteenth-century Germany. This is demonstrated by many texts of the cantatas of Johann Sebastian Bach, such as BWV 82 where the last aria begins with the words *Ich freue mich auf meinen Tod* (I am looking forward to my death) or BWV 170, where the last aria's text is *Mir ekelt mehr zu leben / Drum nimm mich, Jesu, hin! / Mir graut vor allen Sünden, / Lass mich dies Wohnhaus finden, / Wo selbst ich ruhig bin.* (I am disgusted by my life, / thus, Jesus call me now! / All sins do make me shudder / So let me find a dwelling, / where I find peace for me). See: Günther Zedler, *Die erhaltenen Kirchenkantaten Johann Sebastian Bachs (Mühlhausen, Weimar, Leipzig I). Besprechungen in Form von Analysen – Erklärungen – Deutungen* (Norderstedt: Books on Demand Verlag, 2008), 116; Alfred Dürr, *Die Kantaten von Johann Sebastian Bach*, 4th ed. (1971; Munich: dtv, 1981), 309; Wolfgang Steck, 'Die biographische Grabrede. Eine phänomenologische Rekonstruktion ihrer Genese', in *Der 'ganze Mensch.' Perspektiven lebensgeschichtlicher Individualität. Festschrift für Dietrich Rössler zum siebzigsten Geburtstag*, ed. Volker Drehsen, Dieter Henke, Reinhard Schmidt-Rost, Wolfgang Steck (Berlin and New York: De Gruyter, 1997), 272.
[140] Johann Christian Riemann, 16. Juni 1762, in *Soldatenbriefe*, 31–2.
[141] A decent burial is generally seen as important for soldiers. Fleming, *Vollkommene Teutsche Soldat*, 304.
[142] Ibid., 31.
[143] Johann Christian Riemann, 16. Juni 1762, in *Soldatenbriefe*, 32.
[144] See p. 74.

seems to reflect the hierarchies in the rural community and are not connected to their military rank. The NCOs write mainly to their families, and it is the educated privates and the sons and relatives of the village administrators, part of the well-off peasant elite, who collect news from their fellow soldiers and write it down for the relatives and friends at home.

We will now see how the soldiers present their experience of combat, how these letters can be analysed to produce substantial findings about the actual feelings and thoughts of their writers in combat situations, and how they contribute to an analysis of the emotions of a larger number of soldiers during battle.

Sheltered by the Almighty: How should one read the sources?

We will first examine the genesis of a soldier's letter before reviewing the influences on the writing strategies that explain the soldiers' presentation of combat. In order to analyse the soldiers' letters, we can draw on four studies: the reflections of Klaus Latzel on soldiers' letters of the modern age;[145] Jan Peters'[146] book on peasants' ego-documents from the early modern era; and the works of Michael Kauppert and Reinhart Kosselleck respectively on the generation of experience.[147]

During the Seven Years' War, the production of a soldier's letter had four distinct phases:

1. *witnessing*. From the myriad sensations assailing a soldier in battle situations, certain incidents are stored in his memory. That means that the writer sees and senses thousands of shots fired, and dozens of men maimed and killed, but will remember the death of one or two comrades only.
2. *creating sense*. The writer consciously or unconsciously makes sense out of what he has witnessed. He then interprets the death of comrades in his immediate surrounding as the result of a tactical situation and / or divine intervention. Note that this individual creation of sense does not mean that the sight of mutilated bodies has not left the soldier shocked and depressed.
3. *developing experience*. This experience is a mixture of the individually created sense and conversations with other soldiers, and field services or sermons. It also develops into a pattern with each and every new encounter; this pattern influences the individual experience and a certain mode of behaviour. For example, the soldier might explain his suffering as divine service, which will be rewarded in heaven. This idea is reinforced by talking to his surviving comrades and the

---

[145] Klaus Latzel, 'Vom Kriegserlebnis zur Kriegserfahrung. Theoretische und methodische Überlegungen zur erfahrungsgeschichtlichen Untersuchung von Feldpostbriefen', *Militärgeschichtliche Mitteilungen* 56 (1997), 1–30.
[146] Jan Peters, 'Zur Auskunftsfähigkeit von Selbstsichtzeugnissen schreibender Bauern', in *Ego-Dokumente. Annäherung an den Menschen in der Geschichte*, ed. Winfried Schulze (Berlin: De Gruyter, 1996), 175–90.
[147] See pp. 12–13.

chaplain. After surviving several battles and having several similar conversations, he reaches the conclusion that God's help and the quality of his unit will help him survive the war.
4. *communication*. He consciously or unconsciously selects a part of his experiences that he communicates to the addressees of his letters. Which experience he relates, and how he does it, depends on him and his intentions towards the addressees.[148]

The last step in particular is influenced by several factors, which Jan Peters calls *Verfremdungsfaktoren* (disassociation factors),[149] which can contribute to the soldiers' hiding their true emotions and actions on the battlefield. For this study, we examined those dissociation factors which could have affected author soldiers in the Seven Years' War. Most of them could have been caused by a general problem rooted in the special nature of the soldier's space of experience, the battlefield. For example:

Inability to relate battlefield experience: The author is faced with a situation that causes fundamental problems of communication. The experience of being exposed to extreme violence on the battlefield simply cannot be related to non-combatants by means of language. Paul Fussell's analyses of the literary production during the two World Wars have demonstrated that even skilled professional authors are unable to make the reader feel what the soldiers felt.[150] Some of the Prussian soldiers are fully aware of this phenomenon when they state that they cannot describe what happened to them and their comrades.[151]

Disassociation factors could also be rooted in the person of the author:

Level of literacy. While some soldiers were able to write, they may have been able to do so only in a very limited sense. Thus, they may not have been able to communicate their emotions.[152] We have found no indication of such a lack of literacy in all the soldiers' letters used for this study, however. They were perfectly able to express their feelings and to reflect on the official interpretations and to communicate their consent or dissent.

The individual reaction to the exposure to extreme violence. We have already shown that the authors were exposed to violence in a way that could have caused severe psychological trauma. During combat, the author would have been under extreme stress, 'like in a frenzy,'[153] and often reflects his sensations only as a chaotic turmoil.[154] The author may also have been confused or traumatized and affected by

---

[148] Latzel, *Vom Kriegserlebnis*, 20–5.
[149] Peters, *Zur Auskunftsfähigkeit*, 175.
[150] Fussell, *Wartime*, 268.
[151] Frantz Reiß, Lobositz, 6. Oktober 1756, in *Briefe*, 30. Letter no. 2 by Corporal Binn, 8. Mai 1757, in *Soldatenbriefe*, 6.
[152] Peters, *Zur Auskunftsfähigkeit*, 175–6.
[153] Bräker, *Arme Mann*, 150.
[154] See: Extrakt Schreibens von Herrn Kistenmacher, Sekretär Sr. Durchlaucht des Herzogs von Bevern, in *Briefe*, 8.

PTSD,[155] as noted in the Introduction. He is exposed to all of that factors that can cause PTSD, often at the same time. When traumatized, certain sensations might have been either erased from his memory or suddenly reappear as a flashback.[156] In line with modern psychological findings, the soldiers actually show radically differing reactions, especially when they write about the death and maiming of others and were not directly involved in the fighting. For example, Sergeant Liebler is overwhelmed by joy that he had been able to watch a battle from afar after the Battle of Lobositz, while the Kalberlah brothers from the same regiment fall into a depression after watching the identical battle.[157] Dominicus gives a very detailed description of his own feelings after the Battle of Kay, while the Zanders keep silent about their role in combat. Thus, individual exposure to extreme violence can encourage as well as discourage the expression of feelings. Thus only the analysis of the individual letters will indicate whether exposure is a dissociation factor.

Thou shalt not kill. Although they were soldiers, and the authorities as well as the regimental chaplains encouraged the soldiers to fight effectively, all of them seem to view the killing of other human beings as sinful or dishonourable. The Zanders are extremely reluctant to write about their personal involvement in a skirmish in October 1756. Although they must have been involved in close combat, they do not mention it.[158] The same is true for Dominicus, who does not mention the hand-to-hand fighting during the Battle of Kay.[159] None of the soldiers of the von Hülsen Regiment, which drove the Austrians off from the Lobosch Hill at bayonet point, do not mention any aggressive action on their own part. This finding is limited to the *Kantonisten*. For the volunteer or officers, one can state the contrary. For example, the volunteer NCO Dreyer, who was a member of a free regiment, describes the killing of enemy soldiers as something exciting and honourable. He even uses casual soldiers' slang when describing the killing of French hussars or the butchering of Russian rapists. This is also true for Lieutenant von Barsewisch, who describes in detail how he orders two of his marksmen to shoot an Austrian officer off his horse and how this is successfully done. Most probably, the *Kantonisten* did not write about it because they were still rooted in the peasant community and subjected to their fellow peasants' judgement at home. For peasants and artisans, contacts to persons whose hands were 'stained with human blood' was dishonourable. The best example is the ambivalent role of the hangman, who was supposed to kill evil-doers for the sake of the community but was nonetheless regarded as a dishonourable person.[160]

---

[155] Prittwitz, *Ich bin ein Preuße*, 95. The soldiers are shocked by a cavalry charge that reminds them of the one which routed them at the Battle of Kolin.

[156] See p. 182. Reiß' fragmentary recollections may have this background.

[157] Kaspar Kalberlah, 11 November 1756, in *Soldatenbriefe*, 28.

[158] C.F. Zander, 17 February 1757, in *Fundstücke*, 49.

[159] Compared to the entry in his diary covering the same battle, Dominicus presents himself as being much more passive and suffering in the letter to his brother. *Tagebuch des Musketiers Dominicus*, 55–60 (diary) and 61–5 (letter).

[160] Jutta Nowosadtko, *Scharfrichter und Abdecker. Der Alltag zweier unehrlicher Beruf ein der frühen Neuzeit* (Paderborn: Ferdinand Schöningh, 1994), 21–4. On the Brandenburg hangmen and the ambivalent character of their dishonour, see Marita Genesis, 'Scharfrichter in der Stadt Brandenburg. Betrachtung eines Berufsbildes' (MA diss., Fachbereich Landesgeschichte des Historischen Instituts der Universität Potsdam, Potsdam 2006), 67–74.

In sharp contrast, the NCOs and officers were only part of the military community and thus judged by their fellow professional soldiers. The soldiers' reluctance to kill enemies with their own hands also reflected the different types of combat, as the light troops had to kill face-to-face in small-scale actions, and the officer had to kill in order to save his men. But the line infantry, including most of the *Kantonisten*, fought anonymously in battalion formations for most of their missions.

Defend your honour and that of your regiment. Soldiers do not relate actions and emotions which go against their honour or that of their regiment. For example, plundering dead enemy soldiers was not mentioned and expressly denied, although we know it was all too common.

There are other factors which directly influence the relation of the soldier's perception of combat:

Social control. Outright lying about one's role in combat was simply not possible as many soldiers wrote home and every man could be sure that any misdeeds would be passed on by other comrades from the same village. This kind of social control existed in a triangle between uncle and nephew Zander and their relatives back home in Nitzahn.[161] Binn's alleged adultery is also proof that dishonourable behaviour – or even the suspicion thereof – would be transmitted home immediately.[162]

God's help and providence. One of the most important factors is the belief that a soldier's survival depended to a large extent on being sheltered by the Almighty.[163] Thus, pointing to the existing dangers of combat was not hidden from the readers. In modern soldiers' letters, the danger, fear and threat of death in combat are downplayed or not mentioned at all in order to console relatives and to show manly behaviour.[164] But in the Seven Years' War, we find detailed descriptions of the danger that the soldiers had been exposed to and the fear they felt. This is a means of showing their relatives, that God is caring for them, even in a hailstorm of bullets. The divinely protected soldier is also a synonym for the honourable soldier.

Need for intercession. Closely linked to belief in God and his support is the need for intercession by the relatives and friends at home. Many soldiers write in detail about their feelings and actions in combat, because they want to encourage their relatives to pray for them.

In conclusion, we can state that the religious faith of the soldiers and their relatives was the strongest incentive to give a detailed account of their fear and suffering. The less

---

[161] C.F. Zander, 21 July 1757, in *Fundstücke*, 55. The *Dorfschulze* had written to the Christian Friedrich that his nephew, Johann Dietrich, had complained that his uncle had been willing to lend money to him. Christian Friedrich denied this and 'hoped that he had not meant it like that'.
[162] Grenadier Dresel is also serving alongside men from his village and region. Kohl, *Ein Brief*, 84.
[163] Schreiben eines Musketiers des Regiments Anhalt zu Fuß 1757, in *Briefe*, 52. Brief des Feldwebels Liebler, in *Briefe*, 47.
[164] Latzel, *Vom Kriegserlebnis*, 22.

religious the soldier was, the less he tended to write about his feelings and individual perceptions during combat. Among our soldier authors, this is only the case with the Zanders, whose descriptions of their battle experience have been lost anyway.

In order to root out the soldiers' emotions and actions in combat, we have to deconstruct the writing process by using the above mentioned model in reverse order. Firstly, the *writing strategies* have to be analysed, according to which the soldiers organize the communicated experience. The strategies are either openly stated by the men or can be deducted by examining the main topics of the communicated experience. The *communicated experience* is the interface between the writing strategies and the perceptions and emotions of the soldier in combat. It is *communicated* because the soldier wants the audience to hear it and to act in a certain way. It is *experience*, because they had experienced a certain number of life-threatening and cruel situations. Thus, the communicated experience also reflects the creation of sense and shows at least one important aspect of the soldier's perceptions during the combat situation.

The soldiers' letters and their emotions in battle

We will now consider those letters which deal with the authors' participation in combat. As the writing strategies are crucial for the analysis of the emotions and actions of the soldiers in combat, we have structured this section according to the different writing strategies of the soldiers. There are four key groups:

1. the letter of Grenadier Adam Becker, which is an exception, as Becker informs his wife about his whereabouts and fighting experience but is concerned only with his wife's pregnancy and her health.
2. the letters and descriptions, mainly by NCOs, who had been watching the Battle of Lobositz, which are excerpts or closely connected to the men's marching diaries and which stress the honour of the Prussian army or their regiment. They are written to unknown addressees or male relatives like fathers and brothers.
3. the Zanders, whose main aim is to keep their place and influence in their rural community by intervening in all family affairs and defending the honour of their regiment.
4. the bulk of letters, mainly written by privates or extremely pious NCOs or an NCO not very fond of his job, whose main writing strategy is to ask for their loved ones' prayers as well as to promote the honour of their regiment and their own honourable behaviour.

We have eighteen letters by fifteen authors that communicate the latters' participation in combat.[165] With the exception of one letter, all are written to family members, with wives being the most usual correspondent.[166]

[165] A skirmish near Salesel in October 1756, siege warfare during the aborted siege of Prague and a Prussian attempt to bring the Austrians to battle in August 1757 near Zittau, three on the Battle of Lobositz, three on Prague, one on Hohenfriedberg, one on Kay and one on Kunersdorf, one on Roßbach and one on skirmishes around Easter 1762.
[166] Three to a nephew of the author, seven to wives, one to 'uncles, nephews, cousins, sisters and friends', one to the brother, one to the mother.

'I get no rest night or day due to your pregnancy': Adam Becker's letter to his wife

Adam Becker, a grenadier of the von Hülsen Regiment, is concerned with his wife's pregnancy only and very upset that he has not been able to write and thus comfort his wife more regularly. His description of the marches and an encounter with 8,000 Austrian light troops is embedded in a writing strategy to apologize to his wife for not writing sooner.[167]

Becker tells his wife that his battalion had been part of the Prussian rearguard of three Prussian grenadier battalions, numbering at most 1,800 men. They had been ambushed by 8,000 Austrian pandurs and hussars. Becker and his comrades were 'shot at all the time' during this skirmish on 29 October 1756 but lost few men and their cannon and *Jägers* killed many pandurs. On 30 October 1756, the grenadiers again advanced but the Austrians retreated.[168] Taking into account that the Prussians lost this encounter,[169] we see that Becker follows a double strategy. On the one hand, he is the only writer of a soldiers' letter in our sample who lies about his combat experience in order to comfort his wife and not to endanger his unborn child. On the other hand, he tries to save the honour of his battalion. He gives a hint at his feelings and writes: 'You can easily imagine how I feel, but I hope that things will get better.'[170] But his feelings concerning her pregnancy are described in much stronger terms, because he stresses, that he can only be comforted by good news from her and the child.[171] In spite of his participation in the fighting, his letter does not contain information about his feelings during combat, as they are overshadowed by his thoughts for his wife and his care for her and the baby.

'One Prussian must always hound three Imperials': The honour of the army as a writing strategy – NCOs on the Battle of Lobositz

The four letters in this section are from a very homogeneous group of writers. Three of them were NCOs from the Alt-Anhalt Regiment. As NCOs, they kept marching-diaries, had a high level of military expertise and were used to reading and writing. It must also be stressed that they had witnessed the battle from afar, although their regiment had been the target of some badly aimed Austrian cannon shots. One letter is addressed to an unknown recipient, one to the NCO's father and one to the writer's brother. The fourth letter does not have a discernible addressee[172] and was written by a private of the von Hülsen Regiment (No. 21) called Joseph Bartholly and is an extract from a longer letter, which has not been preserved.[173] We shall discus this one first, before the other three by Alt-Anhalt's NCOs.

---

[167] Schreiben des Grenadiers Adam Becker, Gottleuba, 18 November 1756, in *Briefe*, 37–8.
[168] Ibid., 38.
[169] Gieraths, *Kampfhandungen*, 132.
[170] Ibid.
[171] Adam Becker, 18. November 1756, in *Briefe*, 38–9.
[172] The person addressed is called '*Ew.*', an abbreviation for *Euer* (your, in the sense of your highness, your lordship) but no person is mentioned.
[173] Extrakt Schreibens eines Soldaten Hülsischen Regiments Namens Joseph Bartholly. Im Lager bei Lobositz, 1. Oktober 1756., in *Briefe*, 32–33.

While all other letters contain religious expressions or show the authors' piety, Bartholly does not use even one standardized phrase. Bartholly does also not mention himself, while other writers give detailed accounts of their own actions and those of their comrades. Above all, Bartholly had been in the thick of battle, but does not mention anything about it. The reader is merely informed that the author's regiment 'suffered heavily, because we stood directly against the enemy's cannon and had to endure their gunfire all day long'.[174] The text reflects the position of the author's regiment and is written from the point of view of the Prussian infantry on the left wing. The defeat of the Prussian cavalry is missing altogether.[175] It seems as though Bartholly wanted to relate the overall course of the battle to a person of higher rank in order to stress his regiment's honour. He does this by pointing to the suffering of his unit and stressing the steadfastness of the Austrians.[176] He uses a style that reminds us of regimental journals or official relations. Concerning combat, these and Bartholly inform their readers about the positions and movements of the armies and certain units and about the losses.[177] It could well be that this is an extract from a marching diary[178] that Bartholly used to inform his unknown superior.[179]

The writing strategy in the NCOs' letters is most clearly expressed by the anonymous writer of the first letter of the General Staff's collection, who starts his letter with a small verse:

Triumph, Victoria! Conquered are the enemies,
One Prussian must always hound three Imperials.[180]

The honour of the Prussian army is also stressed at the beginning of another anonymous NCO's letter to his father:

The first of October, which was with God's help so glorious a day for our Prussian arms, causes me to relate the following, according to my filial piety and most obedient promise.[181]

---

[174] Ibid., 32.
[175] *Der Siebenjährige Krieg*, ed. Großer Generalstab (Die Kriege Friedrichs des Großen, vol. 3), vol. 1, 272–6.
[176] Joseph Bartholly, 1. Oktober 1756., in *Briefe*, 32–3.
[177] 'Tagebuch eines Offiziers vom Alt-Schwerinschen Infanterieregiment, welches die Feldzüge von 1756 bis 1763 enthält', in *Sammlung*, vol. 1 (Dresden: Waltherische Hofbuchhandlung, 1782), 472. J.F. Seyfarth, *Geschichte des Füsilier Regiments von Kleist* (Halle/Saale: Trampe, 1767), 14–15. 'Nachrichten von den Feldzügen von 1756 bis 1763 das von Mahlensche Dragonerregiment betreffend', in *Sammlung*, vol. 5 (Dresden: Waltherische Hofbuchhandlung, 1785), 511.
[178] Kloosterhuis, *Donner*, 142.
[179] As the same might be true for the extract of a letter from Jakob Angerstein to his wife that was written about two weeks before the Battle of Prague. Extrakt Schreibens des Musketiers Jakob Angerstein aus Wernigerode an seine Frau. (Vom Regiment Hülsen), in *Briefe*, 39–40. See also Von einem Unteroffizier [C.G. Klauel] Anhaltischen Regiments, datirt Lobositz, 6. Oktober 1756, in *Briefe*, 24, directly mentions his diary.
[180] Beschreibung der Lobositzer Bataille, datirt 1. Oktober 1756. Von einem [anonymen] Unteroffizier anhaltischen Regiments, in *Soldatenbriefe*, 1.
[181] Von einem [anonymen] Unteroffizier des Anhaltischen Regiments, datirt Lobositz, 6. Oktober 1756, in *Briefe*, 21.

C.G. Klauel, the third NCO, summarizes his strategy at the end of his letter:

> ...and we have in this battle not achieved more than to crown our old glory with new laurels, to chase them away, which is a really a masterpiece, and made them somewhat fearful on the first reception. Because the Pandurs have never been remunerated like this so far.[182]

All three authors relate the troop movements in detail, and we learn that the unsuccessful Prussian cavalry charges[183] and the successful (but dearly won) infantry assault on the Lobosch mountain[184] and the following storming of Welhotta and Lobositz play a central role.[185] Adding to the day's glory are the accounts of the king's presence,[186] who was guarded by the Alt-Anhalt Regiment,[187] and of the good dispositions[188] and fighting capacities of the Austrians,[189] but also their dishonourable refusal to surrender in a hopeless situation.[190]

Although some of these features are also terrifying, the authors make it clear that they relate them to stress the honourable nature of the Prussian actions. The anonymous learned NCO from Alt-Anhalt calls the bloody assault on the Lobosch-mountain 'tedious work'[191] and does not use any adjectives or expressions, which show any emotions in the face of danger. Quite the contrary, he stresses his 'luck' to have been able to view a battle from afar and tells his unknown reader in Latin that he

> played a twofold role on this occasion: body, outer appearance and arms were military, but my spirit dwelled on Pufendorff's description of the warlike deeds of Charles [X] Gustav[192] and I thought of all defeats and battles, which are described there like cast in iron.[193]

---

[182] [C.G. Klauel], datirt Lobositz, 6. Oktober 1756, in *Briefe*, 28.
[183] Beschreibung der Lobositzer Bataille, datirt 1. Oktober 1756., in *Soldatenbriefe*, 3. (Description of the Battle of Lobositz, dated 1 October 1756). Von einem [anonymen] Unteroffizier des Anhaltischen Regiments, datirt Lobositz, 6. Oktober 1756, in *Briefe*, 22. (By an anonymous NCO of the Anhalt Regiment, dated 6 October 1756.). [C.G. Klauel], datirt Lobositz, 6. Oktober 1756, in *Briefe*, 27.
[184] Beschreibung der Lobositzer Bataille, datirt 1. Oktober 1756, in *Soldatenbriefe*, 2. Von einem [anonymen] Unteroffizier des Anhaltischen Regiments, datirt Lobositz, 6. Oktober 1756, in *Briefe*, 22. [C.G. Klauel], datirt Lobositz, 6. Oktober 1756, in *Briefe*, 27.
[185] Beschreibung der Lobositzer Bataille, datirt 1. Oktober 1756, in *Soldatenbriefe*, 4–5. [C.G. Klauel], datirt Lobositz, 6. Oktober 1756, in *Briefe*, 28.
[186] Beschreibung der Lobositzer Bataille, datirt 1. Oktober 1756, in *Soldatenbriefe*, 3–4. Von einem [anonymen] Unteroffizier des Anhaltischen Regiments, datirt Lobositz, 6. Oktober 1756, in *Briefe*, 23–4.
[187] Ibid., 24.
[188] [C.G. Klauel], datirt Lobositz, 6. Oktober 1756, in *Briefe*, 26–7, 28–9.
[189] Beschreibung der Lobositzer Bataille, datirt 1. Oktober 1756, in *Soldatenbriefe*, 4. Von einem [anonymen] Unteroffizier des Anhaltischen Regiments, datirt Lobositz, 6. Oktober 1756, in *Briefe*, 23. Both anonymous NCOs stress the new training of the Austrians and their steadfastness.
[190] Beschreibung der Lobositzer Bataille, datirt 1. Oktober 1756, in *Soldatenbriefe*, 5.
[191] Ibid., 2.
[192] The NCO refers to Samuel Pufendorf, *De Rebus a Carolo Gustavo Sveciae Rege Gestis Commentariorum* ... (Nuremberg: Christoph Riegel, 1696).
[193] Ibid., 7.

Two near-misses make him thank God for his survival, but he stresses that he does this not out of his 'love of my worldly life, but out of love for my little children'.[194]

The other anonymous NCO gives a more emotional description. He calls the numbers of the Austrian guns shocking[195] and their positions dreadful.[196] The enemy's artillery fire was terrifying, but he stresses that 'we did not let ourselves be bothered by it' and that the Prussian infantry advanced 'not fearing any danger'.[197] When summing up and stressing the honourable nature of the Prussian effort, he denies any feelings of fear:

> Our army must be credited with the undeniable testimony of having fought like heroes for the honour of God and the wellbeing of the country, of having solely relied on the protection of the Almighty and having rushed into the greatest danger so joyfully, that almost no officer had been able to hold them back.[198]

The denial of fear on the Prussian side is due to their non-involvement in serious combat and the writing strategy of augmenting the army's and regiment's honour. Yet the use of emotional adjectives indicating the terrifying sight of the Austrian guns may be interpreted as a hint that the NCO did feel some fear when perceiving the enemy cannon but formed a different experience some time later after not having been exposed to the cannonade, having survived and having been part of the victorious side.

C.G. Klauel, the third NCO of Alt-Anhalt, praises the 'bravery' of the men, who stormed the Lobosch mountain and calls the Austrian grapeshot aimed at the Prussian cavalry 'frightening'.[199] He explains that his regiment had been exposed to a heavy cannonade and that he thanks God for having protected him in his fourth battle, but mentions no feelings or thoughts at all.[200]

All three might have felt fear when they were exposed to the Austrian artillery barrage. But as they were not hit, and only the grenadiers and the men carrying cartridges to the left wing suffered losses, they formed an experience which followed traditional literary patterns of journals and battle-descriptions that proclaimed the glory of the victorious Prussian army.

Christian Friedrich Zander: Defending and strengthening his position in his rural community through the honour of his regiment

The letters of C.F. Zander cover a skirmish near Salesel in October 1756, and constitute the most extensive surviving description of their combat experience by one of the

---

[194] Ibid., 5.
[195] The German word is *erstaunend*, which in eighteenth-century German means that the sight makes the blood freeze. See p. 98. Von einem [anonymen] Unteroffizier des Anhaltischen Regiments, datirt Lobositz, 6. Oktober 1756, in *Briefe*, 21.
[196] Ibid., 22.
[197] Ibid.
[198] Ibid., 23.
[199] [C.G. Klauel], datirt Lobositz, 6. Oktober 1756, in *Briefe*, 27.
[200] Ibid., 29.

Zanders.²⁰¹ Siege warfare during the aborted siege of Prague in May and June 1757, and a Prussian attempt to bring the Austrians to battle in August 1757 near Zittau, mainly present the regiment's endurance under cannon-fire. None of Johann Dietrich's surviving letters contains information about their participation in combat. There were other letters by the two musketeers, which probably covered the Battles of Lobositz, Roßbach and Leuthen. We know only from Prof. Schultze's account that 'the king was always in the front ranks together with [the soldiers]'.²⁰² But it is doubtful that the two musketeers wrote extensively about these battles, as one of the main strategies of their correspondence is to avoid giving detailed information about their participation in combat.²⁰³ The principal subjects of their letters are their and their relatives' health²⁰⁴, all matters concerning the farm²⁰⁵ and family at home, including minor disputes amongst the relatives,²⁰⁶ and care for the younger members of the family.²⁰⁷ Other important themes are asking for material support from home and exchanging information about their whereabouts and the regiment's 'honour status' as a means of supporting the family at home.²⁰⁸ Concerning the war, they hope for a quick cessation of hostilities and that peace will prevail.²⁰⁹ They clearly see the overwhelming power of Prussia's enemies, which they sometimes fear²¹⁰ and sometimes see as a chance for ending the war soon, even at the cost of a Prussian defeat. The fear that other relatives are amongst the 'young lads' being brought from the *Kanton* to the front also plays a prominent role.²¹¹ Concerning their life in the field, they stress the quality of their regiment, their individual hardships and their suffering, being 'treated worse than a dog . . . one could think, that no human being would be able to endure it, we could not even clean ourselves and were eaten up by the lice'.²¹² Religion plays a secondary role for the Zanders and unity in prayer is definitely not amongst the aims stated in their

---

²⁰¹ C.F. Zander, 17 February 1757, in *Fundstücke*, 49.
²⁰² *Fundstücke*, 105.
²⁰³ *Fundstücke*, 91. They write several times that they are not able to report anything about the war and Christian Friedrich's account of the skirmish at Salesel is written more than three months after the fighting.
²⁰⁴ For the sake of traceability, the Zanders' letters will be quoted using their number in the German edition in this chapter and in all places where a large number of letters has to be cited. The pages will be given in brackets. All letters are thus to be found in *Fundstücke*. Also, for the sake of traceability, the letters from the collections of the General Staff and Georg Liebe are cited by their German titles, which should make them easier to find in their German editions. C.F. Zander, no. II (22), IV (26), VI (28), VII (33), VIII (38), XIII (47), XVI (53), XVII (61), XIX (64–5), XXI (71), XXII (74), XXVI (81). J.D. Zander, no. IX (42), X (45), XV (50), XX (68).
²⁰⁵ Including how to fertilize and raise animals: C.F. Zander, no. XIII (47), no. XXV (78), no. XXV (78); or care for the farm hands: C.F. Zander, no. XIX (65), no. XXI (73), no. XXII (76–7).
²⁰⁶ As they are well informed about everything going on home, Christian Friedrich can reprimand his younger brother for not intervening in a quarrel between Christian Friedrich's aunt and brother-in-law. C.F. Zander, 17 February 1757, in *Fundstücke*, 47–8. See p. 201.
²⁰⁷ C.F. Zander, no. VIII (38). Christian Friedrich reprimands his nephew for overexerting 'little Fred' (*Kleiner Fritze*).
²⁰⁸ J.D. Zander, no. IX (40–41). Zander wants to support his relatives' attempt to get back draft-horses, which had been given to the army, by approaching the king, who is favourable to the regiment because of its service during the Battle of Lobositz.
²⁰⁹ C.F. Zander, no. VII (32), XVI (56), XIX (65), XXI (73). J.D. Zander, no. IX (41)
²¹⁰ J.D. Zander, no. IX (41), XV (52)
²¹¹ C.F. Zander, no. VII (31), no. XIX (65), no. XXI (71–2), no. XXVI (81). J.D. Zander, no. XII (45–6).
²¹² C.F. Zander, no. XXVI (81), no. XXII (74–5) and J.D. Zander, no. XX (68).

letters.²¹³ They open their letters with a relatively formal 'God be with you' or 'Jesus be our greeting'²¹⁴ and often thank God with a few words for their and their relatives' good health.²¹⁵ Religious allusions become more numerous when they are exposed to hardships or disease.²¹⁶ It is especially noteworthy, however, that they do not offer a single word of gratitude to the Almighty when they are survive a combat situation. There is only one passage which suggests that Christian Friedrich sees prayer as a means of assuring God's help, when he exhorts his nephew to pray in order to be assisted by the Almighty²¹⁷ and when he sends greetings to 'old Mr. Wilbergen, wishing that he may busily pray for us so that we return in good health'.²¹⁸ There are some passages which show the Zanders' anti-Catholic feelings, such as when they relate that six wagons with thumb-screws had been discovered and publicly exhibited, as the enemy wanted to use them for 'bringing the people to the Catholic faith',²¹⁹ or complain about Hungarian-speaking Catholics in Moravia, saying that they are 'arch-Catholics and when they bury one [of their kind], they play horns, trumpets and trombones'.²²⁰

As a soldier's honour is increased by the *success of his unit* and his *individual suffering*, there is no cultural framework that prevents him from writing about frightening experiences or his genuine terror. This is underlined by Christian Friedrich's description of the Battle of Kolin. As the musketeers of the regiment were not present, he had to rely on second-hand information, probably from his comrade Spellerholtz, who was amongst the regiment's grenadiers. The grenadiers had taken part in the battle, 'of whom not many had survived'.²²¹ The description follows contemporary literary conventions of depicting a battle, and is thus similar to regimental diaries or historiography. It stresses the enemies' well-chosen positions, which proved impossible to attack. The narrative's focus is on the movements of the Prussian army's two wings. Christian Friedrich tells his readers that in spite of all obstacles, the Prussian infantry on the left wing had already driven the enemy right wing out of its positions and captured some cannon. The Prussian defeat is explained by the Prussian cavalry's refusal to charge. In order to defend the honour of his regiment and the infantry as a whole, Zander stresses that not many of the regiment's grenadiers²²² had survived and

---

²¹³ There is only one passage where Christian Friedrich asks his nephew to greet 'old Mr. Wilberg and ask him to busily pray for us, that we return in good health'. C.F. Zander, no. VII (33). The passage shows that the idea is not alien to them, but they do not deem it a main concern of their letters to make their relatives pray for them.
²¹⁴ In every letter.
²¹⁵ C.F. Zander, no. IV (26), VI (28), VII (31), VIII (38), XIII (47), XVI (53–4), no. XXI (71). J.D. Zander, no. IX (40), X (45).
²¹⁶ Christian Friedrich then offers some words of gratitude to God, but includes no long phrases or citations from the Bible. C.F. Zander, no. XVI (61), XIX (65). Johann Dietrich is only slightly more verbose. J.D. Zander, no. XX (68).
²¹⁷ C.F. Zander, no. XXV (78).
²¹⁸ C.F. Zander, no. VII (33).
²¹⁹ J.D. Zander, no. IX (42).
²²⁰ C.F. Zander, no. XXII (77). In mid-eighteenth-century Protestant Germany, brass instruments were not used for burial or Passion music.
²²¹ C.F. Zander, no. XVI (54).
²²² The grenadiers formed a converged grenadier battalion together with the grenadiers of Regiment No. 26 (von Meyerinck). They had indeed been able to drive the Austrian right wing out of its positions but were totally unsupported and then defeated. http://www.kronoskaf.com/syw/index.php?title=13/26_Finck_Grenadiers (accessed 21 October 2018). Showalter, *Frederick*, pos. 2912–18.

that the king had cursed the cavalry, threatened to make them musketeers[223] and called the officers '*Hundsfütter*'[224] and 'eels'.[225] In addition to representing a conventional description, it contains the king's devastating critique of the cavalry's refusal to defend the infantry's honour.[226] It also shows that in the eyes of the brave commoner Zander, the noble officers of the cavalry had lost their honour, as no honourable man of any estate could have been called a *Hundsfott* without immediately challenging the offender to a duel. But a duel was out of the question when the offender was the king, when his orders, according to Zander,[227] had been ignored, and when he had been insulted by his cavalry officers' misconduct and utter cowardice.

Christian Friedrich wrote the longest description of their actual participation in combat in a letter to his nephew from Dresden, on 17 February 1757. A complete translation of the letter can be found in Appendix 2.

> Dear nephew, you asked me to tell you what it was like when I was with the commando and what happened in Bohemia. The commando was 200-men-strong and we were ordered to the village of Salesel.[228] This [village] was located on the Elbe river and on the other side of the Elbe were pandurs and Hungarian infantry.[229] There was already a commando [unit] from another regiment in the village. When we relieved them, they told us that they had shot across the river several times, but the enemy had not shot back. We occupied the village with four pickets. The pandurs and Hungarian infantry attacked us with 800 men at two o'clock in

---

[223] As the service as cavalryman was easier and less dangerous, being made a musketeer was a common punishment for the cavalry.

[224] *Hundsfott / Hundsfut*: literally 'vagina of a dog'. It was one of the most degrading swearwords in the Prussian army and in eighteenth-century Germany.

[225] The German original has *al*. Most probably Zander means *Aal* (eel), which as a swearword means an envious or fraudulent person. *Zedler's* 1 (1732), 16.

[226] The infantry's courage was actually beyond doubt. See: Tempelhof, *Geschichte*, vol. 1, 214–15.

[227] Modern descriptions of the battle show that a part of the Prussian cavalry under Krosigk and Seydlitz had behaved very well, but the bulk had remained more or less inactive. Duffy, *Frederick*, 128. See also: Tempelhof, *Geschichte*, vol. 1, 218.

[228] Zander writes 'SALLEISEN'. The village is called *Dolni Zálezly* today and lies about seven kilometres to the South of Aussig in the Czech Republic. He most probably describes a night action, which took place on 21–2 October 1756. Gieraths, *Kampfhandlungen*, 48.

[229] Pandurs is a Prussian name for the Austrian *Grenzregimenter* (borderers). These were men from the Hapsburg Balkan areas, bordering on the Ottoman Empire. During the first years of the War of the Austrian Succession, these were irregular troops but had been organized into regular regiments by the end of this conflict. They fought in open order on the battlefield and were extensively used in the Little War of raids and skirmishes. Their uniforms were different from other Austrian troops as they wore a shako instead of a tricorn and elements of the traditional garb common to the areas from which they had been recruited. The Hungarian infantry was regular line infantry recruited in the Kingdom of Hungary ruled by the Habsburgs. Their uniform was mainly like that of the German troops but had some elements of the traditional Hungarian garb. They were used as line infantry but also in the Little War. See Frank Wernitz, *Die preußischen Freitruppen im Siebenjährigen Krieg 1756–1763. Entstehung – Einsatz – Wirkung* (Wölfersheim-Berstadt: Podzun-Pallas, 1994), 12. http://www.kronoskaf.com/syw/index.php?title=Banal-Grenzinfanterieregiment_nr._1 (accessed 15 October 2018). Jacob de Cogniazo, *Geständnisse eines Oestreichischen Veterans in politisch-militärischer Hinsicht auf die interessantesten Verhältnisse zwischen Oestreich und Preußen, während der Regierung des Großen Königs der Preußen Friedrichs des Zweyten : mit historischen Anmerkungen gewidmet den königlich preußischen Veteranen / Von dem Verfasser des freymüthigen Beytrags zur Geschichte des österreichischen Militär-Dienstes*, vol. 3 (Breslau: Löwe, 1790), 256–7.

the morning and we were only 200-men-strong. It was so dark that you could not see a soul, but they could see us with our white lapels and cartridge-pouch straps very well. When they came, our sentinel asked who was there and they answered: 'deserters'[230] until they were near enough to open fire immediately and the sentinels were still in the guard room and not even able to reach their muskets. When they came out of the guard room, they were immediately shot dead before we could even reach our guns. We had a cannon with us, where the major was. The other pickets retreated there, and the firing lasted until daybreak. We suffered 32 men wounded or dead and Captain Miltnitz.[231] Nobody was killed or wounded from our company, why we drank nothing but wine and the king gave us one *Reichsthaler* beer-money[232] for each man, five *Groschen* for [each man of the regiment] Prince of Prussia,[233] the major 1,000 *Reichsthaler*, the captain 500 *Reichsthaler*, and the Lieutenants and ensigns 250 *Reichsthaler*.[234] I would have liked to write more but about it but I do not have enough time.[235] Dear cousin, do not worry about us that much, there are many honourable and brave men amongst us.[236] Finally, I send greetings to everybody and remain your faithful uncle until I die.

---

[230] They pose as Austrian deserters who want to change sides. Using this stratagem was against the rules of war and shows the dishonourable behaviour of the Austrians, especially their light troops, whom the Prussians hated. 'Tagebuch eines Offiziers vom Alt-Schwerinschen Infanterieregiment, welches die Feldzüge von 1756 bis 1763 enthält', in *Sammlung*, vol. 1, 451. Ulrich Bräker, *Der arme Mann*, 150; Lemcke, *Kriegs- und Friedensbilder*, 26.

[231] The same Lieutenant 'Miltnitz' whom the Dorschulze had bribed to achieve the dismissal of his brother (see p. 197). His name was Friedrich Bogislav von Miltitz and he died of the wounds received during this skirmish. We are indebted to Prof. Jürgen Kloosterhuis for this information. Another Miltitz, Philip Siegmund, appears in a quarrel about promotions in 1774 and is dismissed due to invalidity in 1777. Rolf Straubel, *"Er möchte nur wißen, daß die Armée mir gehöret" Friedrich II. und seine Offiziere. Ausgewählte Aspekte königlicher Personalpolitik* (Berlin: BWV, 2012), 207.

[232] *Biergeld* in the original. It is the early modern equivalent of the modern German *Trinkgeld* (drink-money), which is a tip: money given by a customer to a service provider who has done a good job. https://gfds.de/trinkgeld/ (accessed 16 October 2018).

[233] Regiment No. 18.

[234] This is an indication that Zander's numbers are no exaggeration. Gifts like these were extraordinary, especially the *Reichsthaler* for each man of the Itzenplitz regiment. The von Meyerinck Regiment (No. 26) received 1,500 *Reichsthalers* in total for all its privates after it had contributed to the success at Leuthen by fighting in the vanguard alongside the Zanders' regiment. As Meyerinck had lost 464 men (including fourteen officers) in this battle, and a regiment numbered about 1,400 privates at this time, each man got roughly 1.5 *Reichsthaler*. http://www.kronoskaf.com/syw/index.php?title=Meyerinck_Infantry (accessed 16 October 2018). Barsewisch, *Kriegs-Erlebnisse*, 41. Möbius, *Mehr Angst*, 118–19.

[235] Given the amount of time Zander spends on the quarrel between his brother-in-law and his aunt, this remark is proof of the fact that he does not *want* to get into the detail of what must have been a very brutal encounter, including close combat. He only mentions the circumstances that highlight the *enemies' dishonourable behaviour*, and his regiment's *honourable bearing*: the numerical superiority of the enemy, and the king's gratitude. The other recurring theme is the *suffering of the soldiers*, who had been visible to the enemy by their white lapels and strings. We should mention, that the 'pandurs' wore darker uniforms of blue and red, while almost all Hungarian infantry regiments (with the exception of No. 2, who wore uniforms identical to the 'pandurs' until 1757) wore white coats, which were even clearer targets than the Prussian lapels and strings. http://www.kronoskaf.com/syw/index.php?title=Meyerinck_Infantry (accessed 16 October 2018).

[236] The meaning of the German original is not clear. Most probably Zander wants to convey that there are many honourable and brave fellows amongst his comrades and that they contribute to the Zanders' chance of survival.

It is striking that the author makes no religious allusions, not even a brief remark thanking God for his surviving the action. The enemy is depicted in the darkest terms. The pandurs are not only light troops despised by the Prussians[237] but also use dishonourable tactics to surprise the Prussians and do not even leave them enough time to get their muskets – the Prussians are killed without having had any chance of defending themselves. The Prussians are also disadvantaged by their white lapels and strips, which make them visible even in the dark. Out-witted and easy targets, the Prussians are also outnumbered 4:1, but they win, which is proven by the royal presents of wine and money. C.F. Zander gives an indirect answer to the question of how the Prussians were able to defeat the enemies' superior force when he tells his nephew that he and his other nephew are with 'honourable and brave' men. These are values which have already earned them the king's favour, and which also strengthen their position in civil society. The ending phrase 'until I die' might be an indication that Christian Friedrich[238] is still moved when he writes about the nightly encounter, as he does not use this ending in other letters, even those in which he writes about his unit being shot at. It is difficult to understand why he does not write anything else about his or his nephew's experience in combat. It seems unlikely that the Zanders misbehaved or were cowardly, as this would have been made known in the village by the other soldiers from Nitzahn. Moreover, Christian Friedrich tells his nephew, that Johann Dietrich argued with the captain about an acquaintance being transferred to the grenadiers. He could not have done this if he or Christian Friedrich had acted in a cowardly fashion some months before. The most likely explanation is that the Zanders had been involved in close combat and do not want to tell their relatives how they killed enemy soldiers. This supposition is supported by Frederick II himself, who praised the conduct of the commanding officers von Syburg and the Zanders' acquaintance, Captain von Miltitz during this action and underlined that the Prussians had chased the pandurs away with bayonets and musket-butts.[239] The extraordinary rewards paid by the king show that a simple fire-fight at night is not what took place – there must have been extensive fighting and Christian Friedrich's silence on it is another proof for the assertion that honour was gained by the success of the unit and not individual fighting skills. Thus, Zander does not talk about his feelings and we can assume only from his closing phrase that he felt fear, but he could well also have felt a certain bloodlust to avenge the death of his ignominiously slaughtered comrades.

In another letter, dated 21 July 1757, Christian Friedrich tells his nephew that the Austrians shot at him and his comrades while they were besieging Prague and 'could have killed all of us in our tents'.[240] After the Prussians had raised the siege of Prague,

---

[237] 'Tagebuch eines Offiziers vom Alt-Schwerinschen Infanterieregiment, welches die Feldzüge von 1756 bis 1763 enthält', in *Sammlung*, vol. 1 (Dresden: 1782), 451. Bräker, *Arme Mann*, 150; Lemcke, *Kriegs- und Friedensbilder*, 26.
[238] *Fundstücke*, 96.
[239] Frederick II, 'Relation de la campagne 1756', in *Politische Correspondenz Friedrichs des Großen*, ed. Johann Gustav Droysen, vol. 14 (Berlin: Duncker und Humblodt, 1886), p. 93.
[240] C.F. Zander, 21 July 1757, in *Fundstücke*, 55.

the Austrians made a sortie and 'pursued our men and wounded and shot dead many [of them]'.[241] Again, the suffering of the men is at the centre of Christian Friedrich's re-telling, as are those events which endangered him and caused fear.

His description of an attempt by the king to force the Austrians into battle in mid-August 1757 is more detailed. According to Zander, the town of Zittau had been taken by the Austrians due to the forcibly recruited Saxon regiments[242] who let the Austrians into the town after three previously unsuccessful attempts. He then tells his nephew that the enemy burnt the entire town and that the Prussians wanted to engage battle, but the enemy had a swamp in front of them and were entrenched. Nevertheless, the Austrians opened fire with their cannon on the von Itzenplitz Regiment.

> Our regiment and that of Prince Ferdinand[243] were the vanguard. After we had marched up and formed up for battle, they shot amongst us with cannon, we did not care for it and did not return fire. They did not hit any of our men, but of Ferdinand's they killed many.

They withdrew and came to halt next to the guards, where they were able to talk to 'uncle Bährend' and Valentin Zander.

> We had to lie on the ground next to our muskets all night long, while it was raining, so that we were soon soaked through ... The king wanted to attack them, but the General Field-Marshals dissuaded him. At noon, we left our tents and they started to fire again and shot with cannon balls over our heads ...

The enemy declined the king's challenge to come out for battle and the Prussians marched back. Pandurs attack the Prussians constantly while they are marching away, 'but they did not come into the open field but stuck to the woods next to us. Our Free Party[244] had to grapple with them, we did not care for it ...'

Again, the enemy is depicted as rule-breaking and even inhuman, as they raze to the ground the small Saxon town of Zittau for no reason. But when the king and the entire army arrive, the Austrians are too cowardly to take up the challenge and come out for battle. Zander also evaluates the tactical situation very carefully, especially when he tells his readers that the 'General-Field-Marshals' dissuade the king from attacking the entrenched Austrian positions. The pride of his regiment is clear, as he tells us the honourable parts of the story, that von Itzenplitz is in the vanguard and next to the guards. Only trustworthy and effective regiments are chosen to be in the vanguard; the guards always occupy the most honourable place and thus being next to the guards means being near the king. Above all, note that Zander tells his nephew and

---

[241] Ibid., 55.
[242] The Zanders depict the forcible recruitment of the Saxons realistically and knew that these units were unreliable. *Fundstücke*, 98.
[243] Alt-Braunschweig, No. 5. Stationed in Magdeburg, it was also considered to be one of the elite regiments of the Prussian army.
[244] *Frei Regimenter* (free regiments). Units comprising volunteers entirely (*Freiwillige* in German). Light troops raised to combat the Austrian light troops.

family that he and his comrades 'did not care' when they were shot at with cannonballs. Clearly we do not know whether this is true or not, but even if Zander were frightened, he stresses that the men stood tall and showed no fear. In those days, soldiers had to stand upright when under artillery fire in order not to be surprised by attacking enemy cavalry. The same is true for the depiction of the retreat, when von Itzenplitz again 'does not care' that the pandurs were attacking and left it to the Prussian light troops to deal with the problem. Again, the passive courage of Christian Friedrich and his comrades is emphasized and this time underlined by stressing their 'cool' conduct. As being afraid was not shameful for the soldiers, we have to assume that Zander stresses that he and his comrades were able to overcome their fear and behave courageously.

'Now, have God in your mind and include me in your prayers': Intercession and honour

Pray for us: Intercession as a writing strategy

Of the remaining eleven letters, seven are addressed to the soldiers' wives, one to a mother, one to a brother, one to 'uncles, nephews, cousins, sister and friends' and one to an unknown relative. The letters to the soldiers' wives and to the brother share a common writing strategy. The men's combat experience is communicated with the aim of showing how God protected the soldiers amidst myriad threats to their lives. Thus, they try to bond with their relatives at home and ask them to thank God for his protection and above all urge their families to pray for them. Their letters aim to secure their relatives' intercession.

Pleading for their family to intercede is not a standard phrase, as the soldier authors see God's help and support as vital for their survival. Most soldiers are convinced that God is responsible for victory or defeat and thank the Lord for a Prussian victory. Many of them believe in not only the Almighty's *general* intervention on their behalf, but also in very concrete divine actions in favour of the Prussian army. Barthel Linck from the Alt-Anhalt Regiment writes to his wife that: 'finally, God made the right wing of the Austrians waver, due to our continuing sighs [prayers] … and I can honestly assure you that we continuously sent our sighs to God, to give power and strength to our comrades to conquer our enemies.'[245] Musketeer Damian Friedmeyer of the von Hülsen Regiment writes to his wife on 17 October 1756 that the collapse of a Saxon pontoon bridge had been brought about by God.[246] Friedmeyer also stresses that God shows his might by giving victory to the Prussians and their king as a result of 'our prayer and ongoing intercession'.[247] An anonymous private of the Alt-Anhalt Regiment holds a similar belief. As he writes to his wife on 9 May 1757 after the bloody Battle of Prague: 'It pleased me very much that the army of Prince Moritz prayed for us and lifted their hands up to God.'[248] The sentence needs some explanation. The corps of

---

[245] Barthel Linck, 3. Oktober 1756, in *Briefe*, 13–14.
[246] Extrakt Schreibens eines Soldaten, Namens Damian Friedmeyer, Hülsischen Regiments. Dresden, den 17. Oktober 1756, in *Briefe*, 36.
[247] Ibid.
[248] Schreiben eines Musketiers des Regiments Anhalt zu Fuß 1757, in *Briefe*, 52.

Prince Moritz had been ordered to cross the Moldau (Vltava in Czech) and support the other corps of the Prussian army in their desperate fight against the entrenched Austrians. But a lack of pontoon bridges[249] – or bad planning[250] – meant they were not able to intervene and could only fire some cannon shots at the Austrians. The musketeer is no military naïf and knows very well to judge a tactical situation.[251] Taking this into account, his lack of criticism for the non-intervention of the reinforcements of Moritz' corps and his praise for their intercession show that for him, prayer is a serious part of military activity and God's resulting help more precious than thousands of well-trained soldiers.

A moving example of a letter aiming to secure a relative's intercession is Dominicus' note to his brother. The carnage caused by the Russian artillery[252] left him shattered and unable to pray:

[I] was so full of sorrow that I could not give thanks to God nor sing a song of praise [to him]. Help me with that, my friends! To thank God that he safeguarded me and ask him to further safeguard me due to his grace, because it[253] has not come to an end, yet.[254]

Sergeant Liebler from the Alt-Anhalt Regiment (No. 3) took part in the bloody storming of the Austrian positions in the last phase of the Battle of Prague and praises the Lord for his protection while urging his wife to pray for him:

For all the promises of God in him are yea, and in him Amen[255], I had much trouble in my heart, but although my faith was very small, I always had God's assurance in me: when a thousand shall fall to thy left, and ten thousand to thy right hand, it shall but not come nigh thee[256] ... My dear wife, give thanks to the Lord, especially, because he has truly given me back to you.[257]

The seriously traumatized musketeer Frantz Reiß urges his wife to pray for him in the end of his letter: 'Now, have God in your mind and include me in your prayer, that the loving God may guard me further on, as I include you and the child in my prayer.'[258] Reiß also shows most clearly that intercession, and giving thanks to God, as writing

---

[249] Johann Wilhelm von Archenholz, *Geschichte des Siebenjährigen Krieges in Deutschland von 1756–1763 (1793)*, in *Aufklärung und Kriegserfahrung. Klassische Zeitzeugen zum Siebenjährigen Krieg*, ed. Johannes Kunisch (Frankfurt/Main: Suhrkamp, 1996), 58. See: Der Siebenjährige Krieg, ed. Gr. Generalstab, vol. 2 (Die Kriege Friedrichs des Großen, vol. 3), 147.
[250] Retzow, *Charakteristik*, vol. 1, 102.
[251] Schreiben eines Musketiers des Regiments Anhalt zu Fuß 1757, in *Briefe*, 50.
[252] Dominicus' perception is shared by Retzow, who underlines the murderous execution of the Shuvalov howitzers. Retzow, *Charakteristik*, vol. 1, 182.
[253] Dominicus' life.
[254] Kerler, *Tagebuch des Musketiers Dominicus*, 63.
[255] 2 Cor. 1.20.
[256] Psalm 91.7.
[257] Schreiben des Feldwebels Liebler, den 7. Mai 1757, in *Briefe*, 45.
[258] Frantz Reiß, 6 October 1756, in *Briefe*, 32.

strategies necessitate the communication of gruesome and perilous experiences and perceptions:

> I could tell you who had been killed or wounded, but I do not want to grieve any human being by [doing] that. It is enough that you know that God has until now spared my life and that I am still hale and hearty. All this you can tell to Ramse's wife, and also tell her, that her husband had been in such danger, that a cannonball hit his musket from his shoulder into a thousand pieces, but that thanks to God remained unharmed together with his son and still until now is fresh and healthy, because we share a tent. I have already written a letter together with Ramse to you on the 30 of September, but do not know whether you have received it. Thus, Ramse and I do not ask for anything more than that you thank God for yours and mine health and that you do not think that it[259] had been child's play.[260]

Similar strategies are used by the other writers, who urge their relatives to intercede on their behalf.[261]

While twentieth-century soldiers tend to downplay (or leave out altogether) the mortal dangers of combat, the early modern Prussian soldiers are keen to communicate these in order to show God's protection[262] for them and thus console their relatives. As they are convinced that prayers can influence God's actions, the soldiers' description of their perilous position also supports their aim to make their relatives pray for them and their further survival. It is not only their physical survival, which is at stake on the battlefield, but also their social survival as they have to defend their honour.

'The king was very cheerful with us': Honour as a writing strategy

We have already seen how the preservation of the honour of the regiment is core to the Zanders' and the NCOs' writing strategies. But also those soldiers for whom intercession and thanking God are their main writing strategies want to defend their and their regiment's honour.

Frantz Reiß gives a horrible and very detailed description of the death of his comrade Krumpholtz, who was shot several times in the head when he was standing next to Reiß.[263] He even becomes angry with his wife about the horror he had had to witness during battle. He points out to his wife that the king

> was very cheerful with us. On Sunday, the 3rd of October, he was with us and visited company after company and thanked us for our bravery. He said, that he

---

[259] The battle.
[260] Frantz Reiß, 6. Oktober 1756, in *Briefe*, 31.
[261] See also Barthel Linck, 3. Oktober 1756, in *Briefe*, 15. Von einem Unteroffizier des Alt-Anhaltischen Regiments [J. S. Liebler, son of G.S. Liebler], in *Briefe*, 16. XV Schreiben eines Musketiers des Regiments Anhalt zu Fuß 1757, in *Briefe*, 52. Kaspar Kalberlah, 11. November 1756, in *Soldatenbriefe*, 28.
[262] Lt. Seiler, 8. November 1757, in *Soldatenbriefe*, 35–6.
[263] Frantz Reiß, 6. Oktober 1756, in *Briefe*, 30.

would make us enjoy [his favour] all his life and promised that we would not be sent into the thick of it again, as we had lost so many men.[264]

Dominicus, who describes the disaster at Kunersdorf, stresses his plight too. In the end, he describes how the king turned their defeat into an honourable sacrifice:

> The king was at the front all the time and said: 'Children, do not leave me!' Two horses were shot from under the king and in the end, he grasped a flag[265] from Prince Henry's regiment and said: 'Everybody, who is a brave soldier, follow me!' Everybody who had cartridges [left] went confidently [with him]. It is said, that he had finally given the order 'wheel to the right!' and said: 'Retreat, children!'[266]

Sergeant Liebler gives a detailed account of his actions during the Battle of Prague. He takes part in three unsuccessful assaults with his (third) battalion of the Alt-Anhalt Regiment and a grenadier battalion. There is no doubt that Liebler deems his actions honourable as he asks his wife in a post-script: 'Let my dear sibling read this letter, no one else, because it would only be judged as boasting.'[267] An anonymous musketeer from the same regiment also gives a detailed description of his participation in the Battle of Prague, which culminates in his battalion clearing the way for another unit, which finally drives the Austrians off their position.[268] Corporal Binn writes in his last surviving letter about his thoughts before the Battle of Kunersdorf, when he asks God to give him and his comrades courage to 'attack our enemies' and that he will not spare the 'tyrants' but 'do what righteous soldiers are supposed to do in battles'.[269]

Other soldiers also show their eagerness to defend their honour and that of their regiment.[270] Concerning the communication of their battle experience, it is crucial to note that suffering,[271] the containment of fear and running a reasonable risk are at the heart of their concept of honour.

As noted above, unity by mutual intercession and the intercession of their relatives are crucial for the soldiers. As they are at the core of their writing strategies, they also determine what the men decide to *take out* of their perceptions and experiences. Unlike modern soldiers, they stress the danger they have been in and the violence they have been exposed to. The logic behind this is that the more they were threatened by the enemy, the more God has intervened to protect them, and will hopefully intervene

---

[264] Ibid., 31.
[265] In Prussia, each company had a flag but there were no regimental or battalion colours. The five flags of the companies that made up a battalion were positioned in the centre of the battalion and guarded by the colours platoon.
[266] Kerler, *Tagebuch des Musketiers Dominicus*, 64.
[267] Brief des Feldwebels Liebler, in *Briefe*, 47.
[268] Schreiben eines Musketiers des Regiments Anhalt zu Fuß 1757, in *Briefe*, 51.
[269] Letter no. 10 by Corporal Binn, 20. Juli 1759, in *Soldatenbriefe*, 22.
[270] Barthel Linck, 3. Oktober 1756, in *Briefe*, 12. Johann Christian Riemann, 16. Juni 1762, in *Soldatenbriefe*, 32. Lt. Seiler, 8. November 1757, in *Soldatenbriefe*, 36.
[271] J.S. Liebler describes the hardships of marching: Von einem Unteroffizier des Alt-Anhaltischen Regiments [J. S. Liebler, son of G.S. Liebler] nach Halle, in *Briefe*, 17. The hanging of three deserters is contrasted with the honourable behavior of the army as a whole. Ibid., 19.

again subsequently to bring them home safely. This focus on the soldiers' individual risk is crucial for the men's selection of those combat experiences that they communicate to their relatives.

Sources of danger: Experiences and perceptions

The men convey those aspects that soldiers perceive as threatening, namely the size of the enemy force, their zeal to fight the Prussians and in particular the quality of the enemy's well-chosen positions. We can conclude this not only from the men's writing strategies of the men, but also from the fact that those involved in heavy fighting were simply not able to perceive anything beyond than their immediate surroundings,[272] or at best the march into the killing zone.

Dominicus begins his description of the Battle of Kay (23 July 1759) by telling his brother that the Russians used 'all sorts of rogue stuff, which is not allowed in war.[273] They load their cannon with chain-shot[274], pieces of raw iron and whole bags with small musket balls[275], of which they put 100 [into their smaller] and 2 to 300 into their heavy pieces; and when these go off, there is real thunder.'[276] Later on, he mentions the advantageous position of the Russians, which meant that the Prussian artillery could not follow the infantry.[277] His report of the Battle of Kunersdorf (12 August 1759) underlines the enemy's savvy entrenchments and details the differing effects of the Prussian and the Russian ammunition:

> The dead, who lay there, were terrible to behold, and believe me! it is certain, that where 6 of ours lay, there lay 10 of theirs. Because, what we hit, we hit for sure.[278] They fired case-shot, which wounded many, but did not kill them.[279]

Barthel Linck, who had been present at the Battle of Lobositz as a musketeer in the Alt-Anhalt Regiment (No. 3) gives a detailed description of the troop movements, stressing the Austrian army's intimidating positioning and strength as well as the Prussians' courage. The detail of his narrative is mainly due to the fact that his regiment was only shot at by Austrian cannon and had not been directly involved in small-arms combat or close combat. Thus, he had been able to watch the battle from above and afar. Like Dominicus, he stresses the dishonourable fighting methods used by the Austrians,

---

[272] Frantz Reiß, 6. Oktober 1756, in *Briefe*, 30. *Friedrich der Grosse – Gespräche mit Catt*, ed. Wilhelm Schüßler (Wiesbaden: Dietrich'sche Verlagsbuchhandlung), 237. *Tagebuch des Musketiers Dominicus*, 32, fn. 4).
[273] The German original has *Schelmezeug* for 'rogue-stuff'. In Early Modern German, *Schelm* means hangman and thus a person without honour. It is a grave insult. It must not be confused with the modern German meaning of *Schelm*, which is a jester or joker or a term of endearment for children.
[274] Two cannon balls linked by a chain. These were normally used on ships to destroy the enemies' sails and rigging.
[275] These are even heavier and more deadly than normal case or grapeshot.
[276] Letter from Musketeer Dominicus, 25 August 1759, in *Tagebuch des Musketiers Dominicus*, 61.
[277] Dominicus' letter is translated in Appendix 2, pp. 178–81.
[278] The Prussians killed the enemies they hit.
[279] Letter from Musketeer Dominicus, 25 August 1759, in *Tagebuch des Musketiers Dominicus*, 64.

who pretend to surrender but then shoot at their captors, and when made POWs, use highly insulting swearwords about their Prussian captors. One of their troopers even attacked several Prussian squadrons (!) alone 'using all kinds of horrific invectives and swearwords but was cut into pieces by our men immediately'.[280]

Frantz Reiß from the von Hülsen Regiment (No. 21) limits his long description to communicating his personal risk and the horrible death of his comrade Krumholtz:

> Thus, the *Bataille* [battle] began at 6 o'clock in the morning and lasted with thundering and firing until 4, where I was in such danger, that I cannot thank God enough for my good health. The first cannon shots hit our Krumpholtz,[281] who stood close to me, through the head and took half his head away, and Bode[282] [was hit by Krumpholtz's] brains and piece of his skull and his musket [was shot] from his shoulder and broke into a thousand pieces, but – thanks to God – [he] remained unscathed. Now, dearest wife, what happened, I cannot describe by any means, as the shooting was so intense from both sides, that no one could understand a word from anybody else, and we did not see one thousand bullets, but many thousands. Towards afternoon, the enemy took flight and God gave victory to us.[283]

The dreadful sight of the elevated and well-chosen positions of the Austrians during the Battle of Prague is related by all writers who mention this encounter. Sergeant Liebler tells his wife about the morning of 6 May 1757:

> Here we saw the entire enemy army marching towards their positions on many mountains and elevations ... And it would have been impossible to attack them here...'[284]

He goes on to explain to her his battalion's unsuccessful attack, and his participation in two subsequent assaults by another musketeer battalion and a grenadier battalion respectively. Liebler stresses all the threatening aspects of the fighting, like the inability of the Prussian cannon to follow and support the infantry attack, the 'hailstorm of bullets', the death of many comrades and in the end his severe contusion, which hindered him from taking any further part in hostilities.[285] Liebler also relates that he found two abandoned colours of his battalion and made a soldier carry them to safety. All these aspects are fear-inspiring and an indication that fear was Liebler's main emotion during combat. At the same time, his actions and thoughts show that his religious belief enables him to cope with his anxieties. Thus, he writes about the third

---

[280] Barthel Linck, 3. Oktober 1756, in *Briefe*, 14.
[281] Probably a relative or close friend from the village of Reiß. His wife seems to know him. Krumpholtz is a common family name in the region around Halberstadt and Wernigerode in today's Saxony-Anhalt.
[282] Another comrade, also probably a relative or close friend, as his wife knows him, too.
[283] Frantz Reiß, 6. Oktober 1756, in *Briefe*, 30–1. The entire letter is in Appendix 2.
[284] Schreiben des Feldwebels Liebler, 7. Mai 1757, in *Briefe*, 46.
[285] Ibid., 47.

and most murderous attack: 'here I learned what it meant "that who sits under the shield of the Lord, etc."'[286]

A musketeer of the same regiment writes that 'we recognized that they were drawn up in four lines[287] and that they had planted so many mountains with cannons, that it was terrifying to behold'.[288] He gives a vivid description of the attack launched by his own battalion:

> Our battalion had not suffered anything so far and all cannonballs had flown over our heads. Finally, we were also going to feel the heat of the cannonade, as fate led us in front of a high mountain, which was planted with many cannons, which cruelly fired at us with grapeshot. Notwithstanding this, we advanced against the enemy batteries with fixed bayonets, and although our battalion was almost incapable of standing and many were forced to retreat, another battalion came to relieve us and this attack made the enemy flee ignominiously and abandon their cannon.[289]

Even Corporal Nikolaus Binn, who was not directly involved in the fighting on the hills, remembers the hilltop positions of the Austrians with a shudder. His regiment, the cuirassier von Driesen Regiment (No. 7), was on the right wing of the Prussian position and lost eight men that day.[290] He writes to his wife that the Austrians 'had such an advantageous position, where they stood, as they had never had before, they occupied medium-height mountains, which could almost not be climbed by any human being and they were all entrenched. Our infantry had to push them off [the heights] with their bayonets. Thus, you can imagine, how many of our men this cost. The mountains were like the highest towers.'[291] His tone becomes even more drastic at the end of his letter: 'This battle was in front of Prague on the white mountains, but they can now be called red mountains, as they are stained with blood.'[292] That the enemies' positions on the hilltops were especially frightening for the soldiers is underlined by the hussar general Warnery in his description of the Prussian advance to the battlefield of Leuthen (5 December 1757): 'The entire army rejoiced [when seeing that the enemy's positions were at ground-level], as the infantry had feared to find the enemy in an entrenched camp.'[293]

Damian Friedmeyer, a private from the same regiment, only mentions the 'redoubled [twice as strong as the Prussians] and advantageous [well-positioned] force' of the

---

[286] Psalm 91.1. The King James Bible reads: 'He that dwelleth in the secret place of the most High shall abide under the shadow of the Almighty.' The German translation by Martin Luther, the one Liebler knew, uses the words '*wer unter dem Schirm des Höchsten sitzet*', which stresses the 'shielding' aspect and does not encompass any hiding place.

[287] Four lines of battalions. The normal order of battle consisted of two lines of battalions, e.g. fourteen battalions in the first line and twelve in the second line, about 150 metres behind the first line.

[288] Schreiben eines Musketiers des Regiments Anhalt zu Fuß 1757, in *Briefe*, 50.

[289] Ibid., in *Briefe*, 51–2.

[290] Maximilian Ritter von Hoen, *Die Schlacht bei Prag am 6. Mai 1757*, Streffleurs Militärische Zeitschrift 1/2 (1909): 230. Duffy, *Frederick*, 49 (map).

[291] Letter no. 2 by Corporal Binn, in *Soldatenbriefe*, 6–7.

[292] Letter no. 2 by Corporal Binn, in *Soldatenbriefe*, 7–8.

[293] Warnery, *Feldzüge*, vol. 1, 224.

Austrians and thanks God 'that he has not struck me as hard as many of us.'[294] Friedemeyer's hand had been wounded,[295] but he seems to have been cheerful as he deemed his wound negligible in the face of the lethal dangers he had been facing during the storming of the Loboschberg.

The soldiers' related experience mainly comprises those events which instilled fear into them and which they perceived as life-threatening. This shows that the main emotion they felt during combat was fear. Their psychological processing differs from man to man. For example, while Sergeant Liebler seems to cope quite well due to his conviction that the Lord saved him and points to his brave rescue saving of two of the regiment's colours, Frantz Reiß is deeply shaken and starts to quarrel with his wife. Yet all of them stress that they had been able to cope with their fear and fight honourably. Another key emotion is probably a hatred of the enemy as many soldiers describe the Austrians, Russians and French not only as having superior numbers and positions but fighting without honour and breaking the rules of war.

'God is a relief in greatest distress': Creating sense of perceptions and emotions in combat

In order to get even closer to the soldiers' emotional life,[296] we will now turn to the direct expression and communication of their feelings in the letters. The men are able and more than willing to communicate emotions. For example, most of them mention their joy at receiving good news from home:

> Your letter from 19 September had only reached me by Mr. Gerecke on the 5 of October, wherein I see that you and the boy are still in good health, which I learned with great joy from the bottom of my heart.[297]

Corporal Binn communicates mixed feelings, when he writes to his wife about his son's writing skills:

> When I get these letters, I am joyful, but when I look through them and see that they do not get better (...)[298] and that they are not able to compose the letter in the style of a scribe, I get so angry that I want to go up the wall.[299]

Emotions and thoughts during combat are also mentioned explicitly by some of the writers. Dominicus is one of them: 'What terrified us the most: as soon as we had passed, a powder-wagon was set on fire by enemy shot, which caused seven dead and

---

[294] Damian Friedmeyer, den 17. Oktober 1756, in *Briefe*, 34.
[295] Ibid., 35.
[296] Peters, *Wegweiser*, 235.
[297] Frantz Reiß, 6. Oktober 1756, in *Briefe*, 29. Adam Becker, 18. November 1756, in *Briefe*, 37. Letter no. 4 by Corporal Binn, in Soldatenbriefe, 11. Letter no. 10 by Corporal Binn, in Soldatenbriefe, 21. Joachim Diederich und Ertmann Kamiet, 1. März 1757, in *Soldatenbriefe*, 27. Johann Christian Riemann. Sommer 1762, in *Soldatenbriefe*, 33.
[298] Unreadable in the original.
[299] Letter no. 8 by Corporal Binn, in *Soldatenbriefe*, 18.

three wounded.'[300] Frantz Reiß tells his wife that he 'did not think of anything else than God, you and the child, which were [his] greatest pains'.[301] Reiß was obviously in pain and thought of God to console him[302] and his agony were aggravated by thinking of his wife and child and their fate should he die.

Sergeant Liebler uses religious language to express his feelings:

> I had much sorrow in my heart, but although my faith was very small, I always had God's assurance in me: when a thousand shall fall to thy left, and ten thousand to thy right hand, it shall but not come nigh thee. Yea, I have seen with mine eyes, how the enemies of the Gospel are rewarded.[303]

Liebler feels depressed with sorrow but also hatred for the 'enemy of the Gospel'. Other soldiers use certain emotional adjectives to characterize perceptions or incidents that also address their feelings explicitly. Several authors use the adjective *erstaunlich* (astounding / stunning) to describe an enemy position,[304] certain encounters[305] or the sight of a battlefield.[306] The word *Erstaunen* has the following meaning in eighteenth-century German: 'a spasm...an unnatural movement, where the nerves and membranes are contracted and released'.[307] *Erstaunliche* perceptions were not to be taken lightly in mid-eighteenth century German territories. The regimental chaplain Carl Daniel Küster tells his readers about the horrible end of General von Kleist: 'This meritorious general died from smallpox long after the war.[308] He got contaminated by the shudder [the result of *Erstaunen*], which had grasped him when he beheld the corps of a smallpox victim.'[309]

Two men write about religious verses they thought of during combat. Barthel Linck tells his wife:

> The verse, you sent to me in your last letter, 'Jesus help [me in] winning, Jesus help fighting, Jesus help beating, make the en'my retreating' strengthened me mightily

---

[300] Kerler, *Tagebuch des Musketiers Dominicus*, 32.
[301] Frantz Reiß, 6. Oktober 1756, in *Briefe*, 32.
[302] Above, Reiß writes that keeping God at the forefront of his mind had been the 'only consolation' during the bloody battle. Ibid., 30. Thus, 'greatest pains' cannot include his thoughts of God, but only those of his wife and child.
[303] G.S. Liebler, in *Briefe*, 45. It is a paraphrase of Psalms 94.19 and 91.7–8. It is especially interesting how he changes 91.8. While the German Bible uses the term *Gottlosen* (ungodly, wicked), Liebler makes it fit the Catholic Austrian enemy by calling them *Feinde des Evangeliums* (enemies of the Gospel), as the Protestants saw the Gospel as the only authoritative source of Christian belief and accused the Catholics of setting the pope's words above the word of God.
[304] Schreiben eines Musketiers des Regiments Anhalt zu Fuß. 1757, in *Briefe*, 50.
[305] Corporal Binn on the Prussian bombardment, von Schweidnitz 1758. Letter no. 7 by Corporal Binn, in *Soldatenbriefe*, 16. J.S. Liebler, son of Sergeant Liebler on the cavalry action at Lobositz. Von einem Unteroffizier des Alt-Anhaltischen Regiments nach Halle, in *Briefe*, 18.
[306] Letter no. 6 by Corporal Binn. 1758, in *Soldatenbriefe*, 6. Frantz Reiß, 6. Oktober 1756, in *Briefe*, 30.
[307] *Zedler's*, 6 (1733), 1179. In today's German, *erstaunlich* describes a far less dangerous emotion like 'wondering'.
[308] Of Hubertusburg, 15. Februar 1763.
[309] *Officier-Lesebuch*, vol. 5, 156, fn. *).

during the battle, when I also remembered the wars of the Old Testament, especially the examples of Joshua and Gideon.[310]

Sergeant J.S. Liebler, son of G.S. Liebler, asks his wife to teach the following verse to their child: 'God is our confidence and strength, a relief in greatest distress, which struck us, therefore we are not afraid.'[311] We cannot be completely sure of course, but it could be that Liebler thought of it himself while under artillery fire at Lobositz.

The emotions of enemy soldiers are expressed directly in two letters. Corporal Binn writes after the Prussian victory of Hohenfriedberg to his wife about the Austrians: 'This time, we terrified them in such a manner, that I do not believe, they will be able to withstand us as long as I live.'[312] NCO Müller from the von Hülsen Regiment describes the Austrians after their defeat at Prague as 'terrified and discouraged'.[313]

On all levels, experience, related perceptions and directly expressed feelings, fear dominates completely. The men also communicate that they coped with their fear and sometimes even mention religious verses as a means to achieving this end. Loathing of the enemy and his dishonourable way of fighting is also mentioned, but never directly expressed.

Statements about soldiers' emotions in combat

Analysis of the soldiers' letters has shown that their writing strategies and audiences forbid the expression of certain feelings like hatred, rage or bloodlust. Yet the high casualty rates and some massacres of fleeing (or even surrendering) troops show that these feelings were not alien to mid-eighteenth-century soldiers. Thus, other sources from officers and chaplains and printed memoires of soldiers have to be studied. Their military writings, historical or theoretical, were aimed at finding solutions to military problems and had to rely on realistic descriptions of combat situations. As they were published, the authors would have been accused of forgery and lies if they had invented an unrealistic picture of the soldiers' behaviour. Concerning the soldiers' emotions, four different groups of sources can be distinguished.

1. **Military history and theory, including journals and regimental diaries.** Most eighteenth-century military writers paid little attention to common soldiers' feelings. But generals still working in the field knew that their emotions played a crucial role and had to be studied carefully. One of the most famous captains of the age,[314] the French Marshal Maurice de Saxe, an illegitimate son of

---

[310] Barthel Linck, 3. Oktober 1756, in *Briefe*, 15.
[311] Von einem Unteroffizier des Alt-Anhaltinschen Regiments [J. S. Liebler, son of G.S. Liebler] nach Halle, in *Briefe*, 20.
[312] Letter no. 1 by Corporal Binn, in *Soldatenbriefe*, 4–5.
[313] Schreiben des Unteroffiziers Müller vom Hülsenschen Regiment an seine Frau, datirt vor Prag, den 15. Mai 1757, in *Briefe*, 59.
[314] De Saxe won the last great victories of the French army of the Bourbon kings during the War of the Austrian Succession: Fontenoy (1745), Rocoux (1746) and Laffeld (1747). See: Browning, *The War of the Austrian Succession*, 206–13 (Fontenoy), 282–6 (Rocoux), 313–17 (Laffeld).

Augustus the Strong of Saxony,[315] criticized the 'scientific' military theoretician Jean Charles, Chevalier Folard, who took as his point of departure that the soldier was always brave. But according to de Saxe, the opposite was true, and the courage of the troops could change from day to day. Explanations for this were rare and had to be searched for in the hearts of men, in de Saxe's view, and he went on to stress that the soldiers' emotions and courage were the most important, subtle and basic part of the 'business' of war.[316] Nevertheless, most writing officers do not discuss this question in detail but mention the soldiers' feelings and emotions only in the context of tactical considerations. It is also noteworthy that the regimental journals – and some military historians – describe certain military situations in an emotional way. For example, when a unit had sustained severe losses, the authors write that it 'had suffered much'.[317] Sources with this kind of 'emotional' wording can also contribute to an analysis of the men's emotions in battle.

2. **Diaries and memoires written by officers.** In this book, the memoires and diaries of two Prussian officers have been used. They were lieutenants or ensigns during the war. The diary of Lieutenant Jakob Friedrich von Lemcke of the Alt-Anhalt Regiment (No. 3) has survived in an extremely truncated edition from 1909.[318] Ernst Friedrich Rudolf von Barsewisch, from the von Meyerinck Infantry Regiment (No. 26), also kept a diary.[319] It is certain that Barsewisch's text was based on his marching-diary and that he inserted new sections into it.[320] The memoires of Carl Wilhelm von Hülsen were written for his children after the war.[321] They were most probably written after 1788, as this was the year of the first edition of Archenholz' *History of the Seven Years'*

---

[315] Karl Ludwig Wilhelm von Pöllnitz, *Das Galante Sachsen* (Dortmund: Harenberg, [1735] 1979, 155.
[316] Duffy, *Military Experience*, 240.
[317] Tagebuch eines Offiziers Alt-Schwerinschen Regiments, in *Sammlung*, vol. 1, 194. Tagebuch des Majors Maximilian von Bornstädt, in *Sammlung*, vol. 4, 17, 45. Beschreibung der Feldzüge von 1744 und 1745, wie auch 1756 bis 1763 von einem Offizier des Anhaltschen Regiments, in *Sammlung*, vol. 4, 65. Tagebuch von den Feldzügen der Grenadierkompagnien des Gräfl. Anhaltschen Füselierregiments von 1744 bis 1763, in *Sammlung*, vol. 4, 179, 184. Bericht des Obristen von Carlowitz, in *Sammlung*, vol. 4, 222. Journal des jetzigen Tauenzienschen Regiments, in *Sammlung*, vol. 4, 454. Journal des Knobelsdorfschen Infanterieregiments, in *Sammlung*, vol. 4, 599, 603. J.F. Seyfarth, *Geschichte des Infanterie-Regiments von Anhalt-Bernburg*, 52, 84. Bemerkungen über das Journal der Preußisch. Campagne von 1756 und 1757 im 4ten Stück der Bellona, in *Bellona*, vol. 8, 29. Rezension der 'Commentaires sur les Institutons militaires de Vegége'; par M. le Comte Turpin de Crissé Lieutenant-General etc. Paris, 1783, in *Bibliothek für Officiere*, vol. 1, 109. See: Relation von der Schlacht bei Hastenbeck, in *Neues Militärisches Journal*, vol. 1, 212. Beschreibung der Schlacht bei Lafeld, in *Neues Militärisches Journal*, vol. 1, 82. Ueber den Angrif der Cavalerie, in *Neues Militärisches Journal*, vol. 1, 95. Einige Bemerkungen über die Schlacht bey Hastenbeck, in *Neues Militärisches Journal*, vol. 1, 251. [Frederick II], Relation von der Schlacht bei Lissa, in *Neues Militärisches Journal*, vol. 5, 242, 244.
[318] Lemcke, *Kriegs- und Friedensbilder 1725-1759* (Osnabrück: Biblio, 1971), VII.
[319] Ernst Friedrich Rudolf von Barsewisch, *Meine Kriegs-Erlebnisse während des Siebenjährigen Krieges 1757-1763. Wortgetreuer Abdruck aus dem Tagebuche des Kgl. Preuß. General-Quartiermeister-Lieutenants* (Berlin: Verlag L. von Warnsdorff, 1863).
[320] Barsewisch writes about his regiment, 'which is now called Woldeck' (7). Thus, his insertion must have been made between 1778 and 1789 (see: Gieraths, *Kampfhandlungen*, 590, 2).
[321] [Carl Wilhelm von Hülsen], *Unter Friedrich dem Großen. Aus den Memoiren des Ältervaters 1752-1773*, ed. Helene von Hülsen (Osnabrück: Biblio, [1890] 1974), 3.

War.[322] Von Hülsen not only refers indirectly to this text,[323] but has also copied entire passages from Archenholz's book. This is especially true for the Battle of Roßbach, in which von Hülsen himself had not participated.[324] Christian Wilhelm von Prittwitz penned the most detailed descriptions of the psychological dimensions of combat in the Seven Years' War by an officer. He was a lieutenant in the von Bevern Regiment (No. 7) and became a member of the Herrnhuter congregation of brethren. Bearing witness to their own lives was a crucial part of the Herrnhuters' faith.[325] His frank descriptions of his own fear, and even his panic, might also have been due to the fact that he loathed his vocational choice, but are not out of line with findings on other officers and armies:[326]

> When I had become sixteen years of age and my brother fourteen and a half, we were asked, which profession we wanted to choose, if we wanted to study or become soldiers? Out of these two alternatives only one could be chosen, as no other one [than the military career] was left for a young nobleman, although it was perfectly possible that – as was the case with us – he was fit for neither one and did not possess the qualities for none of them. Admittedly, we would have preferred to study theology, which we liked very much. But as we lacked the necessary level of prior knowledge and also knew, how expensive this would be..., we decided... to agree to the second proposal and take the soldiers' estate.[327]

3. **Published memoires written by privates.** These are the reminiscences of Ulrich Bräker (1735–98), a young Swiss, who joined[328] the von Itzenplitz Regiment just before the Seven Years' War and deserted during the Battle of Lobositz. He became famous as an enlightened Pietist writer in later life.[329] In his autobiography, he presents himself as having been tricked into Prussian service and was thus presented as the archetype of those young men who were fooled and pressed into military service in the eighteenth century. For the critics of Frederick II, Bräker became the chief witness for the inhumanity of the Prussian army,[330] while the king's defenders and admirers regarded him as a liar and perjurer. Jürgen Kloosterhuis has shown in his careful study of Bräker's memoires that neither

---

[322] Kunisch, *Aufklärung*, 757.
[323] Hülsen, *Unter Friedrich*, 89.
[324] Compare ibid., 53–9 with Archenholz, *Geschichte*, 106–14.
[325] Irina Modrow, 'Religiöse Erweckung und Selbstreflexion. Überlegungen zu den Lebensläufen Herrnhuter Schwestern als einem Beispiel pietistischer Selbstdarstellungen', in *Ego-Dokumente*, ed. Winfried Schulze, 121–30.
[326] Russian officers also expressed their fear openly. Denis Sdvidzkov, *Letters from the 'Prussian War': The People of the Russian Imperial Army in 1758* (Moscow: New Literature Review, 2019; Ibid., 'Landschaft nach der Schlacht. Briefe russischer Offiziere aus dem Siebenjährigen Krieg', in *Forschungen zur Brandenburgischen und Preußischen Geschichte*, 22, vol. 1 (2012): 33–56. We thank Ilya Berkovich for the information on Sdvidzkov's newest book.
[327] Prittwitz, 'Ich bin ein Preuße', 17.
[328] Although Bräker presents his joining the regiment as a trick, it was in fact not. Kloosterhuis, *Donner*, 151.
[329] Holger Böning, *Ulrich Bräker. Der Arme Mann aus dem Toggenburg – Eine Biographie* (Zürich: Orell Füssli Verlag, 1998), 100, 108.
[330] Kloosterhuis, *Donner*, 165.

assertion is true. Bräker is a reliable source in terms of his perceptions and their presentation, but his contribution must be viewed in the context of other sources. When this is done, a much more differentiated picture of the Prussian army, and one of its elite regiments, emerges.[331]

Joseph Ferdinand Dreyer, whose memoires had been published in 1810, was the exact opposite of Bräker. Born in Alsace, he had joined the Prussian service voluntarily. The title of his memoires is somewhat misleading, as he began his career as a drummer (due to his short stature[332]) but was soon transferred to a light battalion, where he served during the Silesian Wars. His book is a conservative reaction to Prussia's crushing defeat at the hands of Napoleon in 1806. For example, Dreyer contrasts the piety and obedience of Frederick II's soldiers to the 'disobedience' of the losers of Jena and Auerstedt.[333] Both Bräker and Dreyer want to present themselves as reliable eye-witnesses and convince others of their respective viewpoints. In both cases this requires a good amount of honesty, especially concerning their emotions during combat. Otherwise any reader with professional knowledge of soldiering would have dismissed them immediately as liars.[334]

4. **The writings of staff-chaplain Carl Daniel Küster.** Küster not only harboured an excessive interest in the emotional life of officers and soldiers alike, but was also in a perfect position to gain this insight given that he himself took part in the fighting at Hochkirch in 1758. Being a chaplain, the soldiers talked to him about their emotions more frankly than they may have done to other people. Küster was also the editor of the 'Officers' Reading Book', through which he propagated an enlightened Christian military ethos. His texts combine a solid knowledge of military life with the aim of educating young officers.

We will use Küster's terms and concepts to organize the information contained in the above-mentioned sources about soldiers' emotions in battle: 'human fear' (*Menschenangst*), 'cannon-fever' (*Kanonenfieber*), 'panic' (*panisches Schrecken*; literally 'panic scare'), 'heat' (*Hitze*) and 'pugnacity' (*Kampflust*).

Human fear and cannon-fever

Ulrich Bräker gives a detailed description of his feelings in his autobiography:[335]

> We were advancing all the time and all my courage went completely into my boots. I would have liked to hide myself in the womb of the earth and a similar fear, yeah, deadly pallor could be seen in all faces, even of those, who normally crow about their courage[336] ... [when we met the enemy] I myself was drunken of rage

---

[331] Ibid., 170.
[332] Dreyer, *Leben*, 14.
[333] Ibid., 22.
[334] Ibid., 15–16.
[335] See also: Kloosterhuis, *Donner*, 173–9.
[336] Bräker, *Arme Mann*, 147.

and heat and not knowing scare and fear fired all my 60 cartridges one after the other until my musket was half-annealing and I had to drag it behind me by its string.[337]

Bräker's description of his fear resembles the common definition of his time as presented in Zedler's *Encyclopaedia*: 'Fear of death, when the cold sweat of death breaks out, and the heart wants to sink into the deepest water and mud.'[338] Dreyer, who was a highly motivated soldier, also speaks about his fear on the morning of his first battle:

> A fool, who pretends that he was as dauntless in his first battle as in his tenth. That is not true, and I know at once, what kind of fellow he is. He is a braggart and nothing else. Enough, my heart throbbed as I beat the *reveille* at the morning of this memorable day.[339]

The ensign Barsewisch tells his readers about his own fears before the Battle of Leuthen. He had a nightmare and dreamt that he was lying amongst the Austrians severely wounded and fearing that he would bleed to death.[340] Although Barsewisch writes about his own feelings, this passage shows that even the noble officer views fear as something normal for all soldiers, and which does not injure their honour. This is underlined by Küster, who writes about many conversions with officers of all ranks 'and brave privates' who had told him that fear was a normal feeling in battle and that anybody who denied this was a 'boastful liar'.[341]

All these men – all professionals and serving in elite units of the Prussian army – agree that fear is a normal feeling in battle and does not diminish the honour of the man, who feels it. These men are miles away from later chauvinist ideas of fearless soldiers[342] or 'blonde beasts'.[343] It is also noteworthy that none of them shared the idea that soldiers had been made 'fearless' by the sergeant's stick or brutal punishments meted out to their comrades.

While fear does not set the soldier *hors de combat*, cannon-fever is a more serious emotion and *does* affect their ability to fight. Küster had been in the midst of fighting

---

[337] Ibid., 150.
[338] *Zedler's* 2 (1732), 301.
[339] Dreyer, *Leben*, 15–16. Compare the diary of a Hessian *Jäger* officer, George Beß: 'My children, do not believe, that one does not feel human fear [in combat]. Just imagine, that when the enemy comes marching against you with shining muskets and drawn sabres and you start to think: probably it is only a few minutes and you enter into eternity, – your heart will surely get warm ... I have heard many braggarts, who said: I do not fear any bullet. Alas, these are fools and mostly the worst soldiers and most fearsome men. I say it again: every mortal feels human fear, but it must not make him act badly, because my oath as a soldier tells me to harm my enemy wherever I can.' George Beß, *Aus dem Tagebuch eines Veteranen des siebenjährigen Krieges* (s.l.e.d.), 239.
[340] Barsewisch, *Kriegs-Erlebnisse*, 25.
[341] Küster, *Bruchstück*, 61, fn. *).
[342] See Erich Maria Remarque, *Erich Maria Remarques Roman 'Im Westen nichts Neues'. Text, Edition, Entstehung, Distribution und Rezeption (1928–1930)*, ed. Thomas F. Schneider (Tübingen: May Niemeyer, 2004), 39, 170.
[343] *Nietzsche Wörterbuch*, ed. Nietzsche Research Group (Nijmegen), vol. 1 (Berlin: De Gruyter, 2004), 410. We must draw a clear distinction between Nietzsche's thought and later racist uses.

for several hours during the Battle of Hochkirch,[344] in which the Zanders lost their lives. He writes about his feelings while retreating with the army:

> But it would be the most infamous lie, if I said, that I had had no fear at all. I also felt the so called cannon-fever or battle-shiver[345] in all its might. But God gave mercy and I was grasped by it lately, when I was passing the village of Kitzlitz, when there was almost no mortal danger [to fear] any more. I walked by myself beside the regiment, and quickly an emasculating fear got hold of me and a shock accompanied by a shiver of all my limbs, which could have enabled a weak child to knock me over.[346]

Lieutenant Lemcke seems to have had similar feelings after his left foot had been torn off by a cannon ball during the Battle of Kay, and plundering Russian soldiers were pondering to drag him away or to kill him and one of them wanted him to get up:

> I pointed at my foot, showing them that I was unable to walk, and he took his gun and aimed at me. As I was thus able to look directly into the muzzle of the gun, it was horrible for me to see my murderer so near before me, that I threw myself to the earth and sprawled and lay on my belly. It was as if all my senses had left me and I might have laid there for quite a while being numbed, when a powerful blow from a Cossack's pike woke me up.[347]

Prittwitz had similar feelings after having been wounded and while fleeing together with his regiment during the Battle of Zorndorf, where he 'was grasped by such fear, that [he] without a word left his sword and arrived without any arms at Zorndorf.'[348]

Although cannon-fever disables the soldier, it is admitted by the men and not perceived as dishonourable.

Panic or panic scare

As an emotion, panic is quite similar to cannon-fever,[349] but encompasses a collective element, the panic-stricken mass flight of entire battalions, regiments or even armies.[350]

---

[344] Küster, *Bruchstück*, 44–5.
[345] *Schlachtschauer* in the German original.
[346] Küster, *Bruchstück*, 59–60.
[347] Lemcke, *Kriegs- und Friedensbilder*, 36.
[348] Prittwitz, *'Ich bin ein Preuße'*, 95.
[349] *Zedler's* 35 (1743), 1111 defines *Schrecken* (scare) thus: 'The human being becomes pale in the face, the hands become cold, the pulse becomes weak, one freezes like standing around without any feelings.'
[350] 'Betrachtungen über den Krieg mit den Wilden in Nordamerika', in *Neue Kriegsbibliothek*, vol. 1, 308. 'Schreiben des Marquis von Havrincourt', in *Neue Kriegsbibliothek*, vol. 8, 78. Retzow, *Charakteristik*, vol. 1, 137, 320, 410; Friedrich der Grosse, *Gespräche*, 263. 'Etwas von Regenschirmen', in *Bellona*, vol. 14, 104; 'Betrachtungen des Generalmajors von Stille', in *Sammlung*, vol. 1, 127.

Sometimes, it is referred to as a 'scare'.[351] Küster views fear, cannon-fever and the 'emasculating fear of death' as normal battlefield emotions and explains the way from individual fear to the flight of an entire army:

> When I talked to officers of the highest to the lowest rank as well as to brave privates about the so-called cannon-fever, all of them said with one voice: He, who prides himself on never having felt this shudder of the fear of death in battle, is a boastful liar. But they also said this, and I have also noticed it many times: that the heroes feel it at different times, some at the beginning, some in the middle and some in the end of a battle. Thus, the strong one can support the weak one and a general flight will only develop when this emasculating fear gets hold of the majority of the army and the weak sweep the strong away. There are examples for this emasculating fear gripping one or a few heroes, making them unable to think and to stand their ground and thus taking away the capacity of an entire army to think and stand their ground, which led to the flight of this army, which would otherwise have worked miracles of bravery.
>
> As this cannot be influenced by the commanding general, he has to lift up his eyes to the Lord of Hosts, who can give power and take power according to his plan, where he has written down the fate of man.[352]

Often, panic cannot be explained rationally, so much that it can be used to exculpate the losing side from accusations of cowardice. Professional soldiers give insightful examples for this phenomenon. Tempelhof writes about the Battle of Kunersdorf (12 August 1759):

> As [the Duke of Württemberg, a Prussian general of the cavalry], looked over his shoulder, he recognised that he had been left alone; the entire cavalry had been deterred by enemy fire and stayed behind. Amongst these regiments were some of those, who had given the strongest proof of their fearlessness at Zorndorf.[353] It is often inexplicable, why the soldier surmounts the greatest difficulties on certain occasions and is a hero in the proper sense of the word and does the exact opposite, when the risk is not nearly as high.[354]

Retzow tells of a similar incident at the Battle of Leuthen (5 December 1757):

> On this occasion, an incident occurred, which could have put the hitherto victorious [Prussian, K&SM] army into danger. According to the disposition for

---

[351] 'Anekdoten', in *Neues Militärisches Journal*, vol. 1, S. 273; 'Relation der Bataille bey Rosbach mit Anmerkungen von den Grafen von St. Germain', in *Neues Militärisches Journal*, vol. 5, 213, fn. **); [C. D. Küster], 'Ueber Feigheit, Tapferkeit, Tollkühnheit etc.', in *Officier-Lesebuch*, vol. 2, 92, 99–100; Retzow, *Charakteristik*, vol. 1, 251–52, vol. 2, 108, 112; 'Geschichte des Freyregiments von Hard', in *Sammlung*, vol. 5, 111; Fleming, *Vollkommene Teutsche Soldat*, II, 274.

[352] Küster, *Bruchstück*, 61, fn. *)

[353] At Zorndorf, the Prussian cavalry had saved the day by a ferocious charge on the Russian left wing, which was taken down in extremely brutal hand-to-hand fighting. Showalter, *Frederick*, pos. 3861.

[354] Tempelhof, *Geschichte*, vol. 3, 221.

the battle, the left wing was to hold itself back all the time; but the enemies' movement suddenly brought it near the Austrians. Until now, it [the Prussian left wing] had been out of the enemies' reach altogether. The unexpected cannon-fire had a disconcerting effect on it and a panic scare made six battalions turn without any need and seek shelter behind a nearby Brechhaus.[355]

Another statement by Retzow is even more in accordance with Küster's observation:

Even the most well trained and brave army can be defeated when surprise, like for example at Roßbach,[356] causes a so-called panic scare, and the tactical capabilities of the commanders are very limited.[357]

Hülsen also cites Roßbach as an illustration of how impossible it was to cope with a mass panic:

The battle was decided so swiftly that even the conquered did not claim the honour of having put up strong resistance but excused themselves by claiming [to have suffered] a panic scare.[358]

It should be added that there were also quite rational reasons for a panic or panic scare and the disintegration of entire regiments or armies. Thus, the flight of the Prussian army at Kunersdorf was caused by the frightful losses it had suffered, and the men's total exhaustion after being involved in six solid hours of slaughter.[359] In many cases it was not the total number of losses that had the biggest impact, but rather the anticipation of the living that they were the next to be killed or maimed.[360] This was probably the real reason for the French and Imperial collapse at Roßbach. The casualty rates at Prague point in the same direction. The von Winterfeld Regiment (No. 1) lost 1,100 of its men (about two-thirds of its total strength) in successfully driving back the Austrians from a number of entrenched positions. The grenadier battalions of the Prussian left, which had fled in the initial phase of the battle, lost 'only' 240 men per battalion (about one-third of their total strength).[361]

---

[355] Retzow, *Charakteristik*, vol. 1, 251. Retzow explains the term *Brechhaus* (lit.: breaking-house): This is the Silesian term for houses in which flax was dried and broken down, and which were erected in the open country to minimize the fire hazard.

[356] At Roßbach on 5 November 1757, the Prussians ambushed a French and Imperial army, which was twice as large as the tiny Prussian army and put it to flight after only 90 minutes of fighting. Showalter, *Frederick*, pos. 3326–8.

[357] Retzow, *Charakteristik*, vol. 1, 209.

[358] Hülsen, *Unter Friedrich dem Großen*, 57. It can be doubted, that the French really offered this as an excuse, as Hülsen copied the greater part of his Roßbach account from Archenholz. But this is of secondary importance here, as the crucial message is that mid-eighteenth-century officers could view a panic scare as an excuse for a most humiliating defeat.

[359] Duffy, *Frederick*, 187–8.

[360] One of the most careful and insightful debates on the causes of military panics is to be found in John Keegan's Face of Battle: John Keegan, *The Face of Battle. A Study of Agincourt, Waterloo and the Somme* (1976; London et al., Pimlico 2004), 170–7.

[361] Hoen, *Die Schlacht bei Prag*, 412.

Heat

'Heat' is one of the most widely used terms for describing emotions and physical reactions of soldiers in combat in German eighteenth-century military sources. With the exception of the soldiers' letters, it can be found in all the other types of sources, including Bräker's memoires. Zedler's encyclopaedia offers the following definition: 'Burning is a mightily excited warmth in the human body, caused by too powerful a movement of the animal spirits or particles of sulphur in the human blood.'[362] A detailed description in the military context can be found in Carl Daniel Küster's text 'On the days of battle as so-called "hot" days':

> The days of battle can justly be called hot days, not only in summer but also in autumn or winter; and experience shows that the hours of combat are very hot hours even during the coldest nights in winter. The most violent physical and psychical efforts [of the combatants, K&SM] and the continuous fire of cannon and muskets indeed cause the most extreme heat imaginable.
>
> The 5 November 1757, when the French were put to flight at Roßbach, was a very cold autumn's day. The advancing Prussian right wing had to cover no more than 10,000 feet; yet, you felt more heated during the march than on a humid summer's day. Both armies saw the white of the enemies' eyes and one can easily imagine that the sight of so many murderous muzzles and the beginning fray caused the most heated motion in everybody; the faces of all officers and privates were glowing; and some, who shook my hand, convinced them that they were literally burning. An old grenadier said: 'Today, everything will depend on the question, who will be able to remain heated longer, us or the enemy. The French attack in heat, but soon get cool again. As soon as their heated fever attack is over, they fall victim to the cold like the feeble flies in autumn. We Prussians will stay heated until the French will have cooled down.' But the regiment of this grenadier did not participate in the actual fighting. It was the regiment von Leps, now von Manstein from Westphalia.[363] The French, who had initially advanced so heatedly, did not even dare to launch a single attack, but soon took flight. The battle started at three o'clock and came to an end before five o'clock. The most heated work of the cavalry lasted three quarters of an hour, the cannonade one and a half hours and the musket fire not 20 minutes; it seems unbelievable, yet, it is true, that a mere six [Prussian, K&SM] battalions opened fire at all …
>
> A similar emotion could also be detected on the day before, the 4 November 1757. Because from 7.00 am, when it was still dark, to 10.00 am, the army was drawn up in order of battle and so near the large French army, that both forces could have reached each other with small arms fire. Everybody eagerly awaited the order to attack at any moment. But the king gave the order to march off and many assured me, that these three hours of restless waiting had been far more heated,

---

[362] *Zedler's* 2 (1732), 1284.
[363] Otto Friedrich von Leps was actually Chef between 1735 and 1747. At the time of the Battle of Roßbach, the regiment's chef was Friedrich Ludwig von Kleist, who was killed in action at Breslau on 22 November 1757. Gieraths, *Die Kampfhandlungen*, 33. It is the Dominicus' regiment.

than some of the most heated days of battle. But the battlefields of Kolin and Zorndorf in June 1757 and August 1758 showed, how big the impact of heat was before the weather got cold.[364] Because then many corpses were found, which did not display any wounds, but the men had been suffocated by inner and outer heat alone.[365]

Küster's description of heat covers two semantic fields. First, the heat of the body described by Küster is caused by an adrenaline rush, which in its turn is triggered by stress and the fear of death.[366] This can even lead – in extreme cases – to physical collapse of the body and even death. Second, there is a discussion of the tremendous military usefulness of the body's heat, which Küster puts into the mouth of an 'old grenadier'.[367] The man repeats an eighteenth-century stereotype about the French, when he tells Küster that they become heated easily but also cool down very quickly.[368] If he had followed the common European eighteenth-century century tropes, he should have juxtaposed the French hot flush to the Prussian / German / British coolness.[369] But Küster's grenadier uses an interesting phrase and tells him, that the Prussians will in fact keep their heat longer and thus fight more effectively than the French. Here, heat becomes an emotion, and one that enables the soldiers to fight. This meaning of heat in Küster's text has much in common with Bräker's description, that he was 'drunken of rage and heat … not knowing scare and fear'.[370] Here, heat is an effective means of fighting the soldiers' fear.

Turning to the texts by officers and from military history, we can discern two contexts in which 'heat' is used. First, it is used to describe a fast and successful attack; 'liveliness' might be used as a synonym.[371] Second, too much heat can lead to tactical blunders and the unit's defeat, such as when they charge too rashly and are ambushed as a result.[372] Thus, heat was positive *as long as* it made the soldier fight and charge without making him lose control. If the latter occurred, the emotion had become counterproductive. While the heat of the common soldier was a double-edged sword,

---

[364] The formulation is strange in the German original too. Küster is referring to the heat during the summer months.
[365] Carl Daniel Küster, 'Von den Schlachttagen, als sogenannten heißen Tagen', in *Officier-Lesebuch*, vol. 2, 82–5.
[366] Dean, *Shook over Hell*, 54–5; McPherson, *Für die Freiheit sterben*, 531.
[367] This can be a means of making Küster's own observation sound more reliable. Yet the few mistakes in his account make it plausible that Küster really heard something the like from a veteran. If that is true, the man was a musketeer of the regiment no. 9. During the Battle of Roßbach, the regiment was positioned on the left flank of the first line. Counting from the left, it formed the seventh and eighth battalion of the first line. The grenadiers of the regiment did not take part in the battle (Duffy, *Frederick*, 360), but this does not mean that Küster invented the 'old grenadier', as he uses this term as a collective term for all Prussian infantrymen as well as for the real grenadiers. Küster, *Bruchstück*, 201, 39.
[368] Retzow, *Charakteristik*, vol. 1, 207; See also: Tempelhof, *Geschichte*, vol. 1, 225; Berenhorst, *Aus dem Nachlasse*, 134;
[369] Fleming, *Vollkommene Teutsche Soldat*, 40; Möbius, *Haß*, 142, 145.
[370] See p. 102.
[371] 'Journal des Feldzugs von 1758', in *Bellona*, vol. 12, 68; 'Anmerkungen', in *Bellona*, vol. 2, 76; 'Relation, in *Bellona*, vol. 7, 45 and 46.
[372] 'Fortsetzung', in *Bellona*, vol. 10, 4.

an officer had to stay cool all the time. Again, Küster gives a good example of this. He tells his readers about a Prussian lieutenant who was 'very experienced concerning tactics'. This man had dreamt that he had silently approached, attacked and captured an enemy post of 300 men in cold blood with no more than 30 Prussians. 'Doing this, he had shown so much caution and cold-blooded bravery that he would surely be unable to develop and carry out such an operational plan off the cuff when he was awake; because he was lacking, he had to admit, the cold blood necessary for it. His lively blood became so hot during an enemy attack that his thoughts came into his head too fast.' That is why he decides to practise cold-blooded – that is, composed – behaviour, because 'it is most necessary for a commanding officer to train himself to stay composed and alert in the turmoil of cannon and musket fire'. He must remain calm, in this way, during the siege of Olmütz, which also 'puts life into his men'. When the Austrians make a sortie, he keeps calm, has his men light two flares and orders them to form a line thirty-strong and 'beat two marches'[373] whereby they advanced 'very slowly and in good order and without firing'. Thus, the enemy was deceived and the lieutenant honoured by his commander.[374]

Pugnacity

The heat caused by stress could contribute to the soldiers being overwhelmed by the desire to fight. Again, Küster gives an insightful description and analysis of this emotion:

> *Batailliren* (doing battle)[375] is *Lust und Unlust* (pleasure and displeasure)[376] [at the same time], I often heard this saying from leaders and privates alike and I must confess, that initially, I thought it totally unbelievable how cruel scenes of murder in battle could be a source of pleasure. I thought, that there must be a distinctive driving force in the minds of the fighting men during battle. I made inquiries regarding this paradoxical state of mind in private conversations with officers and privates. But I only found a satisfactory explanation after I had been an eye-witness and participant of the afflictions and mortal dangers as well as of the pleasures of battle at Prague, Roßbach and Hochkirch. It is impossible for the soul to remain in a state of excessive abhorrence, painfulness and sadness without becoming totally inactive. That is why she looks for a ray of light in these moments of fearsome darkness by the pleasure given to her by the vision of victory. Even the strongest soul of a hero feels pain and sadness before and during the bloody fighting, which can only be surmounted by the powerful instinct of self-preservation and the delightful vision of victory. Without this counter-tension, doom or flight would be

---

[373] Thus, they pretend to belong to two different units.
[374] 'Ein Traum', in *Officier-Lesebuch*, vol. 2, 103–05.
[375] The most appropriate English translation for the French loanword *bataillieren* (from French *bataille* with the German ending *-en*: to do something) is 'doing battle' in the sense of fighting in a battle.
[376] The German word *Lust* (lust, pleasure) is used in the sources, but there is no similar sounding English equivalent to the early modern German *Unlust* (displeasure, non-fulfillment of one's lust). *Zedler's* 49 (1743), 1867–8.

unavoidable. But the hero fears shame more than danger and the probability of victory caused by brave fighting revives the entire soul.

Of course, these main feelings and also a host of different by-feelings like revenge etc. occur in so many modes as the ways of thinking of the combatants differ; and not all driving forces have an equal moral value.[377]

Some officers occasionally write about the soldiers looking forward to doing battle with an particularly detested enemy. This was especially true at the well-documented Battle of Zorndorf, against the Russians. Archenholz writes about the Prussian thirst for revenge: 'Never did an army feel more thirst after a blood-fight than the Prussian one at this time.'[378] Hülsen stated the same in a paraphrased version of Archenholz's statement.[379] Prittwitz, who is always honest about his own feelings, does not share this view of the days before Zorndorf:

> Since the departure from our winter quarters bordering on Swedish Pomerania, we had not been threatened by any danger, but now we came into a state similar to that before the Battle of Kolin, where everybody had to fear for his life as we were confronted with a mighty and numerous enemy we were about to fight.[380]

Frederick II, himself eager to annihilate the Russian forces, noted a similar mood amongst his troops when they were singing hymns while marching towards the Russian positions: 'My rascals are frightened ... because they sing psalms by Clement Marot.'[381] The contradiction between Archenholz and Hülsen on the one side and Prittwitz and the king on the other can be resolved in two ways. On the one hand, Archenholz and Hülsen might simply have invented the zeal of the Prussian troops, probably in an *ex post* attempt to explain the extremely violent destruction of the Russian left wing by the Prussian cavalry.[382] On the other hand, both sides might have been telling the truth about how they felt, and these emotions were not contradictory, but rather situated on different levels. An indication of this can be found in the diary entry by von Barsewisch concerning the Battle of Leuthen. He tells his readers about the army's mood after Frederick's speech to his generals before the battle, which was conveyed to the rest of the troops by the officers:

> As the major part of the army, which had been brought by his majesty from Saxony, had always been victorious against the Imperials [Austrians] and as we had just

---

[377] [C. D. Küster], 'Einige psychologische Erfahrungen über Vergnügen und Misvergnügen', in *Officier-Lesebuch*, vol. 2, 88–9.
[378] Archenholz, *Geschichte*, 156.
[379] Hülsen, *Unter Friedrich*, 86.
[380] Prittwitz, *Ich bin ein Preuße*, 87.
[381] Friedrich der Große, *Gespräche*, 231. Clement Marot (1496–1544) was the most famous French poet of the first half of the sixteenth century. He translated many Biblical psalms into French, and his translations of the psalms of David were at the core of the Genevan Psalter, which had also been translated into German. It is not clear whether Frederick genuinely recognized a psalm by Marot or merely wanted to show off and meant 'hymns'.
[382] Duffy, *Frederick*, 167, 169–71.

won so glorious a victory at Roßbach a mere three weeks ago, the whole army was more than willing to obey this order[383] and was prepared to defeat the enemy.[384]

We can imagine that even the privates seated around the campfires were *publicly* reassuring each other that they would fight with zeal to overcome the Austrians – as they had reassured each other that they would pay the Russians back for their cruel treatment of the civilian population around Küstrin – Barsewisch's *private* feelings during the night before the battle were rather different:

> For my part, I was troubled by a frightening dream, in which I was right among the Imperials and severely wounded so that my blood flowed out of my body and I feared to bleed myself to death. This fear woke me up and I was happy that it had not happened in reality, although I immediately told myself, that there was to be a battle on this day and that it boded no good for me.[385]

Barsewisch's description shows that the army's readiness to fight in the days before the battle must not be confused with 'fearlessness' or even joyfulness directly before combat or on the field of battle. That the army wanted to fight, and was probably even convinced that it would win,[386] is underlined by the low number of deserters, which was unusual before a major battle.[387] This kind of mood *could* lead to battle-lust but could also change and give way to a panic scare as described by Retzow, when the infantry of the Prussian left started to run away.[388] In his description of the initial charge of his regiment at the head of the army at Leuthen, Barsewisch shows how battle-lust could develop. As this is one of the most detailed descriptions of a unit's combat behaviour during the Seven Years' War, we want to present its translation at length.

Lieutenant von Barsewisch's description of his regiment's charge at Leuthen

As Barsewisch was the ensign carrying the colours of the colonel's company (*Leibkompanie*) of one of the regiments forming the vanguard, he was thus at the head of the advancing army; the king himself instructed him to march in the direction of the enemies' entrenchments.[389]

> As soon as 'go on' was ordered, I advanced directly towards the enemy entrenchment. The bell had just tolled half past twelve ... The enemy stood still and did not disturb us in our military order until we had come close to within 200 metres away

---

[383] In his speech, Frederick had told his generals that the Austrians were three times as strong as the Prussians.
[384] Barsewisch, *Kriegs-Erlebnisse*, 24.
[385] Ibid., 31.
[386] Warnery, *Feldzüge*, vol. 1, 224.
[387] 'Journal des Füselierregiments von Jung-Braunschweig', in *Sammlung*, vol. 2, 154.
[388] Retzow, *Charakteristik*, vol. 1, 250–1.
[389] Barsewisch, *Kriegs-Erlebnisse*, 32.

from them. It has to be remarked, that his Majesty sent an aide-de-camp several times, to order us to advance not that hastily but slowly. Our soldiers would have preferred to attack the enemy running at full speed, so that our lieutenant colonel von Bock and the other battalion commanders had enough to do to dissuade the troops from advancing too hastily, which had to be done partly by kindness and partly by force ... As we had come near the enemies' entrenchments and were 200 paces away from them, we came upon a small ditch lined by willows. Now, our commander shouted: 'Gunners, unlimber and open fire!' When our gunners were about to fire their guns, with which they could not have passed the ditch easily, anyway, the enemy started to greet us with seven cannon shots, and our gunners answered their fire immediately, so that we nearly opened our fire together with them. Their seven shots did considerable damage to us, as they were all aimed at the ditch. Their entrenchment was manned with Württemberg grenadiers, who had white coatings drawn over their shiny caps.[390] They began to fire their muskets together with their cannon. But their musketry had little effect, which was either due to the low quality of their cartridges or their taking aim too low. We answered this fire as soon as we had jumped over the ditch with a volley from our muskets and wounded many brave Württemberger. Our artillery had demolished two enemy cannon with their first round. Our stout-hearted soldiers had run out of patience by now and ran towards the enemy with the utmost bravery and lowered bayonets, so that the enemy could just fire one more volley until we were upon them. Their grenadiers fired bravely at us and had fallen on their knee behind their entrenchments and did not want to yield. But as our soldiers rushed at them with loud cries and lowered bayonets, they either had to yield or die. As they had now jumped up in order to yield and tried to get to safety by getting over the causeway behind their entrenchment, our men bode them farewell with their muskets [in such a devastating manner], that ten to twelve of them, officers, NCOs and privates, were shot dead and lay one on top of each other, at each entrance into the woods [behind the entrenchments and the causeway, K. & S.M.], where they had tried to escape. [Now the attacking regiments are supported by a battery of ten heavy guns,] so that the guns could reach the fleeing enemies even when they were stumbling into their second line of battle. Even there, they had not reached a safe place to settle and had to leave many more fatalities on their flight.

Meanwhile, we had taken the entire entrenchment and the causeway, which was in between us and the enemies' second line of battle. We had some minutes to reorder our storming soldiers, make them load their muskets and to get our field-pieces to our battalion. In order to get them men lingering behind the woods into the ranks again, I and the [ensign] von Unruh held our flying colours high into the air. The call "Lads, follow your colours" remined many a tardy soldier of his duty. When a considerable number had rallied around the colours and the remaining

---

[390] The army of the Duchy of Württemberg had Prussian-style uniforms and the grenadiers wore mitre caps with a brass shield. In order to avoid confusion with the Prussians, they wore a white covering over the top.

men had been kept from further plundering the enemy dead and been led though the wood, they were formed into files as orderly as possible in the face of the enemy. As soon as we had left the wood, we met the enemies' second line of battle, which was just 200 paces away from us and advancing against us. As our lines had been reordered, the officers commanded 'Fire! Fire!'. But the enemy immediately fired back as our fire had halted his advance. There, colours in hand, I fell down to earth like dead as a musket bullet had pierced the left side of my neck and had traversed my flesh next to my throat and the carotid artery[391] – Arteria carotis – and got stuck between my shoulder blades in my back. [Now, the Prussians outmanoeuvred the enemies' second line of battle and beat it and also routed the third enemy line. When Moritz von Anhalt-Dessau came up with reinforcements,] he cried out to our soldiers: 'Lads, you have enough honour! Go back to the second line of battle!' But our lads answered: 'We would be *Hundsfötter*[392] if we went back to the second line. Give us cartridges[393], give us cartridges!'[394]

Barsewisch's account is instructive in that it shows how the soldiers switch from fear to heat and then to a frenzied lust for combat, and how they interact with their officers during the attack. First, the soldiers' fear of the enemies' fire makes them advance too fast and they have to be held back by the officers. After a first volley by the entire battalion, which is fired from a short distance, they cannot be held back and start an intense attack, which drives the Württembergers out of their positions.[395] Then, during a lull in the fighting many soldiers try to plunder the dead and wounded. Later the men become even more heated as they defeat the second line of enemy troops. Their victory over the third line, as well as comparatively light losses,[396] arouse their bloodlust and lead to the frenzy described by Küster.

This desire for combat was quite rare amongst the infantry; indeed it was a phenomenon normally associated with the cavalry. After having beaten an enemy unit, the troopers could almost become drunk with their success and fight on, either following the fleeing enemy or attacking other units. Their elevated position, and the speed of their attacks, played a crucial role in such actions. The desire to spill enemy blood could actually become so contagious that even men who were not supposed to fight would ride into the fray. This happened to the regimental chaplain Balke of von

---

[391] The repetition of the name of the artery sounds strange in English, but its German name is not borrowed from Latin but a German word, *große Kopfader* in early modern and *Halsschlagader* in modern German.
[392] *Hundsfott / Hundsfut*. See p. 206.
[393] A clear indication that the men had run out of ammunition.
[394] Barsewisch, *Kriegs-Erlebnisse*, 32–7.
[395] It was recognized by the high command that ordered advances with shouldered muskets and without firing – such as those ordered by the king before Prague – were no longer possible. As Winterfeld wrote to the king in August 1757: 'We cannot get through with shouldered muskets and without shooting, because now our men rely too much on their 60 cartridges: you can surely make them fire volleys by the whole battalion, as soon as they reach the enemy. Thus, we confuse the enemy and our men near him more easily as they rely on shooting and are amused with it.' August von Janson, *Hans Karl von Winterfeld, des grossen Königs Generalstabschef* (Berlin: G. Stilke, 1913), 372.
[396] Christopher Duffy, *Friedrich der Große und seine Armee* (1974; Stuttgart: Motorbuch, 1978), 352.

Seydlitz's cuirassiers (No. 8), who 'forgot his chaplain's gown and took part in attacking the enemy'.[397]

Bloodlust was often the end result. The most common occurrence of this was a successful cavalry charge against enemy infantry, when the troopers pursued the panic-stricken foot-soldiers and cut them down without giving quarter. This merciless slaughter was caused by the psychological implications of a cavalry charge. During the charge, the troopers were more or less defenceless and easy targets for the enemies' muskets and cannon. If a horse fell, its rider could be killed or break his back. At the same time the adrenaline levels rose due to the speed of the charge, excitement, stress and the shouting of the troopers.[398] The charge was a game of nerves as horses were only rarely made to ride into the enemy infantry, and the attacking cavalry could only hope to make the infantry panic before any collision could take place.[399] But when the infantry broke and fled, the situation for the attacking cavalry changed in the twinkling of an eye. The threat was gone, and the trooper could use his elevated position to cut down those who had been shooting at him seconds before.[400] One of the rare situations when cavalry and infantry fought in a bloody melee occurred at Zorndorf.[401] Tempelhof gives a vivid description of the frenzy:

> It seemed as both parts had decided to give no quarter.[402] Ziehten's hussars cut their way through the encircling infantry several times and the cuirassiers seemed to draw renewed strength from butchering the enemy infantry.[403]

Here, the carnage was precipitated by the order to give no quarter and the impossibility for the Russians to flee. Behind all this were alleged violations of the customs of war. In the eyes of the king, the Russians had committed various atrocities against the civilian population while the Russians saw the Prussian order to give no quarter as a crime against their men. One other violation of the rules of war, and which led to bloodthirst on one side, was the refusal to surrender in a hopeless situation. As this meant an unnecessary loss of life, the perpetrators had forfeited their right to be taken prisoner and the anger of the victors could turn into a bloodthirsty slaughter.[404] A desire to kill the enemy could also emerge from rivalries between certain regiments and corresponding insults to the honour of the unit, which might trigger a desire for revenge.[405]

---

[397] 'Das Tagebuch des Feldpredigers Balke', ed. Emil Buxbaum, *Internationale Revue über die gesammten Armeen und Flotten* 3/4 (1885): 15.
[398] Warnery, *Bemerkungen*, 111.
[399] See: Duffy, *Frederick*, 64.
[400] Möbius and Möbius, *Rossbach*, 23.
[401] Duffy, *Frederick*, 169.
[402] In fact, the king had explicitly given the order to give no quarter to the Russians, whom he hated. The Russian soldiers were informed about this and answered by shouts of: 'We won't give quarter either!' Retzow, *Charakteristik*, vol. 1, 325; Warnery, *Feldzüge*, vol. 1, 260; Prittwitz, *Ich bin ein Preuße*, 93–4; Hülsen, *Unter Friedrich dem Großen*, 86.
[403] Tempelhof, *Geschichte*, vol. 2, 227.
[404] The massacre of the surrendering Prussians after the last and hopeless stand at Landshut (1760) is a gruesome example of this. Retzow, *Charakteristik*, vol. 2, 203.
[405] The massacre of French *carabiniers* during the Battle of Krefeld (23 June 1758), due to a rivalry between them and the Prussian dragoons. Tempelhof, *Geschichte*, vol. 2, 120.

Barsewisch's account of the initial stages of the Battle of Leuthen has already shown that the soldiers' emotions were by no means numbed by drill but an essential factor in combat and one that every commander had to take into account. We will now have a look at the Battle of Prague and the Little War to further investigate the role of the privates and NCOs in combat.

Prague and the 'Little War': Successfully formed instincts?

The following paragraph will look at the behaviour of the soldiers in combat. We will investigate how training, orders and the men's own perceptions and feelings interacted.

The Battle of Prague

The Battle of Prague offers many insights as it is well documented and most men fighting in it had been carefully drilled before the Seven Years' War. We also know that Frederick II had given the explicit order to advance with shouldered muskets and lowered bayonets in order to drive the Austrians off their positions. Thus, we have a clear picture of the high command's expectations and can consider the soldiers' compliance or non-compliance. Concerning the overall course of the battle, we followed the research of Maximilian von Hoen, whose criticisms of the General Staff's other detailed account have been proved correct. He also had more sources to draw on, such as the 1787 survey of Austrian officers and privates who had survived the battle.[406] A collection of helpful maps can be found on www.kronoskaf.com.[407]

The Battle of Prague[408] (6 May 1757) was the largest – and one of the bloodiest – battles of the Seven Years' War. The Prussian army comprised 47,000 infantrymen and 17,000 horsemen, totalling about 64,000 soldiers. The Austrians had only slightly less men[409] and were entrenched on the hills in front of the city 'like on the battlements of the Temple at Hierosolyma'.[410] The Prussian high command considered an attack on the right Austrian wing the only promising way of driving the Austrians from their positions. Thus, the Prussian left tried to outflank the Austrian right. The king's page von Puttlitz gives an account about Frederick's tactical directives just before the battle:

> The king had told the officers that they would lose their honour and reputation if they permitted the soldiers to open fire and he had spoken of [dishonourable] dismissal, if any one of them should be found guilty of tolerating this; instead,

---

[406] Hoen, *Die Schlacht bei Prag*, 2, 198.
[407] http://www.kronoskaf.com/syw/index.php?title=1757-05-06_-_Battle_of_Prague (accessed 7 November 2018). As the maps follow the General Staff's account, there are minor inaccuracies, but the maps give the best overview to be found online.
[408] Maximilian Ritter von Hoen, Die Schlacht bei Prag am 6. Mai 1757, *Streffleurs Militärische Zeitschrift* 1, no. 2 (1909): 197–234 and no. 3 (1909): 377–416; *Der Siebenjährige Krieg*, ed. Großer Generalstab, vol. 2 (Berlin: Mittler, 1901), 120–47; Duffy, *Frederick*, 116–22.
[409] *Der Siebenjährige Krieg*, vol. 2, 127.
[410] Berenhorst, *Betrachtungen*, 94. Hierosolyma: Jerusalem.

everybody was to advance up to 150 paces from the enemy with shouldered muskets, then, bayonets lowered and push into the enemy with the bayonet and drive them off, then open fire and the cavalry cut them down!⁴¹¹

The first Prussian infantry attack was carried out by fourteen battalions on the left wing. After the Prussian outflanking manoeuvre had been accomplished, the commander of the left wing, Count von Schwerin, had to move quickly because the Austrians had started to move troops to their right in order to repel the Prussian attack. Thus, he gave the order to wheel into line formation and prepare for the charge. Unfortunately, he mistook some drained carp ponds for meadows; his men got into difficulty and had to form their lines under Austrian fire. Even worse, the main body of the Prussian artillery were trapped in Unter-Poczernitz and only a few artillery pieces were able to support the attack. They were no match for the well-positioned Austrian batteries. The advancing Prussian infantry showed the same desire to get into the killing zone as quickly as possible, just as their comrades at Leuthen would some months later:

> [Schwerin and Winterfeld had ordered] that the infantry spare their fire and push into the enemy with lowered bayonets. Executing this order as well as trying to get out of the enemies' cannonade, the infantry advanced at too fast a pace. Therefore, and because of the unfavourable terrain, they were not able to keep their lines in the most accurate order.⁴¹²

Hence, the Prussian battalions were not able to form a coherent line; some of them lagged behind to the right, while others were directly behind the battalions that ought to have been next to them. That is why the Austrians thought they had been attacked by two Prussian lines of battle.⁴¹³ The Prussian troops showed the heat expected by the king in his deliberations about the charge with cold steel⁴¹⁴ and advanced as fast as possible. While they were doing this, the enemy's heavy guns fired a hailstorm of artillery fire and Austrian reinforcements arrived at the scene. The ensuing situation was judged in a completely different way by the commanding general, von Winterfeld, on the one hand, and by his grenadiers on the other hand. Winterfeld thought that the Austrian reinforcements' manoeuvres to form a coherent line were the first signs of the

---

⁴¹¹ 'Aus den Erinnerungen eines Leibpagen des Großen Königs (Puttlitz)', ed. Curt Jany, *Hohenzollernjahrbuch* 16 (1912), 78. Berenhorst, who fought in the Alt-Anhalt Regiment in the battle, confirms this view (Berenhorst, *Betrachtungen*, 115), as does Tempelhof (*Geschichte*, vol. 1, 152). Warnery and Retzow followed Tempelhof: Warnery, *Feldzüge*, vol. 1, 98; Retzow, *Charakteristik*, vol. 1, 100. The General Staff made Schwerin responsible for the order: *Der Siebenjährige Krieg*, vol. 2, 132. As the General Staff obviously tried to shift blame away from the king, they followed Gaudi (Friedrich Wilhelm Ernst von Gaudi, *Abschriften des Journals vom 7 jährigen Kriege von von Gaudi für 1757*, vol. 1 (1836: Manuscript), 76), who wrote about a corresponding order from Schwerin and Winterfeld. Actually, there is no contradiction between the versions, as a direct order by the king *had* been transmitted to all officers and Schwerin and Winderfeld also deemed it sensible to attack as quickly as possible in order to drive off the Austrians before their reinforcements arrived.
⁴¹² Gaudi, *Journal 1757*, vol. 1, 76.
⁴¹³ Hoen, *Die Schlacht bei Prag*, vol. 3, 387.
⁴¹⁴ See pp. 48–50.

enemy's wavering and potential retreat.[415] As a result, he tried to urge his men on. But losses were also mounting amongst the generals encouraging their men go on. Fouqué and Kurssell were seriously injured and some time later Winterfeld got a bullet through the neck. The grenadiers took a more realistic tack. They had already felt the 'heat' of the Austrians' cannonade. When they were within 200 paces of the enemy's positions, the Austrians fired their muskets and light artillery accompanying the infantry battalions. The intensity of the fire and the attendant number of wounded or dead prompted the Prussian soldiers to abandon their bayonet charge; they opened fire in order to minimize the threat posed by the Austrian bullets. The officers' attempts to drag them forward only made things worse:

> The battalions began to crowd around their colours, lost firepower due to this and offered massive targets to the enemy and were shot up by the artillery.[416]

The end of this first Prussian attack is described by Gaudi:

> As our infantry's order was not the best while the enemy held his position in well-ordered ranks, our fire was delivered standing and without our men gaining ground. And as we suffered a lot, especially by the enemy's canister fire, and as the Fouqué Regiment came upon a battery of 14 cannon and lost very many men due to this fire. This regiment gave way first and this was the signal for the regiment von Schwerin as well as the grenadier battalions Oestereich, Waldow, Möllendorf, Kahlden, Plötz and Burgsdorff, which formed the left wing of the infantry, turned their backs on the enemy and went back scattered.[417]

The situation had been exacerbated by Catholic recruits to the Prussian Fouqué Regiment changing sides in the midst of combat and opening fire on their former comrades.[418]

The flight developed into a panic scare. Winterfeld gives a vivid description of the moments after he was injured, and the flight of the Prussian infantry:

> When life was coming back to me after a few minutes, and I lifted my head up, I could not see any of our men around or next to me, but everybody was running for their lives and retreating. The enemies' grenadiers were some 80 paces in front of me but halted and did not dare to follow [our men]. I picked myself up as well as my weariness allowed me to do, and caught up with our confused lump, but neither pleas nor threats could make a single man turn his face to the enemy or stop running away.[419]

---

[415] Hans Karl von Winterfeld, 'Relation von der Bataille bei Prag', in Janson, *Hans Karl von Winterfeld*, 436.
[416] Hoen, *Die Schlacht bei Prag*, vol. 3, 390.
[417] Gaudi, *Journal 1757*, vol. 1, 76–7.
[418] Duffy, *Frederick*, 117.
[419] Winterfeld, *Relation*, 436.

After some time, the men did stop and formed ranks again. Field Marshal Schwerin tried to lead his regiment forward once more, seizing one of its colours and riding ahead. After a few metres' progress, he was hit by five canister bullets and fell dead from his horse. His men ran away. They had to be stopped by some regiments of hussars and forced back into some semblance of order.[420]

The Austrians had moved forward[421] and occupied a line north of Sterbohol. They were now facing the second battle line of the Prussian left wing and the Prussian artillery, which had now arrived. A prolonged fire-fight ensued. The Austrians suffered from a shortage of ammunition,[422] while fresh Prussian regiments under the command of Lieutenant-General von Bevern appeared on the their right flank. Led by Colonel von Hertzberg, the first battalion of the Darmstadt Regiment – and shortly thereafter the Prince of Prussia Regiment – began to fire at them with canister bullets from their battalion-pieces and their muskets. This manoeuvre forced the Austrians to retreat.[423] Musketeer Dominicus was a member of the infantry's von Kleist Regiment (No. 9). This unit was in the second line of those regiments that followed Herzberg's battalion and took part in the bitter struggle for the Austrian rear positions following the retreat from the line north of Sterbohol.[424] Dominicus writes about his experience at Prague:

> After we had run[425] [for about five minutes], the Austrians and us opened fire with the muskets,[426] we drove them off the first mountain, where we captured a cannon. There were still tents and kettles with soup on the fire at the foot of the hill. Still further at the bottom of the ravine between the hills, there was a village and it was burning. We ran past above the village, where they had posted themselves [in such a way] that we were just able to hit their heads. We drove them off. On this mountain, my musket's muzzle was shot off, [but I] did not recognize this until I wanted to reload. [This] Went[427] on for some time, there lay a soldier, [who] had his [musket] in his arms and was dead; I took it. Meanwhile we had reached the third mountain, where we were soundly greeted with canister from six cannon, there we had to wheel to the right.[428] It was like they had pelted us with peas, [and they] shot

---

[420] *Der Siebenjährige Krieg*, vol. 2, 133.
[421] Hoen, *Die Schlacht bei Prag*, vol. 3, 389–90.
[422] Ibid., 392–3.
[423] Ibid., 396–7.
[424] Kerler, the editor of Dominicus' diary, errs when he claims that Dominicus and his regiment had been involved in the first attack of the Prussian infantry. *Tagebuch des Musketiers Dominicus*, 16, fn. 3 and 4 and 17, fn. 1. Modern research has shown that his regiment had not been deployed here (Duffy, *Frederick*, 351.). If that had been the case, Dominicus would have written a most boastful fairytale much removed from his down-to-earth descriptions of the Battles of Kay and Kunersdorf.
[425] Most probably Dominicus means that they had advanced quickly.
[426] The soldiers and officers follow the kind of projectiles shot at them carefully: first roundshot, then canister from the cannon and in the end musketry. This is also a way of measuring the distance to the enemy as well as calculating the risk of being killed or severely wounded. Roundshot is deadly but does not hit very many men. Canister from a distance causes minor wounds and canister and musketry from 80 metres and below can inflict fatal injuries.
[427] Dominicus leaves out the personal pronoun 'I' several times.
[428] 'Wheel to the right' is the euphemism for 'retreat' or 'flee'.

through my camisole[429] and knapsack. When we went back, the second line of battle arrived, who drove them back soon. By that time, they departed. Then we shouted *Victoria*.[430]

After the defeat of the Austrian right wing, the Prussians had to drive their enemies off one elevated position after the other until the entire Austrian army fled into Prague.[431]

The operations of the Alt-Anhalt Regiment (No. 3) are particularly well-documented. Three eye-witness accounts in addition to that of Berenhorst have survived:

1. Ensign von Lemcke was with the first battalion.[432]
2. The anonymous musketeer who describes his experience of the battle most probably also served in this battalion.[433]
3. Sergeant Liebler wrote two letters about his role in the battle to his family. He was with the third battalion of the regiment.[434]

Figure 2.1 Charge of the third battalion of the Alt-Anhalt Regiment at the Battle of Prague. © Jorge M. Corada.

---

[429] Waistcoat, vest.
[430] Literally: 'There was Victoria.' *Victoria!* was the German speaking armies' victory cry during the seventeenth and eighteenth centuries.
[431] Duffy, *Frederick*, 119, 348–9.
[432] Lemcke was near Colonel von Manstein when the latter was killed. (Lemcke, *Kriegs- und Friedensbilder*, 28.) Manstein was with the first battalion when he was mortally wounded. (Seyfarth, *Geschichte des Infanterie-Regiments von Anhalt-Bernburg*, 205).
[433] His description of the first attack of the battalion matches Lemcke's. Schreiben eines Musketiers des Regiments Anhalt zu Fuß 1757, in *Briefe*, 51–2.
[434] Schreiben des Feldwebels Liebler, 7 May 1757, in *Briefe*, 48.

'The second battalion could not get at the enemy due to a burning village and lost very few men.'[435]

The regiment took part in the last stage of the battle, when it had to drive the Austrian defenders off their elevated positions east of Hrdlorez and Maleschitz.[436] The first assault of the regiment is related by the anonymous musketeer:

> Finally, we were also going to feel the heat of the cannonade, as fate led us in front of a high mountain, which was planted with many cannons, which cruelly fired at us with grapeshot. Notwithstanding this, we advanced against the enemy batteries with fixed bayonets, and although our battalion was almost incapable of standing and many were forced to retreat, another battalion came to relieve us, and this attack made the enemy flee ignominiously and abandon their cannon.[437]

Lemcke's description of the attack reads thus:

> Now, an aide-de-camp of the king appeared with the order, that our battalion was to scale a high mountain to our right, from where the enemies were firing at our right flank and dislodge them from there. Whereupon we started to climb the mountain and had already come out of the shooting sector of their cannon[438] without firing a shot, when we were ordered to wheel to the right[439] and a battalion of grenadiers, which had been behind us, had the honour to conquer this mountain without much effort. This expedition had cost us half of our battalion's strength.[440]

Sergeant Liebler gives a detailed description of the first attack of the third battalion of the Alt-Anhalt Regiment:

> Now it was the turn of our battalion. We came upon one of the highest elevations, where they greeted us with many cannons. Notwithstanding, we had to go on and

---

[435] Seyfarth, *Geschichte des Infanterie-Regiments von Anhalt-Bernburg*, 52.

[436] The General Staff claimed that it took part in a major Prussian offensive against the Austrian divisions of Wied and Baden-Durlach south of Kej. (*Der Siebenjährige Krieg*, vol. 2, 139.) This view had already been refuted by von Hoen. (Hoen, *Die Schlacht bei Prag*, vol. 3, 405, fn *.) The General Staff (*Der Siebenjährige Krieg*, vol. 2, 139.) misinterprets a passage by the anonymous musketeer, when he states that many men were lost due to the order to attack with cold steel. (Schreiben eines Musketiers des Regiments Anhalt zu Fuß 1757, in *Briefe*, 51.) The musketeer explicitly meant other Prussian units and not his own. Lemcke relates that a dispersed battalion of fusiliers caused disorder in the third battalion, which was marching in front of his unit. But there were no units wearing mitrecaps (which made them distinguishable as fusiliers or grenadiers) in the vicinity. (Jany, *Geschichte der Preußischen Armee*, vol. II, 400 and fn. 46–9 on 400. Duffy, *Frederick*, 351.) Liebler writes about the tents of Austrian cavalry, he had been passing (Schreiben des Feldwebels Liebler, in *Briefe*, 47), but there were no cavalry tents near Kej.

[437] Schreiben eines Musketiers des Regiments Anhalt zu Fuß 1757, in *Briefe*, 51–2.

[438] Due to the height of the mountain, and to the impossibility of lowering the guns beyond a certain point, there was a blind angle in front of the guns that covered a considerable distance.

[439] Retreat.

[440] Lemcke, *Kriegs- und Friedensbilder*, 27.

advance until we were able to shoot with small arms, because our cannon had not been able to follow us up the mountain.[441] Here was just a pure hailstorm of bullets, one after the other was cut down and in the end, we had to retire in the greatest disorder. Thus, another regiment [marching at] our side had to advance towards this position, and I went forward again, too, together with a number of brave soldiers and advanced to the foot of the mountain. Alas, again to no avail; everybody was dispersed by the uncountable cannon shots and we also retired. Here, I found two of the colours of our battalion[442] and made a soldier carry them away.[443] Now, a battalion of grenadiers had to go forward, together with which I was again driven away on the orders of General von Ingersleben[444] and had to follow into the grapeshot and here I learned what it meant 'that who sits under the shield of the Lord, etc.'[445] Because a cannister ball hit my breastbone, [it] made me think that I would have to die. But the bullet had not penetrated [my breastbone], [thus] I went back a few steps and stood still in this hail of bullets until the grenadiers also had to retreat from this [enemy] battery[446] (this was only one battery). Now, our first battalion[447] came up from the low terrain [in front of the battery] and it was led by Prince Henry[448] in person in the face of the most violent fire. I was not able to breathe. Hence, I stood still and saw how it[449] had to leave this mountain.[450]

The infantry's use of bayonet (1st battalion Alt-Anhalt) as well as musket (3rd battalion Alt-Anhalt and Dominicus' Jung-Kleist Regiment (No. 9) show that there was neither a Prussian doctrine of always attacking with cold steel and without firing, internalized by all soldiers, nor an unquestioned observance of the king's orders to

---

[441] This means that not even the small Prussian three- and six-pounder regimental pieces could be used, while the Austrians were able to use their regimental and their heavy twelve-pounders with deadly effect.
[442] Every infantry battalion had five colours from the five companies forming the battalion.
[443] Behind the lines, because while on the field, lying on the ground, they risked being taken prisoner. Liebler also shows that he does not use the danger of the colours being captured as a pretext for evading further combat. Rescuing the colours was in itself an honourable act, and worth mentioning in regimental histories. Zielsdorf, *Erinnerungskulturen*, 72.
[444] Johann Ludwig von Ingersleben (1703–57). Commander of the Guard (Rgt. 15/I) and the riflemen (*Jäger*). He was wounded during the battle. He was close to Prince Henry of Prussia, which might explain why he was in the vicinity of Liebler's regiment (Rgt. 3), as this was part of Prince Henry's brigade. Anton Balthasar König, Johann Ludwig von Ingersleben, in *Biographisches Lexikon aller Helden und Militairpersonen, welche sich in Preußischen Diensten berühmt gemacht haben*, vol. 2 (Berlin: Arnold Wever, 1789), 207–09.
[445] Psalm 91.1. The King James Bible reads: 'He that dwelleth in the secret place of the most High shall abide under the shadow of the Almighty.' The German translation by Martin Luther, known by Liebler, uses the words '*wer unter dem Schirm des Höchsten sitzet*', which stresses the shielding aspect but does not extend to any hiding place.
[446] A number of cannons.
[447] Liebler's regiment (Anhalt, No. 3) had three battalions, while most infantry regiments had only two.
[448] Prince Henry of Prussia, younger brother of Frederick the Great and one of his best generals. He was Liebler's brigade commander.
[449] The Austrian battery.
[450] Schreiben des Feldwebels Liebler, in *Briefe*, 47.

attack without firing.[451] Quite the contrary: in spite of the king's threats to ignominiously cashier every officer who allowed his men to fire, units *did* use their muskets and shot at the enemy. What can be seen is a flexible use of different tactics that took into account the soldiers' emotions. The Prussians even used stratagems that went against the customs of war that had nothing to do with the most honourable charge with cold steel. The above-mentioned[452] defection of parts of the Silesian-Prussian Fouqué Regiment to the Austrians during the initial Prussian assault on the Austrian right, had obviously convinced the Austrians that there were more Catholic recruits in Prussian regiments who were eager to fight for the Catholic Empress-Queen rather than for the detested Frederick. Some shrewd Prussian battalion commanders made good use of this belief when attacking an Austrian redoubt (temporary fortification) between the ponds of Kej and Hlaupetin. An Austrian eye-witness gave the following account of the event:

> During this action, something special happened. Before attacking, an enemy battalion had advanced towards us with colours and muskets shouldered upside down[453] and the officers had signalled amity by waving their handkerchiefs. For this reason, it was forbidden to fire cannon as well as muskets, as this battalion was taken for [Prussian] deserters [changing to our side]. They advanced up to the foot of the hill close to a causeway. To their right was a small mill and to their left a small wood, where a commando of Croats had posted itself. As soon, as the enemy battalion had passed the causeway, they turned around their muskets and drove the Croats back by their fire.[454]

The Prussian tricking of their well-entrenched Austrian opponents hints at the real problem at Prague and shows that there was no dysfunctional royal doctrine followed by blindly obedient officers and drill-numbed privates. The tactical situation and the terrain were simply not favourable for the Prussians, as they had to attack uphill. In such a situation, a bayonet charge was also favoured by other experts,[455] as uphill fire was never as effective as downhill fire. Yet the Prussians met conditions that favoured the use of muskets and in both cases – attack with cold steel and by fire – the soldiers' emotions and assessments played a crucial role. And not only in the sense that the officers had to take into account their mood and actions, but also in the more obvious sense that the soldiers had the final say in the matter. Again we must stress that when

---

[451] The General Staff even wrote of a deep-rooted belief, shared by the soldiers, that nobody could withstand their bayonet charges. *Der Siebenjährige Krieg*, vol. 2, 139. Many other authors agree that the terrible Prussian losses at Prague were caused by Frederick's bayonet-doctrine: Hoen, *Die Schlacht bei Prag*, vol. 3, 408; Warnery, *Feldzüge*, vol. 1, 100; Archenholz, *Geschichte*, 56; Jany, *Geschichte*, vol. 2, 404. Duffy, *Frederick*, 117; Nosworthy, *Anatomy*, 145.

[452] See p. 117.

[453] The acknowledged sign for surrendering.

[454] Hoen, *Die Schlacht bei Prag*, vol. 3, 403–04.

[455] Johann Gottlieb Tielke, 'Von dem Angriff und Vertheidigung der unverschanzten Berge und Anhöhen', in Ibid., *Beyträge zur Kriegs-Kunst und Geschichte des Krieges von 1756 bis 1763 mit Plans und Charten*, vol. 1 (Freyberg: Barthelische Schriften, 1775), S. 61.

their final word (as it were) had been to run away, there is no indication, that they were punished for cowardice. The king seems to have known that they had been right, and that standing firm would have meant death.

A short survey of tactics used in other battles hints at the same direction. Frederick's dispatches before the Battle of Kolin (18 June 1757) do not mention any orders for the tactics to be used at battalion level.[456] During the battle, the Prussian battalions used a variety of tactics:[457] the von Bevern Regiment (No. 7) fired several short-range volleys and later on used platoon fire to get rid of Austrian cavalry.[458] Before the vanguard's attack at Leuthen, Frederick again gave a direct order to attack with the bayonet. But, as we have seen from Barsewisch's account of the battle, the actual advance was a complex mixture of the king's orders, the battalion-commanders' attempts to maintain a well-ordered line of battle, and the soldiers' different actions to save their lives and gain honour. To be sure, they did fire a battalion-volley contrary to the king's orders. But the monarch did not mind at all and the regiment was showered with fourteen medals *pour le mérite* for the officers and 1,500 *Reichsthaler* for the surviving privates.[459] The king's later criticism of attacking with cold steel, formulated in 1758, did not make his subordinates stop using it. On 9 October 1759, General Wunsch carried out a bayonet charge of the entire line of battle against a far superior Austrian force at Zinna, near Torgau.[460] We have already mentioned the charge of the Alt-Anhalt Regiment (No. 3) during the Battle of Liegnitz (15 August 1760). Infuriated by the loss of their honour during the siege of Dresden, the battalion advanced against Austrian cavalry, fired a devastating volley and then charged the enemy's cavalry with cold steel, dispersing the Austrian cavalry.[461] Four Prussian battalions stormed an enemy circle of waggons with bayonets lowered and without firing a single shot on 15 September 1761.[462] Thus, Prussian battalions attacked with cold steel,[463] but it was more common for them to advance up to the lethal distance of their muskets and then fire one or more battalion-volleys.[464] Other formations, like the

---

[456] Warnery, *Feldzüge*, vol. 1, 137; Retzow, *Charakteristik*, vol. 1, 126; Max Duncker, 'Die Schlacht von Kollin', in Ibid., *Aus der Zeit Friedrichs des Großen und Friedrich Wilhelms III. Abhandlungen zur preußischen Geschichte* (Leipzig: Duncker und Humblot, 1876), 47–109.

[457] Maximilian Ritter von Hoen, 'Die Schlacht bei Kolin am 18. Juni 1757', *StreffleursMilitärische Zeitschrift* 1, vol. 4 (1911): 595. Prittwitz, *Ich bin ein Preuße*, 60.

[458] Prittwitz, *Ich bin ein Preuße*, 57–9.

[459] Barsewisch, *Kriegs-Erlebnisse*, 41.

[460] Warnery, *Feldzüge*, vol. 2, 29–35; Tagebuch eines Offiziers, in *Sammlung*, vol. 1, 568; Tagebuch von den Feldzügen der Grenadierkompagnien, in *Sammlung*, vol. 4, 181. Wunsch is said to have beaten the 12,000 Austrians commanded by St. André with a mere 3,500 to 5,000 Prussians. He formed only one line of battle and the battalions were ordered only two ranks deep in order not to be outflanked. http://www.kronoskaf.com/syw/index.php?title=1759-09-08_-_Combat_of_Zinna (accessed 08 November 2018).

[461] http://www.kronoskaf.com/syw/index.php?title=1760-08-15_-_Battle_of_Liegnitz (accessed 08 November 2018).

[462] Tagebuch der Unternehmungen des General-Lieutenants Dubislav Friedrich von Platen, in *Sammlung*, vol. 3, 7–8.

[463] Der Siebenjährige Krieg, vol. 3, 73–5; Retzow, *Charakteristik*, vol. 1, 62–3; Extrakt Schreibens von Herrn Kistenmacher, in *Briefe*, 10.

[464] Prittwitz, *Ich bin ein Preuße*, 56–7.

square, were also used,[465] and Prussian line infantry could also be seen fighting in open order.[466]

The Little War

Besides line regiments, European eighteenth-century armies included light cavalry and infantry. These forces had to cover the main armies' operations, collect information about the enemy, hinder him from foraging and secure the supply routes of their own forces. This included a multitude of combat operations, ranging from small skirmishes to small scale raids.[467] Most historians agree that the Prussian regulars, especially the infantry, had been of little use in what is known in German as the Little War, as they were trained only to fight in the line of battle in close order formations and had to be monitored by their officers to prevent desertion.[468] Frank Wernitz summarized this position in his in-depth study of the Prussian light free-regiments:

> The preconditions [for raising light Prussian infantry formations] were extremely disadvantageous. Thus, the kingdom was totally lacking an ethnic group, which was as used to the Little War as the 'borderers' [German *Grenzer*: light infantry from the Habsburg regions bordering the Ottoman Empire, also called Croats or Pandurs.] or [Russian] Cossacks. Training some regular regiments to fight as *chasseurs* was unthinkable. Apart from the danger of mass desertions, the officer corps of the time would have been unable to meet demands, which literally turned all military views and dogmas upside down.[469]

First, we should look at the 'views and dogmas' concerning the Little War by reviewing the positions of Frederick II. In his *Generalprincipien* from 1748,[470] he describes the light troops of the Austrians, 'which surround their army like fog and let

---

[465] Hoen, *Die Schlacht bei Kolin*, vol. 5, 794–5, fn. *); Retzow, *Charakteristik*, vol. 2, 202–03; Fortsetzung des im ersten Theil abgebrochenen Tagebuchs, in *Sammlung*, vol. 2, 45; Journal von der Expedition des Generallieutenants von Platen, in *Sammlung*, vol. 3, 250; Geschichte des Freyregiments von Hard, in *Sammlung*, vol. 5, 225–7; Geschichte und Feldzüge des Dragonerregiments von Borke, in *Sammlung*, vol. 5, 385–7; Berichtigungen über die Journals der Collberger Campagne, in *Sammlung*, vol. 5, 487; Warnery, *Feldzüge*, vol. 2, 5; Journal des Feldzugs von 1758, in *Bellona*, vol. 12, 95; Journal des Feldzugs von 1759, in *Bellona*, vol. 16, 60.; Tagebuch eines Kön. Preußischen Officiers, in *Bellona*, vol. 1, 74; *Tagebuch des Musketiers Dominicus*, 23.

[466] Ferdinand von Braunschweig, 'Réflexions et anecdotes vraies, mais hardies sur la campagne de 1756', in *Urkundliche Beiträge und Forschungen zur Geschichte des Preußischen Heeres*, vol. 4 (Berlin: Mittler, 1902), 31; *Der Siebenjährige Krieg*, vol. 1, 278.

[467] Tagebuch des Husarenregiments von Belling, in *Sammlung*, vol. 3, 286–376; Martin Rink, 'Der kleine Krieg. Entwicklungen und Trends asymmetrischer Gewalt 1740 bis 1815', *Militärgeschichtliche Zeitschrift* 65 (2006): 355–88.

[468] Rink, *Der Kleine Krieg*, 375; Duffy, *Friedrich der Große und seine Armee*, 80; Kunisch, *Der Kleine Krieg*, IX; Hans Bleckwenn, *Altpreußische Uniformen 1753–1786* (Dortmund: Harenberg, 1981), 121.

[469] Frank Wernitz, *Die preußischen Freitruppen im Siebenjährigen Krieg 1756–1763. Entstehung – Einsatz – Wirkung* (Wölfersheim-Berstadt: Podzun-Pallas, 1994), 12.

[470] General Principles of War concerning the Tactics and Discipline of the Prussian Troops. Frederick II, 'Generalprincipien des Krieges in Anwendung auf die Taktik und auf die Disciplin der preussischen Truppen', in *Ausgewählte kriegswissenschaftliche Schriften Friedrichs des Großen*, ed. Heinrich Merkens (Jena: Costenoble, 1876), 1–120.

no one through without searching him'.⁴⁷¹ Below, he writes under the headline 'Precautionary measures to be applied against Hussars [light cavalry] and Pandurs [light infantry] when retreating':

> Hussars and Pandurs are only feared by those, who do not know them ... Our troops do not have to fear that they stage any serious attacks; but as their manner of harassing [our men] does impede the march of the troops and people are killed by them, who are lost most unnecessarily, I will explain the best way of to keep them away. If you retreat on plains, you chase off the Hussars by firing some cannon shots at them and the Pandurs by ordering your hussars or dragoons to charge them, as they are very afraid of them.⁴⁷²

How the Prussian light troops should act against the Hussars and Pandurs is explained by the monarch in another paragraph:

> Our manner of taking a position held by their light troops is to force it; as their method of fighting consists in dispersing their men, they cannot hold out against regular troops. You must not engage in a fire-fight with them; you just cover the flanks of the corps, which marches against them, and when you attack them with resolution, you chase them wherever you want. Our dragoons and hussars attack them in good order, sabre in hand. They cannot stand attacks like these; they were always beaten, regardless of their numbers, which were always favourable to them.⁴⁷³

According to Frederick, the Prussians' problems concerning the Little War were rooted in the number of the light troops and the related costs. The Austrian army's 'borderers' offered a pool of recruits who could be used in the Little War. Moreover, their life in the border regions provided a good part of the training necessary for skirmishing and commando actions.⁴⁷⁴ Thus, the problem was not the Prussian infantry's lack of training or tactical deficiencies, but that it was more expensive than the Austrian light troops. Pandurs and Croats had not received a training that came anywhere close to that of the Prussian line infantry. Replacing an injured Prussian soldier was much more expensive than drafting in one of Maria Theresa's borderers.

The Prussian army mainly relied on its hussars during the Little War.⁴⁷⁵ During the Seven Years' War they became all-rounders capable of every kind of task from scouting to vanguard duties.⁴⁷⁶ Dragoons could play a similar role. They could be used to back

---

⁴⁷¹ Frederick II, *Generalprincipien*, 58.
⁴⁷² Ibid., 71–2.
⁴⁷³ Ibid., 73.
⁴⁷⁴ Jacob de Cogniazzo, *Geständnisse eines östreichischen Veterans in politisch-militarischer (!) Hinsicht auf die interessantesten Verhältnisse zwischen Oestreich und Preußen, während der Regierung des Großen Königs der Preußen Friedrichs des Zweyten mit historischen Anmerkungen gewidmet den königlich-preußischen Veteranen von dem Verfasser des freymüthigen Beytrags zur Geschichte des östreichischen Militär-Dienstes*, vol. 3 (Breslau: Gottlieb Löwe, 1790), 256–7.
⁴⁷⁵ Rink, *Der Kleine Krieg*, 363.
⁴⁷⁶ Tagebuch des Husarenregiments von Belling, in *Sammlung*, vol. 3, 286–376.

up the hussars by charging ordered enemy cavalry or forming a line of retreat. They were also used like the hussars.[477] On certain occasions, cuirassiers were used to support the hussars.[478]

The Prussian infantry's role in the Little War is of special importance for our investigation. The so-called free-regiments were supposed to be the backbone of the infantry in the Little War. But although they were constantly increased in number during the war, from four to fourteen, they were never able to reach the numbers of the Austrian or Russian light troops. Nevertheless, they played a significant role in the last major battle of the war at Freiberg in Saxony (29 October 1762).[479] Frederick II called them *execrables Geschmeiß* (detestable scum).[480] Even if their balance sheet was more favourable than the king's insult might suggest, they were by no means the backbone of Prussia's Little War effort.[481] The von Hardt Free Regiment took part in eighty-four missions during the war,[482] twice as many as the majority of regular infantry regiments, but most free regiments did not take part in more actions than the regulars.

It was the musketeers, fusiliers and above all the grenadiers who fought Frederick's skirmishes and commando actions. That they were by no means limited to fighting large-scale battles, is proven by the fact, that the regulars' encounters in the Little War outnumbered their participation in battles nine to one.[483] The recruitment of shorter and stronger men for the grenadiers, as commanded in the 1726 *Reglement*, indicates that these soldiers had to march longer distances than the musketeers and fusiliers. However, they received no special training and we might even suppose that it was not always best men who were handed over to the grenadier companies.[484] Thus the question remains: what made them elite troops often able to beat numerically superior contingents of Pandurs and Croats? Matthias Ludwig von Lossow, an insightful Prussian lieutenant-general, pointed out that the grenadiers' elite status was above all a question of attitude:

> The peculiarity of these grenadiers was mainly rooted in a mere opinion, as it were not always the choice men, concerning their height, who were selected as grenadiers. But it was this opinion alone, which made the grenadier feel better than other soldiers and that this type of troops felt elevated to a higher rank. The grenadiers were often entrusted with the *tour de force* and very rarely did they betray this trust. I do not know of any occasion when a grenadier battalion was

---

[477] Geschichte und Feldzüge des Dragonerregiments von Borke, in *Sammlung*, vol. 5, 293–436; Gieraths, *Die Kampfhandlungen*, 230–60.
[478] Fortsetzung des Journals des Feldzugs im Jahr 1758, in *Bellona*, vol. 9, 33–6.
[479] Fortsetzung des im ersten Theil abgebrochenen Tagebuchs, in *Sammlung*, vol. 2, 94–101.
[480] Duffy, *Frederick*, 314.
[481] Gieraths, *Kampfhandlungen*, 326–40.
[482] Ibid., 329–30.
[483] Wolfgang Petter, 'Zur Kriegskunst im Zeitalter Friedrichs des Großen', in *Europa im Zeitalter Friedrichs des Großen. Wirtschaft, Gesellschaft, Kriege*, ed. Bernhard R. Kroener (München: Oldenbourg, 1989), 266–7.
[484] See p. 202.

rebuked by the monarch; on the contrary, there are [many] examples, where the grenadiers of the Seven Years' War showed extraordinary devotion.[485]

There are also no indications that the grenadiers were chosen from amongst the veterans of the musketeers and fusiliers.[486] Their prowess in combat stemmed from their elite status, their fear of losing it and from a process of learning-by-doing. Their use in the Little War amounted to a daily training regime for all kinds of martial activities. The fusilier regiments raised after 1740 were not light troops in the strict sense of the word – their men and muskets were smaller than those of the musketeers, but their training was similar to them.[487]

The efficiency of the Prussian army in the Little War was a result of combined arms operations. The outer ring of troops screening the marching columns of the army or of a foraging detachment was formed by hussars. They were also the 'sensors' of the army. They were backed up by squadrons of dragoons, cuirassiers or even larger detachments of hussars, which could come to their aid at any time. These were followed by infantry, mainly grenadiers but also musketeers or fusiliers, who were able to attack enemy infantry in terrain unsuited for cavalry. Light troops or sharpshooters were supported by heavy infantry and troops formed up in line.[488] It was exactly this system of mutual support that military experts regarded as the heart of Prussia's successes in the Little War. Warnery and Cogniazzo agree that the Croats (and especially their grenadiers) were brave and knew their trade, but 'it is to be remarked, that the Croats were badly led during the entire war; seldom were they supported and it is unbelievable, how many of them were cut down by the Prussian hussars'.[489] The Prussians were also able to use tactics in the Little War that were typical of large-scale actions. Well-ordered infantry formed up in line were able to drive pandurs and Croats out of their positions, who were fighting in open order. We might assume that the prevailing theory of eighteenth-century European officers that infantry in close order was superior to a force in open order[490] was no stereotype. The regular infantry drill gave the units a cohesion they needed for the Little War; everything else could be learned in combat.[491]

---

[485] Lossow, *Denkwürdigkeiten*, 96–7.
[486] There seem to have been different modes of recruitment. Johann Friedrich Seyfarth, *Geschichte des Füsilier-Regiments von Lossow* (Halle / Saale: J. G. Trampe, 1767), 15.
[487] Duffy, *Friedrich der Große und seine Armee*, 105.
[488] Tagebuch des Generalmajors von Dewitz, 1741, in *Sammlung*, vol. 1, 64; Tagebuch des Generalmajors, Henning Otto Dewitz, in *Sammlung*, vol. 1, 146–7; Tagebuch eines Offiziers Alt-Schwerinschen Regiments, in *Sammlung*, vol. 1, 203; Bericht von der Action bey Katholisch-Hennersdorf, in *Sammlung*, vol. 1, 411; Tagebuch eines Offiziers vom Salmuthschen Regimente, in *Sammlung*, vol. 1, 582–3; Journal des Füselierregiments von Jung-Braunschweig, in *Sammlung*, vol. 2, 258; Tagebuch der Unternehmungen des General-Lieutenants Dubislav Friedrich von Platen, in *Sammlung*, vol. 3, 15; Bericht von der Unternehmung des Prinzen Heinrich in Franken, in *Sammlung*, vol. 3, 395–6; Beschreibung der Feldzüge von 1744 und 1745, wie auch 1756 bis 1763, in *Sammlung*, vol. 4, 61; Gechichte des Königl. Generallieutnants, Herzog Friedrich von Braunschweig Durchl. Infanterieregiments, in *Sammlung*, vol. 4, 561.
[489] Warnery, *Feldzüge*, vol. 1, 81.
[490] Nosworthy, *Anatomy*, 38.
[491] Bericht von der Unternehmung des Prinzen Heinrich in Franken, in *Sammlung*, vol. 3, 377–8.

Summary

The overview of the soldiers' emotions and thoughts in battle has revealed a number of typical feelings. The most basic sensation is fear, accompanied by different ways of coping with that fear in order to survive without losing one's honour. This kind of fear does not numb the soldiers, as they are perfectly capable of reflecting on their and their comrade's situation and even influencing the tactical execution of an order, as shown by the charge of Barsewisch's regiment in the Battle of Leuthen. As long as the soldier keeps functioning, being fearful does not injure his honour. The soldiers cope with it by prayer and their sense of honour. The loss of relatives, friends and brutal fighting in particular could leave them shocked and psychologically wounded; indeed many showed symptoms of what we would call PTSD today.

Another basic emotion is heat, which can keep fear at bay but also lead to overreactions, which endanger the fighting ability of the formation. Heat is also at the root of a lust for combat and even bloodlust. These elements are not mentioned in the soldiers' letters, probably due to the predominant feeling of fear and their religious writing strategies, which stress the men's suffering for their honour, the service and their relatives.

The analysis of different combat situations demonstrated that drill and subordination did not make the men numbed automatons. Instead, their emotions played a major role in combat, where tactical decisions were made in a triangle between the high command, the officers on the spot and the men in the ranks, whereby the latter had the last say. Their training gave them the competence to use a set of flexible tactics. Their instincts were successfully formed, not just as mere receivers and executors of commands but as human beings, who wanted to survive with their honour intact and a place in heaven secured.

3

The Components of Prussian Honour

What Made the Men Fight?

The impact of the tactical situation in a given combat setting on the soldiers' feelings and their behaviour have been discussed in Chapter 2. We will now turn to the different mental, psychological and material influences on the men. At the core of them were religion and a multifaceted concept of honour.

The honour of professionalism and the soldiers' estate

In early modern estate-based societies, soldiers' professional honour was closely linked to their estate. Thus, Prussian soldiers sang the second verse of the hymn *O God, You Pious God* when they were marching towards the field of battle:

Make, that I do with zeal,
What I'm supposed to do,
Where your command does lead me
As man of my estate,
Make, that I do it soon,
As I am ordered to,
And when I do it, grant,
That it is all done well.[1]

Important aspects of the honour of the soldiers' estate and its inextricably intertwined religious aspects[2] are summarized in Johann Christian Riemann's letter to his sister, in which he writes about the pain caused by his brother's death:

---

[1] Jany, *Geschichte*, vol. 2, 453. *Gib, daß ich tu' mit Fleiß, Was mir zu tun gebühret, Wozu mich dein Befehl In meinem Stande führet! Gib, daß ich's tue bald, Zu der Zeit, da ich soll, Und wenn ich's tu', so gib, Daß es gerate wohl!* (Translation by K. and S. Möbius.)

[2] This is typical for the German-speaking realm. Ludolf Pelizaeus, 'Die zentraleuropäische Entwicklung der Begriffe "Ehre", "Disziplin" und "Pflicht" im Spiegel von Militärschriftstellern und Reglements 1500–1808, in *Ehre und Pflichterfüllung*, 34.

> Let us comfort ourselves with our brother's honour, he has left his glory in this world, that as a faithful soldier he shed his blood courageously and bravely and lost his life for his right, for his king's honour, for his fatherland and its allies and for the good of us all. May our gracious God give him eternal bliss for this, he has escaped all hardships and has gone to a place, where all war and war cries have an end. No cannon blast can frighten him any more.[3]

Riemann summarizes central aspects of the soldier's honour: loyalty, bravery, defence of his own rights, of the king's honour, of the fatherland, his comrades and the common good. According to Lutheran and Pietist doctrine, all this was to be rewarded in heaven. Note how Riemann prioritizes and formulates the elements of his brother's honour. Before citing the different aspects of his honour, he stresses that his brother's honour and glory are based on his death. This unusual aspect of the soldiers' estate is also stressed by von Lossow:

> I do not want to deny that the official, the merchant, the burgher and the peasant must have a vivid sense of honour, but this is different from that of the soldier, for whom, correctly understood, the contempt for his own life is the most important component of his honour.[4]

First, Riemann mentions his brother's faithfulness as a soldier. It is not by chance that Riemann uses the German word *Kriegsknecht* (lit.: war-servant), which is borrowed from Martin Luther's translation of the Bible[5] and would not have been a common mid-eighteenth-century German word for 'soldier'. By using this word, he stresses that the service given as a member of the soldiers' estate is divine,[6] and that a faithful and courageous soldier would gain a celestial reward after his earthly death.[7] He then mentions courage and bravery, two essential qualities of the soldier, which make his estate and occupation different from all others, and in Prussia *superior* to them. It is particularly interesting that Riemann next refers to brother's 'right' (*Recht*), which means his special legal and social status.[8] The honour of the king is important for two reasons. On one hand, the king stands at the top of the estates' pyramid of honour; his subordinates' honour is rooted in his. And the soldier has direct influence on the king's honour, as a military setback is seen as a blow to that,[9] which in turn also affects the soldiers' prestige.[10] Next comes the fatherland, which at that time meant the region of one's birth in the German-speaking realm.[11] The idea of the soldier defending the

---

[3] Brief des Musketiers Johann Christian Riemann, in *Soldatenbriefe*, 32.
[4] Lossow, *Denkwürdigkeiten*, 57.
[5] The King James Bible translates the word as 'soldier' in John 19.2.
[6] This is also in accordance with the German mid-eighteenth-century notion of honour. Pelizaeus, *Die zentraleuropäische Entwicklung*, 34–35.
[7] Fleming, *Der Vollkommene Teutsche Soldat*, 11.
[8] Fleming, *Der Vollkommene Teutsche Soldat*, 104.
[9] Tempelhof, *Geschichte*, vol. 1, 123; Retzow, *Charakteristik*, vol. 1, 426.
[10] This idea was shared by the Saxons, for example, and seems to be a common idea in mid-eighteenth-century Europe. 'Disposition des Herzogs von Sachsen-Weissenfels', in *Sammlung*, vol. 1, 324–5.
[11] *Zedler's* 46 (1745), 737–8.

fatherland and thus being entitled to an honourable burial and memory was already a common idea but it is not Riemann's main interpretation of a soldier's death.[12] The next term needs some explanation, as Riemann is the only soldier who mentions the *topos* of Prussia's few allies and it may be a hint at a sermon held at a soldier's funeral or during an hour of prayer. Finally, he reminds his readers that his brother died for 'the good of us all'. Again, Riemann draws upon a biblical *topos*, the death of Jesus for his friends and mankind.[13] Thus he underlines the inextricable link between his profane and sacred duties. Concerning the question of the honour of the soldiers' estate, it is also striking that Riemann mentions institutions and concepts defended by his brother. He died in defence of his social status (right), the king's honour and other human communities. The incentive is not so much an increase in honour but the *defence of an existing state of honour*.

The soldiers' estate basically consisted of two other estates: the officers and the other ranks, which corresponded to the nobility to, and the commoners (peasantry / artisans and merchants) in civil life. Modern research has shown that honour was not exclusive to the nobility;[14] artisans and peasants saw themselves as honourable too and zealously defended their honour.[15] As noted in the Introduction, the soldiers' experience of campaigning – and more precisely of the battlefield – set him apart from the other estates. Their service meant not only being confronted with most gruesome forms of violence and death,[16] but also that they might lose their honour in the twinkling of an eye, should they not be able to act effectively in the face of extreme danger: 'A disheartened and timid soldier is the most despicable and miserable creature under the sun and not worth, that the sun shines on him ... [cowardice] is the most abominable vice of all ... He, who does not do his duty in battle ... must be executed by an infamous death or at least dishonoured as a rogue for ever.'[17] The soldiers' letters provide important answers to the question of which behaviour was considered as honourable and which as cowardly. We have already been able to demonstrate that showing fear in itself was seen as normal and that soldiers were expected to cope with that fear.[18] They were not expected, however, to fight to the death in hopeless situations.[19] Indeed, putting their lives in danger in such circumstances could even mean missing out on any hope of

---

[12] Fleming, *Vollkommene Teutsche Soldat*, 375.
[13] John 6.51; 10.11–15; 13.1; 15.13.
[14] The nobility's self-perception of being the only estate with honour does not reflect the other estates' view of themselves. See Carmen Winkel, 'Zwischen adliger Reputation und militärischer Subordination. Normative Ehrvorstellungen und soziale Praxis im preußischen Offizierskorps', in *Ehre und Pflichterfüllung*, 111.
[15] Berkovich, *Motivation*, 170–1; Gerd Schwerhoff, 'Early Modern Violence and the Honour Code: From Social Integration to Social Distinction?', *Crime, Histoire & Sociétés* 17, vol. 2 (2013): 27–46; Jutta Nowosadtko, 'Stand und Ehre', in *Lesebuch Altes Reich* (Bibliothek Altes Reich 1), ed. Stephan Wendehorst and Siegrid Westphal (München: de Gruyter, 2006), 146–53; Richard van Dülmen, *Kultur und Alltag in der Frühen Neuzeit, vol. 2 Dorf und Stadt 16.–18. Jahrhundert*, 3rd ed. (1992; Munich: Beck, 2005), 111, 194; Lossow, *Denkwürdigkeiten*, 57.
[16] Lossow, *Denkwürdigkeiten*, 57.
[17] Fleming, *Vollkommene Teutsche Soldat*, 99. Literally, Fleming writes that the coward must at least 'be made a rogue'.
[18] See p. 103.
[19] *Prussian Infantry Reglement of 1743*, 255.

clemency from the enemy, as was the case for the Prussian rearguard under the command of Colonel von Below during the last phase of the Battle of Landeshut in 1760. They were outnumbered and two Prussian squares had already surrendered, but they tried to fight on and escape. When they had run out of ammunition, they threw away their muskets, asked for mercy and were butchered by Austrian cavalry.[20] Units that left the field in hopeless situation were not punished, like the Prussian grenadiers of the left wing at the Battle of Prague or the men from Liebler's battalion who fled the Austrian volleys at the end of this particular confrontation.[21] C.F. Zander tells his nephew that the king rebuked the cavalry for not attacking at Kolin, but not the infantry, which had been forced to retreat.[22] The passage from Zander's letter shows also that those who fell back or refused to charge *without good reason* were dishonoured and had to face not only the permanent wrath of the king but also their comrades' contempt. This was also the case with the Alt-Anhalt Regiment, which lost its laces and swords for alleged cowardice during an Austrian sortie at Dresden in 1760. It was only able to restore its reputation by a frenzied charge at the Battle of Liegnitz some weeks later.[23] The East Prussian regiments that fled during the Battle of Zorndorf had to wait until 1773 until they were 'restored to something like favour.'[24] A brave soldier defending his honour had to hold out for three enemy attacks or three honourable and / or successful attacks of his own unit. This unwritten law was based on the psychological assumption that no reasonable commander could ask more from a soldier. After three encounters, his mental strength would have been spent – no one could reasonably ask more from him. Lieutenant von Hülsen makes this clear when he describes the breakdown of his regiment (von Below, No. 11) during the Battle of Zorndorf on the left wing of the Prussian army:

> As the common man[25] had beaten *three enemy lines* of battle and saw the fourth line facing him as well as another enemy force threatening his back, he stopped listening to the cries of the surviving officers but retreated in the direction of our right wing, which started its operations at the same time. It is impossible for infantry to fight with more head and heart than ours had done until this moment ... Now, my soul became as sad as it had been cheerful before. I trampled on the colours I had taken from the enemy, because it was impossible to make the men stand. Of what use are trophies for the fugitive?'[26]

Küster cites privates from the second battalion of the Markgraf Karl Regiment (No. 19), who were defending the churchyard of Hochkirch against vastly superior Austrian forces:

---

[20] Retzow, *Charakteristik*, vol. 2, 203.
[21] Schreiben des Feldwebels Liebler, in *Briefe*, 47.
[22] C.F. Zander, 21 July 1757, in *Fundstücke*, 54.
[23] Archenholz, *Geschichte*, 186. Retzow, *Charakteristik*, vol. 2, 244.
[24] Showalter, *Frederick*, pos. 3892.
[25] The privates.
[26] Hülsen, *Unter Friedrich dem Großen*, 90.

When the Austrians staged the second assault on the churchyard and [the Prussian commander], Major von Langen, refused to capitulate, brave privates said: 'This is right, *three times*, that is the Prussian watchword, as long as they have not stormed the churchyard for a third time and we have defended ourselves bravely, we do not have to give up.'[27]

The situation for the Prussians became untenable, but Langen refused to surrender and escaped with a few survivors after a last stand. He was wounded eleven times[28] and captured by the Austrians. After his death, the Austrians buried him with military honours.[29] Although Langen had been in an impossible situation, his men and the Austrians knew that the welfare of the army had depended on the defence of the churchyard. Therefore, his behaviour was not regarded as foolish but rather as a tactical necessity, and thus highly honourable.[30] We have already seen how Sergeant Liebler had taken part in three attacks during the Battle of Prague. He writes at the end of his letter that his wife should not tell anybody about his behaviour, because everybody would think he is boasting. This remark shows once more that three attacks are the maximum to be expected of a brave soldier and represent an honourable feat of arms.[31]

The execution of the difficult but effective platoon fire under battle conditions was regarded as especially praiseworthy. The case of the first battalion of Guards (No. 15) is especially instructive. The battalion had managed two complete rounds of platoon fire during the Battle of Mollwitz (10 April 1741), losing many men in the process but nevertheless contributing to the Prussian victory by adhering to their instructions. Platoon fire was very effective, and the soldiers practised it daily, but it was extremely difficult to fire even one round of platoon fire under actual battle conditions. The king led the battalion to the drill square and made it fire two rounds of platoon fire every year on the anniversary of the Battle of Mollwitz.[32]

The adherence to certain rules of honourable behaviour during combat, such as using only allowed ammunition[33] and sparing the life of wounded and helpless enemies,[34] was of crucial importance, because actions to the contrary would make soldiers lose the right[35] to being taken prisoner if they themselves threw down their arms if routed. Capture was not desirable at all,[36] but naturally most soldiers preferred it to death. Being captured with your honour intact increased the chances of survival.

All soldiers stress the hardships of marching and campaigning:

---

[27] Küster, *Bruchstück*, 189.
[28] Herbert J. Redman, *Frederick the Great and the Seven Years' War, 1756–1763* (Jefferson, NC: McFarland & Co., 2015), 241.
[29] Geschichte des Königl. Generallieutnants, Herzog Friedrich von Braunschweig Durchl. Infanterieregiments, in *Sammlung*, vol. 4, 560.
[30] Showalter, *Frederick*, pos. 3985; Duffy, *Frederick*, 169.
[31] Schreiben des Feldwebels Liebler, in *Briefe*, 47.
[32] Zielsdorf, *Militärische Erinnerungskulturen*, 230.
[33] Tagebuch des Musketiers Dominicus, 61.
[34] Schreiben des Feldwebels Liebler, in *Briefe*, 34.
[35] Cogniazzo, *Geständnisse*, vol. 3, 162.
[36] Letter no. 10 by Corporal Binn, 20 July 1759, in *Soldatenbriefe*, 22; Von einem Unteroffizier des Alt-Anhaltischen Regiments, in *Briefe*, 16; Beschreibung der Lobositzer Bataille, in *Briefe*, 5.

Gracious God, our life was that of a dog and even worse, even in rain or snow we had to march on. At night at 7, 8, or 9, we had reached our quarters. But the company had only one house, which was occupied by the captain and the lads were driven upwards like cattle on a paddock and had to care for themselves. One crept into this dark corner, the other one into another, sometimes we build huts and made fire, when the cold became too strong. But we burned off our clothes when we tried to get warm near the fire and did not get any warm food for 5 or 6 days.[37]

On one hand, the soldiers write about the extremely hard conditions of their daily life, because their life *was* hard. But as they write about the horrors of combat, they also stress the pain of the endless marches in heat and cold and always with just enough food to ensure their survival. The men suffer for their relatives and this suffering is honourable.[38]

The physical defence of their homes, and above all of their friends' and the families' lives, was an important part of the soldiers' honour. For example, Corporal Binn tells his family that a Prussian defeat in the coming battle (Kunersdorf) against the Russians would be 'very bad for you and us' and because of that he hopes that God gives him and his comrades the 'courage to attack our enemy'.[39]

Comradeship plays an important role as the group of *Kantonisten* from a certain village or small area are part of the soldiers' social network that links him to his home. The letters contain the names of numerous men who use them as a means of sending greetings and information to their relatives living in the same village as the authors' relatives. Unfortunately, we do not know much about the social network of the *Ausländer*. It might be that the comrades quartered with them played an important role, as Bräker indicates. The tent comradeship or other small units like the mess,[40] so important for other armies,[41] are hardly ever mentioned. This is also true for the soldiers' descriptions of combat. The death of a relative or friend from the village can leave a soldier emotionally devastated but is never used as an incentive to (for example) fight on or take revenge.[42] Dominicus mentions the gruesome death of men marching near him and is deeply shocked, but these men remain anonymous and there is no indication whatsoever that they were personal friends of his, from his town or another small group of soldiers.[43] Liebler, in fact, has no problem whatsoever with his comrades' death, as he quotes the biblical verse 'when a thousand shall fall to thy left, and ten thousand to thy right hand, it shall but not come nigh thee'.[44] The incentives to fight on

---

[37] J.D. Zander, probably spring 1758, in *Fundstücke*, 68. All letters are full of descriptions of these hardships.
[38] Zielsdorf, *Militärische Erinnerungskulturen*, 69.
[39] Letter no. 10 by Corporal Binn to his wife, 20 July 1759, in *Soldatenbriefe*, 22.
[40] The group of soldiers, which prepared their meals together.
[41] Berkovich, *Motivation*, 215–16.
[42] Frantz Reiß, 6. Oktober 1756, in *Briefe*, 30–1; Brief des Musketiers Johann Christian Riemann, 1762, in *Soldatenbriefe*, 33–5.
[43] *Tagebuch des Musketiers Dominicus*, 63.
[44] Psalm 91.7. Brief des Feldwebels G. S. Liebler, in *Briefe*, 45.

are either to be found on the individual or the regimental level: individual survival, salvation of one's soul and defence of one's honour, and defence of the regiment's honour, which was the social space of honour for the soldier. But in the end, the Prussian *Kantonisten's* incentive to fight was self-centred and became collective only when other people were needed to reach the individual's goals.[45]

Religion

The intimate connection between religion and honour, so typical for the German realm at this time, has already been mentioned. Religion linked the different aspects of the soldiers' affiliation to their estate, which culminated in the oath the men had sworn to keep.[46] Soldiers had to fight courageously for the honour of God[47] and doing their duty would mean their soul reached heaven, as Johann Christian Riemann points out when struggling with his brother's death in the passage cited at the beginning of this chapter.[48]

Religious verses and considerations were in the men's minds when they were exposed to death, as has been shown above. Küster mentions another important aspect of the link between religion and honour:

> Such a rational religiosity is more important for the warrior estate than for any other estate, because the trade of the officer and the soldier is of such a nature that they need it most, because only their religion can compensate them for what they sacrifice to the fatherland and mankind. Only very few of them win glory and posthumous glory.[49]

Being rewarded in the afterlife was a strong incentive to fight on and thus keep one's honour intact. To know that one's death would be the end without any reward would have made the men feel hopeless, and provided reasons for desertion. That religious beliefs can be a strong support in the fight against fear and depression has been shown by modern psychiatric research.[50] Küster also stresses it:

---

[45] Again, the NCOs of light units and the officers seem to be much closer to their comrades. George Beß, an NCO from the Brunswick *Jägers*, sees the 'friendship amongst the Jaegers and the ambition, to excel in bravery and save their brothers' as the basis of their extraordinary courage. Beß, *Aus dem Tagebuch*, 195–6.
[46] *Tagebuch des Musketiers Dominicus*, 63.
[47] Fleming, *Vollkommene Teutsche Soldat*, 99.
[48] Brief des Musketiers Johann Christian Riemann, in *Soldatenbriefe*, 32.
[49] Carl Daniel Küster, 'Religiosität im Kriegerstande', in *Officier-Lesebuch*, vol. 1, 145.
[50] Raphael Bonelli, Rachel E. Dew, Harold G. Koenig, David R. Rosmarin, and Sasan Vasegh, 'Religious and Spiritual Factors in Depression. Review and Integration of the Research', *Depression research and treatment* 7 (2012): 4; Alexander Moreira-Almeida, Harold G. Koenig and Giancarlo Lucchetti, 'Clinical implications of spirituality to mental health: review of evidence and practical guidelines', *Revista Brasileira de Psiquiatria* 36 (2014): 177.

Every kind of danger makes the human being adhere to his religion more strongly than in peacetime. The dangers of war, which are more perilous than any others, produce this enforced adherence most strongly and most certainly. There are difficult times and critical situations, when the soldier clings to his religion with all his soul. His religion might be utterly repugnant, yet, it must not be touched, if you do not want to insult the spirit of its adherent and to destroy his courage.[51]

The soldiers' letters show that the men feel protected[52] by a well-meaning, 'gracious' God and this positive attitude helps them to deal with the traumatizing and depressing experiences of war. This finding is also supported by modern psychological research.[53]

Religious considerations were also important for fighting the fear or death in a combat situation. Barsewisch[54] summarizes the use of religious thoughts to avoid a shameful flight:

I was convinced that my life was in God's hands, that he could save it, while I held out at my [extremely dangerous] post and that he could take it from me when I fled.[55]

Being in the hands of a gracious God was one aspect of religiosity that could help the men stay on the field. Another was the idea that not fulfilling one's duties as a soldier would make God punish one in the afterlife. This idea was shared by many soldiers – but not all of them. Küster tells his readers about the desperate fighting at Hochkirch and the flight of some men:

Some cowards had gone back and hidden themselves in the cooking-holes. Brave privates grumbled at them and the officers pushed them back into the line by force. I went back a few steps behind the battalion's front and said with a loud voice: 'Children, I do not know you, but God knows you! Whoever is shot dead in the cooking-hole, dies a deserter, a bad man and sins in the last moment of his life; whoever dies, where his profession calls him to be, will do something good in the end. Do not leave your brave comrades, it is more secure here, at the front, than in the back.' And some of them came back, indeed. But one of the cowards threw a pike at me, which, thank goodness!, missed me.[56]

---

[51] Carl Daniel Küster, *Religiosität*, 146–7.
[52] Schreiben des Feldwebels Liebler, in *Briefe*, 45; Küster, *Bruchstück*, 61.
[53] 'Better adjustment was related to a number of coping methods, such as benevolent religious reappraisals, religious forgiveness/purification, and seeking religious support. Poorer adjustment was associated with reappraisals of God's powers, spiritual discontent, and punishing God reappraisals.' Kenneth I. Pargament, Lisa M. Perez, and Harold Koenig, 'The many methods of religious coping: Development and initial validation of the RCOPE', *Journal of Clinical Psychology* 56, vol. 4 (2000): 519–43, 519.
[54] Although Barsewisch is an officer, we can assume that his way of thinking was also that of many of the writing soldiers, as they shared the idea that God would treat them according to his plan.
[55] Barsewisch, *Kriegs-Erlebnisse*, 104.
[56] Küster, *Bruchstück*, 42.

At the core of the Prussian soldiers' faith was the belief that honourable service for the king was also divine service and would lead directly to heaven. Hymns and prayers helped the soldiers to cope with the fear of death. It is especially interesting to see that there was also a deep sense of fighting a holy war against Catholics. The language of the Bible was also a means to allow communication between the men and their families about the horrors of combat. Prayers by their relatives or fellow soldiers were seen as a means of influencing the outcome of a battle and of helping the soldier to survive.

National and cultural concepts

The Prussian colours displayed the motto *Pro Gloria et Patria* (For glory and fatherland) from 1740 on. Frederick II had chosen this motto ahead of his fathers, *Nec Soli Cedit* (He does not yield to the sun). *Nec Soli Cedit* had been directed against France, as the sun was the symbol of the French kings. As Frederick had allied himself with France against Austria, the former motto would have been inappropriate and *Pro Gloria et Patria* reflected his motivations quite accurately. Thirsting for glory was regarded as a virtue in eighteenth-century Europe, especially for kings and commanders, and Frederick possessed that thirst to an extreme degree.[57] Serving the fatherland was a key component of this glory, as far as the ruler was concerned. We cannot be sure, however, whether this was also true for the ordinary soldier.

Concerning this issue, four different themes occur, which touch upon national and cultural issues:

1. Defence of the fatherland as a part of a soldier's estate's duties;
2. the idea that *Kantonisten*, as *Landeskinder* (children of the land or natives of a region) were better fighters than the *Ausländer*, or mercenaries;
3. the idea that certain regions bred particularly effective soldiers;
4. the hatred of other nations as an incentive to fight on.

Defence of the fatherland

None of the soldiers writes about serving the Prussian state or Prussia or Brandenburg. They do not have a name for the entity that we call 'Prussia'. They do use the word *Vaterland* (fatherland), but this must not be confused with a nineteenth- or twentieth-century concept of fatherland or nation. The meaning prevalent in the mid-1700s was that of the home *region* of a person, characterized by a common language, customs and food. It acknowledges that serving the *Vaterland* is honourable and that people have certain obligations towards its other inhabitants.[58] The word does crop up in some of the letters. Riemann mentions it as an entity that his brother died for, and Binn asks God to be merciful towards 'the dear fatherland' threatened by the 'tyrannical' Russian

---

[57] Luh, *Der Große*, 9, 53.
[58] *Zedler's Universal Lexicon* 46 (1745), 737–8.

enemy.[59] Sergeant Liebler also exclaims that he would have been prepared 'to sacrifice my body and life in greatest distress for the well-being of our *Land* (country or region) and my dear relatives'.[60] Both Riemann and Liebler mention the *Vaterland* together with their comrades and relatives, which stresses the typical German mid-eighteenth-century meaning of *Vaterland* as 'home region'. Some of the soldiers also stress the very concrete need to defend their home regions against enemies, who are ready to plunder[61] and commit atrocities.[62]

The military efficiency of *Kantonisten* / *Landeskindern*

As noted in earlier chapters, the so-called *Ausländer* troops were very far from being the riff-raff of Europe that they were often assumed to be: many of them were in fact Prussian subjects or had been born in bordering areas.[63] Yet it is true, that the *Kantonisten* of a regiment all hailed from the same region and those of a company from a certain number of villages. Tempelhof sees them as the backbone of the army and writes about the Prussian regiments just prior to the Battle of Leuthen:

> When you investigate the condition of the Prussian army, it is no problem to convince yourself that the king was to beat the enemy, wherever he would meet him. It consisted, with few exceptions, of *Landeskindern*, as most of the *Ausländer* had deserted, and those of them who were left had adopted the character of the nation.[64]

Kantonisten had almost no opportunity to desert and wherever they were despatched on army duty remained part of their old community. That said, there is no actual proof to support Tempelhof's assertion here: Lossow, whose knowledge of the army was just as expert as Tempelhof's, regards long-serving and naturalized *Ausländer* as the core of the army. Given the fact that between one-third to one-half the army was made up of *Ausländer*, it is impossible to draw a distinction between *Ausländern* and *Landeskindern* as both were part of the tactical body of the battalion or squadron.

Certain regions breed good soldiers

Frederick II – and some of his generals – valued soldiers from Magdeburg, Pomerania and Brandenburg greatly.[65] Officers seem to have agreed that men from the West Slavic minority of the Sorbs, who lived in Brandenburg, were 'the best infantrymen in the world', as they were totally obedient to their king.[66] The von Meyerinck Regiment (No. 26)

---

[59] Letter no. 10 by Corporal Binn, in *Soldatenbriefe*, 22.
[60] Von einem Unteroffizier des Alt-Anhaltischen Regiments, in *Briefe*, 16.
[61] Von einem Unteroffizier Anhaltischen Regiments, in *Briefe*, 5.
[62] Letter no. 10 by Corporal Binn, in *Soldatenbriefe*, 22; Letter by Kaspar Kalberlah, in *Soldatenbriefe*, 29–30.
[63] Lossow, *Denkwürdigkeiten*, 2–7.
[64] Tempelhof, *Geschichte*, vol. 1, 323.
[65] Ibid., 67.
[66] Warnery, *Feldzüge*, vol. 1, 98.

consisted of seven Sorbian and three German companies and was considered to be one of the best in the army.[67] But there were also *Ausländer*-only regiments that fought with distinction, such as the dragoons of the von Borke[68] Regiment or the guards.[69]

National hatred as an incentive to fight

As there is no mention of a Prussian nation in the soldiers' letters and thus no positive identification with it, the question remains whether there were national stereotypes and antitypes that encouraged the men to take part in the fights against an inveterate enemy.[70] In the later part of the eighteenth century, it was above all the Battle of Roßbach that military writers regarded as Frederick's greatest triumph – and first and foremost as a *pan-German* victory over the hated French.[71] Archenholz, author of the first (1788) bestseller on the Seven Years' War, wrote:

> All German tribes, large or small, and regardless of faction, *Reichstags*-decisions and their individual interest, were satisfied with this victory over the French, which they viewed as a national triumph.[72]

And a triumph it was: 22,000 Prussians had beaten about 40,000 French and *Reichstruppen* (Imperial troops), routing them totally in less than ninety minutes of combat. But it is still doubtful, whether Roßbach was really perceived as a *national* triumph at the time of the battle.[73] Contemporary German-language journals simply mention or reprint the sermons but do not give any accounts of the battle.[74] Prussian sermons also mentioned nothing but the fact that the battle had been won, but did stress God's help and even called for pity for the slain enemies.[75] Ludwig Gleim, the most famous Prussian patriotic poet – was the author of the 'Prussian War Songs in the

---

[67] Barsewisch, *Kriegs-Erlebnisse*, 34.
[68] Geschichte und Feldzüge, in *Sammlung*, vol. 5, 293–436.
[69] Tempelhof, *Geschichte*, vol. 1, 329.
[70] Gerd Baumann, 'Grammars of Identity / Alterity. A Structural Approach', in *Grammars of Identity / Alterity. A Structural Approach*, ed. Gerd Baumann and Andre Gingrich (New York and Oxford: Berghahn Books, [2004] 2006), 19.
[71] Katrin and Sascha Möbius, 'Rossbach: el engaño perfecto', *Desperta Ferro* 24 (2016): 20–7.
[72] Archenholz, *Geschichte*, 115.
[73] Showalter calls it a 'sweet revenge' for French misdeeds during the reign of Louis XIV but challenges a 'bandwagon effect in Frederick's favour among the lesser German states'. Showalter, *Frederick*, pos. 3393.
[74] A search in the research database 'Scholarly journals in the Age of Enlightenment' (http://www.gelehrte-journale.de/startseite/ (accessed 22 November 2018)) found no results for any articles in German journals. The first entries start in the 1770s.
[75] Christian Diederich Wilcken, *Drey Predigten von denen durch Ihro Majestät den König von Preußen erhaltenen grossen Siegen bey Roßbach, und Lissa und der Wiedereroberung der schlesischen Hauptstadt Breslau* (Halle / Salle: Gebauer, 1758), 8; Adolph Dietrich Ortmann, *Adolph Dieterich Ortmanns, Inspektors zu Belitz, Sieges-Predigt wegen der Schlacht bey Roßbach gehalten über Jesaia 26.v.20 in der Kirche zu Belitz* (Berlin: Christian Voß, 1757), 7, 26, even calls for pity for the vanquished; Johann Peter Süßmilch, *Johann Peter Süßmilchs, Königlichen Ober-Consistorial-Raths und Probsts zu Berlin, Danck- und Sieges-Predigt Wegen des Am 5ten Novembr. 1757 bey Freyburg Denen Königlich-Preußischen Waffen über die vereinigte Französische und Reichs-Armee verliehenen Höchstwichtigten Sieges* (Berlin und Schwabach: Enderische Buchhandlung, 1758), 1–12.

Campaigns of 1756 and 1757 by a Grenadier' – wrote a poem celebrating the victory. Although he praises Frederick as the defender of German 'freedom',[76] he ridicules the other German states and their contingents more than he does the French.[77] Goethe, whose *Dichtung und Wahrheit* (*Poetry and Truth*) had been cited in support of Roßbach being Germany's great awakening, gives a detailed account of the factional struggles in Frankfurt am Main during the Seven Years' War but writes nothing that could be interpreted as national triumphalism. It seems that the contemporaries' customary mockery of the vanquished after a humiliating defeat was reinterpreted in the late eighteenth or nineteenth century as a nationalist anti-French-sentiment.

For our purpose, it is important to ascertain whether Prussian soldiers felt a nationalistic hatred for the French. Friedrich Wilhelm von Gaudi, aide-de-camp of the king, wrote in his diary about the slaughter of the fleeing French cavalry and infantry by the Prussian horsemen:

> [The reason was] the natural hatred of the common man in Germany, above all of the Magdeburgers, Brandenburgers and Pomeranians, against everybody who even has a French name. They feel this hatred in the depth of their hearts and imbibe it with their mother's milk. They do not know the reason for it and when you urge them to express one, they say that a Frenchman is not even able to speak German. That this hatred was real was more than revealed during today's battle, because our troops did not limit themselves to doing their duty and to advance against the enemy courageously, but anyone who looked carefully could see that they fought with real anger. The behaviour of the cavalry was the most obvious proof for this when it cut down the enemy infantry, as the officers had great difficulty in making the common man give quarter [that is, to spare surrendering Frenchmen].[78]

Gaudi's verdict is clear; he was an eyewitness and wrote directly after the battle, so ostensibly there is no reason to doubt his account. Yet the letters of Dominicus[79] and Lt. Seiler[80] do not mention anything like national hatred, and while other officers present at the battle may mock the French[81] they do not mention anything like Gaudi's take on events.[82] There is no doubt that the French infantry was indeed routed and massacred,[83] and there is ample proof that many Germans disliked the French, but it is surely implausible to suggest that the only reason troopers and grenadiers of the Brandenburg

---

[76] Which is Prussian propaganda, claiming that Maria Theresa wanted to enslave Germany and make it Catholic by force. The claim has nothing to do with claiming a 'German' victory over the French. Blanning, *Frederick*, 220.

[77] Johann Wilhelm Ludwig Gleim, *Sieges-Lied der Preußen nach der Schlacht bei Roßbach* (Berlin, 1757).

[78] Gaudi, *Journal*, vol. III, 668–9.

[79] Dominicus does have ethnic prejudices, and is often anti-Semitic, but he says nothing derogatory about the French. *Tagebuch des Musketiers Dominicus*, 83.

[80] Letter by Lt. Seiler, in *Soldatenbriefe*, 35–6.

[81] Barsewisch, *Kriegs-Erlebnisse*, 20.

[82] Tagebuch des Majors Maximilian von Bornstädt, in *Sammlung*, vol. 4, 25–6.

[83] Showalter, *Frederick*, pos. 3374; Blanning, *Frederick*, 219.

monarchy's core provinces hated the French was because 'they do not speak German'. Anti-French stereotypes were available throughout society: they were regarded as warmongers, arrogant snobs, light-hearted and 'unsteady', and scornful of everything German. Above all, the French army had taken part in atrocities and plundered and looted their way through German lands.[84] But these aspects are not mentioned in the soldiers' letters. There might be something else behind Gaudi's story. The Prussians had massacred the fleeing French and knew that this was against the 'rules' of war. Gaudi asked some of the Prussian troopers who had taken part in the slaughter why they had behaved in that way, and they cited their ignorance of the French language, which meant they did not understand that the enemy soldiers were surrendering. This explanation is supported by other testimonies pointing to the problems stemming from the Prussian's ignorance of the enemy's language at Roßbach.[85] It is thus even more doubtful that the Prussian troops were full of anti-French hatred.

Anti-Russian sentiments *can* be traced in the soldiers' letters, however. Both Binn and Kalberlah call them 'tyrannical enemies' or 'tyrants', and Kalberlah supposes that they 'eat young children'.[86] The Battle of Zorndorf and especially the destruction of the Russian right wing by Prussian cavalry and the stubborn advance of the Forcade and Prince of Prussia Regiments on the Prussian right were seen as the result of the Prussian soldiers' hatred of an enemy, that had devastated their home provinces so brutally.[87] Both officers and common soldiers wrote about the anger of the privates who had seen the destruction left in the Russian army's wake.[88] In fact, most atrocities had been committed by the Russian irregulars and magnified by Prussian propaganda.[89] There is no doubt, however, that Zorndorf was one of the most brutal battles of the eighteenth century.[90] The soldiers' rage was mainly due to the genuine chaos caused by the Cossacks and the mismanagement of the Russian high command,[91] they had seen for themselves that the king's order to kill the Russians and to cut off their lines of retreat could be ascribed to a thoroughly negative, not to say racist, image of the Russian nation. Like Voltaire,[92] Frederick was convinced that the Russians were uncivilized scum. He continued to hold this view even after Zorndorf, where the

---

[84] Blanning, *Frederick*, 220; Geschichte des Freyregiments von Hard, in *Sammlung*, vol. 5, 108.
[85] Möbius, *Haß*, 126–7. Note in particular the anecdote that the Prussians had been informed of the French intention to establish their winter-quarters in Brandenburg (which would include co-opting the inhabitants' goods, of course). Now, the French were crying 'quarter' to show their willingness to surrender and the Brandenburgers felt mocked and went on killing them until some French, who spoke German, were able to point out to the furious Prussians, that it was no mockery, but the traditional cry for mercy. Although the anecdote is unbelievable to the absurd, it points to the same issue: the massacre needed a justification, and this could be provided by the language barrier.
[86] Brief des Soldaten Johann Kaspar Kalberlah, in *Soldatenbriefe*, 29; Letter no. 10 by Corporal Binn, in *Soldatenbriefe*, 22.
[87] Tempelhof, *Geschichte*, vol. 2, 229; Friedrich der Große, *Gespräche*, 236; Retzow, *Charakteristik*, vol. 1, 318.
[88] Blanning, *Frederick*, 230.
[89] Christopher Duffy, *Russia's Military Way to the West: Origins and Nature of Russian Military Power 1700–1800* (Abingdon: Routledge, [1982] 2017), 103.
[90] Duffy, *Frederick*, 169–70.
[91] See ibid.
[92] Voltaire, *Histoire de Charles XII, Roi de Suede*, (1731; Amsterdam 1733), 24–6.

Russians had come so close to beating him.[93] Much of the ferocity of the battle was due to Frederick's order to give no quarter, which had caused the Russians to stand and fight on even in hopeless situations.[94] The king was so eager to annihilate the Russian army that he consciously let the opportunity pass to take the Russian train.[95] Had he done so, he could have starved his adversary Count Fermor into submission. But Frederick wanted to drown the Russian army in blood and even ordered his hussars to kill wounded enemy troops. And here is the difference to the rank and file: they were both appalled by the atrocities and afraid of the Russian army. Depending on the tactical situation, fear or rage got the upper hand. The foot regiments of the left Prussian wing fled before the Russian infantry, while the Prussian cavalry fought with desperate courage and butchered their enemies. Ultimately some Prussian infantry regiments simply disobeyed the king's orders to massacre the wounded Russians and even defended wounded Russian fellow-infantrymen against the Prussian hussars trying to kill them.[96] That the Prussian privates did not have an entrenched cultural image of the Russians is underlined by the fear instilled in them by the Battle of Zorndorf.[97] Unlike Frederick, they did not view the Russians as rabble but instead dreaded their steadfastness.[98] Later on, Prussian privates tended to respect their Russian adversaries as effective soldiers,[99] a more realistic view than that of the king.[100]

If the Prussian rank and file had an arch-enemy, it was the Austrians. The soldiers' letters are full of complaints about the Austrians acting against the customs of war during and especially after the Battle of Lobositz. They are accused of killing their own wounded, of being ordered to give no quarter and of attacking their Prussian captors after having been taken prisoner.[101] Liebler calls them 'the enemies of the Gospel'.[102] The mixture between the hatred fuelled by years of conflict and religious hatred is underlined by the shouts of the Normann dragoons, when they broke into the right wing of the Austrians at Kolin: 'You Austrian rascals, Catholic dogs!'[103] The Prussian rank and file harboured a strong dislike for the Austrian light troops,[104] whom many Prussians saw as the lowest of the low.[105] These were often killed in cold blood and even their wounded were not spared.[106]

---

[93] Showalter, *Frederick*, pos. 3866.
[94] Retzow, *Charakteristik*, vol. 1, 317–18; Prittwitz, *Ich bin ein Preuße*, 86.
[95] Blanning, *Frederick*, 230.
[96] Prittwitz, *Ich bin ein Preuße*, 99.
[97] Duffy, *Frederick*, 171.
[98] Tempelhof, *Geschichte*, vol. 3, 216.
[99] This is underlined by Dresel's very sober evaluation of the strategic situation in May 1759, which mentions the Russians but puts them on an equal footing with the Austrians. Kohl, *Ein Brief*, 83.
[100] Frederick W. Kagan, 'Russia's Geopolitical Dilemma and the Question of Backwardness', in *The Military History of Tsarist Russia*, ed. Frederick Kagan and Robin Higham (New York and Houndsmills: Palgrave, 2002), 253.
[101] Beschreibung der Lobositzer Bataille, in *Soldatenbriefe*, 5; Barthel Linck, 3. Oktober 1756, in *Briefe*, 13–14; Schreiben des Feldwebels G.S. Liebler, in *Briefe*, 34.
[102] Letter of Sergeant G.S. Liebler, 7 May 1757, in *Briefe*, 45.
[103] Hoen, *Die Schlacht bei Kolin*, vol. 4, 582; See also: Sikora, *Disziplin*, 285–7.
[104] Von einem Unteroffizier [C.G. Klauel] Anhaltischen Regiments, in *Briefe*, 28.
[105] Bericht des Hauptmanns von Billerbeck, in *Sammlung*, vol. 1, 130.
[106] Tagebuch eines Offiziers vom Alt-Schwerinschen Infanterieregiment, in *Sammlung*, vol. 1, 451; Bräker, *Arme Mann*, 150; Lemcke, *Kriegs- und Friedensbilder*, 26.

In summary, national stereotypes or hatred were not the principal incentives for Prussian privates to fight and win. Defending the fatherland was amongst their duties, but it was understood as defending their family and community and not the Prussian state. Their assumed hatred for the French is more than dubious and the Russians were feared by the men but there was no loathing to compare to that displayed by the king and the 'enlightened' thinkers. When the king ordered the killing of wounded men, the Christian beliefs of many infantrymen prevailed and prompted them to ignore the king's orders. If there was an arch-enemy for the Prussian privates, it was the Austrians. This hatred was fuelled by the religious differences and the permanent wars against Austria.

Gender and honour

The soldiers' letters shed some light on the relationships between them and their wives. As a result of each couple's dynamics, there are differences in their relationships. Frantz Reiß is infuriated with his wife as he thinks that she cannot understand his mental pain after the murderous fighting at Lobositz; Adam Becker is concerned only with his wife's pregnancy; and Sergeant Liebler talks to his spouse as if they were at a prayer meeting in their house in Halle. Corporal Binn is annoyed with his wife when he sees their son's poor spelling, but begs her like a naughty boy not to believe rumours about his infidelity. Concerning the description of the soldiers' battle experience, it is striking that they provide detailed descriptions of combat in letters to their wives and in one case, to a mother. They expect their wives to understand military terminology and to be able to follow the explanation of a professional battle plan. Above all, they want to bond with their wives, and ask them to remember them in their prayers. Concerning military knowledge, there is no difference between these letters and those written to fathers, brothers or comrades not fighting at that time. The wives of the writing soldiers appear as members of the soldiers' estate. Apart from the fact that women could not become soldiers, no distinction is drawn between the men and women of this estate by our letter-writers.

As noted in earlier chapters,[107] women were a permanent and important part of 'camp society'.[108] Women worked as sutlers, followed their husbands or friends or visited, as was the case for many *Kantonisten*, their men on campaign. They were important for the campaign economy too, as it was the women who traded all kinds of plundered goods[109] and could even sell ice to the men drawn up for battle in the summer, just before the first shots were fired.[110] Other than the very few women who fought in men's clothes,[111] the battlefield proper was the only male domain in European

---

[107] See pp. 26–7.
[108] Bernhard R. Kroener, '"... und ist der Jammer nid zu beschreiben." Geschlechterbeziehungen und Überlebensstrategien in der Lagergesellschaft des Dreißigjährigen Krieges, in *Landsknechte, Soldatenfrauen und Nationalkrieger. Militär, Krieg und Geschlechterordnung im historischen Wandel*, ed. Karen Hagemann and Ralf Pröve (Frankfurt am Main: Campus, 1998), 279–96.
[109] Dispositionen des Königl. Preußischen Feldmarschalls Grafen von Schwerin, in *Bellona*, vol. 4, 20.
[110] Prittwitz, *Ich bin ein Preuße*, 56.
[111] Rudolf Dekker, Lotte van de Pol, *Frauen in Männerkleidern, Weibliche Transvestiten und ihre Geschichte*, (Berlin: Wagenbach, 1990), 22.

eighteenth-century military life. This has to be kept in mind when the soldiers' concepts of gender and their role in combat are discussed.[112] During the late Middle Ages[113] and the epoch of the French Revolution and Napoleonic Wars,[114] courage, military efficiency and masculinity were synonyms and *männlich* (male) was a common adjective to describe brave and courageous behaviour. This is definitely not the case in Prussian mid-eighteenth-century sources, however. In fact 'male' does not appear in a single letter, diary or memoire. When soldiers describe efficient military behaviour, they use the words 'brave' (*brav*),[115] 'courageous' (*tapfer*),[116] 'heroic' (*heldenmäßig*)[117] or 'honourable' (*ehrlich*).[118] The attributes 'like lions' (*wie die Löwen*)[119] or 'lionlike' (*löwenmäßig*)[120] were also commonly used to describe the extraordinary courage of soldiers.

The very few passages in which 'male' is used by Prussian officers and the chaplain Küster were printed between the mid-1780s[121] and the early 1800s.[122] Küster uses the word 'emasculating' in the already-cited passage on cannon-fever: 'There are examples for this *emasculating* fear gripping one or a few heroes, making them unable to think and to stand their ground.'[123] Here, 'emasculating' describes a physical condition that deprives the soldier of his two most important abilities, namely to think and to hold his ground.[124] This fear in itself is does not harm the honour of the soldier, as Küster calls

---

[112] On Prussia, see Möbius, „Bravthun", 79–96.
[113] Dritte Fortsetzung der Detmar-Chronik, erster Theil von 1401–38, in *Die Chroniken der deutschen Städte*, vol. 28 (Leipzig: Hirzel, 1902), 370. Korner, Hermann, Chronica Novella (Hannoveraner Handschrift), 99 r, 102 l, 107 r, 108 v, 109 r, 111 v, 116 r, 174 r, 178 v, 216 r, 218 r, 230 r, 232 r; Magdeburger Schöppenchronik, in *Die Chroniken deutschen Städte*, vol. 7 (Leipzig: Hirzel, 1869), 409.
[114] Karen Hagemann, Der "Bürger" als "Nationalkrieger". Entwürfe von Militär, Nation und Männlichkeit in der Zeit der Freiheitskriege, in *Landsknechte*, 87–90; Karen Hagemann, 'Of "Manly Valor" and "German Honor": Nation, war and masculinity in the age of the Prussian uprising against Napoleon', *Central European History* 30, no. 2 (1997): 187–220; Ute Frevert, 'Das Militär als "Schule der Männlichkeit". Erwartungen, Angebote, Erfahrungen im 19. Jahrhundert', in *Militär und Gesellschaft im 19. und 20. Jahrhundert*, ed. Ute Frevert (Stuttgart: Klett-Cotta, 1997), 145–73.
[115] Extrakt Schreibens von Herrn Kistenmacher, in *Briefe*, 9; Von einem Unteroffizier Anhaltischen Regiments, in *Briefe*, 23; Schreiben des Feldwebels Liebler, in *Briefe*, 47. See also: *Tagebuch des Musketiers Dominicus*, 64; Beß, *Aus dem Tagebuch*, 195–6; Hülsen, *Unter Friedrich dem Großen*, 88; Bernhard R., Die Geburt eines Mythos – die „schiefe Schlachtordnung". Leuthen, 5. Dezember, in Schlachten der Weltgeschichte. Von Salamis bis Sinai, ed. Stig Förster, Markus Pöhlmann, Dierk Walter (Munich: C. H. Beck, 2001), 182.
[116] Brief des Musketiers Johann Christian Riemann, in *Soldatenbriefe*, 32; Barsewisch, *Kriegs-Erlebnisse*, 33–7.
[117] Von einem Unteroffizier des Alt-Anhaltischen Regiments, in *Briefe*, 19.
[118] Hülsen, *Unter Friedrich dem Großen*, 78, 88.
[119] Barthel Linck, 3. Oktober 1756, in *Briefe*, 12–13.
[120] Von einem Unteroffizier des Alt-Anhaltischen Regiments, in *Briefe*, 19.
[121] Journal von der Expedition des Generallieutenants von Platen, in: *Sammlung*, vol. 3 (1783), 250; Tempelhof, *Geschichte*, vol. 2 (1785), 20.
[122] Retzow, *Charakteristik*, vol. 1, 108 and 251.
[123] Küster, *Bruchstück*, 60.
[124] Ein Traum stimmte einen Officier im siebenjährigen Kriege zur kaltblütigen Tapferkeit, in *Officier-Lesebuch*, vol. 2, 103–05; Tempelhof, Geschichte vol. 3, 117–18. This is also underlined by the other passage, where Küster uses *mannhaft*. He attributes *mannhafte Klugheit* (masculine prudence) to the king for making his army hold its ground against the attacking Austrians. Küster, *Bruchstück*, 98.

the men struck by it 'heroes'. The meaning of 'manly' as being able to think and act effectively under pressure can also be found in the only use of this word in the journals of the different units. An officer named Seehausen was attacked near Treptower Deep on 26 October 1761. He had forty men with him. In order to repel an attack by a far larger enemy force, he made his men form square 'and defended himself in a manly fashion'. He was only captured after his men had spent all their cartridges and no reinforcements could be brought in.[125] The use of 'manly' in the sense of 'being able to think' can also be found in Zedler's *Encyclopaedia*: '... In a moral sense, manliness is a state of mind, where you do not plan or do something, which is not suited for someone, who is able to use his wits maturely.'[126] Zedler's definition of 'Weib' (wife, woman) does not contain any pejorative hints or allusions to cowardice or an inability to think.[127] Thus, a concept of an especially male soldiers' honour is missing in the few passages where the word is used. Yet it remains to be seen whether there is a juxtaposed concept of female cowardice in the sources. Küster presents two women who are confronted with soldiers affected by combat. One of them is an anonymous burgeress, in whose house the army surgeon has set up his equipment. Initially, she is shocked by the wounded soldiers, 'these objects of pity', but then she starts making bandages by tearing apart one of her husband's shirts.[128] Here, Küster describes a courageous and passionate person. The second woman portrayed by Küster is the wife of General Graf von K**.[129] K** was fighting the French in 1795 and had written to his wife saying how upset he became when he thought of her pain should he die or be seriously injured. The general had obviously told her that it had distressed him to imagine her as a female weeping and longing for his return. His wife is furious with him and writes the following poem:

> I am womanly! I weep! Long
> for you! No!
> Be brave! You do not live for me right now,
> But only for the fatherland.[130]

She repeats her husband's characterization of her, which equals being a woman with weeping for her husband, but then rejects it angrily. Küster presents a women of the soldiers' estate who despises stereotypes and does her share in encouraging her husband to fight bravely. Our analysis of the soldiers' communication with their wives at home points in the same direction. The soldiers wanted their spouses to pray for them and thus help to save their lives and their honour.[131]

It is also noteworthy that the symbols of dishonour and cowardice have nothing to do with making the soldiers less 'male'. Instead, they lose the attributes of their honour.

---

[125] Journal von der Expedition des Generallieutenants von Platen, in *Sammlung*, vol. 3, 250.
[126] *Zedler's* 19 (1739), 173.
[127] *Zedler's* 9 (1735), 1767.
[128] Küster, *Bruchstück*, 135.
[129] General Count of K**.
[130] Heldenlied an den General Gr. von K**, in *Officier-Lesebuch*, vol. 3, 184–6.
[131] See p. 90.

As Frederick II threatened his infantry before the Battle of Leuthen: 'Every battalion of infantry which even hesitates while advancing loses its colours and the swords and its laces will be cut off.'[132].

Being a soldier of Frederick II did not encompass any notion of manliness or virility in combat in the modern sense of the word. There is no male component in their concept of honour in battle.[133] This rests on their alignment to the estate of which their women are a part.[134] What we can deduce from the letters is the idea of a good husband – and thus a good man. When Binn defends himself against accusations of unfaithfulness, he stresses that even in his youth he had not been a womanizer.[135] Obviously, it is not 'manly' for him as a *Kantonist* to have extra-marital girlfriends.[136] For Adam Becker, it is manly to care for his wife during her pregnancy and to put her fears and emotions ahead of his own. Being a good husband and a man means taking care of his wife and family.[137]

The soldiers' interactions with their officers

The Prussian king was simultaneously head of state and head of the army. He was the source of his subjects' honour[138] and, as the 'anointed of the Lord', under God's own protection.[139] Being near the king[140] or talking to him[141] was always important and honourable for the men.[142] At the same time it was their duty to defend his honour in return.[143] Defence of the king's honour meant nothing less than winning, as a defeat stained that honour. This is reflected in Dreyer's statement: 'We beat the enemy out of our sense of duty and obedience to our superiors and the king.'[144] If both the king and

---

[132] Retzow, *Charakteristik*, vol. 1, 242.
[133] Research on Britain points into a similar direction. There, violent behaviour was less and less considered to be male over the eighteenth century. Robert Shoemaker, 'Male honour and the decline of public violence in eighteenth-century London', *Social History* 26, no. 2 (2001): 190–208.
[134] *Zedler's* 9 (1735), 1767. Even if the king does not acknowledge the affiliation of poor *Kantonisten'* wives to the soldiers' estate, the women themselves and their husbands do so. See p. 143.
[135] See pp. 143–4.
[136] Unlike the noble cavalry general, Friedrich Wilhelm von Seydlitz. This shows a crucial difference between the commoners' code of honour and idea of manliness and the noble code of honour. Showalter, *Frederick*, pos. 3304.
[137] These findings correspond to the more general research on gender roles in the early modern era. A binary model of male and female = e.g. warrior and housewife, is not typical for the eighteenth century. Martin Dinges, 'Einleitung: Geschlechtergeschichte – mit Männern!', in *Hausväter, Priester, Kastraten. Zur Konstruktion von Männlichkeit in Spätmittelalter und Früher Neuzeit*, ed. Martin Dinges (Göttingen: Vandenhoeck und Ruprecht, 1998), 10–19.
[138] Winkel, *Zwischen adeliger Reputation*, 113; Blanning, *Frederick*, 27.
[139] The anonymous educated NCO from the Alt-Anhalt Regiment writes about a failed enemy attempt on the king's life and exclaims: 'Thus the Lord protects his anointed!' Beschreibung der Lobositzer Bataille, in *Soldatenbriefe*, 2.
[140] Ibid., 2–3.
[141] Barthel Linck, 3. Oktober 1756, in *Briefe*, 12; Frantz Reiß, 6 October 1756, in *Briefe*, 31; *Tagebuch des Musketiers Dominicus*, 59.
[142] Von einem [anonymen] Unteroffizier des Anhaltischen Regiments, 6 October 1756, in *Briefe*, 23–4.
[143] Brief des Musketiers Johann Christian Riemann, in *Soldatenbriefe*, 32. This was also the case in other armies. Disposition des Herzogs von Sachsen-Weissenfels, in *Sammlung*, vol. 1, 324–5.
[144] Dreyer, *Memoiren*, 22.

his men wanted to maintain their honour, both had to fulfil their obligations on the battlefield. The men had to fight effectively and bravely, and the king had to lead them competently. This reciprocal relationship is also reflected in the sources. Leading an army in the Seven Years' War basically meant two things. On the one hand, the commander had to organize an effective fighting force and direct its movements on the battlefield as effectively as possible. On the other hand, he had to act as an example of courage and composure and be alongside his men to encourage them and remind them of their honour. As Frederick and his generals were still in the 'stone age of command',[145] the actual tactical leadership of a battle could end after the drawing-up of battle orders. Even Frederick II could not assure that these initial orders were carried out correctly,[146] however, and a battle could go awry almost from the very beginning. In the case of the Battle of Kolin, it was the king himself who had changed his orders, swapping from a flanking movement to a frontal assault against the elevated Austrian positions. This already problematic move was undermined by communication problems, as the king had to effectively order the change of direction himself.[147] The outcome was Frederick's first major defeat and death, injury or captivity for about 14,000 of his men.[148] The soldiers' assessment of the king as a military leader is rather mixed. Johann Christian Riemann cites the motto of the Prussian army, which was used as a cry of hope in the face of a multitude of enemies during the war: 'God and Frederick are still alive!'[149] It indicates that the men saw Frederick at least as a guarantee against losing the war. NCO Liebler calls the king 'wise' when he praises his ability to thwart the Austrian plans just before the Battle of Prague.[150] The anonymous musketeer of Liebler's Alt-Anhalt Regiment does the same[151] but later presents a rather lukewarm analysis of the attacks on the Austrian positions. In his opinion, these were successful but also cost many lives, because of the [royal][152] order to attack with the bayonet.[153] Three other soldiers tell their relatives about the king being dissuaded from attacking elevated enemy positions by his generals.[154] This contradicts the General Staff's assessment that the soldiers had 'blind trust' in their king.[155] The soldiers mean it as a criticism, as they characterize the positions that Frederick wants to attack as unassailable.

---

[145] The phrase was coined by Martin van Crefeld. Showalter, *Frederick*, pos. 6506.
[146] This was the case at Zorndorf, where the two battle lines of the left wing lost contact and thus allowed the Russians to defeat them. Showalter, *Frederick*, pos. 3796.
[147] Ibid., pos. 2861–74.
[148] Ibid., 2937.
[149] Johann Christian Riemann, 16. Juni 1762, in *Soldatenbriefe*, 34–35; Barsewisch and Küster also cite it. Barsewisch, *Kriegs-Erlebnisse*, 23; Küster, *Bruchstück*, 73–4.
[150] Im Lager bei Prag, den 7. Mai 1757, Brief des Feldwebels G.S. Liebler, in *Briefe*, 46.
[151] Schreiben eines Musketiers des Regiments Anhalt zu Fuß, in *Briefe*, 50.
[152] The musketeer does not mention the king explicitly but knows that orders like this could only be issued by the king himself. Otherwise, he would have noted the name of the general who had given the order.
[153] Ibid., 51.
[154] Beschreibung der Lobositzer Bataille, datirt 1. Oktober 1756, in *Briefe*, 4; Lt. Seiler, 8 November 1757, in *Soldatenbriefe*, 36; C.F. Zander, 16 September 1757, in *Fundstücke*, 62.
[155] *Briefe*, VI.

The king's second duty – setting an example to his men – was unequivocally cherished by them. The Zanders and Dominicus tell their relatives that the king had always been with them on the front line.[156] Barsewisch confirms this by underlining that the king's presence in his regiment contributed to the men holding fast even when under fire.[157] Yet this noble example was often in vain. At Kolin, the king tried to rally some men to renew the attack, but the troops fell back and his aide-de-camp had to ask him: 'Sire, do you want to take the battery by yourself?'[158] At Zorndorf, Frederick grasped the colours of a company of the fusilier von Below Regiment but 'this gesture was as futile as most of its kind. He could scarcely be seen through the dust, and his voice was lost in all the din.'[159] In the final stage of the Battle of Kunersdorf, Frederick addressed his soldiers: 'Everybody who is a brave soldier, follow me.' Dominicus writes that all those who still had cartridges followed confidently. When the situation became untenable, the king commanded 'retreat, children'.[160]

Being near the king as the 'anointed of the Lord' was a source of honour and often strengthened the men's determination to fight. Frederick was also seen as a guarantee against losing the war, even though his attacks against well-entrenched Austrian forces at Prague and Kolin were criticized by the men.

Regarding the role of the king in combat, we have to stress that the king sets an example and appeals to their sense of honour by telling them that 'brave soldiers' will follow him. Therefore, those who failed to follow the king were not brave and thus dishonoured. He also calls the men his 'children', which stresses a bond between him and the men and his function as care-giver and their guardian.

This function of the commander as competent care-giver and protector is also reflected by the other communications between officers and soldiers that appear in the sources. The themes of the 'brave soldier' and the soldiers being their commander's 'children' appear there too. Warnery tells his readers about the death of Field Marshal von Schwerin in the Battle of Prague:

> [Schwerin] hurried [towards his retreating men], grabbed the colours and shouted: 'Those, who are brave men, follow me!' All officers and the greater part of the soldiers did so. Then he was killed by a canister ball and his regiment thrown back so far, that Winderfeld, its division commander, had a lot of trouble stopping it and nearly lost his voice shouting at the men.[161]

Both Retzow and Duke of Bevern's secretary write about the duke's conversation with his men during the Battle of Lobositz, when the von Bevern Regiment had rallied on a hill after having run out of ammunition:

---

[156] *Fundstücke*, 105; *Tagebuch des Musketiers Dominicus*, 65.
[157] Barsewisch, *Kriegs-Erlebnisse*, 74.
[158] Showalter, *Frederick*, pos. 2924.
[159] Duffy, *Frederick*, 167.
[160] *Tagebuch des Musketiers Dominicus*, 64.
[161] Warnery, *Feldzüge*, vol. 1, 99–100.

'Children,' the Duke shouted, 'shoot, for God's sake, shoot, advance!' 'Alas, dear father,' the lads replied, 'what shall we do? We have no more powder and have to let them shoot us here without resistance!' 'What?,' the Duke shouted, 'do you have no bayonets? Stab the dogs to death!'[162] These words, spoken by a commander in whom the soldier had complete trust, were like God's own words for the Prussians. They immediately closed ranks and encouraged by the example of their officers, they attacked with fury ... Like a torrent, they hurled themselves down the Loboschberg and everybody had to yield to their furious bravery.[163]

'Children' was not only used by officers to invoke a close relationship between them and their adult subordinates. During the siege of Schweidnitz in 1762, a superior used it in a literal sense:

the regiments used to besiege the fortress were amongst the worst of the entire army and almost entirely composed of children. One day, the garrison staged a sortie and some of the Prussian soldiers began to cry. The colonel commanding the trenches feared that they might do something worse [flee, K. & S.M.], [but] did not abuse them, not even with words but shouted: 'Cry as much as you want, my children, but open fire and do not run away.' His gentle behaviour made them fight as good soldiers.[164]

Küster's relation of the desperate fighting at Hochkirch gives another vivid example of the encouragement provided by the officers and, in this case, the regimental chaplain:

I stood next to Captain von Vittinghofen. He and I encouraged the men to stand fast until we were ordered to move[165] ... The air was full of the cries of brave officers and privates, who shouted: "children, stand! Comrades, hold the line, our relief will come soon!" I added my voice to theirs and shouted: 'Children, do your duty, God will help us, the king will soon be there with relief.'[166] When the Prussians were retreating from the battlefield, Küster was with the rear-guard commanded by Colonel von Saldern. His regiment's front was attacked by enemy infantry and Austrian cavalry moved in to attack its right flank. Now, some privates said: 'Now the last bread has been baked, the infantry in front and the cavalry attacks our flank.' Others answered them: 'Let them come, we are also here!' I replied: 'God is

---

[162] Extrakt Schreibens von Herrn Kistenmacher, in *Briefe*, 10.
[163] Retzow, *Charakteristik*, vol. 1, 63.
[164] Warnery, Feldzüge, vol. 2, 217; Cogniazzo, *Geständnisse*, vol. 4, 194–5. Cogniazzo doubts Warnery's story. He agrees that there were boys of only fifteen years of age in Prince Henry's regiment in particular, but strongly refutes the suggestion that these boys cried. In order to dismiss Warnery's story, he points to different heroic feats of arms performed by the Prussian infantry during the last phase of the war. But there is no contradiction, because Warnery does not challenge the general quality of the Prussian infantry. It seems as though Cogniazzo is annoyed by the idea that the Austrians should have been beaten by crying children.
[165] Küster, *Bruchstück*, 44.
[166] Ibid., 37.

also there, his scare can drive them back!' ... Colonel von Saldern, who had observed the enemies' movements rode up to our line calmly and said: 'When they come, we will thoroughly brush them so that they will not think of coming back again!' He ordered the gunners to unlimber and to open fire, so that the enemy knew we had artillery with us. The ruse worked, the Austrian cavalry withdrew, and the Prussians could leave the field.[167]

Religious references were also used by officers. Hülsen tried to rally his men during the Battle of Zorndorf by shouting: 'Victoria, lads! Victoria! In God's name, go on. It will soon be over!'[168] Dominicus relates a similar cry by Prince Friedrich Eugen von Württemberg during the Battle of Kunersdorf: 'Go on, in God's name, they are already retreating!'[169]

A last method of influencing the men involved displaying extreme 'coolness'. Barsewisch gives an striking example of this kind of behaviour during the Battle of Hochkirch. His regiment, von Mayerinck, stood against superior forces of Austrian infantry in a protracted fire-fight. The officers had left their assigned positions as four lieutenants were not to stand together when the battalion was lined up for battle. The soldiers were firing on their own and the officers did not shout orders at them, but rather tried to put up a show of coolness:

> I had the honour that when the battle had just begun, a bullet pierced my hat just above my head and went through the tip, another one followed not long after the first one and went through the large brim on the right side of my hat, so that it fell off my head. I asked the two von Hertzberg brothers, who stood nearby: 'Gentlemen, shall I put the hat on again, which the Imperials are desiring so much?' 'Yes, of course,' they said, 'the hat is honourable for you.' The oldest von Hertzberg took out his snuffbox and said: 'Gentlemen, take a pinch of Contenance!'[170] I joined them, took a pinch and said: 'Yes, here we need Contenance.' Von Unruh followed me and the youngest of the von Hertzberg brothers took the last pinch. As soon as the oldest von Hertzberg had taken his pinch out of the box and wanted to bring it near his nose, a musket bullet came and went right into the upper part of his forehead. I stood close by him, looked at him, he cried out loudly: 'Lord Jesus!', turned around and fell down dead. His fall made a great impression on me ... as I had to step back, to allow the body to drop to earth.[171]

In spite of Hertzberg's gruesome death, the show seems to have made the intended impression on the soldiers and contributed to the regiment not running away in spite of only 360 men escaping the slaughter.[172]

---

[167] Ibid., 57–8.
[168] Hülsen, *Unter Friedrich dem Großen*, 89.
[169] *Tagebuch des Musketiers Dominicus*, 60.
[170] This is probably a pun on the word *Contenance* (countenance), which could also have been a brand of snuff.
[171] Barsewisch, *Kriegs-Erlebnisse*, 77–8.
[172] http://www.kronoskaf.com/syw/index.php?title=Meyerinck_Infantry (accessed 15 November 2018).

Officers were to lead their men by example and did so. This ranged from keeping cool under fire to riding in front of the men with the colours of a company and encouraging them to go on. The encouragement of the officers correspond to the findings about the soldiers' feelings and thoughts manifested in their letters. When the officers invoke God, they appeal to the religious thoughts of the soldiers, who entrust their lives to God's mercy and do not want to break their oath. When they call upon the bravery of the men, they call upon the men's honour. And when the officers point out that relief is on the way or that the enemy is already retreating, they appeal to their wish to survive.

Music: The fine-tuning of military honour

The military music of the Prussian army symbolized the fine-tuning of military honour.[173] Every branch of the service had its own instruments, and these reflected the branch's position on the military scale of honour. Particularly prestigious instruments and military marches could be awarded to a regiment in recognition of its exemplary bravery. At the same time, different kinds of music were used to encourage the men to fight.

Instruments

Orchestra instruments in the late baroque era each had a place in the musical scale of honour.[174]

1. The most honourable instruments were the kettledrums and trumpets, which were often used together in sacred and secular music. The trumpets symbolized God, worldly authorities[175] and war.[176]
2. Next were the transverse flutes, which symbolized angels and the sphere between God and men.[177]
3. Third came the oboes, which represented mankind.[178]

---

[173] Möbius, *Ein feste Burg*, 261–90.
[174] Nikolaus Harnoncourt, 'Die Blasinstrumente im Instrumentarium Bachs', in *Beiheft zu: Das Kantatenwerk* 14 (1976): 3–5.
[175] Alfred Dürr, *Die Kantanten von Johann Sebastian Bach* (Munich: dtv Bärenreiter, [1971] 1981), 297; see also In Defence of the Knightly Art of the Trumpet: Caspar Hentschel's *Oratorischer Hall vnd Schall/ Vom Löblichen vrsprung/lieblicher anmuth vnd empfindlichen Nutzen Der Rittermessigen Kunst der Trommeten* (Berlin: George Runge, 1620), ed. Peter Downey (Lisburn, Northern Ireland: Downey Editions, 2017), 2, 18–19.
[176] Christoph Wolff, *Johann Sebastian Bach* (Frankfurt am Main: S. Fischer, 2000), 31; In Defence of the Knightly Art, 25.
[177] A well-known example is the aria 'Aus Liebe will mein Heiland sterben' in Bach's St. Matthew Passion, where the super-human nature of Christ's sacrifice is underlined by the absence of the basso continuo and an obligato transverse-flute. Emil Platen, *Johann Sebastian Bach. Die Matthäus-Passion. Entstehung, Werkbeschreibung, Rezeption*, 2nd ed. (1991; Kassel et al.: Bärenreiter, dtv, 1997), 50.
[178] The baroque score has the trumpets first, then the kettledrums, then the flutes, oboes and strings. See e.g. the score of the 'Gloria' of Bach's Mass in B minor. http://www1.cpdl.org/wiki/images/5/5b/Ws-bwv-232d.pdf (accessed 19 November 2018). Ludwig Prautzsch, *Bibel und Symbol in den Werken Bachs* (Norderstedt: Books on Demand, 2000), 73; Meinrad Walter, *Johann Sebastian Bach: Weihnachtsoratorium* (Kassel: Bärenreiter, 2006), 93;

Prussian military bands of the different regiments played the following instruments:

- cavalry: trumpets and kettledrums for the cuirassiers; oboes, drums and kettledrums for the dragoons;[179] trumpets for the hussars.
- infantry: fifes and drums for the grenadiers; a trumpet,[180] oboes and drums for the musketeers and fusiliers.

With the exception of the infantry's trumpets, the instruments were similar to those used by most European armies since the late 1600s.[181]

The cuirassiers were the most honourable branch of the service.[182] Every company of a cavalry regiment had its own trumpeter. In addition, every regiment had a staff trumpeter and a set of kettledrums, which were assigned to the company owned by the regiment's chef, the *Leibkompanie*.[183] The range of the ventless trumpets was not limited to the triads needed for playing signals during combat. In the highest register, the clarion, the baroque trumpet could not only play triads, but also complete scales. Thus, it could be used to play the tunes of military marches.[184] With careful training, trumpeters were able to produce sharp or flat notes. These notes sounded quite brash, and were used to symbolize terror or the devil when used in sacred music.[185] The trumpet was the queen of baroque instruments, and the most honourable instrument. The kettledrums were also part of the trumpet ensemble in civil society and in the church. Together with the standards, they were the symbols of the cuirassier regiment's honour and officially counted as trophies of war when captured.[186]

As the dragoons were originally mounted infantry that travelled on horseback but fought on foot, they used the same instruments as the musketeers. Every regiment had four oboes and fifteen drums. As the dragoons had become some kind of all-round cavalry by the time of Frederick II and could play a decisive role in battle,[187] they were allowed kettledrums.[188] The instruments reflect the dragoons' status of honour between the heavy cavalry and the infantry, as the oboes rank third in the ranking of honour of baroque instruments but the kettledrums are in first places along with the trumpets.

The hussars were the backbone of Prussia's effort in the Little War and were also used on the battlefield to great success. Although below the dragoons on the scale of honour, their only musicians were trumpeters.[189] This was due mainly to their role in

---

[179] This was due to the fact that the dragoons had been mounted infantry in the seventeenth century.
[180] Achim Hofer, *Studien zur Geschichte des Militärmarsches*, vol. 1 (Tutzing: Schneider, 1988), 231–3.
[181] Werner Braun, Entwurf für eine Typologie der "Hautboisten", in *Der Sozialstatus des Berufsmusikers vom 17. bis 18. Jahrhundert*, ed. Walter Salmen (Basel: Bärenreiter, 1971), 50.
[182] Frank Wernitz, *Die Armee Friedrichs des Großen im Siebenjährigen Krieg* (Eggolsheim-Berstadt: Podzun-Pallas, 2002), 47.
[183] *Prussian cavalry Reglement of 1743*, 3–5.
[184] Hofer, *Studien*, vol. 1, 213.
[185] Johann Sebastian Bach, *Kantate „Schauet doch und sehet, ob irgendein Schmerz sei"* (BWV 46), ed. Arnold Schering (London et al. s.d.), V, 32–40.
[186] Joachim Toeche-Mittler, *Armeemärsche. Die Geschichte unserer Marschmusik* (Neckargmünd: Spemann, 1975), vol. III, 31.
[187] Bericht, in *Sammlung*, vol. 1, 320. von Hoen, *Die Schlacht bei Kolin*, vol. 4, 582; Bericht, in *Sammlung*, vol. 2, 581–2.
[188] Jany, *Geschichte*, vol. II, 84.
[189] Ibid., 84.

the Little War and the need to fight in open order. Thus they needed instruments that could be heard over long distances. That this was a necessity and no upgrade in honour was underlined by the king's refusal to grant them the honourable kettledrums.[190] These were awarded only to the Black Hussars, who were allowed to keep the kettledrums of an Austrian cuirassier regiment that they had captured at Katholisch-Hennersdorf in November 1745.[191]

The grenadier companies had two fifers (*Pfeifer*) each.[192] These stressed the honour of the grenadiers and their elite status vis-à-vis the musketeers and fusiliers, as the flutes ranked second in the baroque hierarchy of instrumental honour.[193] In addition, the grenadiers had the right to play a special march. It differed from the normal marches of the musketeers as the short notes were played on the rim and not the head of the drum.[194] Musketeer regiments could be awarded the right to play the grenadier march as a special reward.

As the musketeers ranked below the grenadiers, it was only logical that their instruments were also less honourable than the flutes, and thus they used oboes. Every regiment had six oboe players, three per battalion.[195] Yet it seems that sometimes all six oboe players were concentrated behind the colours in the middle of a battalion.[196] The oboists were organizationally attached to the staff of the regiment. The same was true for the trumpet played by one of the oboe players since the days of the Soldier King.[197] As this trumpet was awarded to the entire regiment, musketeers and grenadiers alike, it did not improve the *musketeers'* rank on the scale of honour but that of the entire infantry. It reflected the honour of the infantry, and ultimately of the whole field army, that all branches of the service were allowed to use the most honourable queen of instruments.[198]

Compared to modern military orchestras, these regimental bands were small and scarcely able to rouse the spirits of all men in a battalion when marching towards the enemy with all eighteen drummers of the battalion beating the charge. Yet the marches they played were important for the regiment's honour. The Alt-Anhalt Regiment, for

---

[190] Toeche-Mittler, *Armeemärsche*, vol. III, 31.
[191] Peter Panoff, *Militärmusik in Geschichte und Gegenwart* (Berlin: Karl Siegismund, 1938), 87; http://www.kronoskaf.com/syw/index.php?title=Ruesch_Hussars (accessed 19 November 2018).
[192] Constantin Kling, *Die Infanterie-Regimenter. Allgemeine Bemerkungen* (Weimar: Buch- und Steindruckerei von Putze und Hölzer, 1902), 153.
[193] The musketeers had lost their fifers in 1749 as they were told to work as carpenters for manning the battalion pieces. Peter. C. Marten, *Die Musik der Spielleute des altpreussischen Heeres* (Osnabrück: Biblio, 1976), 27; Jany, *Geschichte*, vol. 2, 184.
[194] Marten, *Die Musik*, 68.
[195] The *Reglement* erroneously calls the musicians of the musketeer battalions 'Pfeiffers', the traditional name for the fifers. *Prussian Infantry Reglement of 1743*, 4.
[196] http://www.kronoskaf.com/syw/index.php?title=Prussian_Line_Infantry_Drill (accessed 19 November 2018).
[197] Achim Hofer, 'Zur Erforschung und Spielpraxis von Märschen bis um 1750', in *Militärmusik und „zivile" Musik. Beziehungen und Einflüsse*, ed. Armin Griebel and Horst Steinmetz (Uffenheim: Forschungsstelle für fränkische Volksmusik, 1993), 48–9.
[198] Only the garrison regiments had no oboists and only their grenadiers had two fifers for each company. *Prussian Reglement for the Garrison Regiments of 1743*, 4; a royal decree from 1755 cut this number to one fifer per company, but was not carried out. Jany, *Geschichte*, vol. 2, 184, fn. 12.

example, had a march that could be played by infantry and cavalry alike. (Playing a cavalry march was regarded as especially honourable.[199])

Infantry marches were characterized by 'military' dotted rhythms and major triads.[200] The warlike trumpet could add fanfare-like triads or even join in playing the melody.[201] Normally, the melody was played by the oboes, while the bassoons played the bass part in unison or in two parts when the band played together.

Musicians

Some of the musicians were black Africans. For example, the *Pfeifer* (fifers) of the Potsdam Giants were slaves bought in the Netherlands or England. Upon their arrival in Prussia, they were taught German, baptized and given German names. Legally, they were freed and theoretically had the same rights as other non-noble subjects of the king. There were twenty-three of these former slaves in the army at the end of Frederick William's reign.[202]

A good part of the oboists were trained by the famous Gottfried Pepusch,[203] who headed the *Hautboistenschule* (oboists' school) located in the military orphanage in Potsdam[204] and also played for the king himself.[205] The *Hautboisten-Premiers* (first oboes) of the military bands led the other oboists and had to be good composers as well in order to entertain their regimental chefs.[206]

Some the drummers also came from the military orphanage in Potsdam. During the reign of the Soldier King, orphaned boys were taught to play the drum by older invalid drummers and at the same time taught to write and read in order to join one of the regiments of the elite Potsdam garrison. Under Frederick II, the orphanage degenerated and became a prison-like institution which supplied cheap labour to the nearby factories.[207] The king was not interested in educating the orphans and music and drumming lessons were pretty much abandoned. Other drummers were recruited like other soldiers and were often smaller than the regular musketeers.[208] The oboists were paid four *Reichsthalers* a month, the regimental drummer three *Thalers* and twelve *Groschen*. They were thus on an equal footing with the best paid subaltern officers. The ordinary fifers and drummers got as much money as the musketeers, two *Reichsthalers* a month.[209]

---

[199] Seyfarth, *Geschichte des Infanterie-Regiments von Anhalt-Bernburg*, 9.
[200] Hofer, *Geschichte*, vol. 1, 289–342, esp. 317.
[201] Ibid., 318–19, 348.
[202] http://potsdam-geschichte.de/stadt-abc/mohren/ (accessed 19 November 2018). See also: Küster, *Bruchstück*, 49.
[203] The brother of John Christopher Pepusch, who composed the Beggar's Opera. Bruce Haynes, *The Eloquent Oboe: A History of the Hautboy 1640–1760* (Oxford: Oxford University Press, 2001), 345.
[204] Braun, *Entwurf*, 46.
[205] The Soldier King had a strong liking for Handel's operas. Friedrich Christoph Förster, *Friedrich Wilhelm I. König von Preussen*, vol. 1 (Potsdam: Ferdinand Riegel, 1834), 303.
[206] Hofer, *Geschichte*, vol. 1, 321.
[207] René Schreiter, 'Das Große Militärwaisenhaus zu Potsdam 1724–1952. Ein Kapitel preußisch-deutscher Erziehungsgeschichte', *Militär und Gesellschaft in der frühen Neuzeit* 7, no. 1 (2003): 77.
[208] Dreyer, *Leben*, 15.
[209] *Prussian Infantry Reglement of 1743*, 479–80.

The role of the musicians in combat

When the battalion was drawn up for battle, the oboists were positioned behind the colours platoon in the middle of the formation, while the drummers marched behind the two flanking platoons.[210] The regimental drummer had to be near the commander riding in front of the centre of the battalion to convey his commands to the other drummers and men.[211] The *Reglement* of 1726 orders the battalions to advance against the enemy with 'arms shouldered, colours flying and music playing'.[212] But when the actual battle started and the musketeers had to fire, everybody had to be silent and the musicians had to stay behind the battalion together with the chaplains and field-surgeons. Nobody was allowed to carry the wounded to safety; only officers could order their servants accompany them to the dressing station.[213] The role of the musicians changed in 1742, when Frederick II ordered the 'oboists, drummers and fifers' to 'bring the wounded to the circle of waggons'.[214] The regimental drummer had to stay with the commander and a certain number of drummers seem to have stayed with the battalion, too, as they were ordered to beat the drums, when the unit had to advance after firing.[215]

In battle, the musicians had two main tasks. First, they had to support the orders given by the commanders. This was especially true for the cavalry, where the volume of the kettledrums[216] and the characteristic sound of the trumpets[217] could communicate orders over a distance in a way the human voice could never match.

Second, the music served to combat the soldiers' fears and to raise their spirits. This could be done by the beating of drums and playing of marches while advancing against the enemy. Given the small size of the regimental bands and the minimal volume of the instruments, however, the effect must have been rather limited. Another kind of music was more effective, though, as it chimed with the men's religious beliefs. Dreyer writes that 'we went into battle with [the hymn] *Ein feste Burg ist unser Gott* (*A mighty fortress is our God*) on our lips and ended it with *Nun danket alle Gott* (*Now thank we all our God*).[218] The playing and singing of hymns during the advance is well documented[219] and we have a detailed account of the hymns played and sung while the Prussian infantry was closing in on the Russian forces at the Battle of Zorndorf. A Protestant chaplain on the Russian side wrote about the moment when he heard the Prussian musicians:

> We had already heard the dreadful noise of the Prussian drums but were not yet able to discern their music. But they come closer and closer in a solemn march,

---

[210] Marten, *Die Musik*, 25.
[211] Johann Conrad Müller, *Der Wohl exercirte Preußische Soldat* (Schaffhausen, 1759), 39.
[212] *Prussian Infantry Reglement of 1726*, 358.
[213] Ibid., 363.
[214] Marten, *Die Musik*, 26.
[215] *Prussian Infantry Reglement of 1743*, 70–2.
[216] Percival Kirby, 'The Kettle-Drums: An Historical Survey', in *Music & Letters* 9 (1929): 34–43.
[217] Harnoncourt, *Blasinstrumente*, 3–5.
[218] Dreyer, *Leben*, 22.
[219] Jany, *Geschichte*, vol. 2, 453.

now we hear their oboists, they play: *Ich bin ja Herr in deiner Macht (I am, my Lord, just in thy power)*. Speaking of this music, not a single word about my feelings. Everybody capable of human feelings will not think it unbelievable, that this melody caused me the most intense sentiments of melancholy ever after in my life.[220]

The hymn was also noticed on the Prussian side:

While the regiments were drawing up, Frederick realized that one of the regimental bands was playing a somewhat special but extraordinary solemn march. 'What is that?,' he asked a general in his vicinity, who was visibly moved by listening to the music of the passing regiment. 'It is the melody of the hymn, *Ich bin ja Herr in deiner Macht*,' answered the general. Also moved, the king repeated these words and listened most attentively to the music...[221]

Soldiers also sang hymns while marching into battle on the same day.[222] The lyrics of the hymn *Ich bin ja Herr in deiner Macht* bear closer examination:

Ich bin ja, Herr, in deiner Macht,
du hast mich an das Licht gebracht,
du unterhältst mir auch das Leben;
du kennest meiner Monden Zahl,
weißt, wann ich diesem Jammertal
auch wieder gute Nacht muss geben;
wo, wie und wenn ich sterben soll.

I am, my Lord, just in thy power,
You brought me to the light,[223]
You also do maintain my life,
You know the number of my months[224],
You know, when I good night must wish,
To this vale of tears,
Where, how and when I have to die,
Thou, father, knowest more than well.[225]

The entire hymn is centred around the expectation of death. It corresponds to the analysis of the soldiers' letters, which are dominated by the fear of death and religious

---

[220] Christian Täge, *Christian Täge's ehemaligen Russischen Feldpredigers, jetzigen Pfarrers zu Pobethen, Lebensgeschichte. Nach dessen eigenhändigen Aufsätzen und mündlichen Nachrichten bearbeitet von August Samuel Gerber* (Königsberg: Göbbels und Unzer, 1804), 181.
[221] Cited after: Wolfgang Venohr, *Der große König* (Bergisch Gladbach: Bastei Lübbe, 1997), 165.
[222] Friedrich der Große, *Gespräche*, 231.
[223] You gave birth to me.
[224] The number of my days.
[225] Translation by K. and S. Möbius.

Figure 3.1 Oboists of the von Bevern Regiment (No. 7) during the Battle of Zorndorf. © Jorge M. Corada.

comfort. As the Prussian army had no equivalent to the Catholic benediction of the soldiers that prepared them for death in battle, the men themselves started singing the hymns to calm their nerves.[226]

On the eve of a victory, the soldiers also sang hymns to thank God for 'having survived this great and murderous day', as Retzow put it after the Battle of Leuthen, when the men sang the famous hymn *Nun danket alle Gott*.[227] A similar scene took place after the Battle of Roßbach:

> It is noteworthy, that almost all regiments and [grenadier][228] battalions sang songs of praise and thanksgiving and had good reason to do so. Only a brute could not have been moved by this display of gratitude to our gracious God. Lest we forget, how piously His Excellency Prince Moritz [von Anhalt-Dessau] behaved on this occasion.[229]

---

[226] This was probably what Frantz Reiß meant when he complained about having been sent to the slaughtering block or scaffold, without knowing what was to come.

[227] Retzow, *Charakteristik*, vol. 1, 251–3; Bernhard R. Kroener, ,"Nun danket alle Gott." Der Choral von Leuthen und Friedrich der Große als protestantischer Held. Die Produktion politischer Mythen im 19. und 20. Jahrhundert', in *'Gott mit uns.' Nation, Religion und Gewalt im 19. und frühen 20. Jahrhundert*, ed. Gerd Krumeich and Hartmut Lehmann (Göttingen: Vandenhoeck & Ruprecht, 2000), 108.

[228] See: Tempelhof, *Geschichte*, vol. 1, 274.

[229] Maximilian von Bornstädt, Tagebuch, in *Sammlung*, vol. 3, 26.

While soldiers themselves sang hymns after a victory, ritual of singing and playing the *Te Deum Laudamus*[230] was a highly official act, which was performed not only by the victorious army but also in churches throughout the victor's and his allies' countries.[231] It stressed the victor's honour and was always performed by a festival orchestra with trumpets and kettledrums or, as in the case of Graun's *Te Deum* for the victory at Prague, with horns and oboes. The army sang the *Te Deum* for the victory at Lobositz two days after the battle

> ... accompanied by the sound of trumpets and kettledrums, and I can honestly assure you that I have never before seen such a devotion throughout our entire army. Our colonel von Bredow lifted up his eyes to heaven and beat his breast, when the verse *Nun hilf uns Herr, den Dienern Dein, die mit Deinem theuren Blut erlöset sein!* (Now help us, Lord, we are thine servants and have been redeemed by your precious blood) was sung.[232]

The official act to celebrate for the king's glory[233] was very intimate and emotional for the surviving troops. That they sang so many hymns on the battlefield of their own volition shows a religious soldiers' culture that was closely linked to the men's feelings and fears.

Music as a reward

Two of the most honourable rewards of the Prussian army were the awarding of the right to play the grenadier march or to keep and use kettledrums captured from enemy regiments. It is also noteworthy that these were the only rewards for the *collective* regiment. All other rewards were given to the regiment or battalion but later on distributed to individual soldiers. It is another indication of the Prussian army's special esteem for the infantry that the grenadier march was regarded as even more honourable than the *Reutermarsch* (march of the cuirassiers). The dragoon von Holstein-Gottorp Regiment (No. 9)[234] was awarded the right to keep the kettledrums taken from the French regiment Roussillon during the Battle of Krefeld (23 June 1758) and to beat the *Reutermarsch* on them. 'But concerning the right to beat the grenadier-march on its drums, the regiment will have to wait until it will have further distinguished itself in

---

[230] 'Der König an den Staatsminister Grafen von Podewils', in *Friedrich der Große. Denkwürdigkeiten aus seinem Leben nach seinen Schriften, seinem Briefwechsel und den Berichten seiner Zeitgenossen*, ed. Franz Eyssenhardt, 2nd ed.(1886; Leipzig: Fr. Wilh. Brunow, 1910), 367.

[231] Bernhard Jahn, 'Die Medialität des Krieges. Zum Problem der Darstellung von Schlachten am Beispiel der Schlacht bei Lobositz (1.10.1756) im Siebenjährigen Krieg', in *"Krieg ist mein Lied" Der Siebenjährige Krieg in den zeitgenössischen Medien*, ed. Wolfgang Adam and Holger Dainat in cooperation with Ute Pott (Göttingen: Wallstein, 2007), 97–8.

[232] Barthel Linck, 3. Oktober 1756, in *Briefe*, 14–15; Von einem Unteroffizier Anhaltischen Regiments, in *Ibid.*, 24; Schreiben des Feldwebels Liebler, in ibid., 55. These instances after the Battles of Lobositz and Roßbach are well documented.

[233] Jürgen Luh, *Der Große. Friedrich II. von Preußen* (München: Siedler, 2011), 63.

[234] Gieraths, *Die Kampfhandlungen*, 252–4.

future battles.'[235] And it did so during the Battle of Minden (1 August 1759), where it took four enemy battalions prisoner and captured ten cannon. Unfortunately it is not known whether the regiment really was awarded the grenadier march, but we can be certain that its men received several thousand *Reichsthaler*.[236] The example shows that the infantry's grenadier march ranked higher than the *Reutermarsch* of the cuirassiers. Frederick II awarded the grenadier march to a good number of regiments. The infantry von Schlichting Regiment (later von Kanitz, No. 2) earned the right to beat it after its decisive action at Hohenfriedberg (4 June 1745).[237] The dragoon Bayreuth Regiment (No. 5) gained this and numerous other rewards for its famous charge that led to the collapse of the Austrian infantry.[238] All infantry regiments engaged in the Battle of Kesselsdorf (15 December 1745) and the dragoon von Bonin Regiment (No. 4) were awarded the grenadier march,[239] as did the infantry after the Battle of Hohenfriedberg.[240]

In summary, then, singing and even playing hymns were common means for the soldiers to encourage themselves and prepare for the probability of death while marching towards the enemy and onto the battlefield. During direct advances under enemy fire, regimental bands played martial marching tunes characterized by C and D major triads which, according to the musical doctrine of the day, aroused warlike feelings. Each branch of the service had instruments that matched their status on the army's scale of honour. Being awarded instruments that were very high in the hierarchy of instruments (trumpets, flutes, kettledrums), and above all the right to beat the grenadier march, increased the regiment's honour and were thus also an incentive to fight effectively.

Material incentives

The most common material incentives for soldiers were plunder or rewards in cash. Plundering in itself was not dishonourable,[241] but it is obvious from our soldiers' letters that they did not like to talk about it. Some mention booty like fur from enemy caps,[242] a musket or other pieces of equipment,[243] but as a whole they indicate the infantry and line cavalry had very limited chances for plunder.[244] Corporal Binn proudly tells his

---

[235] Panoff, *Militärmusik*, 88.
[236] *Stammliste aller Regimenter und Corps der Königlich-Preußischen Armee für das Jahr 1806* (1806; repr., Osnabrück: Biblio, 1975), 241.
[237] http://www.preussenweb.de/regiment1.htm. (accessed 20 November 2018).
[238] Jany, *Geschichte*, Bd. 2, 138.
[239] Marten, *Die Musik*, 66–7.
[240] Seyfarth, *Geschichte des Infanterie-Regiments von Anhalt-Bernburg*, 43.
[241] Barthel Linck, 3 October 1756, in *Briefe*, 14. Barthel Linck tells his wife that a Prussian lieutenant had been given the sword, sash and sword of an Austrian general, whom he had taken prisoner 'according to the customs of war', but the Austrian had roguishly fired a pistol at him. See also Barsewisch, *Kriegs-Erlebnisse*, 28.
[242] Beschreibung der Lobositzer Bataille, datirt 1. Oktober 1756, in *Soldatenbriefe*, 6.
[243] Letter no. 3 by Corporal Binn, in *Soldatenbriefe*, 8.
[244] Frantz Reiß, 6. Oktober 1756, in *Briefe*, 32.

wife this after the Battle of Prague,²⁴⁵ but some months later he did send a belt and a musket that can only have been party of such ill-gotten gains.²⁴⁶ Even if looting were an incentive to fight on, it was not considered honourable and can therefore be dismissed in our context.

Much more important for the soldiers' honour were the rewards earned by privates from successful regiments or from units that had been able to capture enemy colours, standards or kettledrums. These were the traditional trophies in early modern European warfare, as their capture normally meant the end of the enemy unit as a coherent fighting force. As privates were normally not promoted for especially honourable actions, the payment of money and the distribution of wine²⁴⁷ were the king's means of showing his esteem. These presents were collective payments, distributed equally amongst the surviving privates of a unit. This was mainly due to the common way of fighting in formations that could defeat an enemy formation and then capture its key effects.

The 1726 *Reglement* promises the privates money for trophies and this passage is literally copied in its 1743 incarnation:

> If a common soldier captures a colour, standard of kettledrum from the enemy, he shall always get a good amount of money for it; but when it is an officer or NCO, he will recommend himself by this and there is no doubt, that he will be promoted.²⁴⁸

Corresponding payments were also paid, as was the case after the Battle of Kesselsdorf (15 December 1745), for example.²⁴⁹ Money could also be given to the men of especially successful regiments for outstanding behaviour in combat. These were the so called *Douceurgelder* (gratuities).²⁵⁰ Thus the men of a squadron of the dragoon von Borcke Regiment received one *Reichsthaler* for every private and 100 for every lieutenant for their achievements in the skirmish at Zarnewanz.²⁵¹ C.F. Zander writes to his nephew that after the night action described in his letter, the major received 1,000 *Reichsthaler*, the captain 500, every lieutenant and ensign 250 and every private one *Reichsthaler* or five *Groschen* depending on the regiment.²⁵²

Other types of gratuity were the two kinds of *Winterdouceurs* (winter gratuities). One of them was money given to the men of successful units, when they went into their winter quarters.²⁵³ The other one was given to the officers of all regiments that had not dishonoured themselves.

One reward specific to the Seven Years' War was *Kanonengeld* (cannon money). Their introduction was linked to the psychological effect on the men of the

---

[245] Letter no. 2 by Corporal Binn, in *Soldatenbriefe*, 7.
[246] Letter no. 3 by Corporal Binn, in *Soldatenbriefe*, 8.
[247] C.F. Zander, 17 February 1757, in *Fundstücke*, 50.
[248] *Prussian Infantry Reglement of 1726*, 363; *Prussian Infantry Reglement of 1743*, 274.
[249] Geschichte und Feldzüge des Dragonerregiments von Borke, in *Sammlung*, vol. 5, 311.
[250] Bericht des Obristen von Carlowitz, in *Sammlung*, vol. 4, 227; Barsewisch, *Kriegs-Erlebnisse*, 24; C.F. Zander, 17 February 1757, in *Fundstücke*, 50.
[251] Geschichte und Feldzüge des Dragonerregiments von Borke, in *Sammlung*, vol. 5, 359.
[252] Zander, 17 February 1757, in *Fundstücke*, 50.
[253] Tagebuch eines Preußischen Offiziers über die Feldzüge von 1756 bis 1763, in *Sammlung*, vol. 2, 391.

Austrians' devastating cannon fire. Frederick II told his private secretary de Catt in late April 1758:

> I encourage my soldiers ..., I reward them, and when it is necessary, I promise them these rewards already in advance to encourage them. They feared the [enemies'] cannons after the Battle of Breslau;[254] then, I promised 100 ducats[255] for every cannon taken by a Prussian soldier and this was wonderfully successful. It is so advantageous to know the hearts of men and to know what makes them do their duty.[256]

Indeed, this money was first paid to the von Kahlden grenadier battalion after the Battle of Breslau. It was the only battalion to receive *Kanonengelder* after this battle.[257] Frederick announced the payment of 100 ducats for each enemy cannon in his speech before the Battle of Leuthen.[258] The amount of 100 ducats is verified by a letter from Major von Heyden to Prince Moritz von Anhalt-Dessau on 3 January 1758, in which he reminded the commander of the promised 100 ducats for every cannon captured from the Austrians.[259] Unfortunately, there is no explanation in our sources for why the von Oestenreich grenadier battalion[260] received only 50 ducats for each cannon,[261] and why this amount seems to have become normal from 1758 onwards. For example, after the Battle of Liegnitz (15 August 1760), the king paid the promised gratuities to the officers 'and to the regiments [privates] for every cannon 137 *Reichsthaler* and 12 *Groschen* and for every colour and standard 50 *Reichsthaler*' two days after the battle.

Honourable actions of brave privates and NCOs could lead to an offer of an officer's commission. As we do not possess the regiments' files, we do not have any numbers, but it seems that these offers were rather exceptional. Some privates declined the promotion and took money instead. Three of the five common soldiers who had been made such an offer preferred cash. Thus, Sergeant Hochleitner from the dragoon von Borcke Regiment (No. 7) declined a lieutenant's commission after his courageous behaviour in a skirmish on 25 September 1762 and took 100 *Reichsthaler* instead.[262]

Their preference for monetary reward can be explained by the fates of the non-noble NCO Zander of the von Graevenitz infantry regiment (No. 20), who was promoted to captain in 1741 for his extraordinary role in the taking of the fortress of Brieg, and of Grenadier David Krauel from the von Kahlbutz grenadier battalion in 1744.

---

[254] A Prussian army under the command of the Duke of Bevern was defeated at Breslau on 22 November 1757.
[255] One ducat equalled *c.* 2 ¾ *Reichsthaler*. Thus, a cannon could earn a unit *c.* 275 *Reichsthaler*.
[256] Friedrich der Grosse, *Gespräche*, 43; Tempelhof, *Geschichte*, vol. 1, 241.
[257] Bericht des Obristen von Carlowitz, in *Sammlung*, vol. 4, 228–9. Georg Karl von Carlowitz became commander of this battalion in 1759; it had been commanded by Henning Alexander von Kahlden between 1756 and 1757. Gieraths, *Kampfhandlungen*, 566 and 574.
[258] Barsewisch, *Kriegs-Erlebnisse*, 25.
[259] Jany, *Geschichte*, vol. 2, 451, fn. 136.
[260] On the name see: Gieraths, *Kampfhandlungen*, 580.
[261] Journal des Oesterreichischen Grenadier-Bataillons, in *Sammlung*, vol. 5, 86.
[262] Geschichte und Feldzüge des Dragonerregiments von Borke, vom Jahr 1717 da es gestiftet worden, bis zum Julius 1784, in *Sammlung*, vol. 5, 392. Another case is described on p. 311.

NCO Zander had disguised himself as a Catholic monk as part of the efforts to capture Brieg in 1741. The king gave him a captaincy in the garrison regiment stationed in Breslau / Wroclaw. He was treated very poorly by the regiment's upper-class officers, however, and not just because of his lowly origins but also due to the fact that he came from another unit. Normally, vacant officers' positions were filled with the most senior noble officer or noble NCO from the next lower rank; for example, when a captain was killed, the most senior first lieutenant got his commission. This was an iron rule that not even the king could break[263] and neither Frederick nor Leopold von Anhalt-Dessau could save Zander from being bullied. In the end, the exemplary Zander had to quit the service and Frederick could do no more than grant him an annual pension of 200 *Reichtsthaler* and free housing in the city Magdeburg.[264]

David Krauel had been the first Prussian soldier to enter the Ziska redoubt on the mountain of the same name when it was stormed in September 1744. Two days later, he was ennobled – named 'Krauel vom Ziskaberg' – and transferred to the von Byla grenadier battalion as an officer. He was most probably bullied by his noble fellow officers, as he was transferred subsequently to the garrison battalion of Lieutenant General de la Mott in Geldern.[265] Without doubt, this was a demotion. He was probably transferred once more after the relocation of his regiment to Magdeburg and served in the *Neue Garnison Land-Regiment Nr. 3*,[266] which was also stationed in Magdeburg.[267] There, he held the rank of a lieutenant before his death in 1771.[268]

Privates could also rise to the officers' ranks via the normal promotion route, which involved first becoming an NCO and then an officer. But as the king wanted an officer corps consisting of nobles,[269] it was much more difficult for an NCO to rise through the ranks in this way. The *Reglement* provides the following guidelines for non-noble NCOs who aim to become officers:

> If an NCO, who is no nobleman, has got great merits and an open head[270] and a handsome appearance and has at least 12 years of service, he shall be proposed for promotion to second lieutenant of His Royal Majesty.[271]

C.F. Zander tells his nephew of four NCOs who had become officers. One of them had faked his proof of nobility and Zander's frankness about the matter indicates that his superiors knew this type of thing went on, but tolerated it due to the desperate need

---

[263] Hülsen, *Unter Friedrich dem Großen*, 30–4.
[264] Carl Daniel Küster, 'Der Unterofficier Zander vom Grävenitz'schen Regiment geht als verkleideter Pater in die Festung Brieg, und erleichtert die Einnahme im Jahr 1741', in *Officier-Lesebuch*, vol. 1, 174.
[265] Bericht des Obristen von Carlowitz, in *Sammlung*, vol. 4, 210.
[266] The *Landregimenter* (territorial regiments) were made up of Kantonisten, who did not serve in the field regiments but could be used as a reserve for the field regiments.
[267] Gieraths, *Kampfhandlungen*, 316–17 and 324–5.
[268] The short cv is from *Briefe*, 54–5, fn. *. The first transfer is not mentioned there and can be found in the Bericht des Obristen von Carlowitz, in *Sammlung*, vol. 4, 210.
[269] *Prussian Infantry Reglement of 1743*, 442.
[270] Is intelligent.
[271] *Prussian Infantry Reglement of 1743*, 443.

of officers after the bloody battles of the previous year. It is also noteworthy that one NCO could have got a commission 'had he not been married'.[272] The rejection of the married NCO was probably due to the fact that the king did not like his officers to be married and thus forbade young NCOs from finding a wife. Older NCOs were allowed to marry only if the bride was rich:[273] the king was interested in well-off officers because they could help support their unit financially until the king was able to reimburse later. It was generally assumed that married men would think of their wives and children during combat and thus become timid and keener to keep themselves safe rather than behave honourably.

It is striking that Zander does not mention any problems with these NCOs' promotions, which stands in sharp contrast to the treatment meted out to Krauel vom Ziskaberg and the anonymous NCO who had helped to capture the fortress of Brieg. The difference in behaviour by the noble officers might be explained by the different *context*. There was no lack of noble officers in 1741 and 1744 and vacant positions could easily be filled up with those noblemen who were next in the line of seniority. By 1758, however, the situation was completely different. Many noble officers had been killed or maimed and there were simply not enough candidates to fill all vacancies. Thus, the most senior nobles next in line for promotion were not hampered by the newcomer. And if the NCOs were able men, their new noble colleagues knew that it was in their interest to have an experienced colleague marching next to them.

The overview shows that honourable feats of arms of privates and NCOs were linked mainly to material gains. These comprised the possibility to plunder and, more importantly, money paid to the regiments' privates and NCOs for war 'trophies' such as cannon, colours, standards and kettledrums. This prize money was also important because it gave soldiers proof of their own valour, and this could be communicated to relatives at home, thereby increasing their honour and social standing in their community. Promotions to the officer ranks were rare and even promotions to NCO were tempting only for those privates who did not have a well-paying job in civilian life.

Discipline by force

Johan Friedrich von Fleming, Saxon officer and the first German military encyclopaedist, summarized the prevailing eighteenth-century wisdom[274] on the treatment of soldiers who tried to flee in battle:

> A disheartened and timid soldier is the most despicable and miserable creature under the sun and does not deserve for that sun to shine on him ... The poltroon and cowardly wimp ... flees and thinks of nothing else than how he can secure his

---

[272] C.F. Zander, 16 May 1758, in *Fundstücke*, 76.
[273] *Prussian Infantry Reglement of 1743*, 470–1. As NCOs like the Lieblers or the anonymous Latin-speaking NCO of the regiment Alt-Anhalt were married, they had either married well-off women or had already been married before rising to the position of NCO.
[274] Sikora, *Disziplin*, 165; Duffy, *Military Experience*, 220.

life. Out of this followed the greatest damage for the armies and troops, that are supposed to fight and achieve something, as timid minds and people who run like hares have caused the utmost confusion, which in the end became general and allowed the enemy to prevail. Rulers have understood this vice and acknowledged that it is the most abominable vice of all. That is why they made it punishable with death, so that he who does not do his duty in battle, assaults or skirmishes and abandons his post, can be massacred [sic][275] immediately by his superior or another [soldier], or shot, hung or executed by another kind of infamous death or at least for ever dishonoured as a rogue. The soldier who keeps this in mind has all reason to be always brave and courageous and to banish all fear and timidity.[276]

This is also reflected in the Prussian 'orders for the army, when it shall give battle to the enemy', which are part of the Prussian *Reglement*: 'The officers and NCOs must always encourage the men and make things easy for them, and, when somebody starts to flee, pierce the man's ribs with his sword, spontoon or pike'.[277] Similar orders can be found in Austrian regulations from 1741 and 1749.[278] The armies of the French Revolution knew even more drastic punishments and generals of the Republican armies could lose their head for being defeated.[279] Thus, the threat voiced in the *Reglement* can hardly be interpreted as proof for soldiers having no concept of honour and being forced into battle, as we know that the French and Allied armies of the revolutionary and Napoleonic wars were motivated by more than fear.[280] However, we can assume that the Prussian soldiers feared death by the hands of their own superiors or comrades if they tried to break formation and flee. This fear was not limited to the immediate killing of soldiers panicking in battle but also to being executed for deserting during combat. J. S. Liebler, an NCO in the Alt-Anhalt Regiment, tells his wife and relatives about the death of three men who had fled during the Battle of Lobositz (1 October 1756):

> Yesterday, on the second [of October], three men who had deserted and were captured were hung. One of them [was] from Captain Kaehler's company, Schuberth, who had deserted together with Dann.[281] His end was sudden and horrible, because he was told one hour before the execution and he used the most appalling expressions upon hearing it.[282]

---

[275] *Massacriret* in the German original.
[276] Fleming, *Vollkommene Teutsche Soldat*, 99. Literally, Fleming writes that the coward must at least 'be made a rogue'.
[277] *Prussian Infantry Reglement of 1726*, 361; *Prussian Infantry Reglement of 1743*, 273.
[278] Balisch, *Die Entstehung*, 181.
[279] John A. Lynn, *The Bayonets of the Republic. Motivation and Tactics in the Army of Revolutionary France, 1791–94* (Urbana and Chicago: University of Illinois Press, 1984), 25.
[280] Lynn, *Bayonets*, 179.
[281] Obviously, a man Liebler and his relatives know.
[282] Von einem Unteroffizier des Alt-Anhaltischen Regiments [J.S. Liebler, son of G.S. Liebler], in *Briefe*, 19.

Although these men were executed for desertion and not for running away from the enemy, the public execution was still a threat for the other soldiers.[283] In combat situations, four different kinds of direct compulsion by force were commonly used in the Prussian army:

1. *ordering the infantry to fire on fleeing comrades from other units.* There are two instances in the soldiers' letters in which the men are ordered to fire at retreating and fleeing comrades. During the Battle of Lobositz, Frederick II ordered the soldiers of the Alt-Anhalt Regiment to prepare to fire on members of the Prussian cavalry that had been beaten by the Austrians and were fleeing towards the infantry: 'Pay attention to the officers' commands, do not let the cavalry through, shoot them down.'[284] Dominicus writes about an incident during the Battle of Kunersdorf: 'An aide-de-camp came to us and said: "Children! Show yourselves once more,[285] you have always stood your ground, if someone from the front line comes, who wants to retreat, shoot them down!"' But immediately after this order, the regiment had to advance. In both cases these general orders were not carried out. It also has to be stressed that these tactics were not aimed at punishing the fugitives but rather to protect the regiments that were still standing. It was vital that these should not lose their order and be caught in the turmoil of the fleeing front-line units.
2. *positioning the cavalry behind infantry formations.* The Prussian field marshal Lehwald issued an order 29 July 1757 in expectation of a battle against the Russian army. Here, he ordered 'every regiment of hussars to send one squadron behind the second line of battle after having taken up its position ... and when the people [from the second line of battle] do not behave bravely or do not want to advance, to drive them forward'.[286] Lehwald seems to have taken this precaution because the second line of his force consisted of eight garrison battalions[287] that were considered to be unreliable because they contained former Saxon soldiers who had been pressed into Prussian service.[288]
3. *the rounding-up of stragglers by the cavalry.* Lieutenant Prittwitz witnessed this procedure during the Battle of Zorndorf[289] and was himself threatened by Black Hussars after having been wounded during the Battle of Kunersdorf. 'We passed a troop of Black Hussars, the commanding officer thought I was an unharmed deserter and sent two of his men after me, threatening to cut me down, if did not immediately go back into the fray again. But they let me go after I had convinced them of the opposite.'[290]

---

[283] On the British army: Way, *Militarizing*, 356.
[284] Beschreibung der Lobositzer Bataille, datirt 1. Oktober 1756., in *Soldatenbriefe*, 3.
[285] Fight bravely for another time.
[286] Disposition zum Marsch gegen den Feind, in *Bellona*, vol. 5, 53.
[287] *Der Siebenjährige Krieg*, vol. 4, 88.
[288] Bleckwenn, *Altpreußische Uniformen*, 53.
[289] Prittwitz, *Ich bin ein Preuße*, 96–7.
[290] Ibid., 123.

4. *exercising control by having officers, NCOs and privates march behind the formation as ordered in the* Reglement. It seems to have been a regular occurrence for soldiers to be beaten – or threatened with a beating – in order to keep them in formation.[291] Prittwitz relates how he himself threatened his men with death when they were attacked by enemy Cossacks: 'I have to add, that when my men saw, that everybody in their rear was running upon this surprise attack, they were also about to do the same. Being frightened, [that they might actually do this], I took my pistol and pointed to the breast of one of the lads and threatened to shoot him if he did not stand his ground. This had the desired effect, although the pistol was not loaded.'[292]

Prittwitz' claim that the pistol was not loaded[293] opens up the question about whether officers ever did really shoot wavering or fleeing soldiers. Not a single source can prove it definitely, and only Liebler mentions the testimony of an Austrian POW who claimed that his captain had stabbed ten of his soldiers who had tried to escape. But Liebler's witness also stated that the Austrians had been ordered to give no quarter and even drowned hundreds of their own seriously wounded comrades in the nearby River Elbe, which is definitely not true. Thus is seems that this Austrian captive did the same as Prussian POWs who 'invented hundreds of lies to flatter their captors', and cannot be taken as evidence of the actual execution of the order to kill fugitives. But what Liebler's tale does reflect is that in spite of the orders in the *Reglements*, killing one's own men was not seen as something normal or desirable, as it is mentioned in the same breath as giving no quarter and killing wounded men. Both actions were diametrically opposed to the customs of war and the Austrian Cogniazzo compared it to 'scalping the hair from the scull like the *Illinoises* [sic] do'.[294] The reluctance to actually harm their men is underlined by the following incident. Lieutenant von Hülsen's regiment was already drawn up for battle when one of his soldiers asked him for permission to leave his position and rest because the unbearable heat had made him sick. Hülsen answers: 'Shame! I thought, you were an honest man, but now I see, that you are a rascal!' He answered: 'Rely on me, lieutenant, I will be there at the right time.' And the soldier reappeared indeed: 'I am here again, lieutenant.' And Hülsen answered: 'That is honest, Fischer, I will not forget it.'[295] According to the *Reglement*, Hülsen should have beaten him back into the line or even stabbed him for leaving his post, but he did nothing of the like. Obviously, killing soldiers was seen as the last resort rather than an option an officer should consider at the first hint of any wavering. Frederick II's correspondence contains an insightful exchange of letters that helps to solve the riddle of why no source mentions the killing of fugitives. After the Battle of Prague, Major-General Heinrich Adolf von Kurssell complained to Frederick when the king rebuked his entire regiment (No. 37) for having run away during the battle. He

---

[291] Retzow, *Charakteristik*, vol. 1, 251.
[292] Prittwitz, *Ich bin ein Preuße*, 115.
[293] It also reflects Prittwitz's and other soldiers' reluctance to kill people with their own hands.
[294] Cogniazzo, *Geständnisse*, vol. 3, 162.
[295] Hülsen, *Unter Friedrich dem Großen*, 88.

stressed 'that all my captains and subalterns[296] have all distinguished themselves without exception during the first assault as well as during the second cannonade and did everything honour-loving and brave officers had the duty to do.'[297] All the officers had instead complained about the 'very bad behaviour' of the battalion commander. The king replied angrily: 'Why then do you blame the man [Major von Massow, the commander]? For I saw with my own eyes, and to my great disappointment, that all of you ran.'[298] Leaving aside the question of whether Frederick's accusations were justified, the dispute shows why the sources remain silent about the killing of fleeing soldiers: fleeing officers could hardly kill fleeing privates. Panic gripped the unit as a whole and was a collective emotion that would have affected the entire 'tactical body'.[299]

Nevertheless, the threat of violence did play a role in keeping soldiers in line, although it would be methodologically misleading to try to gauge the role of this threat in comparison to other factors. That said, we can assume that it was not the central means of making the men fight and win, or there would be more hints at the actual use of force in the sources. It was used to prevent desertion from the field of battle and to make units stand that were deemed untrustworthy and not bound by a common understanding of honour by the commander. But this also shows that the majority of units was considered loyal and honourable. For them, the threat of cutting down any wavering soldier was a threat aimed at those individuals who were gripped by 'emasculating fear' and who thus might endanger the entire unit. But it seems that the fear of losing their honour contributed more to the men's ability to stand their ground. The 'tactical body' of the battalion was also a 'space of honour'.

Summary

Carl Daniel Küster summarized many of the soldiers' incentives to fight on and defend their honour mentioned in this chapter:

> The precedence given to the brave; the salvation of a post, a city or of an entire country; the promotion of peace; the rewards for heroic courage; the honour of the regiment, or the company; the individual love for the ruler, the general, the commander or friend; the presence of a spectator to whom you want to show your courage; the recapture of a position, which was lost due to a weak or cowardly unit; the castigation of an enemy for his cruelty; a last effort to avenge prior bloodshed;

---

[296] Lieutenants, not to be confused with NCOs.
[297] The high losses of the regiment indicate that its flight was not due to cowardly behaviour. Gieraths, *Kampfhandlungen*, 122.
[298] Carmen Winkel, 'Kriegserinnerungen preußischer Offiziere zwischen Korpsgeist und königlichem Anspruch (1740–1786)', in *Militärische Erinnerungskulturen vom 14. bis zum 18. Jahrhundert. Träger-Medien-Deutungskonkurrenzen*, ed. Horst Carl and Ute Planert (Göttingen: V&R unipress, 2012), 236.
[299] On the 'tactical body': Hans Delbrück, *Geschichte der Kriegskunst im Rahmen der politischen Geschichte*, vol. 3 (Berlin 1923), 374; Georg W. Oesterdiekhoff, *Sozialstruktur und sozialer Wandel. Gesammelte Aufsätze* (Münster et al.: LIT, 2006), 167–8.

the hope of refreshments after toil and trouble; good winter-quarters after a successful campaign – all these ideas stream through the soul of the warrior and encourage him to keep doing his heroic business; however, he can be hit by a bullet or get his head split by a sabre-stroke.[300]

Ironically, the chaplain forgot to list the soldiers' religious belief. The men's focus was on their physical, social and spiritual survival and their Protestant faith was the religious anchor of their duties as members of the soldiers' estate. Everything they did as 'faithful soldiers' defending their and their regiment's honour would guarantee their place in heaven and a blissful afterlife, even if nobody except God remembered their deeds. This was also reflected in the soldiers' music. The men defended and sometimes increased their regiment's honour – as symbolized by certain instruments and marches – and sang hymns as religious preparation for death or as thanks for their survival. Religion and their estate were far more important to the soldiers' decision to fight on than notions of the nation or manliness. Whether or not the 'common man' developed a special aversion to certain enemy nations depended heavily on the actual course of the war and their experience, while a special 'male' connotation of being a soldier is completely absent. Defending their religious honour and that of their estate was closely linked to material incentives ranging from royal favours given to the men and families of especially successful regiments to cash for capturing trophies and to the possibility of plunder. The hope to rise to the post of NCO or even officer was secondary but could have played a more important role than hitherto acknowledged.

Modern psychological research has shown that religion and spirituality are helpful in combating depression and thus also panic attacks.[301] Thus, the incentives for fighting on were very effective.

The network of mentalities, rules and behavioural patterns outlined in this chapter is knit by the authorities as well as the soldiers. The result is a framework accepted by both sides as long as the soldiers agreed to the general framework of their service and the authorities allowed them a limited liberty of action.

---

[300] Carl Daniel Küster, 'Einige psychologische Erfahrungen', in *Officier-Lesebuch*, vol. 2, S. 88–90.
[301] Stefan G. Hofmann, Aleena Hay and Abigail Barthel, *Panic Attacks and Panic Disorder: Symptoms, Treatment, Causes, and Coping Strategies* (https://www.anxiety.org/panic-disorder-panic-attacks (accessed 23 November 2018)). The article includes a list of core articles and books on the subject.

4

Summary

The Prussian soldier of the Seven Years' War was by no means the sense- and nerveless automaton of so many later legends but a human being. He was not only capable of displaying a broad variety of emotions but also demonstrated good military judgement stemming from years of training and experience. This judgement and his feelings often had a decisive influence on the outcome of a battle. At the core of the soldiers' thinking were the defence of their honour, their regiment's honour, and a religious belief that honourable service for the king would ensure them God's protection and a place in heaven. This belief had major psychological implications, as it helped them cope with their fear in battle and the depression caused by the constant threat of death while on campaign.

The majority of the common soldiers of the Prussian army came from the lands of the Hohenzollern monarchy. About 50 to 70 per cent, depending on the phase of the war, were *Kantonisten*, draftees from the recruiting districts (*Kantone*) of the regiments. They were the second, third or fourth sons of peasants and craftsmen and they came from the very centre of Prussian society. The other 30 to 50 per cent were *Ausländer* (foreigners), which meant that they were not *Kantonisten* but mercenaries. That said, most of them hailed from Prussian lands or neighbouring principalities like Mecklenburg; only a minority were foreigners from non-German speaking countries. Many of the *Ausländer* joined the colours for economic reasons, others had an individual inclination to the soldiers' trade and a large number was forceably recruited during the war. Training periods were intense by eighteenth-century standards and ensured the professional functioning of the Prussian battalions. Yet the soldiers had plenty of spare time in which to pursue other occupations via which they could boost their income. Most of the men were quartered in the homes of civilians and were not under the permanent control of their officers. The means of creating totally controlled battle-automatons in peacetime simply did not exist.

The elementary tactics of the Prussian army were the linear tactics applied by all European armies of the time. Battalions of 300 to 1,000 men stood two- to four-ranks-deep in close order and applied different methods of fire to bring as many muskets to bear on a certain point as possible. Permanent drill in formation made the men close their ranks instinctively and fire without harming themselves or their comrades. It also made them trust in the efficiency of their fire and strengthened their believe that collective action was the central tool of individual survival.

The elementary tactics introduced by Frederick II of Prussia before the Seven Years' War were also characterized to a high degree of psychological considerations. He trained the infantry and cavalry to charge with cold steel without firing in order to cause panic amongst the enemy. Concerning his own soldiers, the king wanted to use their interest in their own survival to psychologically prepare them for the bayonet-charge. He did this by pledging that the enemy would not dare to stand fast and that a prolonged standing fire-fight would cost more lives than a lively attack with cold steel.

The soldiers whose letters have survived were almost all private *Kantonisten* or NCOs from the core regions of the Prussian monarchy (today's Saxony-Anhalt, Brandenburg and North-Rhine Westphalia) and from some of the army's most distinguished regiments. Their writing skills were good, which reflected the high level of literacy in these regions. Most of the letters are written to close relatives, particularly their wives. Many writers served as a 'hub' between other men from their village community at the front and their relatives, which is reflected in the greetings and information contained in the letters. This reflected the two 'communities of honour' the soldiers were a part of: their village community and the regiment at the front. Their main writing strategy was to point to their suffering and perilous situations in order to demonstrate God's protection for them and to encourage their relatives intercede for them. This strategy allows a unique insight into their feelings and thoughts during combat.

Soldiers displayed a large variety of emotions in battle. Fear and stress were basic emotions for almost all of them. The adrenaline rush and the strain of combat could lead to 'heat', a well-documented phenomenon that was regarded as effective as it made the soldier fight on. Heat could turn into fury and bloodlust, however. On the other hand, soldiers could be gripped by panic, the so-called 'cannon-fever', which rendered them unable to fight on.

The fear of damaging the honour of the regiment or of the individual soldier represented important incentives to fight. Being dishonoured by running away would also dishonour the family and community at home. Conversely, a regiment's success would have positive implications for the soldiers and their families. When the king was satisfied with them, they might be able to request favours like being spared from contributions, like services or money, to the war effort or even money as a reward for their prowess in battle.

Concerning the soldier's incentives to fight, we encounter other important factors. Religious belief played a major role when the soldiers were fighting their fear in combat situations. They were thus able to console themselves when faced with death and mutilation. At the same time they were encouraged by the Pietist idea that their obedience to their superiors was equal to obedience to God. Fighting effectively was a way of praising God and done for His honour, so they could be assured that their death in combat would lead their soul directly to heaven. God's protection in dangerous situations also showed their families that they were behaving honourably. Making their relatives intercede for them was of the utmost importance, as many soldiers believed that such intercession would increase their chances of being protected by God, or of victory in battle.

The idea of fighting for the nation was alien to the Prussian soldiers. When they mention their suffering for the *Vaterland* (fatherland), they mean their home regions and the people living there. National hatred, which was inextricably intertwined with religious hatred, did play a certain role, however. Some Prussian soldiers saw the Seven Years' War as a war of religion that pitted them as righteous Protestants against Austrian Catholics, and 'barbaric' Russian orthodox soldiers. For most of the common soldiers, their level of hatred for the enemy depended on their experience during the conflict and not on entrenched cultural stereotypes. Thus, the Austrians were their main enemy as scores from former battles had to be settled and revenge taken. The Russians were perceived primarily as 'barbaric', mainly due to Prussian propaganda and to a lesser extent to atrocities committed by some of the Russian auxiliary troops. Later on, the Russians were feared by the Prussian rank and file for their tenacity, but we also find mutual respect, especially amongst the infantry of both sides.

The idea of 'manly' behaviour and male honour in the modern sense is absent in the soldiers' letters and their esteem for their wives – and even their fear of them – is striking. Soldiers are afraid of losing their honour by being accused of unfaithfulness or by not caring for their pregnant wife. Women were present in military life at home and on campaign. The Prussian army was the only one to offer a certain degree of social security to the 'darlings' (*Liebsten*) of the soldiers. Unmarried couples could obtain a certificate from the regimental commander which kept the girl's honour intact while having extramarital sexual relations with a soldier and entitled her to certain low-level benefits in case of war. When women went into the field, they occupied important positions as sutlers (*Marketenderinnen*). All the women in soldiers' families were expected to have a certain knowledge of the martial trade and were thus part of the soldiers' estate. Although the field of battle itself was a male domain, in their letters the soldiers try to relate their experience of battle to their wives and seek their support by intercession. Female is clearly not a negative antitype of male in the soldiers' eyes, because their female relatives are a part of their estate and comrades in prayer.

Officers were one of the main encouraging factors for the soldiers in battle. They had to lead by example and by showing extraordinary feats of courage and coolness. This ranged from courteously offering snuff to the other officers during a standing firefight to a senior general snatching the colours and rallying his wavering men. Although desertion during battle was punished by death, a fleeing regiment would often not be punished at all, especially if the soldiers and the commanders agreed that the regiment had done enough to save its honour. There were no known executions for fleeing in battle, when it was not considered to have been an attempt to desert. And there are no sources confirming the killing of fleeing soldiers by their officers. Officers often threatened to do so but ultimately the battalion was also a common space of emotions and when it took top its heels, officers and men alike ran. Officers' encouraging cheers stressed the family-like nature of the social realm of the regiment, when senior officers called their men 'my children', appealed to the honour of the men, when they called them *Herren* (gentlemen), when they invoked the rivalry between the different arms of the service, not to mention their religious beliefs and their wish to survive.

Music was the fine-tuning of military honour. The distribution of instruments to the different types of regiments was directly linked to the instruments' prestige. The more honourable the arm of the service, the more honourable the instruments its bands were allowed to play. Being allowed to use certain instruments or marching tunes that were normally not used by the given branch of the service also acted as an incentive to fight. When marching onto the field of battle, the soldiers and their bands sang and played hymns to appeal to the Almighty for help and to prepare for the possibility of death. As the Prussian army had no official religious rituals to prepare for battle, the soldiers themselves accorded the singing of hymns a special significance.

Material and financial incentives were also important for the Prussian army. These ranged from certain sums of money given to units that had conquered enemy guns or flags, to promotions linked to higher pay. Although battlefield looting was forbidden officially, many officers allowed their men to plunder the dead as long as this was not detrimental to their fighting capacity. These royal gifts for victory also increased the social capital of honour. Defeat and desertion were punished by the honour of a unit or an individual being diminished or even erased altogether. A regiment that had abandoned its post too early could lose the right to wear its dedicated hats, uniforms and swords, while an individual could be chased away as a dishonoured 'rascal'.

If we link these findings with the social and mental environment of the soldiers, we see a very efficient mixture of relations to basic cultural and mental patterns in early modern Prussian society. Religion and the existence of God are self-evident for the men and it is thus no wonder that the soldiers rely on God and their faith when confronted with death and danger. The idea that doing one's duty to king will be rewarded by God corresponds to a deeply rooted estates-based way of thinking and the specific Prussian variant of Protestant Pietism. The idea of upholding one's own honour as a soldier, the honour of the regiment or the army, and by extension the honour of the monarch, is linked to the military concept of the soldiers' estate, which mainly rested on the soldiers' effectiveness. For its part, this effectiveness was enhanced by the psychological implications of their faith, as it helped to maintain their capacity to fight even when under extreme stress. That none of the men went into war enthusiastically, full of national conceit or hatred for the enemy, also contributed to their efficiency. They did not suffer from a psychological breakdown when their heroic expectations met the cruel realities of war, as was often the case in the wars of the nineteenth and twentieth centuries.

All of this shows that we must refute the image of machine-soldiers beaten into battle by their officers. Instead, we encounter men of flesh and blood with human emotions, who wanted to defend their honour, serve their God and stay alive for their families.

Appendix I

Sources: Regulations, military history and theory, journals

Reglements and orders

First of all, these are the Reglements of 1726[1] and 1743[2] as well as different instructions and orders for officers issued by the king before and during the Seven Years' War:

- 1748: *Instruktion für die Generalmajors der Infanterie*[3] *und Kavallerie* (Instructions for the major-generals of the infantry and cavalry)[4]
- 1746–48 (geschrieben), published in an abridged German version in 1752/53: *Generalprincipien des Krieges in Anwendung auf die Taktik und auf die Disciplin der preussischen Truppen* (General principles of war applied to the tactics and discipline of the Prussian troops)[5]
- 1751: *Lehrgedicht über die Kriegskunst* (Instructive poem on the art of war)[6]
- 1752: *Politisches Testament von 1752* (Political testament of 1752)[7]
- 1755: *Gedanken und allgemeine Regeln für den Krieg* (Thoughts and general rules of war)[8]
- 1758: *Betrachtungen über die Taktik und einzelne Theile des Krieges, oder Betrachtungen über einige Veränderungen in der Art, Krieg zu führen* (Observations on tactics and particular aspects of war, or observations on some changes in warfare)[9]

---

[1] *Reglement vor die Königl. Preußische Infanterie von 1726*, repr. (1726; Osnabrück: Biblio, 1968).
[2] *Reglement für die Königl. Preußische Infanterie* (Berlin 1743).
[3] Frederick II, 'Instruction für die General-Majors von der Infanterie', in *Ausgewählte kriegswissenschaftliche Schriften Friedrichs des Grossen*, ed. Heinrich Merkens (Jena: Costenoble, 1876), 163–76.
[4] Frederick II, 'Instruction für die General-Majors von der Kavallerie', in *Ausgewählte kriegswissenschaftliche Schriften*, 177–96.
[5] Frederick II, 'Generalprincipien des Krieges in Anwendung auf die Taktik und auf die Disciplin der preussischen Truppen', in *Ausgewählte kriegswissenschaftliche Schriften*, 1–120.
[6] Frederick II, *Die Kriegskunst: Lehrgedicht in 6 Gesängen* (Berlin: Heymann, 1842).
[7] Frederick II, 'Das Politische Testament von 1752', in *Friedrich der Große*, ed. Otto Bardong (Darmstadt: WBG, 1982), 174–261.
[8] Frederick II, 'Gedanken und allgemeine Regeln für den Krieg', in *Die Werke Friedrichs des Großen*, ed. Gustav Berthold Volz, vol. 6 (Berlin: Reimar Hobbing, 1913), 87–115.
[9] Frederick II, 'Betrachtungen über die Taktik und einzelne Theile des Krieges, oder Betachtungen über einige Veränderungen in der Art, Krieg zu führen', in *Ausgewählte kriegswissenschaftliche Schriften*, 121–38.

- 1759 (12.2.): *Instruktion für die Generalmajors von der Infanterie* (Instructions for the major-generals of the Infantry)[10]
- 1759 (16.3.): *Instruktion für die Generalmajors von der Cavallerie* (Instructions for the major-generals of the cavalry)[11]
- 1763 (11.5.): *Instruktion für die Commandeurs der Infanterie-Regimenter* (Instructions for the commanders of the infantry regiments)[12]
- 1763: *Instruktion für die Commandeurs der Cavallerie-Regimenter* (Instructions for the commanders of the cavalry-regiments)[13]
- 1768: *Das militärische Testament von 1768* (Military testament of 1768)[14]

Military history and theory

- Tempelhof's *Geschichtes des Siebenjährigen Krieges*[15] (History of the Seven Years' War), which military experts during the late eighteenth century valued as a standard reference.[16] The author was a captain of artillery during the Seven Years' War.
- Cogniazzo's *Geständnisse eines österreichischen Veteranen* (Confessions of an Austrian veteran)[17]. He served in the Austrian infantry as well as the cavalry and was an admirer of Frederick II.[18]

---

[10] Frederick II, 'Instruktionen für die Generalmajors der Infanterie', in *Die Werke Friedrichs des Großen*, 265–8; *Militärische Schriften Friedrichs des Großen*, ed. Adalbert von Taysen (Berlin: Richard Wilhelmi, 1882), 511–18.

[11] Frederick II, 'Instruktion für die Generalmajors von der Cavallerie', in *Militärische Schriften Friedrichs des Großen*, 519–30.

[12] Frederick II, Instruktion für die Commandeurs der Infanterie-Regimenter, in *Militärische Schriften Friedrichs des Großen*, 569–74.

[13] Frederick II, Instruktion für die Commandeurs der Cavallerie-Regimenter, in *Militärische Schriften Friedrichs des Großen*, 574–83.

[14] Frederick II, 'Das militärische Testament von 1768', in *Die Werke Friedrichs des Großen*, 222–61.

[15] Georg Friedrich von Tempelhof, *Geschichte des Siebenjährigen Krieges in Deutschland zwischen dem Könige von Preußen und der Kaiserin Königin mit ihren Alliierten*, 5 vols. (Berlin: Johann Friedrich Unger, 1783–1801).

[16] Carl Daniel Küster, 'Beispiel außerordentlicher Tapferkeit des Majors v. Lange und des Lieutenant v. Marwitz, in Vertheidigung des Kirchhofs bey dem nächtlichen Ueberfall bey Hochkirch', in *Officier-Lesebuch* historisch-militairischen Inhalts, mit untermischten interessanten Anekdoten, vol. 3 (Berlin: Carl Matzdorffs Buchhandlung, 1795), 129; Friedrich August von Retzow, Charakteristik der wichtigsten Ereignisse des siebenjährigen Krieges, in Rücksicht auf Ursachen und Wirkungen, vol. 1 (Berlin: Himburg, 1802), IX, 100, S. 134 fn. *), 229–30, 250; 'Ueber den Angrif der Cavalerie', in *Neues Militärisches Journal*, vol. 1 (1788), 95; 'Woraus kann man den Fortgang, den eine Armee in disem oder jenem Zweige der Kriegskunst macht, am sichersten abhennem?', in *Neues Militärisches Journal*, vol. 6 (1792), 185.

[17] Jacob de Cogniazzo, *Geständnisse eines östreichischen Veterans in politisch-militärischer (!) Hinsicht auf die interessantesten Verhältnisse zwischen Oestreich und Preußen, während der Regierung des Großen Königs der Preußen Friedrichs des Zweyten mit historischen Anmerkungen gewidmet den königlich-preußischen Veteranen von dem Verfasser des freymüthigen Beytrags zur Geschichte des östreichischen Militär-Dienstes*, 4 vols. (Breslau: Gottlieb Löwe, 1788–91.).

[18] Cogniazzo, *Geständnisse*, vol. 1, Vorrede.

- Retzow's *Charakteristik der wichtigsten Ereignisse des Siebenjährigen Krieges* (Characteristics of the most important incidents of the Seven Years' War)[19]. Retzow served as an aide-de-camp during the war. He knew and used the texts of the aforementioned authors and was able to add his own experiences.[20]
- Warnery's *Feldzüge Friedrichs des Zweyten* (Campaigns of Frederick II).[21] The author was an officer of the hussars and rose to the rank of major-general during the war. He was considered an expert on cavalry combat by most other military authors[22] and was recognized by French military authors.[23]
- Archenholz's *Geschichte des Siebenjährigen Krieges* (History of the Seven Years' War)[24]. Archenholz had served in the Prussian army as a captain from 1760 on. His bestseller was written for the broader public and is no military history in the strict sense of the word.
- Tielkes' *Beyträge zur Kriegs-Kunst und Geschichte des Krieges von 1756 bis 1763* (Contributions to the art of war and the history of the war from 1756 to 1763).[25] The author was a Saxon captain of artillery and an acknowledged historian and military theoretician.[26]

A special category of military history are the *Journale* (journals) and diaries of certain units or campaigns.[27] Many of them have been printed in military collections published between the 1770s and 1790s.[28] The former quartermaster of the infantry Alt-Anhalt

---

[19] Friedrich August von Retzow, *Charakteristik der wichtigsten Ereignisse des siebenjährigen Krieges, in Rücksicht auf Ursachen und Wirkungen*, 2 vols. (Berlin: Himburg, 1802).

[20] Vgl. Max Duncker: Die Schlacht von Kollin, in: Ders.: Aus der Zeit Friedrichs des Großen und Friedrich Wilhelms III. Abhandlungen zur preußischen Geschichte, Leipzig 1876, S. 47–109.

[21] Charles-Emmanuel de Warnery, *Feldzüge Friedrichs des Zweyten, Königs von Preußen, seit 1756 bis 1762*, 2 vols. (Hannover: Helwing, 1789).

[22] 'Einige Bemerkungen über die Schlacht bey Hastenbeck und einige Erläuterungen der gegebenen Relationen', in *Neues Militärisches Journal*, vol. 1, 246; 'Rezension zu Warnerys Campagnes de Frederic II', in *Neues Militärisches Journal*, vol. 2, 117; 'Woraus kann man den Fortgang, den eine Armee in diesem oder jenem Zweige der Kriegskunst macht, am sichersten abnehmen', in *Neues Militärisches Journal*, vol. 6, 185; Tempelhof, Geschichte, vol. 1, 166, fn. *).

[23] 'Auszug aus: "Commentaires sur les Institutons militaires de Vegéce; par M. le Comte Turpin de Crissé Lieutenant-General etc. Paris, 1783. II. Tomes en 4', in *Bibliothek für Officiere*, vol. 1, 95.

[24] Johann Wilhelm von Archenholz, *Geschichte des Siebenjährigen Krieges in Deutschland von 1756 bis 1763* (Mannheim: Schwan und Götz, 1788).

[25] Johann Gottlieb Tielke, *Beyträge zur Kriegs-Kunst und Geschichte des Krieges von 1756 bis 1763 mit Plans und Charten*, 6 vols. (Freyberg: Barthelische Schriften, 1775-86).

[26] 'Relation der Schlacht bey Freyberg, zwischen der Preussischen Armee unter dem Prinzen Heinrich und der Oesterreichischen und Reichsarmee unter dem Prinzen von Stolberg, den 29sten Oct. 1762', in *Neues militärisches Journal*, vol. 6, 25.

[27] Most Authors of *Bellona* are known. Those of other important serials, like the *Sammlung ungedruckter Nachrichten* are only partially known. See: Curt Jany, Das Gaudische Journal des Siebenjährigen Krieges. Feldzüge 1756 und 1757 (Berlin: Mittler, 1901), 1, fn. *).

[28] - *Bellona, ein militärisches Journal*, ed. Karl von Seidel, 20 vols. (Dresden: Waltherische Hofbuchhandlung, 1781–87).
- *Bibliothek für Officiere*, ed. Georg von Scharnhorst, 4 vols. (Göttingen: Johann Christian Dieterich, 1785).
- *Sammlung ungedruckter Nachrichten, so die Geschichte der Feldzüge der Preußen von 1740–1779 erläutern*, ed. Gottlob Naumann, 5 vols. (Dresden: Waltherische Hofbuchhandlung, 1782-5).
- *Neue Kriegsbibliothek*, ed. Georg Dietrich von der Gröben, 9 vols. (Breslau: Wilhelm Gottlieb Korn, 1774–81).
- *Neues militärisches Journal*, ed. Georg von Scharnhorst, 13 vols. (Hannover: Helwingsche Hofbuchhandlung, 1788–1805).

Regiment (No. 3) tried to publish histories of all Prussian regiments,[29] but this endeavour was stopped by Frederick II, who did not want the public to see this information.[30]

These sources contain information about:

- the spatial movements of the units;
- information about the careers of the officers;
- losses;
- rewards;
- combat missions;
- tactics used in combat, especially when they were considered to be honourable.

---

[29] Johann Friedrich Seyfarth, *Geschichte des Infanterie-Regiments Friedrich August v. Braunschweig* (Halle / Saale: J.G. Trampe, 1767), V, fn. 1).

[30] Johann Friedrich Seyfarth, *Geschichte des Füsilier-Regiments von Brietzke* (Halle / Saale: J.G. Trampe, 1767), VIII.

Appendix II

Twelve Prussian Soldiers' Letters from the Seven Years' War

Translator's note: the letters are from three late nineteenth-century or early twentieth-century editions and one modern edition: the 'Diary of Musketeer Dominicus', edited by Dietrich Kerler in 1891; the 'Letters of Prussian Soldiers from the Campaigns of 1756 and 1757', edited by the Prussian General Staff in 1901 and 'Prussian Soldiers' Letters from the Province of Saxony[1] in the 18th Century', edited by Georg Liebe. Kerler – and Liebe in particular – offered literal transcriptions of the original letters, while the General Staff carefully modernized the letters' spelling and grammar.

The modern edition of the letters of the Zander cousins, by Christian F. Zander, contains a literal transcription of the letters.[2] We would like to thank Mr. Zander and his publisher, Verlag Dr. Kovač, for the permission to translate three of the letters and to reproduce the facsimile of one letter.

We chose to translate the letters into modern English while trying to preserve the individual style and expressions by the authors. This decision was threefold. First, we wanted to present modern English-speaking readers who are not familiar with the German language with a readable translation that was as close to the original as possible. Second, Early Modern German was one of the least standardized European languages, and this adds to the individuality of the different authors, as we tried to preserve. Third, the alternative of translating into Early Modern English seemed problematic, because the differences between the Early Modern and Modern languages are so extensive that any Early Modern English translation of the German soldiers' letters would end up being far removed from the original.

The soldiers' citations from Martin Luther's translation of the Bible were translated using the King James Bible, because this was the only way to capture the difference between eighteenth- and sixteenth-/early seventeenth-century German.

---

[1] The 'Prussian Province of Saxony' was a province of the Prussian state from 1815 until 1944/45. It comprised the modern county of Saxony-Anhalt, without Anhalt, and parts of Thuringia, around Erfurt, south-west Brandenburg and north-west Saxony.
[2] Christian F. Zander, *Fundstücke – Dokumente und Briefe einer preußischen Bauernfamilie (1747-1953)* (Hamburg: Verlag Dr. Kovac, 2015), 15–113.

The letters

1. Letter from Musketeer Dominicus to his brother written in the camp at Fürstenwalde, 25 August 1759, in *Aus dem Siebenjährigen Krieg. Tagebuch des preußischen Musketiers Dominicus*, ed. Dr. Dietrich Kerler (Munich: C.B. Beck'sche Verlagsbuchhandlung, 1891), 61–6.

Thanks to God's wonderful guidance, I am still healthy. We suffered from great exertions this summer, which were caused by marching as well as hunger and thirst. We marched into Poland, three miles away from Cossel[3], where we met the Russians. We attacked each other constantly. On the 12 July we stood under their guns for the whole day, they shot at us with howitzer grenades[4] all the time, and many of us were wounded. They have a lot of [different] cannon [and] all sorts of rogue stuff that is not allowed in war.[5] They load their cannon with chain-shot[6], pieces of raw iron and whole bags of small musket balls[7], of which they put 100 [into smaller] and two to 300 into their heavy pieces; and when these go off, there is real thunder.[8]

Due to divine intervention, we fought them twice. The first time was at Züllichau[9] on 23 July. Before [the battle] General Dohna[10] had been in command. On the 22nd of July, General Wedel[11] took over command and the old General Dohna left us. According to [the soldiers'] talk and our estimation, Dohna should have attacked the enemy on the plain in front of the bushes[12] and before our actual attack [led by Wedel]. When Wedel arrived, the enemy stood behind the bushes. On the 23rd we marched through the bushes towards them. The cannonade (61–62) was terrifying; they fired their cannon into the trees, so that many trees and branches fell unto us. As soon as we came out of the bush, we took ten cannons. We started to fire our muskets at them, but as we had not been able to drag our cannons through the woods, it was impossible to drive them back because they had two to three

---

[3] Presumably today's Kozle in Poland. Three miles are three German miles, about 22.6 km.
[4] Howitzers were used to fire powder-filled iron balls with fuses. Most of them were not lethal but they did cause significant wounds and were used particularly against enemy cavalry, where the sharp parts of the exploding iron balls wounded and scared the horses.
[5] The German original has *Schelmezeug* for 'rogue-stuff'. In Early Modern German, *Schelm* means hangman and thus a person without honour. It is a grave insult. It must not be confused with the modern German meaning of *Schelm*, which is a jester or joker, and can even be used as a term of endearment for children.
[6] Two cannon balls linked by a chain. These were normally used on ships to destroy the enemies' sails and rigging.
[7] These are heavier and more deadly than normal case or grapeshot.
[8] The use of these types of ammunition was prohibited in the rules of war and gunners using them were normally put to the sword if the enemy got hold of them.
[9] Today's Sulechów in the Polish Voivodship Lubusz. The battle is also known as the Battle of Kay or Paltzig. For more on this battle, see Dennis Showalter, *Frederick the Great: A Military Life*, Kindle edition (London: Frontline Books, [1996] 2012), 4256–75. http://www.kronoskaf.com/syw/index.php?title=1759-07-23_-_Battle_of_Paltzig (accessed 8 August 2018).
[10] General Christoph II. von Dohna-Schlodien (1702–62).
[11] Lieutenant-General Carl Heinrich von Wedel (1712–82). He had explicit orders from the king to attack the Russians immediately.
[12] There were thick woods in front of the Russian wings.

lines, one after the other, [which were] also defended by many cannons. I fired forty-eight cartridges[13] when we had to retreat, and on this occasion I realized how it felt to do so. As soon as we retreated, they started to shout and the Cossacks[14] pursued us. I have been running all my life, but now I did my best[15] and had to carry a heavy load.[16] I was lucky[17] to be the bearer of the kettle[18] and bread for two days and my knapsack. I would have liked to throw them away, but did not have any time to do it, and ran for more than two hours, after which we finally arrived at a pond, where I refreshed myself by drinking unclean water, not only unclean but also thick with dirt, because one could not get there [to the cleaner part] due to the horses.[19] But it tasted very good and did me no harm. We rallied again on a mountain. There was a woman there, and from her I begged some brandy for 10 Sh.,[20] just to refresh myself a little. I have 4 signs that show how miraculously the Lord (62–63) saved me: one bullet went through the tip of my hat, one through the turnback, one went into the butt of my musket and a part of the cover of my cartridge pouch was shot off. While I was standing and loading, a bullet flew just over my hand and bent my ramrod like a fiddlestick. Next to me on my left, the legs of three men were evenly shot off at the same height – there is no doubt that this had been done with chain-shot. The man to my right was wounded and the one next to him killed. I had the same thoughts as King Hiskia: 'The Lord has cut off like a weaver my life, from day even to night wilt he make an end of me.'[21] But I saw that my time had not yet come[22] and was so full of sorrow that I could not give thanks to God nor sing a song of praise [to him]. Help me with that, my friends! To thank God that he protected me and ask him to further safeguard me due to his grace, because it[23] has not come to an end, yet. Many of us defect, but I will not break my oath if God further grants health and life to me, [instead] I will remain faithful to God and the king and will bear the burden as long as God wants me to. I have often experienced many seductions and tribulations, but the Lord God has maintained my good thoughts; and I will lead my life and actions in a way I can answer for to God and man.

The day after the battle, we retreated and crossed the Oder[24] and marched until 6 August, when we reached the king's corps coming from Silesia near the town of

---

[13] Every soldier carried sixty cartridges with him.
[14] Light irregular Russian cavalry. The Prussians feared them because they were said to give no quarter.
[15] He ran as fast as he could. The retreat had obviously become a rout.
[16] Prussian soldiers carried most of their belongings themselves.
[17] Obviously ironic.
[18] The cooking kettle for his tent.
[19] Dominicus seems to have been unable to access the part of the pond with cleaner water as the cavalry's horses were already drinking there. The German original is not clear.
[20] 10 Prussian *Shilling*. The *Shilling* was an East Prussian coin. 270 *Shilling* made one *Reichsthaler*. 3 ½ Reichsthaler were the monthly pay of a Prussian musketeer. http://www.numismatik.realedition.de/preussenI/index.html (accessed 8 August 2018).
[21] Isaiah 38.12. The editor, Kerler, remarked that Dominicus citation was not entirely correct. The King James Bible has: 'I have cut off like a weaver my life: he will cut me off with pining sickness: from day even to night wilt thou make an end of me.'
[22] In the sense of 'my end had not come'.
[23] Dominicus' life.
[24] River rising in the Czech Republic. It forms part of today's Polish–German border.

Müllrose.[25] From there, we marched until the 12th [August 1759], which was the ninth Sunday after Trinity. It was a hard Sunday again and at 10 o'clock, instead of going to church, a great bloodshed commenced (63–64) which lasted until 7 o'clock at night. Our right wing opened the fight with [its] cannon. We had 30 cannons, which were drawn by twelve horses[26] [each], without the other ones, which were six times as many. We beat back their left wing – they had entrenched themselves heavily to the last [part of their position], where we had to drive them out of two redoubts. All the Russians had been beaten, but then eight battalions of Austrian grenadiers arrived, whom we were by no means able to beat.[27] The king was at the front for the whole time and said: 'Children, do not leave me!' Two horses were shot from under him and in the end, he grasped a flag[28] from Prince Henry's regiment and said: 'Everybody, who is a brave soldier, follow me!' Everybody who had cartridges [left] went confidently [with him]. It is said, that he finally gave the order 'wheel to the right!' and said: 'Retreat, children!' Meanwhile, we had to retreat to the Oder. The [numbers of]dead who lay there, were terrible and – believe me! – it is certain, that where six of ours lay, there lay ten of theirs. Because what we hit, we hit for sure.[29] They fired case-shot, which wounded many, but did not kill them. And the better part of our wounded were able to retreat with the army. The Russians are said to have lost 40,000 dead, without the wounded[30]; and I (64–65) do believe it. The king was with us in the morning, just two hours before the battle; while we were marching past [him], he addressed all of us: 'Good morning, children, how are you?' and then in Low German: 'Do you want to eat big beans soon?' We answered: 'Yes.' He said: 'Yes, have some patience for a little while' and he was confident during the conversation.

We lost our Colonel Kikol in the first battle and in the other one Major Reden; Captain Mune and Lieutenant Colonel von Plötz have been severely wounded in the foot and many other officers and soldiers have been injured. When we marched from our winter quarters, our regiment had been forty-two officers and 1,620 privates strong, now we are just twelve officers and 448 privates. Six of the men

---

[25] Small town in the east of the German county of Brandenburg, 15 km away from Frankfurt am Oder.
[26] The heavy Prussian twelve-pounders were drawn by twelve horses. Interestingly, the heavier 24-pounders were drawn by six or eight horses. http://www.kronoskaf.com/syw/index.php?title=Prussian_Cannon#24-pdr_Cannon (accessed 8 August 2018).
[27] Dominicus voices the Prussian and Austrian understanding that the day was lost by the Russians and then won by the elite Austrian grenadiers. In fact, the Prussians were beaten after a ferocious battle around the Kuh-Grund, where the bulk of the allied troops were Russian. For example, Seydlitz's attack was repulsed by the Russian Azov, Second Moscow infantry and First Grenadiers. Christopher Duffy, *Frederick the Great: A Military Life*, Kindle edition (Abingdon and New York: Routledge, [1985] 2016), 187.
[28] In Prussia, each company had a flag but there were no regimental or battalion colours. The five flags of the companies making up a battalion were positioned in the centre of the battalion and guarded by the colours platoon.
[29] The Prussians killed the enemies they hit.
[30] Kerler, the editor of Dominicus' diary, gives 2,614 dead and 10,863 wounded Russians, and 6,048 dead and 11,101 wounded Prussians (fn. 3, p. 64). Dominicus seems to be echoing Prussian rumours or false information spread by the Prussian high command in order to boost spirits after the catastrophic defeat.

from Meinerzhagen and four from Kierspe[31] are still healthy. The Kayser brothers have been severely wounded in the head. I was with Anton [Kayser] while we were retreating, and he was hit under the right eye and the bullet was still lodged in his head; he said that his brother had been shot in the eye. Before we went to Poland, I had been with Schrage in Torgau[32]; [and] because Torgau is no more in our hands, I do not know, where he is now. He had promised me to write to Rönsahl, because I did not have time to do it; I do not know if he has actually done it. I ache to receive a letter from you so that I know how you are, and if the Frenchman has visited you, too, while retreating.[33] I ask you to let my closest relatives read this letter and they should take it as if I had written to every one of them. I am waiting for an answer with the first postal delivery, because (65–66) the mail is getting through again. I remain my dear friends' faithful

J.J. Dominicus

P.S. Our regiment is now called von Schenckendorff.[34] When writing this letter, I had nothing to eat, but tomorrow is bread-day. A pound of pork is 8 Gute Groschen[35] and a jug of beer is 5 Shilling, or you do not get anything. Oh, miserable times!

2. Extract of a letter by a soldier of the Hülsen Regiment called Frantz Reiß, written at Lobositz on 6 October 1756, in *Briefe preußischer Soldaten aus den Feldzügen 1756 und 1757*, ed. Großer Generalstab (Berlin: Mittler, 1901), 29–32.

God be with you! My dearest wife.

Your letter from 19 September reached me via Mr. Gerecke only on the 5 of October, wherein I see that you and the boy are still in good health, which I learned with great joy from the bottom of my heart. I also learned about your vicious quarrel with the neighbour, which was the last part of your letter. O thank our God, that you do not have to suffer a greater danger and no greater harm is done to you. I had thought that you had grown up, I had thought that you were in such a condition that you would no longer regaled me with such antics, but alas, this makes me see that you are in a better condition than me. Thus, I give you this advice: if you have nothing to do, keep God at the forefront of your mind and take a book and pray that you and I may keep our good health. This was our only consolation on Friday, which was 1 October. Now [I] tell you, my dearest child, that we marched from Aussig[36] on Thursday, which was 30 September and marched until midnight. As the day was dawning the next morning, we had to set out again; after we had marched for a quarter of an hour, we had to form a line [of battle].

---

[31] Two villages in the *Kanton* of Dominicus' regiment.
[32] Torgau is a town in Northern Saxony.
[33] Dominicus alludes to the French defeat at Minden (1 August 1759) and the following retreat of the French army.
[34] Major-General Friedrich August von Schenckendorff (1710–80) was now its owner and chef.
[35] In Brandenburg currency, one *Reichsthaler* is equal to twenty-four *Gute Groschen*.
[36] Today's Ústí nad Labem in the north-west of the Czech Republic.

Immediately, even faster than I can tell you about it, the Austrians fired with cannon at us. Thus, the *Bataille* [battle] began at 6 o'clock in the morning and lasted with thundering and firing until 4 [pm], where I was in such danger that I cannot thank God enough for my present good health. The first cannon shots hit our Krumpholtz,[37] who was standing close to me, through the head and took half his head off, and Bode[38] [was hit by Krumpholtz'] brains and pieces of his skull and his musket [was shot] from his shoulder and broke into a thousand pieces, but – thanks to God – [he] remained unscathed. Now, dearest wife, what happened I cannot describe by any means, as the shooting was so intense from both sides, that no one could understand a word from anybody else, and we did not see one thousand bullets, but many thousand. Towards afternoon, the enemy took flight and God gave victory to us. When we came unto the field of battle, there lay not just one but three and four [bodies] on top of each other, some dead because their head had been [blown] away, some with two short legs,[39] their arms [shot] from the body – all told, it was horrible[40] to behold. Now, dearest child, think about this, how we must have felt, led to the slaughtering block with empty stomachs[41] in the morning, not knowing what would happen. We and another three regiments suffered the heaviest losses. Many men from our regiment were left dead. Some companies lost about forty men, but from our company fifteen to twenty men have been killed or wounded. Three died on the field[42] and seven (31) by cannonball[43]. For my part, I thank the almighty God, that he preserved me so wonderfully. I could tell you who had been killed or wounded, but I do not want to grieve any human being by that. It is enough that you know that God has until now spared my life and that I am still well and healthy. All this you can tell to Ramse's wife, and also tell her that her husband had been in such danger, that a cannonball shattered the musket on his shoulder into a thousand pieces, but that thanks to God I can tell her that he and son remained unharmed and up to now are well and healthy, because we all share a tent. I have already written a letter together with Ramse to you on the 30 of September, but do not know whether you have received it. Thus, Ramse and I do not ask for anything more than that you thank God for yours and mine health and that you do not think that it[44] had been child's play. From the officers of our regiment, the oldest,[45] Knigge, has been killed. Colonel Münchow is wounded, and also wounded are Major von Bonin, Captain von Franckenberg, Lieutenant von Bandemer, Lt. von Tettenborn and Lt. Paxleben. The king was very cheerful with

---

[37] Probably a relative or a friend from the village, obviously known to his wife.
[38] Another comrade, also probably a relative or close friend, as his wife knows him too.
[39] Men who had lost their legs during the battle.
[40] Reiß uses the German term *erstaunlich anzusehen*. In contemporary German it means 'astonishing to behold'. In eighteenth-century German, it meant 'a sight that makes one's blood freeze'.
[41] The German original has *nüchtern*. Nüchtern can either mean 'not drunk' or 'empty', 'with an empty stomach'. *Zedler's Universal-Lexicon* 24 (1740), 1589–60.
[42] He means the close-up fighting in which his regiment had been involved.
[43] He means the cannon fire during the beginning of the battle.
[44] The battle.
[45] There were often two or more brothers serving in one regiment, officers as well as common soldiers or NCOs.

us. On Sunday 3 October, he was visited company after company and thanked us for our bravery. He said that he would make us enjoy [his favour] all his life and promised that we would not be sent into the thick of it again, as we had lost so many men. Where we gave battle and kept the field: in front of the town of Lobositz. The Austrians retired into Lobositz and fired at us from the windows and roofs. But when we reached the town, we set it on fire at all four corners. It is impossible for me to describe what happened and it is also unbelievable for those who have not been there. A woman from the Colonel's company[46] will come to you, named Trottin;[47] her husband was shot dead – ask her. There must have been three times more Austrians than us, And they stood their ground like never before. And our host was very small. If God had not been on our side in the game, we would all have perished; but thanks to God, it is finished. Our regiment's thanksgiving text was Romans 8: 36-7.[48]

The Austrians have retreated about three miles towards Budin and they have another army standing at the Silesian border, where our Field Marshal Schwerin is posed against them with 60,000 men. We do not know whether it is over or not. We are still in front of Lobositz on the field of battle, where all dead humans and horses are buried. Dearest child, I could have got about 1,000 *Thalers*,[49] but I thank my God, that I kept my health and did not think of anything else than God, you and the child, which were my greatest pains.[50] Now, have God in your mind and include me in your prayers that the loving God may keep protecting me, as I include you and the child in my prayers. Remember what I wrote at the beginning of this letter and the one I wrote on 30 September, then you will have fortune and blessing and God will bring me back to you at the right time, where we will be happy with each other and in good spirits.

3. Letter of Sergeant G.S. Liebler from the camp near Prague, 7 May 1757, in *Briefe preußischer Soldaten aus den Feldzügen 1756 und 1757*, ed. Großer Generalstab (Berlin: Mittler, 1901), 44–9.

My dearly beloved wife, children and siblings!

The Lord has done great things for us.[51] If he not been on our side, our enemies would have swallowed us up quick.[52] Yea, 'tis of the Lord's mercies (44-45) that we have not been consumed.[53] Alas, sing a joyful Hallelujah, never forget this day,

---

[46] The formulation 'a woman from the Colonel's company' shows the close connection between the soldiers' families and the regiment.
[47] The family name is Trott. The suffix *-in* means in Early Modern German that she is the wife of Trott or a woman from the Trott family.
[48] 36 'As it is written: "For your sake we face death all day long; we are considered as sheep to be slaughtered." 37 No, in all these things we are more than conquerors through him who loved us.' Note that Reiß cited this verse to stress his horror.
[49] Reiß means, that he could have got booty worth 1,000 *Thalers*.
[50] Reiß means that his fear for his wife and his child in case of his death caused him the greatest pain during the battle.
[51] Psalm 126.3.
[52] Psalm 124.1.3.
[53] Lamentations 3.22.

which was terrible, but also highly gratifying for us. Terrible was this day, as an army of one hundred and more thousand waited for us, drawn up in such a manner that you could have thought they would not have yielded a single foot. [And in the end] they had to leave their entire camp together with their tents and 100 and more cannon to us. And at the same time they had to yield their capital Prague to us, to which – or better behind which[54] – they had fled, and which they have to leave now through the help of the almighty God.[55] Ascribe ye greatness unto our God![56] You will surely hear more of all these events,[57] although I am not able to give a thorough account, because this battle is one of the most important that ever happened. I just want, as far as I am able, to inform my dearest loved ones that the merciful God has saved me from all injury during this hard-fought action. And I will not glory in my infirmities,[58] but the great mercifulness of my faithful redeemer as long as I live, yea, I do not want to cease singing of it and to say of it as much as I know of it and understand of it through his mercy. For all the promises of God in him are yea, and in him Amen,[59] I had much sorrow in my heart,[60] but although my faith was very small, I always had God's assurance in me: when a thousand shall fall to thy left, and ten thousand to thy right hand, it shall but not come nigh thee.[61] Yea, I have seen with mine eyes, how the enemies of the gospel are rewarded.[62] My dear wife, give thanks to the Lord, because he has truly given me back to you. There was just a hair between me and death, as I will touch upon shortly. We had reached Budin when I wrote my last letter (I do not know whether or not it has arrived). On the 29th we followed the king and set up camp near a small town called Welwarn.[63] Here the Austrians had wreaked havoc, as we never do. They had cut in two many barrels of flour that they were unable to take with them, spoiled the flour and, in a nutshell, destroyed everything and devastated the town and the surrounding villages. In spite of this, about 100 barrels were left (45–46) for our use, as was the case in Budin. On 30 April, we joined the king's corps again and marched one mile[64] away from Welwarn. On 1 May, as we were about to march against Prague, we were sure that they would hinder our further advance, as their army stood not far away from us; but we did not meet any resistance and set up another camp three miles away from Prague. On the 2nd we advanced further and arrived

---

[54] Liebler juxtaposes fleeing to the town (in the sense of under the walls) to fleeing into it (behind the walls).
[55] Liebler takes wishful thinking for facts. The Austrians are still in Prague. The Prussians would have to lift the siege of Prague after their defeat at Kolin on 18 June 1757 at the hands of Marshall Daun.
[56] Deut. 32.3
[57] Liebler means from other people and sources.
[58] 2 Corinthians 12.5. Liebler writes that he will *not* glory in his infirmities, while the verse reads: 'yet of myself I will not glory, but in mine infirmities'.
[59] 2 Cor. 1.20.
[60] Psalm 94.19. The King James Bible reads: 'In the multitude of my thoughts within me thy comforts delight my soul.'
[61] Psalm 91.7.
[62] Psalm 91.8. Liebler stresses the critique of his enemies, the Austrians, by changing the word 'the wicked' in the original Psalm for 'enemies of the gospel'.
[63] Today's Velvary in the Czech Republic.
[64] A Prussian / German mile is 7,532 km long.

happily at Prague on White Mountain and nobody would have guessed that they would leave it to us. Yet, the whole enemy army had withdrawn [to a position] behind Prague and thus we set up our camp on this side of the town without any enemy resistance. Yea, the king himself was not satisfied that they did not want to give battle and we all seemed to get bored, because laying siege to the town from only one side would have been useless and we thought that we would get into serious trouble here, because food was scarce. On the 3rd we did not do anything until the next day, which was the 4th. Half of the army set out at 6 in the evening, marched back for one hour and camped in the open during the night. On the 5th, we marched [to a position] near the Vltava, pontoon bridges were set up, and we happily set up camp on the other side [of the river]. This was possible because their hussar pickets had been driven back by the riflemen[65] who had crossed the river earlier. At 5 o'clock in the morning of the 6th, the army set out and met the army of Field-Marshall Schwerin, which was already advancing. Here we saw the entire enemy army marching towards their positions on many mountains and high points; they halted on that side of Prague and had left their tents behind them. And it would have been impossible to attack them here, but wise Frederick[66] had a better idea. Our entire army marched away under their very eyes and marched [to a position] behind them, which they would not have believed [that we would do]. This march lasted until 10 o'clock and when about half of the army had reached the other side[67] the king made several battalions attack their left flank, which had to advance, but we kept on marching. These[68] were driven back by heavy fire after half an hour. Then, the entire army wheeled [into line][69] and everybody advanced against their camp. They gave way everywhere and (46–47) we still had not fired a single shot with our battalion, which was also true for the entire right wing, as we had marched to the left and were no longer positioned on the right wing. There were cannon everywhere in front of us and everybody had to give way to us on this side. We had already beaten the left wing of their cavalry and had had to pass their tents, which were still full of [their] equipage, and thus we thought that it would not be our turn [today].[70] Alas, something great had been saved for us, as they had not been attacked in the line[71] and the flanks had been beaten, so they tried to post themselves on all the mountains, but were always driven back. Now it was the turn of our battalion. We came upon one of the highest elevations, where they greeted us with many cannons. Nevertheless, we had to go on and advance until we were able to shoot with small arms, because our cannon were not able to follow us up the mountain.[72] Here was just a pure hailstorm of bullets; one after the other was

---

[65] See pp. 22–3.
[66] King Frederick II of Prussia.
[67] The other side of the town, behind the Austrians.
[68] The charging Prussian battalions.
[69] 'Wheeling' means the process of changing from marching columns into fire-lines.
[70] Liebler uses the German term *daran kommen*.
[71] Their centre had not been attacked.
[72] This means that not even the small Prussian three- and six-pounder regimental pieces could be used, while the Austrians were able to use their regimental cannon and their heavy twelve-pounders with deadly effect.

cut down and in the end we had to retire in the greatest disorder. Thus, another regiment [marching at] our side had to advance towards this position, and I went forward again too, together with a number of brave soldiers, and advanced to the foot of the mountain. Alas, again to no avail; everybody was dispersed by the uncountable cannon shots and we also retired. Here, I found two of the colours of our battalion[73] and made a soldier carry them away.[74] Now, a battalion of grenadiers had to go forward, and along with them I was again driven away on the orders of General von Ingersleben[75] and had to follow into the grapeshot. Here I learned what it meant 'that who sits under the shield of the Lord, etc',[76] because a cannister ball hit my breastbone, and I thought I would die. But the bullet had not penetrated [my breastbone], [thus] I went back some steps and stood still in this hail of bullets until the grenadiers also had to retreat from this [enemy] battery[77] (this was only one battery). At this point our first battalion[78] came up from the low terrain [in front of the battery] and it was led by Prince Henry[79] in person in the face of the most violent fire. I could barely breathe, so I stood still and saw how it[80] had to leave this mountain. And this was only one battery – they still had about twenty of the sort in this area. They had to be driven back by our men (47–48) one after the other, until they had to cede the entire other side of Prague. And this is what my humble self can report and what I have seen. However, many other regiments and battalions have suffered as heavily as ours. Our losses are inexpressible and I am not able to get valid information. From our company alone the following have been wounded: four NCOs, two drummers, sixty-six privates. Eight were killed on the battlefield and four men are missing. The count[81] was wounded thrice and will most probably die, the first count[82] was shot in the face, Lieutenant Colonel Sydow was dangerously wounded in the left arm,[83] Captain Herzberg is dead, Captain

---

[73] Every infantry battalion had five colours from the five companies forming the battalion.

[74] Behind the lines, because while on the field, lying on the ground, they were in danger of being taken by the enemy. Liebler also shows that he does not use the danger of the colours being captured as a pretext for evading further combat. Rescuing the colours was in itself an honourable act, worth mentioning in regimental histories. Frank Zielsdorf, *Militärische Erinnerungskulturen in Preußen im 18. Jahrhundert. Akteure-Medien_Dynamiken* (Göttingen: V&R unipress, 2016), 72.

[75] Johann Ludwig von Ingersleben (1703–57). Commander of the Guard (Rgt. 15/I) and the riflemen (*Jäger*). He was wounded during the battle. He was close to Prince Henry of Prussia, which might explain why he was in the vicinity of Liebler's regiment (Rgt. 3), as this was part of Prince Henry's brigade. Anton Balthasar König, Johann Ludwig von Ingersleben, in *Biographisches Lexikon aller Helden und Militärpersonen, welche sich in Preußischen Diensten berühmt gemacht haben*, vol. 2 (Berlin: Arnold Wever, 1789), 207–09.

[76] Psalm 91.1. The King James Bible reads: 'He that dwelleth in the secret place of the most High shall abide under the shadow of the Almighty.' The German translation by Martin Luther, the one Liebler knew, uses the words '*wer unter dem Schirm des Höchsten sitzet*', which stresses the shielding and does not encompass the sense of hiding place.

[77] A number of cannons.

[78] Liebler's regiment (Anhalt, No. 3) had three battalions, while most infantry regiments only had two.

[79] Prince Henry of Prussia, younger brother of Frederick II and one of his best generals. He was Liebler's brigade commander.

[80] The Austrian battery.

[81] Footnote by the General Staff editors: Captain Count Leopold von Anhalt.

[82] Footnote by the General Staff editors: Major Count Wilhelm von Anhalt.

[83] Footnote by the General Staff editors: Died of this wound.

König was wounded thrice etc. To sum it up: the III. battalion[84] is nearly ruined[85], and for my part, I do not know where to begin with regard to the company. Everything we need to survive has been ruined. We do not have any of the cauldrons, bottles and the like that we need, yet we are required to do everything in the field that we did before [the battle] and everything depends on me now.[86] [I] praise the mercy of the Lord,[87] which makes everything easy for me and all being well I accomplish the most burdensome things in the end. On the evening of the 6th, about 10 pm., after everything had somewhat been restored to order, we moved into our camp and kept quiet until today, which is the 7th [of May 1757]. I can hardly occupy[88] half of the tents, yet I am ordered to have all of them pitched. We surround Prague, Prince Moritz[89] on one side and us on the other side. The siege will begin very soon, because the enemy's left wing has retired into the city and we will still meet stiff resistance. I will end now, because I am so tired that I cannot think anymore. Most holy Jesus, faithful redeemer, into thine wounds I commit myself and my people[90], there we will always find our refuge.[91] If we came together again according to your holy will, we would not cease to thank you unceasingly forever and ever, as I will also not cease to proclaim God's mercy together with my brethren right now. Alas, do it (48–49) all together with me, praise the redeemer, give thanks unto the Lord, for he is mighty and of great power,[92] Hallelujah! Amen.

I am to all my dear family, friends, children and siblings

Sincerely

G.S.L.

P.S. Let my dear sibling read this letter but no one else, because it would only be judged as boasting.

4. Camp in front of Prague, 8 May 1757, letter of a musketeer from the Alt-Anhalt Foot Regiment, in *Briefe preußischer Soldaten aus den Feldzügen 1756 und 1757*, ed. Großer Generalstab (Berlin: Mittler, 1901), 49–53.

---

[84] Liebler's battalion.
[85] Ruined (*ruiniert*) is the eighteenth-century German term for the destruction of a military unit.
[86] Liebler is not boasting; he is the senior *Feldwebel* (sergeant) and responsible for the organization of the company.
[87] Psalm 145.7.
[88] Assign men to the tents.
[89] Moritz von Anhalt Dessau (1712–60), uncle of the owner of Liebler's regiment, Colonel Leopold Friedrich Franz von Anhalt-Dessau.
[90] The German term used by Liebler *die Meinigen* (lit.: those belonging to me) can also be translated with 'my family', but can also include his friends.
[91] Like Psalm 62.8.
[92] Liebler's prayers are reminiscent of Psalm 136.

I had written my letter so far, when the drum was beaten and the sergeants got the order that fifteen battalions of the left wing had to break camp and march.[93] This was on the afternoon of 4 May at 4 pm, when we broke camp immediately and [marched][94] through deep valleys to a mountain near the river Moldau, where we camped under the sky at midnight. It was a cold night and I was so cold that my teeth were chattering in my throat.[95] At daybreak, we marched onto an elevation from where we had to make our arduous path progress along the deep valley of the Moldau, where the pontoon bridges were to be built [to cross the river]. The construction was started and the Halloren[96] did a good job for the second time.[97] Here, I have to marvel at something and cannot understand how an army as strong as that of the enemy allowed us to build pontoon bridges over the water in such a dangerous area that they could have ruined half of our army; but the bridges were ready at 12 o'clock and the army started to cross them. There, everything went on according to our wishes, although some troops of enemy hussars[98] tried their luck against us, but these were soon driven back by our riflemen[99] (49–50). I have to remember that when we marched away from Prague, 40,000 men were left there. After we had crossed the water,[100] we had Prague to our right, where our army camped behind a wooded elevation. The Austrians tried to deceive us when we marched again on 4 May. They pretended to leave Prague and posed as if they had broken camp and marched away, as we were completely able to see their positions[101] on 5 May.[102] But the king, a wise master, had realised what they were up to and as he had reconnoitred the enemy army so well, its strength and the advantageous camp [they had made], it was ordered that upon the issuing of the watchword[103] we would march again tomorrow, which was 6 May. However, we saw the hussars[104] of Schwerin's[105] corps arrive and were well aware that the next day would bring something new for us.[106] During this night, I threw myself into Jesu's wounds and put my fate into the hands of my God. When dawn broke on 6 May, it promised a

---

[93] Address and salutations are missing and the letter reproduced by the General Staff seems to have a first part, written on 4 May 1757, to which this sentence refers. This first part has not been reproduced by the General Staff and is still missing.

[94] The verb is also missing in the in original German version.

[95] This is a literal translation from the German original. The normal German phrase is 'my teeth chattered in my mouth'. It is unclear why the anonymous musketeer uses 'throat'.

[96] *Halloren* is the German term for the inhabitants of the town of Halle / Saale in today's Saxony-Anhalt. Regiment No. 3, Alt-Anhalt, was stationed in Halle / Saale. The composer George Frederic Handel was a native of Halle / Saale.

[97] As the first part of the letter is missing, we do not know what the first good job had been.

[98] Austrian light cavalry from Hungary and the Balkans. They were experienced in the 'Little War'.

[99] Cf. Fn. 65. The German original has *Fußjäger*.

[100] The River Vltava.

[101] The German original has *ihr Lager*. The literal translation of *Lager* is camp. But in Early Modern German *Lager* can also mean 'positions' or 'order of battle'.

[102] The meaning is not clear.

[103] The watchword (*Parole*) was issued at 5 pm every day. *Reglement* of 1743, 226.

[104] Light Prussian Cavalry. Unlike their Austrian counterparts, they were not recruited from Hungary or the Balkans, but from the Prussian homelands and other German states. They had to reconnoitre the enemy's positions but were also used like heavy cavalry in battle.

[105] Kurt Christoph von Schwerin (1684–1757). Prussian Field Marshal. He died at the Battle of Prague.

[106] The last phrase, *uns was Neues bringen würde*, means that a battle would take place.

warm day. Shortly thereafter, we heard a cannon shot, which was the signal for the arrival of General Schwerin's army. Due to this, we broke tents immediately, took our muskets in our hands and marched off to the left, because Prague and the Austrian army – of which some say that it was 198,000 men strong[107] – were to our right. After having passed the fault to our right, we were able to see their positions.[108] We saw that they were drawn up in four lines[109] and that they had planted so many mountains with cannons that it was terrifying to behold. It was impossible to attack them from the front because we saw only deep valleys, ponds and ditches before us and [we] were not able to bring cannon there. It would have been even more impossible to take the mountains to our right, where they had taken up their positions. Hence, General Schwerin marched to the left and we followed his army. There were so many men there, that we could not see the soil beneath our feet but we recognized that there was still a tremendous number of tents in the enemy's camp. Our left wing went on further in order not to attack them frontally but to attack their right wing's flank. It was in the morning, at 8.30 am, when the vanguard under the command of the Duke of Bevern[110] fired the first shot at the enemy. Only then did they begin to (50–51) believe that we were going to attack their huge army as it was arrayed in such an advantageous position. At half past ten, the general cannonade started. We had to cross swamps and ditches one man after the other in order to attack their first line, which stood behind a village where the cavalry had left its tents. This was executed with such bravery, that our left wing chased the enemy's right wing out of position after two hours of combat. Alas, as all the high mountains (of which there were very many here) had been packed with cannon and men and as their camp measured one mile[111] in length and width, many of our men perished. This was also due to the command that our men were not to fire before being ordered to do so, as they were to charge into the enemy [lines] with fixed bayonets.[112] Because of this, many of our men were pitifully maimed, but the enemy had to flee from the bayonets – we would also have beaten them even if the mountains had been twice as high and even if there had been another 120 cannon. Now the major part of the whole army engaged the enemy and you could see one or the other battalion attacking the enemy's batteries on the mountains and it came to the point that fortune and misfortune – yea, the wellbeing of our fatherland[113] or its total ruin – were at stake. This fine and bright day had turned into terrible darkness because the smoke from the gunpowder and the dust of so many men and horses darkened the air so much that you could not see a thing and it seemed

---

[107] In fact, there were around 70,000 Austrians. The source of the number 198,000 is not known, but it clearly shows that the Prussians felt outnumbered.
[108] Again, the musketeer uses *Lager* for 'positions' (see fn. 101).
[109] Four lines of battalions. The normal order of battle consisted of two lines of battalions, e.g. fourteen battalions in the first line and twelve in the second line, about 150 metres behind the first line.
[110] August Wilhelm, Duke of Brunswick-Bevern (1715–81). Prussian Lieutenant-General at the time of the Battle of Prague.
[111] 7532.5 metres.
[112] See p. 115.
[113] The German original has *Vaterland*. In Early Modern German, the term encompasses either the kingdom of Prussia or, more often, the region from which a person comes.

as if the end of the world had come. Our battalion had not suffered anything so far and all cannonballs had flown over our heads. Finally, we were also going to feel the heat of the cannonade, as fate led us in front of a high mountain that was planted with many which fired at us cruelly with grapeshot. Notwithstanding this, we advanced against the enemy batteries with fixed bayonets, and although our battalion was almost incapable of standing and many were forced to retreat, another battalion came to relieve us and this attack made the enemy flee ignominiously (51–52) and abandon their cannon. From this time on, which might have been about 2 o'clock, the enemies were not able to accomplish anything, but were knocked out. Their cavalry was not able to save a single tent. They just saved their shirts on their backs, so to speak. Many of their infantry also had been forced to abandon their tents, [so] we got 120 cannon, all pontoons, and an enormous amount of powder carriages with ammunition and it is said that we captured their entire war chest. If you had seen what mortal danger I and my brother had been exposed to and how the bullets had flown around us like a hailstorm, you would have considered it impossible for us to survive. It was only a matter of a finger's breadth for me and my brother to be sent to the other world by a cannonball. But God sheltered us with his wing and saved my and my brother's life and limbs. Oh my, we are full of gratitude and give thanks on our knees to our creator for his mercy, praise God for his mercy, which he had unto his servants on this day. Surely, the world has never seen such cruel encounters[114] before. We were about 20,000 men and drove their army of 140,000 out of their camp.[115] And these were only those directly engaged, not counting those in Prague or on the mountains around us. Yet they had to be beaten, God could no longer tolerate their haughtiness any more, and thus this mighty army was forced to flee either into Prague or to the left of the city and the latter were shot to pieces by Prince Moritz,[116] who stood on the other side of Prague with 40,000 men while they were retreating. It pleased me very much that the army of Prince Moritz prayed for us and lifted their hands up to God.[117] Oh, if every pious Christian considered how a soldier has to suffer for the fatherland, his heart would swim with tears. Alas, so many honourable children of mothers have found their grave here. I have not slept for nearly fourteen days. Now, it is night in my tent, while I write these lines on my knees and my eyes are so tired that I cannot go on writing. That is, why I will end my letter and [just] add the list of the dead and (52–53) wounded of our company. Tomorrow, on 9 May, our army will shoot *Victoria* with the enemy cannon and our small arms.[118] Dead: our

---

[114] The German original has *Grausamkeitsgefechte*. The musketeer created this word himself; it was not in common German usage during his lifetime. As a result, it has been translated literally.

[115] The numbers are totally false but show one key pillar of the Prussian army's self-image: the enemies' vast superiority in numbers, which is overcome by Prussian courage and professionalism.

[116] Moritz von Anhalt-Dessau.

[117] It is proof of the soldier's devotion that he stresses his satisfaction with the prayers of Prince Moritz's army, which were more important to him than the fact that Moritz's corps was not able to provide the much-needed military support, as it was positioned on the other side of the river and could not cross it.

[118] Most European armies of the time celebrated their victories with shouts of *Victoria!* (victory!), firing their guns (or the captured ones of the enemy) and their muskets and the singing of the *Te Deum Laudamus*, a Christian hymn sung when giving thanks, e.g. for military victories, the birth of an heir to the ruling dynasty.

Field-Marshall von Schwerin, Colonel von Manstein, Captain von Hertzberg. From our company, twelve privates are dead, wounded are: Colonel von Sydow, Major Count of Anhalt, Captain von Anhalt, Captain von König and nine others, whom I will specify later, no time at the moment. From our company are wounded: one NCO and sixty-one privates, of whom some will probably die. While I was writing this in a hurry at 4 o'clock in the morning of 9 May, cannon were heard and we had to line up immediately. More soon.

5. Letter from Corporal Binn, 8 April 1759, in *Preußische Soldatenbriefe aus dem Gebiet der Provinz Sachsen im 18. Jahrhundert*, ed. Georg Liebe (Halle/ Saale: Gebauer-Schwetschke, 1912), 18–19.

May God be with all of you.

My dearest wife and children, I received your letter and learned from it that all of you are still healthy, which gave me great joy. Concerning me, I am, thank God, also still healthy, may [our] good God help you henceforth. My dear wife, I do not know what is going on and why it is that our children do not improve their writing skills (...)[119] When I get these letters, I am joyful, but when I look through them and see that they do not get better (...)[120] and that they are not able to compose the letter in the style of a scribe, I get so angry that I want to go up the wall. Dear wife, it is good that our eldest son is still alive so that he, as he writes, can go to the Lord's Supper next year – but [I wish] he had also learned something. I know very well, my dear wife, that a school[121] where the children are well taught is expensive, alas (18–19), but there is nothing I can do about it: had my parents given me the opportunity to learn something useful, and if I had not inherited anything else from them, I would have been living better and could have supported my family much better than [I am able to do] right now, and our children will say the same when they will be able to fully use their brains and probably be in the same situation as I am, when they will be forced to act exactly like me.[122] Again, I urgently ask you to hire a better teacher and if this does not suffice, I shall have reminded you of it for the last time, because I understand that all my letters and my pleas have been to no avail and of no use. My dear wife, as I was finishing this letter, I got the other one, written on 25 March, attached to which was a parcel with a shirt for Christian Günter. My dearest wife, I send ten *Reichsthaler* to you, which you should use for the school[123] of our children; if I live and stay healthy, I will send more to you. Please be so good as to reply to this letter as soon as you receive it. Dear wife,

---

[119] Unreadable in the original.
[120] Unreadable in the original.
[121] Literal translation from the German original. There were no 'schools' in our modern sense. The word means either a learning group headed by a teacher, or simply a private teacher. First steps towards a school system had been taken by the Soldier King, Frederick William I, but there was still a huge gap between the *Schul-Reglements* (school-reglements) and reality. When Binn writes of a 'school', he most certainly has a private teacher in mind.
[122] ... and become a Corporal in a Prussian Cuirassier Regiment.
[123] Education.

I inform you that I am no longer quartered in Leißling[124] but have been attached to a *Commando*[125] for fifteen days and will most probably not rejoin the regiment until we go to the front. When you answer my letter, write to the regiment and company, then I will surely get the letter; you can address the letter to Nauenburg,[126] where our staff is quartered, and to Prince Henry's army. Even if the regiment has moved on by then,[127] the letter will follow. We will soon go to the front, may God give us fortune and blessing and help all of us, as our enemies are coming up again. My dearest wife, do not blame me for reprimanding you because of our children, I am not angry because of this, but you know how important it is for me and how necessary it is. I remain until then, my dear wife and children, faithful unto death.

Löbiz, 8 April 1759

Corpa[128] Binne.

6. Letter from Corporal Binn, 18 April 1759, in *Preußische Soldatenbriefe aus dem Gebiet der Provinz Sachsen im 18. Jahrhundert,* ed. Georg Liebe (Halle/ Saale: Gebauer-Schwetschke, 1912), 20–21.

May God be with all of you.

Dearest wife and children, as I have the opportunity to . . .[129] I cannot but write to you and it is my soul's desire that I find you healthy and lively. Concerning myself, I am still healthy, thanks to God, may our dear God also help me in the future. My dear wife, I have already told you that I had been detached from the regiment and that I would be joining it after the regiment got its marching orders. But my *Commando*[130] has left its post and returned to the regiment and I am again in my old quarters in Leißling,[131] where I had been quartered well during the last winter, for which reason I had been the envy of my Comrades, who suspect that this is for other[132] reasons. I will tell you what has been said about me. My own quarters are poor and the only good thing I have here in the village is a preacher, who is a very benevolent man. When I came to this village for the first time, I was alone with twenty men and no officer was there. Thus, the man immediately invited me for dinner and we became such close acquaintances that he invited me every day and as the man has grown-up daughters, the fools accuse me [of infidelity]. Should any of the women who had been here[133] gossip about me, I will tell you why

---

[124] Liebe explains: near Weißenfels.
[125] Commando: a small party used for special tasks, ranging from foraging to escorting important people or secret letters.
[126] Naumburg in today's Saxony-Anhalt.
[127] By the time the letter arrives.
[128] Corporal.
[129] Unreadable. He most probably means that he has the opportunity to send a letter to his family via a female person.
[130] See p. 73, fn. 131.
[131] Leißling is near Weißenfels, a town in the south of today's Saxony-Anhalt.
[132] In the sense of other reasons than having been assigned good quarters.
[133] The spouses, sweethearts or relatives of the troopers under Binn's command. As the cavalry is also recruited from *Kantons*, they and Binn come from the same area.

they insult me. That is just the product of envy and, my dear wife, you know my circumstances well and that I have not done things like that[134] in my youth and especially not now, as I am old and my head is white and I told these people[135] straightaway that I had a wife and two grown-up children. These people were very kind to me, I had my food and my coffee [with them] every day. Yea, these people were so kind (20–21) that they could not have treated me more kindly had I been one of their own children. They shared everything with me, I can say that no one has ever treated me as kindly as them. When I had to join the outposts, they thought I would not return and wept like children, and they visited me even when I was three miles[136] away from them. That is why these foolish people cast this suspicion on me and cannot understand what happened. My dear wife, I recently sent 10 *Reichsthalers*[137] to you and hope that you have received it. When you write to me, please tell me if you have received it and also write about everything else that has happened. I cannot tell you anything else other than that we are daily expecting to get our marching orders. All the men from Polkau[138] are still healthy, Christoph Schultz, Carl Milau, Christian Günter send many regards to their families and also godfather Krauße, who is still in Naumburg.[139] In closing, [I send] a thousand greetings to you and the dear children and the whole family and all good friends and if you have not answered my last letter, I hope to hear from you soon. Meanwhile, I do not wish anything more than your dear health and am faithfully yours till death.

Leißling, on the 18th of April 1759.

Corp. Binne

7. Letter from Christian Arnholtz, written in Aussig, 21 September 1756, in *Preußische Soldatenbriefe aus dem Gebiet der Provinz Sachsen im 18. Jahrhundert*, ed. Georg Liebe (Halle/ Saale: Gebauer-Schwetschke, 1912), 25–26.

The editor Georg Liebe remarked of the following letter: 'It is from Zethlingen near Salzwedel. All persons mentioned in them can be traced in the parish records. The letter's author was the son of the *Schulze*[140] Jürgen Arnold and was born in 1730. He must have been enrolled in Regiment No. 27, which had its garrison in Stendal and Gardelegen.'[141]

---

[134] Adultery and casual sexual relationships.
[135] The preacher and his daughters.
[136] A German mile is 7532.5 metres long.
[137] Three and a half *Reichsthalers* was the pay of a common soldier.
[138] Polkau was a small village (today a district of Osterburg in the North of Saxony-Anhalt). It seems to have been Binn's home village.
[139] Naumburg is a town in the south of today's Saxony-Anhalt.
[140] The *Schulze* is the village administrator. Normally from a well-off peasant family, the *Schulze* administers the day-to-day business of a village under noble rule. Ursula Löffler, *Dörfliche Amtsträger im Staatswerdungsprozess der Frühen Neuzeit: Die Vermittlung von Herrschaft auf dem Lande im Herzogtum Magdeburg. 17. und 18. Jahrhundert* (Münster: LIT, 2005), 155.
[141] 24–5.

God be with you.

My dear brother, I now want to write to you and when my short letter finds you and our father and mother and all good friends well, I will be pleased; concerning myself, I am still healthy. My dear brother, Christoph Stendell and Asmus Gerk and Hans Kamieth and Joachim Gille from Grieben[142] and Peter Schultz and Erdmann Kamieth und Heinrich Schultz from Geinnitz, also our Johan Joachim Kamieth and Just Schultz, the *Bombardier*[143] from our village, they all send heartfelt greetings to all their friends and [ask] if they are still healthy, they will heartily welcome it as they are also still healthy. Now, my dear brother, be so kind and pass all this on to those whom I have named in this letter and when you write back, reply together and bring the letter to Gardelegen, to cutler Rinke, who lives in ...[144] God knows that the letter will reach us this way. Now, my dear brother, I would have liked to write more, but we do not know how this campaign will end, because we have marched through Saxony and into Bohemia. At the moment, we are in the camp near a town called Aussig.[145] But we do not have a stable camp: we stand in one place for a few days and then move on. But we don't know ourselves what will happen. Now, my dear brother, ask the cutler in Gardelegen when he leaves [for the army] next time and write an answer to us to say what you are doing. Gerk[146] would like to know if his brother's marriage has already taken place or not. Now, we do not have anything else to mention this time, other than we are all still well and healthy. May our dear God help us further on, as the march into the mountains was so exhausting that we became weary of our lives more than once. By this we end [our letter] and commit you to God.

Aussig, 21 December 1756

Christian Arnholtz

Address: This letter shall get to my brother Christophel[147] Arnholtz from Zetlingen and shall be delivered to the mail ... in Gardelegen.

8. Letter from Kaspar Kalberlah, written between Dresden and Pirna, 26 September 1758, in *Preußische Soldatenbriefe aus dem Gebiet der Provinz Sachsen im 18. Jahrhundert*, ed. Georg Liebe (Halle/ Saale: Gebauer-Schwetschke, 1912), 29–30.

The editor Georg Liebe wrote of the following letter: 'Together with another letter, this one is owned by a farmer in Behnsdorf,[148] near Weferlingen. We are informed about the author by his stepbrother, who wrote into the farm's commonplace book: "1759, on 23 of July, my late brother Johann Jochen Kaspar Kalberlah fell in battle against the

---

[142] Grieben was a village and is today a district of Tangerhütte in the north-east of Saxony-Anhalt.
[143] A specialized artilleryman skilled in the handling of mortars and all kinds of time-fuse-equipped bombs and grenades.
[144] Left out of the original edition.
[145] Today's Ústí nad Labem in the north-west of the Czech Republic.
[146] A fellow soldiers. Gerk is a German surname.
[147] Old German form of Christopher.
[148] Today, Behnsdorf is a part of the municipality of Flechtingen in the north-west of Saxony-Anhalt.

Russians at Zilge[149] near the Polish border, and he served the king of Prussia for 10 years. He was born 4 May 1732."'

> God be with you. Dear father, mother, brothers and sister, brother- and sister-in-law, I got your letter and learned from it that all of you are still healthy. For my part, thanks to God, I am also still healthy and my brother is as well. Dear brother,[150] you informed me that the king had beaten the Russians;[151] we heard of this just two days after the victory [and] how they [the Russians] behaved, how they tortured the people, cut off their hands, threw the womenfolk into the straw and burned them, yeah, they ate young children, stabbed and burned everything in the towns and villages. Pray every day that God does not allow this enemy to become too mighty and conquer us, otherwise we will all fare badly. Dear brother, I inform you that the king has come to our aid with the army, but he is on one side of the Elbe and we on the other.[152] We do not yet know if we get work[153] this year as they do not want to attack us and the king cannot attack them, but if he obtains the smallest advantage, it will start.[154] The king's army and the Austrians can look into each other's camps and attack each other night and day.[155] Now I commend myself and you into the protection of the Most High and remain your faithful son unto the end.
>
> Give my and my brother's regards to father and mother, brothers and sister, brother- and sister-in-law and all good friends and acquaintances. Give also our regards to the chaplain and Mr. and Mrs. Cantor, and commend them into God's protection. Also regards to ... and his wife and children, [I hope] that he is also still healthy and to [his] father and mother and his son Heinrich and all good friends and acquaintances.
>
> In the camp between Dresden and Pirna
>
> 26 September Anno 1758.
>
> Kaspar Kalberlah

9. Letter from Musketeer Johann Christian Riemann, written in the camp of Prätzschendorf, 16 June 1762, in *Preußische Soldatenbriefe aus dem Gebiet der Provinz Sachsen im 18. Jahrhundert*, ed. Georg Liebe (Halle/ Saale: Gebauer-Schwetschke, 1912), 30–3.

The editor Georg Liebe remarks that the letter belonged to the owner of the brickyard in Druxberge bei Magdeburg, Mr. Röber, who was a descendant of Heinrich Röbern, to whom the letter was sent.

---

[149] Battle of Züllichau, where the Russians defeated the Prussians.
[150] We may assume that the brother is the better reader and all participants know that he will read the letter to the other relatives.
[151] The bloody Battle of Zorndorf (25 August 1758).
[152] Kalberlah describes the weeks before the Battle of Hochkirch (14 October 1758), where the Prussians were beaten by the Austrians.
[153] Have to give battle.
[154] Kalberlah means that Frederick II will attack the Austrian army with the aim of a decisive victory.
[155] Kalberlah does not mean large scale attacks but the daily skirmishes between the outposts and light troops.

God be with you

My dear cousins and all dearest friends, especially most beloved sister. It will be dear to me, when these my few lines find you in good health and desired wellbeing. I have been, thanks to God's almighty help, kept mercifully alive and unharmed. But this is a miracle, particularly when I remind myself of the days of Pentecost, which were lamentably gloomy, and which I will remember as long as I live. Cannon and kartouwe blasts were our toll of bells, the sound of drums and trumpets our hymns, march! And quarter! our sermon – and not even enough of our dear bread. Dearest beloved sister and most esteemed friends, with sorrow I have to tell you the sad news that our dear brother Benjamin got the chance to seek a path out of this world and found it during these days of Pentecost. He went from this world to eternity on the evening of 7 June and is buried in the small town of Tumsen[156] between Torgau and Wittenberg. The cause of his death was an unexpected raid of enemy troops on the village of Salteritz,[157] near Geringswalda. There he was shot through his left leg and got a large tumour, which took away from him the light of this world, but he was conscious unto the end. Alas, my gracious God, I wish I was with him, most joyfully I would go this way, so tired I am of my life. My heart wants to burst into a thousand pieces when I read the letter he wrote to me one day before his death and sent to me. He gave me so much pleasure when he came to me in Gera[158] and will cause me much more pain [by his departure]. I will never be able to forget him because we got on so well and one gave comfort to the other. I have described his departure from this world, where he rests, who will tell my people, where I will remain? Yea, now, our gracious God may do this. Let us comfort ourselves with our brother's honour, he has let his glory in this world, that as a faithful soldier he shed his blood courageously and bravely and lost his life for his right, for his king's honour, for his fatherland and his comrades and for the good of us all. May our gracious God give him eternal bliss for this, he has escaped all hardships and has gone to a place where all war and war cries have an end. No cannon blast can frighten him any more. Heartily beloved sister . . .[159] honour our brother's departure and do not forget it, so that you can tell where he remained in this world.[160] I will see if you can tell when I come back to you with God's help. But if we do not meet again in this world, yea, then our gracious God shall arrange it as he pleases, we will surely meet in the other world, where all war and war cries are at an end, it is for sure that we all shall gather there. Our dear

---

[156] Probably Dommitzsch between Lutherstadt Wittenberg (in today's Saxony-Anhalt) and Torgau (in Saxony). Liebe himself was astonished about the spelling but did not make a guess at what the author meant. There is no town or village called 'Tumsen' between Wittenberg and Torgau.
[157] 'Salteritz' is most probably Zetteritz, as it is near Gepülzig, where the official records place the attack on a Prussian train and covering troops under Colonel Dingelstädt by Imperial forces (*Reichstruppen*) and Austrians. Although the Prussian and Austrian records differ substantially on the details, they agree that the Prussians had been forced to retreat in the end. Johann Friedrich Seyfarth, *Geschichte des seit 1756 in Deutschland und dessen angränzenden Ländern geführten Krieges. . .*, vol. 6 (Frankfurt and Leipzig, 1765), 60–4.
[158] A town in the east of today's Thuringia.
[159] Not readable in the original.
[160] He seems to mean that she shall remember where their brother was buried.

brother Benjamin was buried well. He paid the field surgeon in advance, so that he had a good coffin made for him and also took care that he was buried decently in the ground, which pleased me greatly. I commend you, dear sister, and all cousins and all dear friends to God's almighty help and I remain your faithful friend and cousin and my dear sister's faithful brother until my death and when there is the opportunity, help his [the deceased brother's] sad wife and console her, especially, heartily beloved sister, that our brother's blood[161] will not be abandoned. Goodbye, dear friends, goodbye, heartily beloved sister, goodbye, with God's help we will see each other again. If it does not come to pass in this world, it will surely come to pass where our dear brother is.

Johann Christian Riemann, Musketeer in the Highly Esteemed Major-General von Jung Stutterheim's Regiment, in the company of Captain von Borg, between Frauenstein and Döplitzwalda in the camp near Prätzschendorf[162], 16 June 1762.

This letter has to be given to Heinrich Röber and will be sent to him quickly.
My heart into pieces does break
When the seal I onto this make.[163]
In Drucksberge[164]

10. Letter by Christian Friedrich Zander to his brother, Berlin, 15 June 1749, in Christian F. Zander, *Fundstücke – Dokumente und Briefe einer preußischen Bauernfamilie (1747–1953)* (Hamburg: Verlag Dr. Kovač, 2015), 22–3.

Jesus be with you

Most dear brother, I see from your latest letter that you are all healthy, which is heartily dear to us. Thanks to God, we are still healthy. We received the cheese and the peas, but the cheese had been eaten by maggots so much that we were not able to enjoy even half of it. On the 13th of this month, the Major[165] sent a sergeant to fetch me and asked me what I had paid for my dismissal and what you had given to Lieutenant Miltnitz.[166] I told him that I knew nothing of it. He said: 'So you want to deny that again? Your brother paid him 2 *Louisdors*[167] and now you think that Miltnitz could do you a favour because of that? Even if you or your brother paid 100 *Reichsthaler* to the NCOs and Corporals, you could send me a bill for reimbursing you these 100 *Reichsthaler* but then I would treat you like an *Ausländer*

---

[161] His child.
[162] In the southern central region of today's Saxony.
[163] A rhyme in the original.
[164] His native village.
[165] Major von Zastrow. See next letter.
[166] A bribe. The lieutenant is Friedrich Bogislav von Miltitz. He died as captain after the skirmish near Salesel. He was an important contact of the Zanders amongst the officers and highly esteemed by the king. Frederick II, 'Relation de la campagne 1756', in *Politische Correspondenz Friedrichs des Großen*, ed. Johann Gustav Droysen, vol. 14 (Berlin: Duncker und Humblodt, 1886), 93. We are indebted to Prof. Jürgen Kloosterhuis for the information about the death of Bogislav von Miltitz.
[167] *Louis d'or*, a French gold coin.

and keep you here with the regiment forever so that you can earn the money again.'¹⁶⁸ I said: 'I do not want money back, I want to get my dismissal.' [The Major answered:] 'Yeah? Your brother has approached the king and asked that I give back the money that he gave to Major Aschersleben.¹⁶⁹ He can complain before his lord!'¹⁷⁰ He sent me to the Auditor¹⁷¹ whom I had to tell who your lord was and your supreme judge. He may not be any person he likes to note, but you may wish to remind the General,¹⁷² if appropriate, that we do not want the money back, but [my] dismissal, because the king is also said to have granted it.¹⁷³ He asked me also where I kept the dismissal written by Major Aschersleben? I answered that he [von Rastrow] had it, but he said he did not know anything about it. He asked: 'Who do you think gave the dismissal to me?' I said that it had been my brother¹⁷⁴ and he replied that he did not know anything about you giving him the dismissal. You have to write to Mr. Becker,¹⁷⁵ as he had promised to apply to the king. The Major does not go out any more and will probably also get his dismissal.¹⁷⁶ Nobody knows when the review will take place. Neither of us has any more money, [so] you have to send us some – without money you cannot exist. When you sent it, send it to Seiler¹⁷⁷ and send some money to Seiler, too, as he cares so much for us. Greetings to all the others.

Berlin, 15 June 1749

C.F. Zander

---

[168] While the *Kantonists* were able to go home for ten out of twelve months a year after their basic training, the *Ausländer* (mercenaries) had to stay in the garrison at all times. There, they were able to pursue other occupations in their free time or be paid by comrades for taking on their guard duties. See p. 24.

[169] The Zanders had given sixty *Reichsthalers* to Major Aschersleben to secure Christian Friedrich's dismissal. This was not a bribe in the modern sense of the word, but money they had to pay for the dismissal and which Aschersleben could have used to hire another man. The major was Martin Sigismund von Aschersleben. He was killed in the Battle of Kesselsdorf (15 December 1745) leaving the Zanders without the paperwork for their dismissal. We are indebted to Prof. Jürgen Kloosterhuis for the information about Aschersleben.

[170] There were two jurisdictions involved in this case: the military and the civilian. As the brother of Private Zander is not a soldier, the major wants him to complain to civilian authorities and not the king, who is the head of the army and can be approached directly by the soldiers of the elite regiments. The Zanders, on the other hand, thought that the civilian brother's right to approach the king derived from the younger brother being in the army.

[171] The regiment's legal officer.

[172] Philipp Bogislav von Schwerin. He was the owner of the regiment at that time and major-general (Brigade commander).

[173] The meaning of Zander's words is difficult to discern, as he switches between comments and a literal rendition of his conversation with the *Auditor*.

[174] The recipient of the letter, the *Dorfschulze*.

[175] Neither the German editor nor we were able to find out who Mr. Becker was.

[176] The German original is not clear. Zander most probably means that the major will not go to the *Kanton* – and thus to Zander's village – to get new recruits to the regiment. That is why the *Dorfschulze* Zander will not be able to see him, talk to him or bribe him. 'The Major' is most probably Zastrow, who had granted the dismissal (according to Zander).

[177] Probably another soldier or NCO.

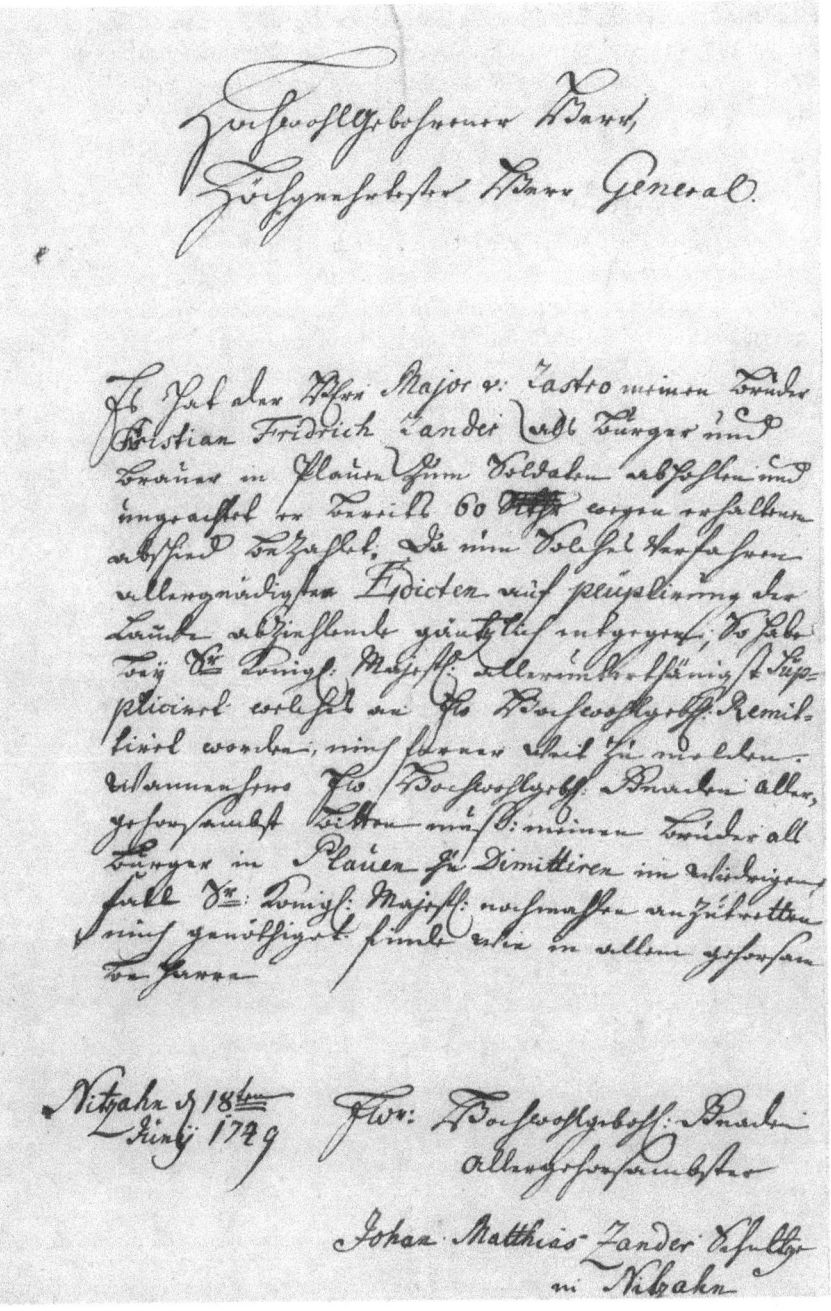

Figure 6.1 Letter from Johan Matthias Zander, Dorschulze of Nitzahn, to Major-General Philipp Bogeslav von Schwerin, Nitzahn, 18 June 1749, in Christian F. Zander, *Fundstücke – Dokumente und Briefe einer preußischen Bauernfamilie (1747–1953)* (Hamburg: Verlag Dr. Kovač, 2015), 25. Reprinted with kind permission of Verlag Dr. Kovač and Christian F. Zander.

11. Letter from Johan Matthias Zander, Dorschulze of Nitzahn, to Major-General Philipp Bogeslav von Schwerin, Nitzahn, 18 June 1749, in Christian F. Zander, *Fundstücke – Dokumente und Briefe einer preußischen Bauernfamilie (1747–1953)* (Hamburg: Verlag Dr. Kovač, 2015), 23–4.

> Your Excellency,
>   Most excellent General.
>   Major von Zastrow had recruited my brother Christian Friedrich Zander, a burgher and brewer from Plaue,[178] as a soldier [to your regiment], though he had already paid 60 *Reichsthalers* for his dismissal. This procedure is totally against the most gracious [royal] edicts for the settlement of the realm.[179] That is why I had most subserviently applied to the king,[180] who has remitted [this issue] to your Excellency, and asked me to approach you. Therefore, I have to request most obediently, that your most excellent grace dismisses my brother as [he is] a burgher of Plaue.[181] Failing which, I would feel obliged to approach His Royal Majesty again while remaining most obedient.[182]
>
> Nitzahn, 18 June 1749
>
> Your excellent Grace's most obedient
>
> Johan Matthias Zander, *Schultze* in Nitzahn.

12. Letter from Christian Friedrich Zander to his nephew Wilhelm, Dresden, 17 February 1757, in Christian F. Zander, *Fundstücke – Dokumente und Briefe einer preußischen Bauernfamilie (1747–1953)* (Hamburg: Verlag Dr. Kovač, 2015), 47–50.

Page 1

> Jesus be our greeting and the gracious God shall be with us,

---

[178] A town in modern Brandenburg, today an eastern district of Brandenburg and der Havel. Plaue is near Nitzahn.

[179] The original German word for settlement is *Peuplierung*. It is a loanword from the French language and means the settlement of new settlers in sparsely populated areas as well as the maintenance of the existing working population in areas where workers were thin on the ground. *Peuplierung* was one of the main aims of Prussia's domestic policy. The *Kantonsystem* was also invented to counter the bad effects of domestic recruitment on the economy. The *Dorfschulze* means that his brother's recruitment is contrary to the edicts and the *Kantonsystem* as he is an indispensable worker and should not be recruited into the army. We should also note that beer is one of the basic foodstuffs of mid-eighteenth-century Europe.

[180] Zander does not use the argument of his brother's status as a soldier, because he knows that the king grants the right to address him directly only to soldiers. Instead, he claims that the major has acted against the king's decrees.

[181] Although Plaue was not exempt from the *Kantonsystem*, it was indeed unusual to recruit a well-to-do burgher who was also from a family with one member already serving in the same regiment.

[182] Zander is clearly trying here to make his threat sound less aggressive. Note how self-consciously Zander writes to a man who ranks well above him.

Dearly beloved nephew Wilhelm, I have learned from your letters, which were delivered to me by the sergeant[183] and Christopher Spellerholtz,[184] that all of you are still in good health, which is very dear to us. Concerning the both of us, we are, thanks to God, still pretty healthy and well, may our gracious God preserve us further. Dear cousin, I am informed by your letter, that you still cope well with the farm, which is very dear to me, but as Spellerholtz told me, you have made a mistake. You had already spread dung[185] on the meadow[186] behind Zander's [farm], but you should do that in Spring and then spread sheep droppings all the way up to the path. And you have to spread dung on the other meadow behind Sperlerholtz[187] in Autumn using rotten dung from the front of the farmyard. Otherwise, there will be no barley. And where you want to sow wheat during the year, you have to use sheep-dung or another kind of good dung. You have to think a bit about everything you do [and remember] how we have done it previously. I do not believe that Christopher[188] will come back from Magdeburg, Spellerholtz said that the other one also had to stay.[189] See to it, that there is no lack of people,[190] otherwise it will be bad for the farm. And take care of the granary: [ensure] that the servants do not steal the grain, as the granary's lock is not very good. You also have to take care that the small horses and the oxen are well fed, otherwise

Page 2

they will not be able to draw [carts and ploughs] in Spring. You write that our brother-in-law, Mr. Dancker has not visited you yet, but aunt Bährend[191] was in Dresden again and she had told us that you had been invited to Förde[192] together with our brother-in-law Dancke and that she had also been there. [She said] that our brother-in-law had mightily pestered her, asking if she could not find a lover. He had been annoyed that she had taken Bährend [as a husband]. [She told us] that Dancker had said: 'Hey, now our little Mary[193] has to travel a lot.'[194] She had been

---

[183] He was either responsible for delivering the mail or had been to Zander's village.

[184] He is most probably another *Kantonist* from Nitzahn. However, it is unlikely that he is a servant of the Zander family, as the editor of the German version assumed (Zander, *Fundstücke*, 120). As a new recruit, it is very unlikely that he would have joined the grenadiers. Most probably he comes from a peasant family in Nitzahn and Zander misspelled the name of a farm in Nitzahn, when he wrote of 'Sperlerholtz'.

[185] The old German word *misten* means to spread muck in modern English. *Zedler's Universal Lexicon*, 21 (1739), 517.

[186] *Mahte* in the German original, and in modern English a meadow. *Zedler's Universal Lexicon*, (56 (1748), 516.

[187] It is not clear if that is also the name of a family's farm or the name of a wood, as -holtz is a German ending meaning 'wood'.

[188] A servant of the Zanders.

[189] The German original is not that clear what this means. Most probably, the men had been recruited or as *Kantonists* called to arms. Zander, *Fundstücke*, 96.

[190] Servants.

[191] The editor of the Zander letters remarks that she was Maria Elisabeth Bährend, *b.* Zander.

[192] Probably a neighbour.

[193] Zander remarks in his edition that Dancker still hassles 'aunt Bährend', whom he had been pestering before. Zander, *Fundstücke*, 48.

[194] Because she has to shuttle between her home and the army to see her husband.

very angry about that and [told us] that you two[195] had surely seen that this had annoyed her but had made the slightest attempt to intervene,[196] although Dancker spoken this type of twaddle not a hundred times, but a thousand times. She had also told you to send her a letter with the clothes but you had neither sent a letter nor the clothes. I would have liked to get a new shirt. We had been given an army shirt, but this was much too small and could not be tucked into our trousers. I sold it for 12 *gute Groschen*.[197] The young lads[198] arrived here in Dresden on the 15th. Spellerholtz was also quartered here until 18 February and was handed over to the grenadiers together with Andreas Bake.[199]

Page 3

Our grenadiers are six miles away from Dresden and they had to go there on 18 February from here. Dietrich[200] had gone to the captain and asked him to leave him [Spellerholtz, K. & S.M.][201] here with us, but the captain replied: 'Had he not been so lazy, I would not have made him put on the blue coat.'[202] I had to join the commando to Bautzen on 13 February, when we escorted four wagons laden with money there. We marched through Bischofswerda. There was a little snow in Dresden but as we marched on the snow became thicker and thicker and in Bautzen, which was seven miles from Dresden, it lay really deep and covered all the fences. We were away for four days. The entire commando was 200 men strong and were quartered in Bautzen for one night. It was even more expensive there than in Dresden. We were quartered in villages for two nights, one of the villages was called Geißmannsdorf,[203] the other one Frankenthal.[204] The peasants were generous with food and shelter. The son of the *Schulze* [village administrator] of Möthlitz died

---

[195] Cousin Wilhelm, the recipient of the letter, and the host 'Förde'.
[196] Against Dancker's pestering.
[197] In Brandenburg currency, one *Reichsthaler* is equal to twenty-four *Gute Groschen*. Thus, the shirt got Zander half a *Reichsthaler*.
[198] In German *junge Burschen*. It is the term for the new *Kantonisten*, who have been brought to serve in the regiment.
[199] Why these men were handed over to the grenadier companies of the regiment is not clear. On the grenadiers, see p. 22.
[200] Johann Dietrich Zander, Christian Friedrich's cousin.
[201] Zander seems to allude to Spellerholtz. It is more likely he is referring to Spellerholtz than to Bake, because the Captain says that he would not have made him wear the 'blue coat' if he had really been that lazy. Bake was a musketeer wearing the 'blue coat' but Spellerholtz came from the same village as the sergeant and could have been the captain's servant. We know from Bräker's memoires that the officers' servants did not wear the regiment's uniform. Ulrich Bräker, *Der arme Mann im Tockenburg*, ed. Eduard Bülow (Leipzig: Georg Wigand's Verlag, 1852), 119. http://gutenberg.spiegel.de/buch/lebensgeschichte-und-naturliche-ebentheuer-des-armen-mannes-im-tockenburg-1825/13 (accessed 14 October 2018). Dietrich Zander was definitely not transferred to another unit, as the editor of the German original presumed. Zander, *Fundstücke*, 97.
[202] 'Blue coat': the uniform of the Prussian army.
[203] About 15 km west of Bautzen.
[204] About three km west of Geißmannsdorf.

here on 13 February. He had been ill for a short time[205] and had been only recently been on guard together with Dietrich.[206] Dear nephew, you asked me to tell you what it was like, when I was with the commando and what happened in Bohemia. The commando was 200 men strong and we were ordered to the village of Salesel.[207] This [village] was located on the Elbe river and on the other side of the Elbe were pandurs and Hungarian Infantry.[208] There was already a commando from

Page 4

another regiment in the village. When we relieved them, they told us that they had shot across the river several times, but the enemy had not shot back. We occupied the village with four pickets. The pandurs and Hungarian Infantry attacked us with 800 men at two o'clock in the morning and we were only 200 men strong. It was so dark that you could not see a soul but they could clearly see us with our white lapels and cartridge-pouch straps. When they advanced, our guard asked who was there and they answered 'deserters'[209] until they were near enough to open fire immediately and the guards were still in the guard room and not even able to reach their muskets. When they came out of the guard room, they were immediately shot dead before we could even reach our guns. We had a cannon with us near the major. The other pickets retreated there, and the firing lasted until daybreak. Thirty-two men were wounded or killed and Captain Miltnitz.[210] Nobody was killed or wounded from our company, [which is] why we drank nothing but wine and the king gave us one *Reichsthaler* beer-money[211] for each man, five *Groschen* for [each man of the regiment of the] Prince of Prussia,[212] the major 1,000 *Reichsthaler*, the captain 500

---

[205] The German original is not clear; it is impossible to ascertain whether he had been ill for four days or if his illness had begun on the day of his death at four o'clock.

[206] Johann Dietrich Zander.

[207] Zander writes 'SALLEISEN'. The village is called Dolní Zálezly today and lies about seven km to the south of Aussig in the Czech Republic. He most probably describes a night action, which took place 21–2 October 1756. Gieraths, *Kampfhandlungen*, 48.

[208] Pandurs is a Prussian name for the Austrian *Grenzregimenter* (borderers). These were men from the Hapsburg Balkan areas, bordering on the Ottoman Empire.

[209] They pose as Austrian deserters who want to change sides. Using this stratagem was against the rules of war and shows the dishonourable behaviour of the Austrians, especially their light troops, whom the Prussians hated. 'Tagebuch eines Offiziers vom Alt-Schwerinschen Infanterieregiment, welches die Feldzüge von 1756 bis 1763 enthält', in *Sammlung Ungedruckter Nachrichten*, vol. 1 (Dresden: Waltherische Hofbuchhandlung, 1782), vol. 1, 451. Ulrich Bräker, *Der arme Mann*, 154. Walz, *Kriegs- und Friedensbilder*, 26.

[210] Presumably the same Lieutenant 'Miltnitz', whom the *Dorfschulze* had bribed to achieve the dismissal of his brother (see p. 87, fn. 231). The lieutenant is Friedrich Bogislav von Miltitz. He died as captain after the skirmish near Salesel. He was an important contact of the Zanders amongst the officers and highly esteemed by the king. Frederick II, 'Relation de la campagne 1756', in *Politische Correspondenz Friedrichs des Großen*, ed. Johann Gustav Droysen, vol. 14 (Berlin: Duncker und Humblodt, 1886), 93. We are indebted to Prof. Jürgen Kloosterbuis for the information about the death of Bogislav von Miltitz.

[211] *Biergeld* – drink-money or tip.

[212] Regiment No. 18.

Reichsthaler, and the lieutenants and ensigns 250 *Reichsthaler*.[213] I would have liked to write more but about it but I do not have enough time.[214] Dear cousin, do not worry about us that much, there are many honourable and brave men amongst them.[215] Finally, I send greetings to everybody and remain your faithful uncle until I die.

Dresden, 17 February 1757

Christian Friedrich Zander.

---

[213] This is an indication that Zander's numbers are no exaggeration. Gifts like these were extraordinary, especially the *Reichsthaler* for each man of the Itzenplitz regiment. The von Meyerinck Regiment (No. 26) received 1,500 *Reichsthalers* in total for all its privates after it had contributed to the success at Leuthen by fighting in the vanguard alongside the Zanders' regiment. As Meyerinck lost 464 men (including fourteen officers) in this battle, and a regiment numbered about 1,400 privates at this time, every man received roughly 1.5 *Reichsthaler*. http://www.kronoskaf.com/syw/index.php?title=Meyerinck_Infantry (accessed 16 October 2018). Barsewisch, *Von Roßbach*, 45. Möbius, *Mehr Angst*, 118–19.

[214] Given the amount of time Zander spends on the quarrel between his brother-in-law and his aunt, this remark is proof of the fact that he does not *want* to get into the detail of what must have been a most brutal encounter, and which included close combat. He only mentions the circumstances that highlight the *enemies' dishonourable behaviour* and the *honourable bearing of his regiment*: The numerical superiority of the enemy, and the king's gratitude. The other theme – shared with other correspondents – is once more the *suffering of the soldiers*, who on this occasion had been visible to the enemy by their white lapels and strings. We should mention, that the 'pandurs' wore darker uniforms of blue and red, while almost all Hungarian infantry regiments (with the exception of No. 2, who wore uniforms identical to the 'pandurs' until 1757) wore white coats, which were even better targets than the Prussian lapels and strings. http://www.kronoskaf.com/syw/index.php?title=Meyerinck_Infantry (accessed 16 October 2018).

[215] The meaning of the German original is not clear. Most probably Zander wants to convey that there are many honourable and brave fellows amongst his comrades and that they contribute to the Zanders' chance of survival.

Glossary

A glossary of German terms and technical terms

Ausländer In the Prussian muster lists, an *Ausländer* (foreigner) was a mercenary, recruited on a contract-basis. The German word is misleading, as while it implies these men came from another country but in fact it means simply that they were not *Kantonisten*. A good number had been born in the lands governed by the Hohenzollern monarchy and many others were from regions bordering on the Hohenzollern lands. Recruiting *Ausländer* took a variety of forms, ranging from signing up voluntarily to a six-year contract to forced recruitment by press gangs.

Bataille Battle. As a French loanword, it was used in eighteenth-century German.

Chasseurs Huntsmen, French loanword for *Jäger*. These small specialist contingents were deployed for reconnaissance, the Little War and commando actions, and were similar to today's special forces. They were armed with rifles like their British equivalent in the rifle regiments.

Dorfschulze Village administrator. Many German villages had a *Dorfschulze*. He was normally from a well-off peasant family which had the trust of the other peasants as well as the noble who owned the land. They had a high level of literacy. Members of *Dorfschulzen* families in the army often served as hubs between the home community and the front by writing collective letters for themselves and other soldiers, which were read to their relatives at home.

Elementarerfahrungen Existential human experiences, which shape the actions and culture of a human being.

Erfahrung Experience. The English term 'experience' covers the German terms *Erleben* (witnessing) and *Erfahrung* (experience). We use 'experience' in the sense of the German word *Erfahrung*. For example, a soldier *erlebt* (witnesses) the death of a comrade, when he is directly present at the moment of the terrible event. He experiences (*macht die Erfahrung*) his comrade's death, when (for example) he writes about it after having – however briefly – reflected and made sense of it / or acknowledged his failure to make sense of it.

Erfahrungsraum Space or realm of experience.

Freibataillon Free battalion. Light Prussian infantry made up of volunteers and POWs.

Füsilier Fusilier. Prussian line infantry made up of smaller men with shorter muskets than the musketeer regiments and a special small mitre cap. Mainly recruited after the accession of Frederick II.

Grenzer Light Austrian troops of Slav origin from the military border to the Ottoman Empire. Also called Croats or pandurs.
Hautboist Oboist. Military *Hautboists* played oboes, bassoons and the trumpet.
Hundsfott Lit.: a dog's vagina. Worst insult in eighteenth-century German.
Immediatverkehr Direct communication. Soldiers of highly esteemed regiments were allowed to communicate with the king directly, overriding the chain of command.
Jäger Lit.: huntsman. Small specialist contingents for reconnaissance, the Little War and commando actions, similar to today's special forces. They were armed with rifles, like their British equivalent in the rifle regiments.
Journal The diary of a unit or campaign.
Kantonist / Inländer In the Prussian muster lists, a *Kantonist* (man from the recruiting region of the regiment, the *Kanton*) or *Inländer* (native) was a draftee. *Kantonisten* were one of two categories to distinguish the origin of a soldier. The regiment as the basic organizational unit had its own area of recruitment from which all male peasants, artisans and small traders who reached a certain height and who had brothers were enrolled at the age of thirteen. Once they reached the age of twenty, they were drilled for two months each year during the summer. Soldiers were obliged to serve in the army between the age of twenty and forty (and sometimes above). Some seem to have been even younger. The regiment and the local authorities would work together to decide which men were actually drafted but typically more than half of those who had been enrolled were able to avoid service.
Land Regiment Provincial regiment. These were seldom used in the field but served as training units for *Kantonisten*, who were later distributed to the line regiments.
Lange Kerls 'Long men', or Potsdam Giants: the Footguards of the Soldier King, Frederick William I. As their name would imply, the king recruited very tall men for this unit. For representative reasons, he kept a detachment comprising men who were at least six feet tall.
Oberkonsistorialrat There is no equivalent term in English. An *Oberkonsistorialrat* is a member of the *Konsistorium*, the highest administrative body of the Lutheran church in a given region or 'church province'. It consisted of theologians and jurists.
Peloton / platoon A Prussian battalion consisted of eight to ten vertical segments or 'platoons'. Each of these segments fired all its muskets (or all muskets of one or two of its three ranks) together when ordered.
Pfeifer Fifer. As a military term, it covered the musicians playing small transverse flutes, fifes, who were attached to the grenadiers.
Reglement Regulation. Term used for all kinds of royal orders in the early modern era. Military *Reglements* covered every single aspect of military life, especially drill, marching and battle procedures, but also pay and conduct.
Soldatenkönig The Soldier King, Frederick William I of Prussia (1688–1740), father of Frederick II.
Spießrutenlaufen Running the gauntlet.
Treffen Line of battle. A European eighteenth-century order of battle had two *Treffen* / lines of battle, consisting of a number of battalions of infantry and squadrons of cavalry. The second line of battle was drawn up 300 paces behind the first one, and formed a parallel with it.

Bibliography

Sources

Archives

Biblioteca Central Militar Madrid
Landeshauptarchiv Sachsen-Anhalt – LHA – Rep. von Bülow
Landeshauptarchiv Sachsen-Anhalt – LHA – Rep. von der Schulenburg
Landeshauptarchiv Sachsen-Anhalt – LHA – Rep. H Harbke
Landeshauptarchiv Sachsen-Anhalt – LHA – Rep. H Stolberg-Wernigerode K.

Reglements

Müller, Johann Conrad. *Der Wohl exercirte Preußische Soldat*. Schaffhausen, 1759.
Prussian Infantry Reglement of 1726 as quoted in the text. Full Title: *Reglement vor die Königl. Preußische Infanterie, Worinn enthalten: Die Evolutions, das Manual und die Chargirung, und Wie der Dienst im Felde und in der Garnison geschehen soll, Auch Wornach die sämtliche Officiers sich sonst zu verhalten haben. Desgleichen wie viel an Tractament bezahlet und darvon abgezogen wird, auch wie die Mundirung gemachet werden soll. Ordnung halber In XII. Theile / ein jeder Theil in gewisse Titules, ein jeder Titul in gewisse Articles abgefasset*. 1726. Reprint, Osnabrück: Biblio, 1968.
Prussian Infantry Reglement of 1743 as quoted in the text. Full title: *Reglement vor die Königl. Preußische Infanterie, Worinn enthalten: Die Evolutions, das Manual und die Chargirung, und Wie der Dienst im Felde und in der Garnison geschehen soll, Auch Wornach die sämtliche Officiers sich sonst zu verhalten haben. Desgleichen wie viel an Tractament bezahlet und darvon abgezogen wird, auch wie die Mundirung gemachet werden soll. Ordnung halber In XII. Theile / ein jeder Theil in gewisse Titules, ein jeder Titul in gewisse Articles abgefasset.* Berlin, 1743.
Prussian Cavalry Reglement of 1743 as quoted in the text. Full title: *Reglement vor die Königl. Preußische Cavallerie-Regimenter. Worinn enthalten: Die Evolutions zu Pferde und zu Fuß, das Manual und die Chargirung, Und Wie der Dienst im Felde und in der Garnison geschehen soll, Auch Wornach die sämtlichen Officiers sich zu verhalten haben. Desgleichen wie viel an Tractament bezahlet und darvon abgezogen wird, auch wie die Mundirung gemachet werden soll. Ordnung halber In IX. Theile / ein jeder Theil in gewisse Titules, ein jeder Titul in gewisse Articles abgefasset.* Berlin, 1743.
Zur Ausbildung und Taktik der Artillerie, edited by Hans Bleckwenn. Münster: Biblio, 1982.

Writings of Frederick II

Frederick II. *Friedrich der Große. Denkwürdigkeiten aus seinem Leben nach seinen Schriften, seinem Briefwechsel und den Berichten seiner Zeitgenossen*, edited by Franz Eyssenhardt, 2nd edn., 1886. Leipzig: Fr. Wilh. Brunow, 1910.

Frederick II. 'Generalprincipien des Krieges in Anwendung auf die Taktik und auf die Disciplin der preussischen Truppen.' In *Ausgewählte kriegswissenschaftliche Schriften Friedrichs des Großen*, edited by Heinrich Merkens, 1–120. Jena: Costenoble, 1876.

Frederick II. 'Instruction für die General-Majors von der Infanterie.' In *Ausgewählte kriegswissenschaftliche Schriften Friedrichs des Grossen*, edited by Heinrich Merkens, 163–76. Jena: Costenoble, 1876.

Frederick II. 'Instruction für die General-Majors von der Kavallerie.' In *Ausgewählte kriegswissenschaftliche Schriften Friedrichs des Grossen*, edited by Heinrich Merkens, 177–96. Jena: Costenoble, 1876.

Frederick II. *Die Kriegskunst: Lehrgedicht in 6 Gesängen*. Berlin: Heymann, 1842.

Frederick II. 'Das Politische Testament von 1752.' In *Friedrich der Große*, edited by Otto Bardong, 174–261. Darmstadt: WBG, 1982.

Frederick II 'Gedanken und allgemeine Regeln für den Krieg'. In *Die Werke Friedrichs des Großen*, edited by Gustav Berthold Volz, vol. 6, 87–115. Berlin: Reimar Hobbing, 1913.

Frederick II. 'Betrachtungen über die Taktik und einzelne Theile des Krieges, oder Betachtungen über einige Veränderungen in der Art, Krieg zu führen.' In *Ausgewählte kriegswissenschaftliche Schriften*. In *Ausgewählte kriegswissenschaftliche Schriften Friedrichs des Großen*, edited by Heinrich Merkens, 121–38. Jena: Costenoble, 1876.

Frederick II 'Instruktionen für die Generalmajors der Infanterie'. In *Militärische Schriften Friedrichs des Großen*, edited by Adalbert von Taysen, 511–18. Berlin: Richard Wilhelmi, 1882.

Frederick II. 'Instruktionen für die Generalmajors der Cavallerie.' In *Militärische Schriften Friedrichs des Großen*, edited by Adalbert von Taysen, 519–30. Berlin: Richard Wilhelmi, 1882.

Frederick II, 'Instruktion für die Commandeurs der Infanterie-Regimenter.' In *Militärische Schriften Friedrichs des Großen*, edited by Adalbert von Taysen, 569–74. Berlin: Richard Wilhelmi, 1882.

Frederick II, 'Instruktion für die Commandeurs der Cavallerie-Regimenter.' In *Militärische Schriften Friedrichs des Großen*, edited by Adalbert von Taysen, 574–83. Berlin: Richard Wilhelmi, 1882.

Frederick II, 'Das militärische Testament von 1768.' In *Die Werke Friedrichs des Großen*, edited by Gustav Berthold Volz, vol. 6, 222–61. Berlin: Reimar Hobbing, 1913.

Officers' ego documents

Barsewisch, Ernst Friedrich Rudolf von. *Meine Kriegs-Erlebnisse während des Siebenjährigen Krieges 1757–1763. Wortgetreuer Abdruck aus dem Tagebuche des Kgl. Preuß. General-Quartiermeister-Lieutenants*. Berlin: Verlag L. von Warnsdorff, 1863.

Lemcke, Jakob Friedrich von. 'Kriegs- und Friedensbilder aus den Jahren 1754–1759. Nach dem Tagebuch des Leutnants Jakob Friedrich Lemcke', edited by R. Walz. *Preußische Jahrbücher* 138 (1909): 19–43.

'Zur Geschichte des Königlich Preußischen Fünften Husarenregiments, genannt Blücher'sches, ehemals Belling'sches.' In *Militärischer Nachlaß des Königlich Preußischen Generallieutenants, Gouverneurs von Königsberg und General-Inspekteurs der Ostpreußischen Infanterie, Viktor Amadäus, Grafen Henckel von Donnersmarck*, edited by Karl Zabeler, vol. 1, 30–42. Zerbst: Kummersche Buchhandlung, 1846.

Scheelen, Ernst Gottlob von. 'Aus Scheelens Tagebüchern'. In *Potsdamer Tagebücher 1740–1756*, edited by Großer Generalstab, 37–109. Berlin: Mittler, 1906.

Hülsen, Carl Wilhelm von. *Unter Friedrich dem Großen. Aus den Memoiren des Aeltervaters. (1752–1773)*, edited by Helene von Hülsen. Berlin, 1890.
'Aus den Erinnerungen eines Leibpagen des Großen Königs. Puttlitz', edited by Curt Jany. *Hohenzollernjahrbuch* 16 (1912), 73–85.
Lossow, Matthias Ludwig von. *Denkwürdigkeiten zur Charakteristik der preußischen Armee unter dem Grossen König Friedrich II. Aus dem Nachlasse eines alten preußischen Offiziers*. Glogau: Carl Heymann, 1826.
Prittwitz, Christian Wilhelm von. *'"Ich bin ein Preuße. . ."' Jugend und Kriegsleben eines preußischen Offiziers im Siebenjährigen Krieg*. Paderborn: Verlag für historische Publikationen und Reprints, 1989.

Soldiers' and NCOs' ego documents

Beß, George. *Aus dem Tagebuch eines Veteranen des Siebenjährigen Krieges*. s.l. & t.
Bräker, Ulrich, *Der arme Mann im Tockenburg*, edited by Eduard Bülow. Leipzig: Georg Wigand's Verlag, 1852.
Briefe preußischer Soldaten aus den Feldzügen 1756 und 1757, edited by Großer Generalstab. Berlin: Mittler, 1901.
Dreyer, Joseph Ferdinand. *Leben und Taten eines preußischen Regiments-Tambours*. 1810. Reprint, Osnabrück: Biblio, 1975.
Fundstücke – Dokumente und Briefe einer preußischen Bauernfamilie (1747–1953), edited by Christian F. Zander. Hamburg: Verlag Dr. Kovač, 2015.
Grotehenn, Johann Heinrich Ludewig. *Briefe aus dem Siebenjährigen Krieg, Lebensbeschreibung und Tagebuch*, edited by Marian Füssel and Sven Petersen. Potsdam: Militärgeschichtliches Forschungsamt, 2012.
Grotehenn, Johann Heinrich Ludewig. *Briefe und kleine Nachrichten, die ich während dem Kriege, welcher sich Anno 1757 im Monat April eräugnete, an meinen Vater geschrieben*, edited by Hans Hölscher. Kirchbrak: publisher unknown, 1991.
Kahl, Rolf Dieter. 'Ein Brief des Wiblingwerder Bauernsohnes Johann Hermann Dresel aus dem Siebenjährigen Krieg.' *Der Märker* 28, vol. 3 (1979): 82–4.
Preußische Soldatenbriefe aus dem Gebiet der Provinz Sachsen im 18. Jahrhundert, edited by Georg Liebe. Halle / Saale: Gebauer-Schwetschke, 1912.
Tagebuch des Musketiers Dominicus as cited in the text. Full title: *Aus dem Siebenjährigen Krieg. Tagebuch des preußischen Musketiers Dominicus*, edited by Dietrich Kerler. München: Beck'sche Verlagsbuchhandlung, 1891.

Regimental histories

Seyfarth, Johann Friedrich. *Geschichte des Füsilier-Regiments von Lossow*. Halle / Saale: J. G. Trampe, 1767.
Seyfarth, Johann Friedrich. *Geschichte des Füsilier-Regiments von Brietzke*. Halle / Saale: J. G. Trampe, 1767.
Seyfarth, Johann Friedrich. *Geschichte des Füsilier-Regiments von Kleist*. Halle / Saale: J. G. Trampe, 1767.
Seyfarth, Johann Friedrich. *Geschichte des Infanterie-Regiments von Anhalt-Bernburg*. Halle / Saale: J. G. Trampe, 1767.
Seyfarth, Johann Friedrich. *Geschichte des Infanterie-Regiments von Braunschweig*. Halle / Saale: J. G. Trampe, 1767.

Contemporary historiography and theory of war

Archenholz, Johann Wilhelm von. *Geschichte des Siebenjährigen Krieges in Deutschland von 1756 bis 1763*. Mannheim: Schwan und Götz, 1788.

Berenhorst, Georg Heinrich von. *Betrachtungen über die Kriegskunst*. 3rd edn., 1797. Leipzig: Fleischer, 1827.

Aus dem Nachlasse von Georg Heinrich von Berenhorst, edited by Eduard von Bülow, vol. 1. Dessau: Verlag von Aue, 1845.

Cogniazzo, Jacob de. *Geständnisse eines östreichischen Veterans in politisch-militarischer Hinsicht auf die interessantesten Verhältnisse zwischen Oestreich und Preußen, während der Regierung des Großen Königs der Preußen Friedrichs des Zweyten mit historischen Anmerkungen gewidmet den königlich-preußischen Veteranen von dem Verfasser des freymüthigen Beytrags zur Geschichte des östreichischen Militär-Dienstes*. 4 vols. Breslau: Gottlieb Löwe, 1788–91.

Fleming, Hans Friedrich. *Der Vollkommene Teutsche Soldat* . . . . Leipzig: Johann Christian Martini, 1726.

Gaudi, Friedrich Wilhelm Ernst von. *Abschriften des Journals vom 7 jährigen Kriege von von Gaudi für 1757*, vols 1–3. Manuscript, 1836.

Gaudi, Friedrich Wilhelm Ernst von. *Journal vom Siebenjährigen Krieg*, edited by Jürgen Ziechmann, vols 7–8. Buchholz: LTR, 1996.

Pöllnitz, Karl Ludwig Wilhelm von. *Das Galante Sachsen*. Frankfurt am Main, 1734.

Retzow, Friedrich August von. *Charakteristik der wichtigsten Ereignisse des siebenjährigen Krieges, in Rücksicht auf Ursachen und Wirkungen*. 2 vols. Berlin: Himburg, 1802.

Retzow, Friedrich August von. *Zusätze und Berichtigungen zur Charakteristik der wichtigsten Ereignisse des siebenjährigen Krieges, in Rücksicht auf Ursachen und Wirkungen*. Berlin: Himburg, 1804.

Täge, Christian. *Christian Täge's ehemaligen Russischen Feldpredigers, jetzigen Pfarrers zu Pobethen, Lebensgeschichte. Nach dessen eigenhändigen Aufsätzen und mündlichen Nachrichten bearbeitet von August Samuel Gerber*. Königsberg: Göbbels und Unzer, 1804.

Tempelhof, Georg Friedrich von... *Geschichte des Siebenjährigen Krieges*. 5 vols. Berlin: Unger, 1783–1801.

Beyträge zur Kriegs-Kunst und Geschichte des Krieges von 1756 bis 1763 mit Plans und Charten, edited by J. G. Thielke, 3 vols. Freiberg: Bartels, 1775.

Warnery, Charles Emmanuel de. *Feldzüge Friedrichs des Zweyten*. 2 vols. Hannover: Helwing, 1789.

Warnery, Charles Emmanuel 'Bemerkungen über die Kavallerie. In Charles-Emmanuel de Warnery, *Des Herrn Generalmajor von Warnery sämtliche Schriften*, vol. 1, 1–184. Hannover: Helwingsche Hofbuchhandlung, 1785.

Contemporary journals, collections and series

Bellona, ein militärisches Journal, edited by Karl von Seidel. 20 vols. Dresden: Waltherische Hofbuchhandlung, 1781–7.

Beyträge zur neuern Staats- und Krieges-Geschichte. 19 vols. Danzig: Schuster, 1757–64.

Bibliothek für Officiere, edited by Georg von Scharnhorst. 4 vols. Göttingen: Johann Christian Dieterich, 1785.

Neue Kriegsbibliothek, edited by Georg Dietrich von der Gröben. 9 vols. Breslau: Wilhelm Gottlieb Korn, 1774–81.

Neues militärisches Journal, edited by Georg von Scharnhorst. 13 vols. Hannover: Helwingsche Hofbuchhandlung, 1788-1805.
Officier-Lesebuch historisch-militairischen Inhalts mit untermischten interessanten Anekdoten, edited by Carl Daniel Küster. 2 vols. Berlin: Carl Matzdorffs Buchhandlung, 1793-6.
Sammlung ungedruckter Nachrichten, so die Geschichte der Feldzüge der Preußen von 1740-1779 erläutern, edited by Gottlob Naumann. 5 vols. Dresden: Waltherische Hofbuchhandlung, 1782-5).

Others

'Das Tagebuch des Feldpredigers Balke vom Seydlitz'schen Kürassierregiment aus den Jahren 1759-1762', edited by Emil Buxbaum. *Internationale Revue über die gesammten Armeen und Flotten* 3, vol. 2. (1884/1885): 15-22, 142-50, 251-8. 3, vol. 3 (1885): 37-43, 139-46. 3, vol. 4 (1885): 29-34, 126-34, 250-5. 4, vol. 2 (1886): 151-65.
[Küster, Carl Daniel]. *Bruchstück seines Campagnelebens im siebenjährigen Kriege*. Berlin: Karl Matzdorffs Buchhandlung, 1791.

Scientific Literature

'*Mit göttlicher Güte geadelt.' Adel und Hallescher Pietismus im Spiegel der fürstlichen Sammlungen Stolberg-Wernigerode: Katalog zur Ausstellung der Franckeschen Stiftungen*, edited by Claus Veltmann and Thomas Ruhland. Wiesbaden: Harrassowitz, 2014.
Balisch, Alexander. 'Die Entstehung des Exerzierreglements von 1749. Ein Kapitel der Militärreform von 1748/49.' *Mitteilungen des Österreichischen Staatsarchivs* 27 (1974): 170-94.
Bartov, Omer. *The Eastern Front, 1941-1945: German Troops and the Barbarisation of Warfare*. Basingstoke: Palgrave, 2001.
Baumann, Gerd. 'Grammars of Identity / Alterity. A Structural Approach.' In *Grammars of Identity / Alterity: A Structural Approach*, edited by Gerd Baumann and Andre Gingrich. New York and Oxford: Berghahn Books, [2004] 2006.
Beirich, Heidi Ly. *The Birth of Spanish Militarism: The Bourbon Military Reforms, 1766-1808*. MA diss. San Diego: San Diego State University, 1994.
Berkovich, Ilya. 'Fear, Honour and Emotional Control on the Eighteenth-Century Battlefield.' In *Battlefield Emotions 1500-1800: Practices, Experience, Imagination*, edited by Erika Kuijpers and Cornelis van der Haven, 93-110. Basingstoke: Palgrave Macmillan, 2016.
Berkovich, Ilya. *Motivation in War: The Experience of Common Soldiers in Old-Regime Europe*. Cambridge: Cambridge University Press, 2017.
Bilder aus der deutschen Vergangenheit, edited by Gustav Freytag. 1859-67. Dachau: OK Publishing / Musaicum, Kindle edition, 2017.
Blanning, Timothy C. W. *Frederick the Great: King of Prussia*. London: Penguin, 2015.
Blanning, Timothy C. W. *The French Revolutionary Wars, 1787-1802*. London: Arnold, 1996.
Bleckwenn, Hans. *Altpreußische Uniformen 1753-1786*. Dortmund: Harenberg, 1981.

Bleckwenn, Hans. 'Bauernfreiheit durch Wehrpflicht: ein neues Bild der altpreußischen Armee.' In *Friedrich der Große und das Militärwesen seiner Zeit*, edited by Johann Christoph Allmayer-Beck, 55–72. Herford: Mittler, 1987.

Bonelli, Raphael, Rachel E. Dew, Harold G. Koenig, David H. Rosmarin and Sasan Vasegh. 'Religious and Spiritual Factors in Depression. Review and Integration of the Research.' *Depression Research and Treatment* 7 (2012): 1–8.

Boning, Holger, *Ulrich Bräker. Der Arme Mann aus dem Toggenburg – Eine Biographie*. Zürich: Orell Füssli Verlag, 1998.

Braun, Tina Braun and Elke Liermann. *Feinde, Freunde, Zechkumpane. Freiburger Studentenkultur in der Frühen Neuzeit*. Münster: Waxmann, 2007.

Braun, Werner. 'Entwurf für eine Typologie der "Hautboisten".' In *Der Sozialstatus des Berufsmusikers vom 17. bis 18. Jahrhundert*, edited by Walter Salmen, 43–64. Basel: Bärenreiter, 1971.

Britain's Soldiers. Rethinking War and Society, 1715–1815, edited by Kevin Linch and Matthew McCormack. Liverpool: Liverpool University Press.

Bröckling, Ulrich. *Disziplin. Soziologie und Geschichte militärischer Gehorsamsproduktion*. München: Verlag Wilhelm Fink, 1997.

Browning, Reed. *The War of the Austrian Succession*. New York: St. Martin's Press, 1993.

Burkhart, Dagmar. *Eine Geschichte der Ehre*. Darmstadt: Wiss. Buchgesellschaft, 2006.

Büsch, Otto. *Militärsystem und Sozialleben im alten Preußen 1713–1807. Die Anfänge der sozialen Militarisierung der preußisch-deutschen Gesellschaft*. Frankfurt am Main: Ullstein, [1962] 1981.

Clark, Christopher. *Iron Kingdom: The Rise and Downfall of Prussia, 1600–1947*. New York: Penguin, 2007.

Cox, Caroline. *A Proper Sense of Honor: Service and Sacrifice in George Washington's army*. Chapel Hill, NC: University of North Carolina Press, 2004.

Cozens, Joe. '"The Blackest Perjury": Desertion, Military Justice, and Popular Politics in England, 1803-1805.' *Labour History Review* 79, no. 3 (2014): 255–80.

Dean, Eric T. Jr. *Shook over Hell: Post-Traumatic Stress, Vietnam, and the Civil War*. Cambridge, MA and London: Harvard University Press, 1997.

Dekker, Rudolf and Lotte van de Pol. *Frauen in Männerkleidern, Weibliche Transvestiten und ihre Geschichte*. Berlin: Wagenbach, 1990.

Delbrück, Hans. *Geschichte der Kriegskunst im Rahmen der politischen Geschichte*, vol. 4. Berlin: De Gruyter, [1920] 1962.

Die Taktische Schulung der Preußischen Armee durch König Friedrich den Großen während der Friedenszeit 1745 bis 1756, edited by Großer Generalstab. Berlin: Mittler, 1900.

Dinges, Martin. 'Einleitung: Geschlechtergeschichte – mit Männern!' In *Hausväter, Priester, Kastraten. Zur Konstruktion von Männlichkeit in Spätmittelalter und Früher Neuzeit*, edited by Martin Dinges, 1–19. Göttingen: Vandenhoeck und Ruprecht, 1998.

Ditcham, Brian G. H. Review of Sascha Möbius 'Mehr Angst vor dem Offizier als vor dem Feind', H-German, April 2008. https://networks.h-net.org/node/35008/reviews/45433/ditcham-m%C3%B6bius-mehr-angst-vor-dem-offizier-als-vor-dem-feind-eine (accessed 29 May 2018).

Doing Culture. Neue Positionen zum Verhältnis von Kultur und sozialer Praxis, edited by Karl H. Hörning and Julia Reuter. Bielefeld: Transcript, 2004.

Dressel, Gerd. *Historische Anthropologie. Eine Einführung*. Vienna: Böhlau, 1996.

Duffy, Christopher. *Friedrich der Große und seine Armee*. German translation. Stuttgart: Motorbuch, 1978.

Duffy, Christopher. *The Military Experience in the Age of Reason*. 2nd edn. London: Routledge, 1998.

Duffy, Christopher. *Russia's Military Way to the West. Origins and Nature of Russian Military Power 1700-1800*. Abingdon: Routledge, [1982] 2017.

Dülmen, Richard van. *Kultur und Alltag in der Frühen Neuzeit, vol. 2 Dorf und Stadt 16.-18. Jahrhundert*. 3rd edn. Munich: Beck, 2005.

Dürr, Alfred. *Die Kantaten von Johann Sebastian Bach*. 4th edn. Munich: dtv, 1981.

Ehre. Fallstudien zu einem anthropologischen Phänomen in der Vormoderne, edited by Dorothea Klein. Würzburg: Königshausen und Neumann, 2019.

Ehre und Pflichterfüllung als Codes militärischer Tugenden, edited by Ulrike Ludwig, Markus Pöhlmann and John Zimmermann. Paderborn: Ferdinand Schöningh, 2014.

Ehre und Recht. Ehrkonzepte, Ehrverletzungen und Ehrverteidigungen vom späten Mittelalter bis zur Moderne, edited by Sylvia Kesper-Biermann. Magdeburg: Meine, 2011.

Ehrkonzepte in der Frühen Neuzeit, edited by Sibylle Backmann, Hans-Jörg Künast, Sabine Ullmann and B. Ann Tlusty. 2nd edn. Berlin: Akademie, 2018.

Ellis, Harold. *A History of Surgery*. London: Greenwich Medical Media Limited, 2002.

Engelen, Beate. *Soldatenfrauen in Preußen. Eine Strukturanalyse der Garnisonsgesellschaft im späten 17. und 18. Jahrhundert*. Münster: Lit Verlag, 2005.

Epistolario español: colección de cartas de españoles ilustres antiguos y modernos, vol. II. Madrid: Imprenta y Estereotipia de M. Rivadeneyra, 1870.

European Warfare 1453-1815, edited by Jeremy Black. London: Routledge, 1999.

Fann, Willerd R. 'On the Infantryman's Age in Eighteenth Century Prussia.' *Military Affairs* 41, no. 4 (1977): 165-70.

Fesser, Gerd. *Die Schlacht bei Jena und Auerstedt 1806*. Berlin: Deutscher Verlag der Wissenschaften, 1986.

Förster, Friedrich Christoph. *Friedrich Wilhelm I. König von Preussen*, vol. 1. Potsdam: Ferdinand Riegel, 1834.

Foyster, Elizabeth A. *Manhood in Early Modern England: Honour, Sex and Marriage*. Harlow: Longman, 1999.

Frevert, Ute. 'Das Militär als "Schule der Männlichkeit". Erwartungen, Angebote, Erfahrungen im 19. Jahrhundert.' In *Militär und Gesellschaft im 19. und 20. Jahrhundert*, edited by Ute Frevert, 145-73. Stuttgart: Klett-Cotta, 1997.

Frevert, Ute. *Gefühlspolitik. Friedrich II. als Herr über die Herzen*. Göttingen: Wallstein, 2012, Kindle edition.

Füssel, Marian. 'Emotions in the Making: The Transformation of Battlefield Experiences during the Seven Years' War (1756-1763).' In *Battlefield Emotions 1500-1800. Practices, Experience, Imagination*, edited by Erika Kuijpers and Cornelis van der Haven, 149-72. Basingstoke: Palgrave Macmillan, 2016.

Fussell, Paul. *Wartime: Understanding and Behavior in the Second World War*. New York and Oxford: Oxford University Press, 1989.

Genesis, Marita. 'Scharfrichter in der Stadt Brandenburg. Betrachtung eines Berufsbildes.' MA diss. Potsdam: Fachbereich Landesgeschichte des Historischen Instituts der Universität Potsdam, 2006.

Gieraths, Günther. *Die Kampfhandlungen der Brandenburgisch-Preussischen Armee 1626-1807. Ein Quellenhandbuch*. Berlin: Walter de Gruyter & Co., 1964.

Gleim, Johann Wilhelm Ludwig. *Sieges-Lied der Preußen nach der Schlacht bei Roßbach*. Berlin, 1757.

Groehler, Olaf. *Die Kriege Friedrichs II.* 4th edn. Berlin (Ost): Militärverlag der DDR, 1986.

Gross, Gerhard P. *The Myth and Reality of German Warfare: Operational Thinking from Moltke the Elder to Heusinger*. Lexington, KY: The University Press of Kentucky, 2016.

Großer Generalstab. *Der Siebenjährige Krieg 1756–1763*. 13 vols. Berlin: Mittler, 1901–14.
Guinier, Arnaud. *L'honneur du soldat: éthique martiale et discipline guerrière dans la France des Lumières*. Ceyzérieu: Champ Vallon, 2014.
Häberlein, Mark and Michaela Schmölz-Häberlein, *Der Siebenjährige Krieg und das Kommunikationsnetz des Halleschen Pietismus,* to be published in *The Seven Years' War 1756–1763: Micro- and Macroperspectives*. Schriftenreihe des Historischen Kollegs München), edited by Marian Füssel. Berlin and Boston, MA: De Gruyter/Oldenbourg, 2019.
Hagemann, Karen. 'Der "Bürger" als "Nationalkrieger". Entwürfe von Militär, Nation und Männlichkeit in der Zeit der Freiheitskriege.' In *Landsknechte, Soldatenfrauen und Nationalkrieger. Militär, Krieg und Geschlechterordnung im historischen Wandel*, edited by Karen Hagemann and Ralf Pröve, 74–102. Frankfurt am Main: Campus, 1998.
Hagemann, Karen. 'Of "Manly Valor" and "German Honor". Nation, War and Masculinity in the Age of the Prussian Uprising against Napoleon.' *Central European History* 30, no. 2. (1997): 187–220.
Hagen, William W. *Ordinary Prussians: Brandenburg Junkers and Villagers, 1500–1840* (Cambridge: Cambridge University Press, 2003).
Hansen, Ernst Willi. 'Zur Problematik einer Sozialgeschichte des deutschen Militärs im 17. und 18. Jahrhundert.' *Zeitschrift für Historische Forschung* 6 (1979): 425–60.
Hariri, Yuval Noah. *The Ultimate Experience: Battlefield Revelations and the Making of Modern War Culture, 1450–2000*. Basingstoke: Palgrave Macmillan, 2008.
Harnoncourt, Nikolaus. 'Die Blasinstrumente im Instrumentarium Bachs.' In *Beiheft zu: Das Kantatenwerk* 14 (1976): 3–5.
Hatton, Ragnhild Mary. *Charles XII of Sweden*. London: Weidenfeld & Nicolson, 1968.
Haynes, Bruce. *The Eloquent Oboe: A History of the Hautboy 1640–1760*. Oxford: Oxford University Press, 2001.
Heil, Wolfgang. 'Die Gemeinen Soldaten – Das Sozialleben der militärischen Unterschicht im altpreußischen Heer und seine Rolle in der altständischen Gesellschaft 1754–1807.' PhD diss. Hagen: Fernuniversität Hagen, 2001.
Heilmann, Johann. *Die Kriegskunst der Preußen unter König Friedrich dem Großen*, vol. 1. Leipzig and Meißen: F.W. Goedsche'sche Buchhandlung, 1852.
Hill, J. Michael. 'Killiecrankie and the Evolution of Highland Warfare.' *War in History* 1, no. 2 (1994): 125–39.
Hoen, Maximilian Ritter von. 'Die Schlacht bei Kolin am 18. Juni 1757.' *Streffleurs Militärische Zeitschrift* 1, vol. 1 (1911): 11–46; vol. 3: 369–404; vol. 4: 581–612; vol. 5: 773–96; vol. 6: 939–58.
Hoen, Maximilian Ritter von. 'Die Schlacht bei Prag am 6. Mai 1757.' *Streffleurs Militärische Zeitschrift* 1, vol. 2 (1909): 197–234 and vol. 3. (1909): 377–416.
Hofer, Achim. 'Zur Erforschung und Spielpraxis von Märschen bis um 1750.' In *Militärmusik und 'zivile' Musik. Beziehungen und Einflüsse*, edited by Armin Griebel and Horst Steinmetz, 41–54. Uffenheim: Forschungsstelle für fränkische Volksmusik, 1993.
Hofer, Achim. *Studien zur Geschichte des Militärmarsches*. 2 vols. Tutzing: Schneider, 1988.
Hofmann, Stefan G., Aleena Hay and Abigail Barthel. *Panic Attacks and Panic Disorder: Symptoms, Treatment, Causes, and Coping Strategies*. https://www.anxiety.org/panic-disorder-panic-attacks (accessed 23 November 2018).
Höhn, Reinhard. *Revolution, Heer, Kriegsbild*. Darmstadt: Wittich, 1944.
http://www.kronoskaf.com
http://www.preussenweb.de

Honour, Violence and Emotions in History, edited by Carolyn Strange. London: Bloomsbury, 2014.

Hurl-Eamon, Jennine. 'Deadbeat Dads? A Closer look at the Married Men Who Joined the Army in Eighteenth-Century Britain.' https://www.youtube.com/watch?v=RM6f4UgWSvI (accessed 22 August 2018).

Hurl-Eamon, Jennine. *Marriage and the British Army in the Long Eighteenth Century: 'The Girl I Left Behind Me'*. Oxford: Oxford University Press, 2014.

In Defence of the Knightly Art of the Trumpet. Caspar Hentschel's *Oratorischer Hall vnd Schall / Vom Löblichen vrsprung / lieblicher anmuth vnd empfindlichen Nutzen Der Rittermessigen Kunst der Trommeten* [Berlin: George Runge, 1620], edited by Peter Downey. Lisburn, Northern Ireland: Downey Editions, 2017.

Isenmann, Eberhard. *Ehre. Die Ehre und die Stadt im Spätmittelalter und zu Beginn der frühen Neuzeit*. Würzburg: Königshausen und Neumann, 2019.

Jahn, Bernhard. 'Die Medialität des Krieges. Zum Problem der Darstellung von Schlachten am Beispiel der Schlacht bei Lobositz. (1.10.1756) im Siebenjährigen Krieg.' In *'Krieg ist mein Lied.' Der Siebenjährige Krieg in den zeitgenössischen Medien*, edited by Wolfgang Adam and Holger Dainat in cooperation with Ute Pott, 88–110. Göttingen: Wallstein, 2007.

Janson, August von. *Hans Karl von Winterfeld, des grossen Königs Generalstabschef*. Berlin: G. Stilke, 1913.

Jany, Curt. *Geschichte der Preußischen Armee*, vol. 2. Osnabrück: Biblio, [1928] 1967.

Jensen, Geoffrey. *Irrational Triumph: Cultural Despair, Military Nationalism, and the Ideological Origins of Franco's Spain*. Reno and Las Vegas: University of Nevada Press, 2002.

Jessen, Olaf. 'Review of Martin Winter, Untertanengeist durch Militärpflicht.' *Militär und Gesellschaft in der frühen Neuzeit* 9, no. 2 (2008): 206–9.

Johann Sebastian Bach, Kantate 'Schauet doch und sehet, ob irgendein Schmerz sei.' BWV 46, edited by Arnold Schering. London et al. s.d.

Kagan, Frederick W. 'Russia's Geopolitical Dilemma and the Question of Backwardness.' In *The Military History of Tsarist Russia*, edited by Frederick Kagan and Robin Higham, 249–58. New York and Houndsmills: Palgrave Macmillan, 2002.

Kauppert, Michael. 'Wie erschließt sich der Erfahrungsraum? Zur Transformation des Lebensweltheorems.' In *Phänomenologie und Soziologie. Theoretische Positionen, aktuelle Problemfelder und empirische Umsetzungen*, edited by Jürgen Raab et al., 243–52. Wiesbaden: Verlag für Sozialwissenschaften, 2008.

Keegan, John. *The Face of Battle: A Study of Agincourt, Waterloo and the Somme*. London: Pimlico, [1976] 2004.

Keegan, John. *The Illustrated Face of Battle: A Study of Agincourt, Waterloo, and the Somme*. Illustrated edn. New York: Viking, [1976] 1989.

Keynes, Katherine M. et al. 'The burden of loss: Unexpected death of a loved one and psychiatric disorders across the life course in a national study.' *American Journal of Psychiatry* 171, vol. 8 (2014): 864–71.

Kirby, Percival. 'The Kettle-Drums: An Historical Survey.' *Music & Letters* 9 (1929): 34–43.

Kling, Constantin. *Die Infanterie-Regimenter. Allgemeine Bemerkungen*. Weimar: Buch- und Steindruckerei von Putze und Hölzer, 1902.

Kloosterhuis, Jürgen. *Bauern, Bürger und Soldaten. Quellen zur Sozialisation des Militärsystems im preußischen Westfalen 1713–1803*. Münster: Selbstverlag des Nordrhein-Westfälischen Staatsarchivs, 1992.

Kloosterhuis, Jürgen. 'Donner, Blitz und Bräker – der Soldatendienst des "armen Mannes im Tockenburg" aus der Sicht des preußischen Militärsystems.' In *Schreibsucht – autobiografische Schriften des Pietisten Ulrich Bräker (1725–1798)*, edited by Alfred Messerli and Adolf Muschg, 129–87. Göttingen: Vandenhoeck & Ruprecht, 2004.

Kloosterhuis, Jürgen. *Legendäre 'lange Kerls'. Quellen zur Regimentskultur der Königsgrenadiere Friedrich Wilhelms I., 1713–1740*. Berlin: Geheimes Staatsarchiv Preussischer Kulturbesitz, 2003.

König, Anton Balthasar. 'Johann Ludwig von Ingersleben.' In *Biographisches Lexikon aller Helden und Militairpersonen, welche sich in Preußischen Diensten berühmt gemacht haben*, vol. 2, 207–9. Berlin: Arnold Wever, 1789.

Koselleck, Reinhart. *Vergangene Zukunft. Zur Semantik geschichtlicher Zeiten*. Frankfurt am Main: Suhrkamp, 1979.

Kriegelstein, Carl Binder von. *Geist und Stoff im Kriege*, vol. 1. Vienna and Leipzig: Wilhelm Braumüller, 1896.

Kroener, Bernhard R. '"Nun danket alle Gott." Der Choral von Leuthen und Friedrich der Große als protestantischer Held. Die Produktion politischer Mythen im 19. und 20. Jahrhundert.' In *'Gott mit uns.' Nation, Religion und Gewalt im 19. und frühen 20. Jahrhundert*, edited by Gerd Krumeich and Hartmut Lehmann, 105–34. Göttingen: Vandenhoeck & Ruprecht, 2000.

Kroener, Bernhard R. 'Die Geburt eines Mythos – die "schiefe Schlachtordnung." Leuthen, 5. Dezember.' In *Schlachten der Weltgeschichte. Von Salamis bis Sinai*, edited by Stig Förster, Markus Pöhlmann and Dierk Walter, 169–83. Munich: C. H. Beck, 2001.

Kroener, Bernhard R. '"... und ist der Jammer nid zu beschreiben." Geschlechterbeziehungen und Überlebensstrategien in der Lagergesellschaft des Dreißigjährigen Krieges.' In *Landsknechte, Soldatenfrauen und Nationalkrieger. Militär, Krieg und Geschlechterordnung im historischen Wandel*, edited by Karen Hagemann and Ralf Pröve, 279–96. Frankfurt am Main: Campus, 1998.

Kroll, Stefan. *Soldaten im 18. Jahrhundert zwischen Friedensalltag und Kriegserfahrung. Lebenswelten und Kultur in der kursächsischen Armee 1728–1796*. Paderborn: Ferdinand Schöningh, 2006.

Kunisch, Johannes. *Das Mirakel des Hauses Brandenburg. Studien zum Verhältnis von Kabinettspolitik und Kriegführung im Zeitalter des Siebenjährigen Krieges*. München und Wien: Oldenbourg, 1978.

Kunisch, Johannes. *Der Kleine Krieg. Studien zum Heerwesen des Absolutismus*. Wiesbaden: F. Steiner, 1973.

Landsknechte, Soldatenfrauen und Nationalkrieger. Militär, Krieg und Geschlechterordnung im historischen Wandel, edited by Karen Hagemann and Ralf Pröve. Frankfurt am Main and New York: Campus, 1998.

Latzel, Klaus. '"Schlachtbank" oder "Feld der Ehre"? Der Beginn des Einstellungswandels gegenüber Krieg und Tod 1756–1815.' In *Der Krieg des kleinen Mannes. Eine Militärgeschichte von unten*, edited by Wolfram Wette, 76–92. 2nd edn. Munich und Zürich: Piper, [1992] 1995.

Latzel, Klaus. 'Vom Kriegserlebnis zur Kriegserfahrung. Theoretische und methodische Überlegungen zur erfahrungsgeschichtlichen Untersuchung von Feldpostbriefen,' *Militärgeschichtliche Mitteilungen* 56 (1997), 1–30.

Lemcke, Jakob Friedrich von. 'Kriegs- und Friedensbilder aus den Jahren 1754–1759. Nach dem Tagebuch des Leutnants Jakob Friedrich Lemcke', edited by R. Walz. *Preußische Jahrbücher* 138 (1909): 19–43.

Linch, Kevin. *Britain and Wellington's Army. Recruitment, Society and Tradition, 1807–15.* Houndsmills and New York: Palgrave Macmillan, 2011.

Lobenstein-Reichmann, Anja. *Sprachliche Ausgrenzung im späten Mittelalter und in der frühen Neuzeit.* Berlin and Boston, MA: de Gruyter, 2013.

Löffler, Ursula. *Dörfliche Amtsträger im Staatswerdungsprozess der Frühen Neuzeit: Die Vermittlung von Herrschaft auf dem Lande im Herzogtum Magdeburg. 17. und 18. Jahrhundert.* Münster: LIT, 2005.

Lorenz, Maren. *Das Rad der Gewalt. Militär und Zivilbevölkerung in Norddeutschland nach dem Dreißigjährigen Krieg. 1650–1700.* Cologne: Böhlau, 2007.

Lynn, John A. *The Bayonets of the Republic. Motivation and Tactics in the Army of Revolutionary France, 1791–94.* Urbana and Chicago: University of Illinois Press, 1984.

Mansfield, Nicholas. *Soldiers as Workers: Class, Employment, Conflict and the Nineteenth-century Military.* Liverpool: Liverpool University Press, 2016.

Marschke, Benjamin. *Absolutely Pietist: Patronage, Factionalism, and State-Building in the Early Eighteenth-Century Prussian Army Chaplaincy.* Tübingen: Niemeyer, 2005.

Marten, Peter. C. *Die Musik der Spielleute des altpreussischen Heeres.* Osnabrück: Biblio, 1976.

McCormack, Matthew. *Embodying the Militia in Georgian England.* Oxford: Oxford University Press, 2015.

McPherson, James M. *Für die Freiheit sterben. Die Geschichte des amerikanischen Bürgerkrieges.* Munich: List and Leipzig, 1988.

Meumann, Markus. '"Jay dit plusieurs fois aux officiers principaux d'en faire des exemples". Institutionen. Intentionen und Praxis der französischen Militärgerichtsbarkeit im 16. und 17. Jahrhundert.' In *Militär und Recht vom 16. bis 19. Jahrhundert,* edited by Jutta Nowosadtko, Diethelm Klippel and Kai Lohsträter, 87–144. Göttingen: V&R unipress, 2016.

Möbius, Katrin and Sascha. 'Rossbach: el engaño perfecto.' *Desperta Ferro* 24 (2016): 20–7.

Möbius, Sascha. '"Haß gegen alles, was nur den Namen eines Franzosen führet"? Die Schlacht bei Rossbach und nationale Stereotype in der deutschsprachigen Militärliteratur der zweiten Hälfte des 18. Jahrhunderts.' In *Gallophobie im 18. Jahrhundert,* edited by Jens Häsler and Albert Meier, 123–58. Berlin: Deutscher Wissenschaftsverlag, 2005.

Möbius, Sascha. '"Bravthun", "entmannende Furcht" und "schöne Überläuferinnen" – Zum Männlichkeitsbild preußischer Soldaten im Siebenjährigen Krieg in Magdeburg, Halle und der Altmark.' In *Leben in der Stadt. Eine Kultur- und Geschlechtergeschichte Magdeburgs,* edited by Eva Labouvie, 79–96. Cologne, Weimar, Vienna: Boehlau, 2004.

Möbius, Sascha. 'Die Kommunikation zwischen preußischen Soldaten und Offizieren im Siebenjährigen Krieg zwischen Gewalt und Konsens.' *Militärgeschichtliche Zeitschrift* 63, vol. 2 (2004): 325–53.

Möbius, Sascha. '"Ein feste Burg ist unser Gott" und "Das furchtbare Lärmen ihrer Trommeln." Preußische Militärmusik in der Kultur des Kampfes in den Schlesischen Kriegen.' In *Mars und die Musen. Das Wechselspiel zwischen Militär und Gesellschaft in der frühen Neuzeit,* edited by Jutta Nowosadtko and Matthias Rogg, 261–90. Münster: Lit Verlag, 2008.

Möbius, Sascha. 'Kriegsgreuel in den Schlachten des Siebenjährigen Krieges in Europa.' In *Kriegsgreuel: Die Entgrenzung der Gewalt in kriegerischen Konflikten vom Mittelalter bis ins 20. Jahrhundert,* edited by Sönke Neitzel and Daniel Hohrath, 185–204. Paderborn: Ferdinand Schöningh, 2008.

Möbius, Sascha. *Mehr Angst vor dem Offizier als vor dem Feind? Eine mentalitätsgeschichtliche Studie zur preußischen Taktik im Siebenjährigen Krieg.* Saarbrücken: VDM / Akademikerverlag, 2007.

Möbius, Sascha. 'Von Jast und Hitze wie vertaumelt. Überlegungen zur Wahrnehmung von Gewalt durch preußische Soldaten im Siebenjährigen Krieg.' *Forschungen zur Brandenburgischen und Preußischen Geschichte, Neue Folge* 12 (2002): 1–34.

Modrow, Irina. 'Religiöse Erweckung und Selbstreflexion. Überlegungen zu den Lebensläufen Herrnhuter Schwestern als einem Beispiel pietistischer Selbstdarstellungen.' In *Ego-Dokumente. Annäherung an den Menschen in der Geschichte*, edited by Winfried Schulze, 121–30. Berlin: De Gruyter, 1996.

Moreira-Almeida, Alexander, Harold G. Koenig and Giancarlo Lucchetti. 'Clinical implications of spirituality to mental health: review of evidence and practical guidelines.' *Revista Brasileira de Psiquiatria* 36 (2014): 176–82.

Muth, Jörg. 'Leuthen: contra una abrumadora superioridad.' *Desperta Ferro: Historia Moderna* 24 (2016): 48–55.

Muth, Jörg. *Flucht aus dem militärischen Alltag. Ursachen und individuelle Ausprägung der Desertion in der Armee Friedrichs des Großen. Mit besonderer Berücksichtigung der Infanterieregimenter der Potsdamer Garnison.* Freiburg in Breisgau: Rombach, 2003.

Nietzsche Wörterbuch, edited by Nietzsche Research Group. Nijmegen, vol. 1. Berlin: De Gruyter, 2004.

Nowosadtko, Jutta. 'Militärjustiz in der Frühen Neuzeit. Anmerkungen zu einem vernachlässigten Feld der historischen Kriminalitätsforschung.' In *Unrecht und Recht. Kriminalität und Gesellschaft im Wandel von 1500–2000. Gemeinsame Landesausstellung der rheinland-pfälzischen und saarländischen Archive*, edited by Heinz-Günther Borck, 638–51. Koblenz: Verlag der Landesarchivverwaltung Rheinland-Pfalz, 2002.

Nowosadtko, Jutta. *Scharfrichter und Abdecker. Der Alltag zweier unehrlicher Beruf ein der frühen Neuzeit.* Paderborn: Ferdinand Schöningh, 1994.

Nowosadtko, Jutta. 'Stand und Ehre.' In *Lesebuch Altes Reich* (Bibliothek Altes Reich 1), edited by Stephan Wendehorst and Siegrid Westphal, 146–53. Munich: de Gruyter, 2006.

Nowosadtko, Jutta. *Stehendes Heer im Ständestaat. Das Zusammenleben von Militär- und Zivilbevölkerung im Fürstbistum Münster 1650–1803.* Paderborn: Ferdinand Schöningh, 2011.

Oesterdiekhoff, Georg W. *Sozialstruktur und sozialer Wandel. Gesammelte Aufsätze.* Münster: LIT, 2006.

Ordenanzas de su Magestad, para el Regimen, Disciplina, subordinacion, y servicio de la Infanteria, Cavalleria, y Dragones de sus Exercitos en Guarnicion, y en Campaña. Dividas en dos Tomos. Madrid: Imprenta de Juan de Ariztia, 1728.

Ortenburg, Georg. *Waffe und Waffengebrauch im Zeitalter der Kabinettskriege.* Koblenz: Bernard & Graefe, 1986.

Ortmann, Adolph Dietrich. *Adolph Dieterich Ortmanns. Inspektors zu Belitz, Sieges-Predigt wegen der Schlacht bey Roßbach gehalten über Jesaia 26.v.20 in der Kirche zu Belitz.* Berlin: Christian Voß, 1757.

Panoff, Peter. *Militärmusik in Geschichte und Gegenwart.* Berlin: Karl Siegismund, 1938.

Pargament, Kenneth I., Lisa M. Perez and Harold Koenig. 'The many methods of religious coping: Development and initial validation of the RCOPE.' *Journal of Clinical Psychology* 56, vol. 4 (2000): 519–43.

Parker, Geoffrey. *The Military Revolution: Military Innovation and the Rise of the West, 1500-1800*. 3rd edn. Cambridge: Cambridge University Press, 1998.

Pelizaeus, Ludolf. 'Die zentraleuropäische Entwicklung der Begriffe "Ehre", "Disziplin" und "Pflicht" im Spiegel von Militärschriftstellern und Reglements 1500-1808.' In *Ehre und Pflichterfüllung als Codes militärischer Tugenden*, edited by Ulrike Ludwig, Markus Pöhlmann and John Zimmermann, 31-45. Paderborn: Ferdinand Schöningh, 2014.

Peters, Jan. 'Zur Auskunftsfähigkeit von Selbstsichtzeugnissen schreibender Bauern.' In *Ego-Dokumente. Annäherung an den Menschen in der Geschichte*, edited by Winfried Schulze, 175-90. Berlin: de Gruyter, 1996.

Petter, Wolfgang. 'Zur Kriegskunst im Zeitalter Friedrichs des Großen.' In *Europa im Zeitalter Friedrichs des Großen. Wirtschaft, Gesellschaft, Kriege*, edited by Bernhard R. Kroener, 266-7. Munich: Oldenbourg, 1989.

Platen, Emil. *Johann Sebastian Bach. Die Matthäus-Passion. Entstehung, Werkbeschreibung, Rezeption*. 2nd edn. Kassel: Bärenreiter, dtv, 1997.

Prautzsch, Ludwig. *Bibel und Symbol in den Werken Bachs*. Norderstedt: Books on Demand, 2000.

Pröve, Ralf. 'Vom Schmuddelkind zur anerkannten Subdisziplin? Die "neue Militärgeschichte" der Frühen Neuzeit – Perspektiven, Entwicklungen, Probleme.' *Geschichte in Wissenschaft und Unterricht* 51 (2000): 598-9.

Pröve, Ralf. *Stehendes Heer und städtische Gesellschaft im 18. Jahrhundert. Göttingen und seine Militärbevölkerung 1713-1756*. München: Oldenbourg, 1995.

Pufendorf, Samuel. *De Rebus a Carolo Gustavo Sveciae Rege Gestis Commentariorum . . .*. Nuremberg: Christoph Riegel, 1696.

Redman, Herbert J. *Frederick the Great and the Seven Years' War, 1756-1763*. Jefferson, NC: McFarland & Co., 2015.

Remarque, Erich Maria. *Erich Maria Remarques Roman Im Westen nichts Neues. Text, Edition, Entstehung, Distribution und Rezeption (1928-1930)*, edited by Thomas F. Schneider. Tübingen: May Niemeyer, 2004.

Rink, Martin. 'Der kleine Krieg. Entwicklungen und Trends asymmetrischer Gewalt 1740 bis 1815.' *Militärgeschichtliche Zeitschrift* 65 (2006): 355-88.

Scheelen, Ernst Gottlob von. 'Aus Scheelens Tagebüchern.' In *Potsdamer Tagebücher 1740-1756*, edited by Großer Generalstab, 37-109. Berlin: Mittler, 1906.

Ross, Stephen T. *From Flintlock to Rifle: Infantry Tactics, 1740-1866*. London: Routledge, 1979.

Schieder, Theodor. *Friedrich der Grosse: ein Königtum der Widersprüche*. Berlin: Ullstein, 1998.

Schreiter, René. 'Das Große Militärwaisenhaus zu Potsdam 1724-1952. Ein Kapitel preußisch-deutscher Erziehungsgeschichte.' *Militär und Gesellschaft in der frühen Neuzeit* 7, no. 1 (2003): 76-8.

Schwerhoff, Gerd. 'Early Modern Violence and the Honour Code: From Social Integration to Social Distinction?' *Crime, Histoire & Sociétés* 17, vol. 2 (2013): 27-46.

Sdvidzkov, Denis. 'Landschaft nach der Schlacht. Briefe russischer Offiziere aus dem Siebenjährigen Krieg.' *Forschungen zur Brandenburgischen und Preußischen Geschichte* 22, vol. 1 (2012): 33-56.

Sdvidzkov, Denis. *Letters from the 'Prussian War': The People of the Russian Imperial Army in 1758*. Moscow: New Literature Review, 2019.

Shalev, Arieh, Israel Lieberzon and Charles Marmar. 'Post-Traumatic Stress Disorder.' *The New England Journal of Medicine* 376 (2017): 2459-69.

Shoemaker, Robert. 'Male honour and the decline of public violence in eighteenth-century London.' *Social History* 26, no. 2 (2001): 190–208.

Showalter, Dennis E. *Frederick the Great. A Military History*. Barnsley: Frontline Books, [1996] 2012.

Showalter, Dennis E. 'Tactics and Recruitment in Eighteenth Century Prussia.' *Studies in History and Politics/Etudes d'Histoire et de Politique* III, no. 3 (1993/1994): 15–41.

Showalter, Dennis E. 'Hubertusberg to Auerstädt: The Prussian Army in Decline?' *German History* 12, no. 3 (1994): 308–33.

Showalter, Dennis E. *The Wars of Frederick the Great*. Boston, MA: Addison-Wesley Longman, 1995.

Sikora, Michael. *Disziplin und Desertion: Strukturprobleme militärischer Organisation im 18. Jahrhundert*. Berlin: Duncker & Humblot, 1996.

Spillmann, Kurt and Kati. 'Friedrich Wilhelm I und die preußische Armee. Versuch einer psychohistorischen Deutung.' *Historische Zeitschrift* 246 (1988): 549–89.

Spring, Matthew H. *With Zeal and With Bayonets Only: The British Army on Campaign in North America, 1775–1783*. Norman, OK: University of Oklahoma Press, 2010.

Stammliste aller Regimenter und Corps der Königlich-Preußischen Armee für das Jahr 1806. 1806. Reprint, Osnabrück: Biblio, 1975.

Starkey, Armstrong. *War in the Age of Enlightenment, 1700–1789*. Westport, CT: Greenwood Publishing Group, 2003.

Steck, Wolfgang. 'Die biographische Grabrede. Eine phänomenologische Rekonstruktion ihrer Genese.' In *Der 'ganze Mensch'. Perspektiven lebensgeschichtlicher Individualität. Festschrift für Dietrich Rössler zum siebzigsten Geburtstag*, edited by Volker Drehsen, Dieter Henke, Reinhard Schmidt-Rost and Wolfgang Steck, 263–304. Berlin and New York: de Gruyter, 1997.

Straubel, Rolf. *'Er möchte nur wißen, daß die Armée mir gehöret.' Friedrich II und seine Offiziere. Ausgewählte Aspekte königlicher Personalpolitik*. Berlin: BWV, 2012.

Stuart, Kathy. *Unehrliche Berufe: Status und Stigma in der Frühen Neuzeit am Beispiel Augsburgs*. Augsburg: Wißner, 2008.

Süßmilch, Johann Peter. *Johann Peter Süßmilchs, Königlichen Ober-Consistorial-Raths und Probsts zu Berlin, Danck- und Sieges-Predigt Wegen des Am 5ten Novembr. (1757 bey Freyburg Denen Königlich-Preußischen Waffen über die vereinigte Französische und Reichs-Armee verliehenen Höchstwichtigen Sieges*. Berlin und Schwabach: Enderische Buchhandlung, 1758.

Toeche-Mittler, Joachim. *Armeemärsche. Die Geschichte unserer Marschmusik*, vol. III. Neckargmünd: Spemann, 1975.

van Dülmen, Richard. *Der ehrlose Mensch: Unehrlichkeit und soziale Ausgrenzung in der frühen Neuzeit*. Köln: Böhlau, 1999.

Verletzte Ehre. Ehrkonflikte in Gesellschaften des Mittelalters und der Frühen Neuzeit, edited by Klaus Schreiner and Gerd Schwerhoff. Cologne, Weimar, Vienna: Böhlau.

Wallmann, Johannes. *Pietismus-Studien. Gesammelte Aufsätze II*. Tübingen: Mohr-Siebeck, 2008.

Walter, Meinrad. *Johann Sebastian Bach: Weihnachtsoratorium*. Kassel: Bärenreiter, 2006.

Way, Peter Way. 'Class and the Common Soldier in the Seven Years' War.' *Labor History* 44, no. 4 (2003): 455–81.

Way, Peter. 'Militarizing the Atlantic World: Army Discipline, Coerced Labor, and Britain's Commercial Empire.' *Atlantic Studies: Global Currents* 13, no. 3 (2016): 345–69.

Way, Peter. 'Rebellion of the Regulars: Working Soldiers and the Mutiny of 1763-1764.' *William and Mary Quarterly* 57, no. 4 (2000): 761–92.

Way, Peter. 'Venus and Mars: Women and the British Army in America during the Seven Years' War'. In *Britain and America Go to War: The Impact of War and Warfare in Anglo-America, 1754–1815*, edited by Julie Flavell and Stephen Conway, 41–68. Gainesville, FL: Florida University Press, 2004.

Wernitz, Frank. *Die Armee Friedrichs des Großen im Siebenjährigen Krieg*. Eggolsheim-Berstadt: Podzun-Pallas, 2002.

Wernitz, Frank. *Die preußischen Freitruppen im Siebenjährigen Krieg 1756–1763. Entstehung – Einsatz – Wirkung*. Wölfersheim-Berstadt: Podzun-Pallas, 1994.

Wilcken, Christian Diederich. *Drey Predigten von denen durch Ihro Majestät den König von Preußen erhaltenen grossen Siegen bey Roßbach, und Lissa und der Wiedereroberung der schlesischen Hauptstadt Breslau*. Halle / Salle: Gebauer, 1758.

Wilson, Peter H.. "Social Militarization in Eighteenth-Century Germany." *German History*, 18, no 1 (2000): 1–39.

Wilson, Peter H.. *German armies. War and German politics, 1648–1806*. London: UCL Press, 1998.

Winkel, Carmen. 'Kriegserinnerungen preußischer Offiziere zwischen Korpsgeist und königlichem Anspruch. (1740–1786)'. In *Militärische Erinnerungskulturen vom 14. bis zum 18. Jahrhundert. Träger-Medien-Deutungskonkurrenzen*, edited by Horst Carl and Ute Planert, 227–44. Göttingen: V&R unipress, 2012.

Winkel, Carmen. 'Zwischen adliger Reputation und militärischer Subordination. Normative Ehrvorstellungen und soziale Praxis im preußischen Offizierskorps'. In *Ehre und Pflichterfüllung als Codes militärischer Tugenden*, edited by Ulrike Ludwig, Markus Pöhlmann and John Zimmermann, 111–26. Paderborn: Ferdinand Schöningh, 2014.

Winter, Martin. 'Desertionsprozesse in der preußischen Armee nach dem Siebenjährigen Krieg'. In *Militär und Recht vom 16. bis 19. Jahrhundert*, edited by Jutta Nowosadtko, Diethelm Klippel and Kai Lohsträter, 187–208. Göttingen: V&R unipress, 2016.

Winter, Martin. *Untertanengeist durch Militärpflicht? Das preußische Kantonsystem in brandenburgischen Städten im 18. Jahrhundert*. Bielefeld: Verlag für Regionalgeschichte, 2005.

Wolff, Christoph. *Johann Sebastian Bach*. Frankfurt am Main: S. Fischer, 2000.

Zedler, Günther. *Die erhaltenen Kirchenkantaten Johann Sebastian Bachs. Mühlhausen, Weimar, Leipzig I. Besprechungen in Form von Analysen – Erklärungen – Deutungen*. Norderstedt: Books on Demand Verlag, 2008.

Zielsdorf, Frank. *Militärische Erinnerungskulturen in Preußen im 18. Jahrhundert. Akteure-Medien-Dynamiken*. Göttingen: V&R unipress, 2016.

Index

abuse, 29, 30, 149
alcoholism, 29
Almodóvar, Duque de, 28
(Alt-)Anhalt, regiment, 10, 31, 60, 61, 66, 68, 71, 80, 82, 83, 91, 93, 94, 100, 119, 120, 121, 123, 132, 147, 153, 157, 161, 162, 164, 165, 170, 187, 209
Alt-Braunschweig, regiment, 64
American Civil War, 15, 41
Anhalt-Dessau, Leopold von (Prussian field marshal), 43, 47, 66, 162
Anhalt-Dessau, Moritz von (Prussian field marshal), 51, 52, 90, 91, 113, 157, 161, 190
Archenholz, Friedrich Wilhelm von (Prussian officer), 100, 110, 139, 175
arms factories, 32
Arnholtz, Christian (Prussian soldier), 70, 71, 193, 194
Arouet, François-Marie *see* Voltaire, 141
artillery, 20, 24, 40, 41, 83, 90, 91, 94, 99, 112, 116, 117, 118, 150, 174, 175, 194
artisans, 15, 24, 25, 77, 131, 206
atrocities, 114, 138, 141, 142, 171
Ausländer (mercenary), 25, 26, 27, 28, 34, 37, 55, 134, 137, 138, 139, 169, 197, 198, 205
Austria, Austrian army, Austrian light troops, 14, 35, 36, 41, 43, 54, 60, 64, 66, 68, 70, 77, 79, 80-4, 88-91, 93-7, 99, 103, 106, 109-11, 115-26, 130-3, 142-3, 147-50, 153, 159, 161, 164-6, 171, 174, 180, 182-6, 188-9, 195-6, 203, 205, 203, 206, 212
authorities, local 24, 26, 27, 206

Barsewisch, Ernst Friedrich Rudolf von (Prussian officer) 11, 77, 100, 103, 100-11, 113, 115, 123, 128, 136, 148, 150, 204, 208

Bartholly, Joseph, (Prussian private) 80-1
Bayonet 39, 42, 43, 48-53, 56, 64, 67-8, 70, 77, 88, 96, 112, 115-17, 120-3, 147, 149, 170, 189, 190
Bayreuth, regiment 159
Becker, Adam, (Prussian grenadier) 79-80, 143, 146
Behnsdorf 71, 194
Belgium 1
benediction 157
Berenhorst, Georg Heinrich von (military theoretician and Prussian officer) 47, 49, 119
Berlin 25, 30, 51, 173-5, 181, 183, 186-7, 197-8, 203
Bevern, August Wilhelm (Prussian general) 118, 148, 189
Bevern, regiment 11, 101, 123, 148, 157
Bible 61-2, 65, 67, 130, 137, 177, 179, 184, 186
Binn, Nicolaus, NCO 59, 69, 70, 78, 93, 96-7, 99, 134, 137, 141, 143, 146, 159, 191-3
birth 130
Bock, lieutenant-colonel (Prussian officer) 112
Bohemia 26, 86, 194, 203
Bonin, regiment 159, 182
booty 25, 159, 183
Borcke, regiment 160-1
bounty 33, 38
Bräker, Ulrich 6, 34, 57-9, 101-3, 107-8, 134, 202-3
Brandenburg 138, 140, 170, 177, 181-1, 200, 202
bravado 17
Breslau, Battle of 70, 161
Brieg 161-3
brigade 53, 186, 198
British army 5
burghers 25-6

canister 40, 51, 117, 118, 148
Capitain des armes 64
caps 22, 112, 159
catholics 85, 137, 171
Catt, Henri de 117, 134, 161
cavalry 20–4, 28, 30, 39, 40–2, 47–8, 50, 53, 54–6, 59, 67, 69, 81–4, 86, 90, 105, 107, 110, 113–14, 116, 124–7, 132, 140–2, 149–50, 152, 154–5, 159, 165, 170, 174–5, 179, 185, 188–90, 192, 206
chaplains 16, 32, 42, 59, 67, 77, 99, 155
Charles XII, King of Sweden 42
children 11, 25, 28, 32, 35–6, 61, 66, 72–3, 83, 93, 100, 136–7, 141, 148–9, 163, 165, 171, 178, 180, 183, 187, 190–3, 195
civilians 17, 33–4, 55, 169
Cogniazzo, Jacob de (Austrian officer and military historian) 127, 166, 174
colours 32, 38, 46, 55, 64, 66–7, 95, 111–13, 117–18, 121–2, 132, 148, 151, 153, 155, 160, 163, 169, 171, 180, 186
conscription 25
contract 37, 98, 205
Cossacks 124, 141, 166, 179
cowardice 123, 131–2, 145
craftsmen 26, 55, 169
Croats 125–7, 206
cuirassiers 23, 39, 114, 126–7, 152, 158–9

Dann (Prussian soldier) 164
death penalty 31
desertion 6, 17, 30, 32, 37, 124, 135, 165, 167, 171–2
diaries 1, 9–10, 15–16, 61, 63, 79–80, 85, 99–100, 175
disabled soldiers 32
divine service 35, 67, 75, 137
Dominicus, Johann Jacob (Prussian soldier) 10, 57, 59, 60, 62–4, 77, 91, 93–4, 97, 118, 121, 134, 140, 148, 150, 177, 180–1
Dorfschulzen (village administrators) 25, 62–3, 205
Douceurgelder (gratuities) 160
dragoons 23, 39, 125, 127, 139, 142, 152
Dresden 26, 66, 86, 123, 132, 175, 194–5, 200, 201–4
Dresel, Johann Hermann (Prussian soldier) 10, 57, 59–60

Dreyer, Joseph Ferdinand (Prussian NCO) 10, 34, 57, 77, 102–3, 145, 155
Driesen, regiment 60, 69, 96
drill 1–2, 4–5, 9, 12, 19, 21, 25, 27–9, 31, 33–5, 37, 39, 44–5, 47, 49, 51, 53, 55, 56, 115, 122, 127–8, 133, 169, 206
drummers 153–5, 186
DSM-5 13
Dutch army 42, 44

ego-documents 9–10, 57, 75
executions 30–1, 171
existential human experiences (*Elementarerfahrungen*) 205

Fatherland 35, 74, 130–1, 135, 137, 143, 145, 170, 189–90, 196
Fermor, Wilhelm von (Russian general) 142
fife, flute 153–5, 159, 206
Fleming, Johan Friedrich von (Saxon officer) 163
flintlock 39
Fontenoy 1
Forcade, regiment 141
Fouqué, Heinrich August de la Motte (Prussian general) 117, 122
Franckesche Stiftungen (Franke Foundation) 67
Frederick II, King of Prussia 2–4, 7, 24, 27, 32, 38, 43, 48–9, 55, 88, 101–2, 110, 115, 124, 126, 137–8, 146–7, 152, 154–5, 159, 161, 166, 173–4, 176, 185–6, 195, 197, 206
Frederick William I, (The Soldier King), King of Prussia 32, 43, 154, 191, 206
Fredrick Augustus II (The Strong), Elector of Saxony, King of Poland 100
free-regiments (Prussian light troops) 126
Freibataillone (free battalions) 23
French army 107, 141, 181
French language 141, 200
French Revolution 4, 35, 144, 164
Freytag, Gustav 58
Friedmeyer, Damian (Prussian soldier) 90, 96
fusiliers 127, 152–3

Gardelegen 60, 71, 193–4
garrison regiments 23
garrison society 26
Gaudi, Friedrich Wilhelm von (Prussian general) 117, 140–1, 175
General Staff 177, 186, 188
Generalprincipien des Krieges (writing by Fredrick II) 124, 173
Geringswalde 73
Gideon 99
God 17, 31, 33, 42, 64–5, 68, 71, 76, 78, 81, 83, 88, 92–3, 95, 97–8, 99, 104, 129–30, 134–7, 139, 145, 147, 150–1, 155, 157, 168–70, 172, 182–4, 187–8, 190–2, 195–7, 200–1
Goethe, Johann Wolfgang von 140
gospel 98, 142, 184
Göttingen 6, 175, 186
Graevenitz, regiment 161
Graun, Heinrich 158
grenadier march 153, 158–9
grenadiers 20, 22, 41, 44, 80, 83, 85, 88, 112, 116–17, 120–1, 126–7, 132, 140, 152–3, 180, 186, 201–2, 206
Grenzer (Austrian light troops) 124, 206
Groschen 154, 161, 181, 202
guards 1–2, 52, 66, 89, 133, 139, 203, 206
Gummersbach 63
Gustavus Adolphus, King of Sweden 42

Halberstadt 60, 64
Halle/Saale 66–7, 176, 188
Hardt, free-regiment 126
Harhausen 63
Heiducks 26
Henry, Prince of Prussia 180, 186, 192
Herrnhuter 101
Hertzberg (Prussian officer) 118, 150, 191
historical anthropology 11
Hitze (heat) 102
Hlaupetin 122
Hochkirch, Battle of 149–50, 174, 195
Hochleitner, Prussian NCO 161
Hohenfriedberg, Battle of 41, 69–70, 99, 159
Holstein-Gottorp, regiment 158
howitzer 40, 178
Hrdlorzez 120

Hülsen, Carl Wilhelm von (Prussian officer) 150, 166
Hülsen, regiment 181
Hundsfott 86, 206
hussars 23, 40, 54, 77, 80, 114, 118, 125–7, 142, 152–3, 165, 175, 188
hymns 159, 168, 172, 196

Immediatverkehr (the soldiers' right to address the king directly) 62, 206
Imperial army 64, 80–1, 106, 110–11, 139, 150, 196
Ingersleben, Johann Ludwig von (Prussian general) 121, 186
intercession 92–3, 170–1
Iserlohn 64
Itzenplitz, regiment 62, 89–90, 101

Jägers (huntsmen, chasseurs) 186, 188, 205–6
Jena and Auerstedt, Battle of 102, 173
Joshua 99
journals 9, 13, 81, 83, 99–100, 139, 145, 173, 175

Kadavergehorsam 37
Kaehler (Prussian officer) 164
Kalberlah, Kaspar (Prussian soldier) 77, 141, 194–5
Kampflust (lust for combat) 102
Kanitz, regiment 159
Kanonenfieber (cannon-fever) 102
Kanonengelder (cannon-money) 161
Kantonisten (cantonists) 15, 20, 24–8, 33–4, 37, 55, 59, 62–4, 71, 77–8, 134–5, 137–8, 143, 169–70, 202, 205–6
Katholisch-Hennersdorf 153
Kay/Paltzig/Züllichau, Battle of 104, 178, 181
Keith, James (Prussian field marshal) 64
Kej 122
Kerl 177–80, 206
Kesselsdorf, Battle of 159–60
Klauel, C.G. (Prussian soldier) 71, 82–3
Kleist, Friedrich Wilhelm von (Prussian general) 98
Kleist, regiment 70, 118
Kolin, Battle of 36–7, 41, 54, 66–7, 69, 85, 108, 110, 123, 132, 142, 147–8, 184

Krauel, David (Prussian soldier) 161–3
Krefeld, battle 158
Krumpholtz (Prussian soldier) 92, 95, 182
Kunersdorf, Battle of 36–8, 64–5, 69–71, 93–4, 105–6, 134, 148, 150, 165
Kurssell, Heinrich Adolf von (Prussian general) 117, 166
Küster, Carl Daniel 9, 11, 14, 57, 98, 102–3, 105–9, 113, 132, 135–6, 144–5, 149, 167, 174
Küstrin 111

Land-regimenter (provincial regiments) 23
Langen, Siegmund Moritz Wilhelm von (Prussian officer) 133
Lehwald, Johann von (Prussian field-marshal) 165
Leibkompanie (colonel's company) 111, 152
Lemcke, Jakob Friedrich von (Prussian officer) 10, 100, 104, 119–20
Lengefeld, Johann Christian Karl von (Prussian officer) 60
Leuthen, Battle of 58, 62–3, 70, 84, 96, 103, 105, 111, 115–16, 123, 128, 138, 146, 157, 161, 204,
Liebe, Georg 10, 57–60, 70, 177, 191–6
Liebler, G.S. (Prussian NCO) 66, 99, 183
Liebler, J.S. (Prussian NCO, son of G.S. Liebler) 35, 60–1, 66–8, 71, 77, 91, 93, 95, 97–9, 119–20, 132–4, 138, 142–3, 147, 164, 166, 183–7
Liebstenschein (sweetheart diploma) 26
Liegnitz, Battle of 67, 123, 132, 161
Linck, Barthel (Prussian soldier) 71, 90, 94, 98
Little War 22–3, 57, 115, 124–7, 152–3, 188, 205–6
Lobositz, Battle of 165, 181, 183
Lossow, Matthias Ludwig von (Prussian general) 126, 130, 138
Lutheran denomination 55, 67, 130, 206

Magdeburg 14, 60, 64, 73, 138, 140, 162, 193, 195, 201
Maleschitz 120
marches, music 109, 151–5, 168
Maria Theresa of Austria, Archduchess of Austria and Queen of Hungary 43, 125

Massow (Prussian officer) 167
Maxen, Battle of 64, 65, 69
Meißen, Battle of 66
memoires 9–11, 13, 15, 57–8, 99–102, 107, 202
Mennonites 25, 31
Menschenangst (human fear) 102
mercenaries 1, 15, 21, 34, 41, 58, 137, 169, 198
Meyerinck, regiment 11, 100, 138, 204
military justice 31
military psychologists 14
military theory/theoreticians 54, 100, 175
Miltnitz (Prussian officer) 87, 197, 203
Minden, Battle of 159, 181
mitre cap 22, 205
Moldau 91, 188
Mollwitz, Battle of 54, 133
Müller (Prussian NCO) 99
Munster 6
musicians 154–5, 206

Napoleon 3, 102, 144, 164
Natzmer, General von 30
Nine Years' War 41–2
Nitzahn 88, 199–201
Normann, regiment 142

oboe 151–4, 158, 206
Old Testament 99
orphanage, Potsdam military 32, 76, 154

pandurs 80, 82, 86, 88–90, 124–7, 203–4, 206
Panisches Schrecken (panic scare) 102
peasants 169, 202, 205–6
Pepusch, Gottfried 154
pietism 67, 172
Pirna 33, 194–5
Plaue an der Havel 62, 200
Potsdam 51, 154, 206
Pour le mérite, Prussian order 123
Prague, Battle of 31, 37, 57, 59–60, 62, 64, 66–7, 70, 84, 88, 95–6, 106, 109, 115, 118–19, 122, 132–3, 147–8, 158, 160, 166, 183–90
praxeological method 11
prayer 65, 68, 79, 84–5, 90–2, 137, 143, 171, 183, 187, 190

Prince of Prussia, regiment 118, 141, 203–4
Prittwitz, Christian Wilhelm von (Prussian officer) 104, 110, 165–6
PTSD (Post-Traumatic Stress Disorder) 73, 77, 128
Pufendorf, Samuel 61, 82
Puttlitz, page of Fredrick II 115

Quakers 25, 31
Quedlinburg 60, 64

Ramse (Prussian soldier) 92, 182
regimental bands 2153, 155–6, 159
Reichsthaler 38, 87, 123, 154, 159–61, 179, 181, 191, 193, 197–8, 200, 202–4
Reiß, Frantz (Prussian soldier) 64–6, 91–2, 95, 97–8, 181–3
Retzow, Friedrich August von (Prussian officer) 105–6, 111, 148, 157, 174–5
Riemann, Benjamin (Prussian soldier) 73
Riemann, Johann Christian (Prussian soldier) 147, 195, 197
right to appeal 31
Rinke, cutler 71, 194
rituals 172
Roßbach, Battle of 140–1, 157, 204
running the gauntlet 2, 29–30, 206
Russian army 14, 64, 66, 72, 77, 91, 94, 104, 110, 124–5, 137, 141–2, 155, 165, 171, 178–80, 195

Saldern, Friedrich Christoph von (Prussian general) 149–50
Salesel 83, 86, 197, 203
Salzwedel 60, 70, 193
Saxe, Maurice de, French Field marshal 99–100
Saxon army 7, 33
Saxony 6, 10, 25, 59–60, 70–2, 100, 110, 126, 170, 177, 181, 188, 192–4, 196–7
Scheelen, Ernst Gottlob von (Prussian officer) 52
Schlichting, regiment 159
Schuberth (Prussian soldier) 164
Schultze, Prof. Friedrich 58, 84, 200
Schweidnitz 149
Schwerin, Kurt Christoph von (Prussian field marshal) 198–200, 203

Seehausen (Prussian officer) 145
self-mutilation 37
Silesia 122, 179, 183
small unit cohesion 5, 20, 134
Spain 4, 16, 43
Spandau 52
Spellerholtz (Prussian soldier) 85, 201–2
standards 160, 163, 169
Sterbohol 118
Stolberg-Wernigerode (noble family) 58–9, 175
sutlers 27–8, 143, 171
Swedish army 42–3, 110
sweethearts 26, 56, 192

Tangermünde 60
Te deum laudamus 158, 190
Tempelhof, Georg Friedrich von (Prussian artillery officer and military historian) 138, 174
tent-comradeship 20–1, 134
Thirty Years' War 1
Torgau, Battle of 37, 65, 71, 73, 123, 181, 196
trauma 15, 76–7, 136
Treffen (line of battle) 41, 206
trophies 160, 163, 168
trumpets 155, 158–9, 196

Unter-Poczernitz 116

Verfremdungsfaktoren (disassociation factors) 76
Vietnam War 15
Vittinghofen (Prussian officer) 149

War of the Austrian Succession 36, 49, 70
War of the Spanish Succession 24, 41
Warnery, Charles-Emmanuel de (Prussian officer and military writer) 127, 148, 175
Weferlingen 71, 194
Welhotta 82
Winterfeldt, Hans Karl (Prussian general) 116–17
Winterfeldt, regiment 106
Wittenberg 73, 196
wives
World War I 14

Wunsch, Johann Jacob von (Prussian general) 123
Württemberg soldiers (fighting with the Austrians) 112–13
Württemberg, Friedrich Eugen von, Duke of Württemberg (Prussian general) 105–50

Zander, Christian Friedrich (Prussian soldier) 197, 200, 204
Zander cousins (Christian Friedrich and Johann Dietrich) 34–5, 38, 58–9, 61–3, 69–70, 77, 79, 84–5, 86, 92, 104, 148, 197–8, 201, 203–4
Zander, Johann Dietrich (Prussian soldier) 10, 26
Zander, Johann Matthias (village administrator) 62
Zander, Johann Wilhelm (village administrator) 62
Zander (Prussian NCO) 161–2
Zarnewanz 160
Zethlingen 70, 193
Ziethen, Hans Joachim von (Prussian general) 114
Zinna, Battle of 123
Ziska mountain 162–3
Zittau 84, 89
Zittemann, Christian (comrade of Ulrich Bräker) 34
Zorndorf, Battle of 70, 72, 104–5, 108, 110, 114, 132, 142, 148, 150, 155, 157, 165, 195

www.ingramcontent.com/pod-product-compliance
Lightning Source LLC
Chambersburg PA
CBHW052059300426
44117CB00013B/2201